# Site Planning for Cluster Housing

# Site Planning for Cluster Housing

## Richard Untermann & Robert Small

Department of Landscape Architecture
Department of Architecture
University of Washington
Seattle, Washington

with assistance by Lynn Lewicki

**VAN NOSTRAND REINHOLD COMPANY**

NEW YORK   CINCINNATI   ATLANTA   DALLAS   SAN FRANCISCO
LONDON   TORONTO   MELBOURNE

Van Nostrand Reinhold Company Regional Offices:
New York  Cincinnati  Atlanta  Dallas  San Francisco

Van Nostrand Reinhold Company International Offices:
London  Toronto  Melbourne

Manufactured in the United States of America

Published by Van Nostrand Reinhold Company
450 West 33rd Street, New York, N.Y. 10001

Published simultaneously in Canada by Van Nostrand Reinhold Ltd.

15  14  13  12  11  10  9  8  7  6  5  4  3  2  1

**Library of Congress Cataloging in Publication Data**

Unterman, Richard.
  Site planning for cluster housing.

  Includes index.
  1. Cluster housing—United States. 2. Home-
sites—United States. 3. Architecture, Modern—
20th century—United States. I. Small, Robert E.,
joint author. II Title.
NA9051.4.U57      711'.58      77-23222
ISBN 0-442-28822-0

# PREFACE

This book is about the process of physically designing cluster housing environments. It was written with a sense of urgency; there is great need for all the participants in the housing industry to develop new and improved skills in the planning and design of this reemerging house/settlement form.

The American pioneer dream of every family living in a single unit dwelling can no longer be sustained. The alarming escalation of human pathology in high-density/high-rise urban housing environments throughout the world has proven that human society cannot yet, and indeed may never be able to, adapt to this settlement form. Not by default then, but for many compelling reasons, the viable alternative of medium-density cluster housing environments has been emerging from the decay of 19th and 20th century American urban and suburban housing environments.

Cluster housing may be found in many environments, in many climates, on many land forms, and may be built of many different materials. It is certainly not a new housing form; its antecedents are found in a very broad range of cultures that span the entire history of man as a builder of human settlements. It is found in many early civilizations in highly refined forms such as Mediterranean hill towns, villages on the African savanna, Arctic Eskimo igloo villages, and southwest American Indian pueblos. There are also many fine contemporary examples of urban cluster housing throughout the world, most of them occurring in the technologically advanced nations of Western Europe. There are few, by comparison, in America itself.

Cluster housing has only recently begun developing as a contemporary residential environment in North America, and it is very likely that, as it becomes understood, it will become accepted by an increasingly larger proportion of the American public. There is a growing public awareness of the urgent need to find an alternative to urban crowding and its resultant social problems. But there is also a growing public awareness of the need to conserve the land, its natural systems, its open space, and its capability to yield sufficient material and energy resources. These two needs, which have seemingly conflicting objectives, must now be perceived as one need with one set of objectives. A close examination of the cluster housing environments reveals it has the potential to meet this set of objectives.

Literature in the area of housing is increasing. There are numerous books and articles written on housing designs and design standards; and there is an encouraging increase in literature on human needs and responses in housing environments. There is, however, very little written on the development of housing environments as a whole. This book applies current theory and information on cluster housing, human needs in housing, and site planning to an action-oriented format intended to aid professionals in designing and implementing housing developments at any scale.

The book places emphasis upon the development of low-rise, medium-density cluster environments that optimize the interrelationship of land form and house form. The cluster environments are planned as components, and groups of components, that fit into the larger scale planning of existing neighborhoods and new communities. As open space/garden apartment-type housing developments, they have characteristics best described as a mixture of Radburn, Reston, Hook New Town, Columbia, Rochampton, and other similar planned residential environments. These developments begin to accomplish, at a reasonable cost, a rich integration of amenity preservation, conservation of open space, efficiency of operation, and personal privacy, identity, safety, and accessibility.

# CONTENTS

# PART ONE-SMALL SITES

# PLANNING CLUSTER HOUSING ENVIRONMENTS

THE CLUSTER HOUSING ENVIRONMENT IS THE MOST
ENDURING FORM OF HUMAN SETTLEMENT

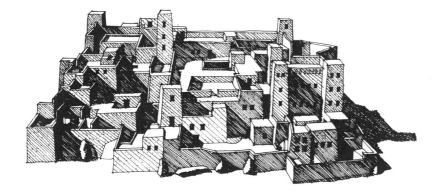

CLUSTER HOUSING IS PRIMARILY
AN URBAN HOUSE FORM

The cluster housing environment is the most fundamental and enduring form of human settlement. It may be simply described as housing that is joined together so that individual units share common walls, floors, and ceilings. More importantly, the individual units share common open spaces and common facilities. Historically, cluster configuration and scale have been limited only by the material resources and the ingenuity of the society building them.

Traditionally, the scale and organization of the cluster settlement described not only the physical setting, but the social setting as well. In a culture whose settlement form was refined over thousands of years, the physical organization became highly structured. This certainly did not mean that house form became rigid; rather each culture conceived order based on its own values.

There are many reasons why cluster housing is a desirable alternative at this time. We are gradually discovering the need to understand what scales and densities of housing will enhance individual privacy and safety while engendering a sense of community. Cluster housing has the flexibility of configuration and scale to be organized into prescribed social groupings. We are discovering that while suburbia is wasteful of land, the urban settlement is far too removed from the land. Between these extremes is cluster housing which can afford a reasonable degree of privacy, private outdoor space, and ground orientation at densities much higher than suburbia. Furthermore, we are discovering that much more social benefit can be gained by aggregating shared open space. Cluster housing has the capability to organize a hierarchy of private, semi-private, and public spaces. Finally, we are discovering that the cost reduction techniques of mass housing can be properly applied to low-rise medium-density housing developments.

## EVOLUTION

Planning new cluster housing environments requires a perspective view of their history. Studying the evolution of cluster housing environments through the ages reveals that they flourished in many stable cultures. Thus, the basic planning principles of cluster housing can most easily be understood by studying the housing environments of these cultures. These cultures have influenced cluster housing in America, which must also be studied.

## NEED

How to meet the need for housing in America is a dilemma shared by the housing industry, the government, and the persons who need housing. As a member of the development team, the site planner has the responsibility to understand the problem and contribute to meeting the need.

## PROCESS

Site planning for contemporary American cluster housing environments has many special requirements. The planning process is a creative decision-making process that is dependent upon the rational interpretation of quantitative and qualitative information.

Cluster housing is primarily an *urban house form* that is adaptable to many different community scales. By drawing upon the best of a rich tradition, it has the potential to become the enlightened compromise between conventional suburban and urban housing environments for which so many Americans are searching.

## THE EVOLUTION OF CLUSTER HOUSING

In primitive cultures the village was often defined by the organization of individual dwelling units into groups to enclose a community space and simultaneously form a defensible enclosure. The main entry of each unit faced into the community space. In some cultures the units were connected to actually form the enclosure, whereas in others they were aligned (not quite connected) to define, but not formally enclose, the community space. Depending upon available material resources and technological skills, the units were one or two stories high.

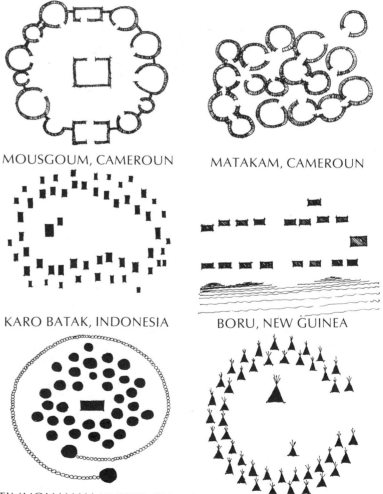

MOUSGOUM, CAMEROUN     MATAKAM, CAMEROUN

KARO BATAK, INDONESIA     BORU, NEW GUINEA

TIMUQUANAN, UNITED STATES    CHEYENNE, UNITED STATES

In time, as the population increased, the village became the town. Although many of the village characteristics remained, the houses were more isolated from the main public spaces. The entry no longer fronted on the main community space, the town center, but on a secondary community space in the form of a pathway or street leading to the town center. The house no longer formed the village wall. It either opened onto an interior court or was surrounded on all but one side by adjacent units. Moreover, improved technology allowed multiple story dwellings to be built to a height of four or five stories.

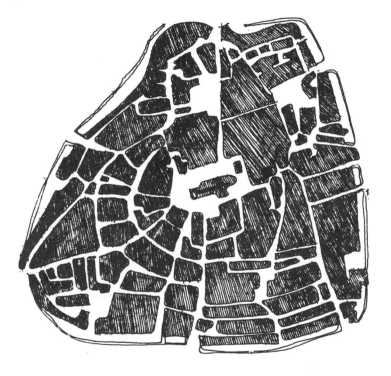

As urbanization throughout the world led to still greater concentrations of population, the urban single-family house cluster reached a high level of refinement and sophistication. In medieval European cities it became still more compact with very narrow frontage on the street and heights of four to five stories. This basic model is the genesis of contemporary European urban housing.

As the city began to be planned, the informal pattern of incremental growth yielded to more formal, large-scale preconceptions of total city organization. Regardless of t pography city streets were arranged in regular geometric patterns, with the rectilinear grid being dominant. The city "block" thus formed became the standard. The cluster form, which had previously been the generator of informal growth and change, was subdued and had to yield to the discipline of the block.

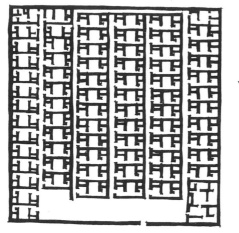

ARMANA—14th CENTURY B.C.

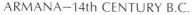

MANNHEIM—18th CENTURY A.D.

MILETUS—5th CENTURY B.C.

CHAN-CHAN—10th CENTURY A.D.

With the beginning of the industrial revolution and the great influx of rural population into the city, this formal massing combined with improved technology in the development of taller residential buildings. Many walk-up tenements, composed of flats, were built to heights of six to eight stories. With this trend the basic values of cluster housing environments were set aside and many of the advantages of urban lifestyle were greatly compromised for those living in tenement housing. The contemporary tenement housing environment, i.e., the apartment house complete with elevators, is a stepchild of the industrial revolution.

The squeezing upward of housing can almost always be correlated with the great demand for land near the urban core, and the land management practices of a given culture. High-rise housing continues to be built in spite of overwhelming evidence that it spawns and sustains many social problems. Efforts to improve upon it seem only to further intensify the

PUEBLO BONITO—12th CENTURY A.D.

problem. Perhaps, then, the problem is the basic assumption that high-rise housing is a humane environment. Interestingly, some ancient civilizations managed to build very large-scale residential environments which seem to be more humane than their contemporary equivalents. Perhaps because our ancestors could not conceive of the technological means to build vertical structures of great height and in great quantity, they were spared the social problems associated with high-rise living.

UGARIT-16th CENTURY B.C.    DENMARK-20th CENTURY A.D.

# CLUSTER HOUSING IN AMERICA

## THE PAST

European colonization of Eastern North America brought with it a set of housing traditions. As urbanization began, the European urban row house was emulated. The villages and towns were tightly knit patterns of single-unit dwellings modeled after an array of European dwellings. An equal variety of European farmhomes was copied in rural areas. Simultaneously, the Spanish colonization in Southwest America introduced the patio and terrace house, which was highly compatible with the adobe house forms of the native Southwest Americans.

For reasons of cultural tradition, climate, landform, materials, and technology, some civilizations built a complex of patio and terrace house clusters as their basic house type. Most of these civilizations continue to build in these forms. The patio house form is still the basic type throughout the hot/dry climate zones. The terrace house form naturally evolved in all the hilly portions of the world. Since many early civilizations chose to build in inaccessible places for defense, there are many enduring examples. The terrace house continues to be the dominant houseform in the hilly portions of the world, but its many advantages are making it an attractive alternative in many other parts of the world.

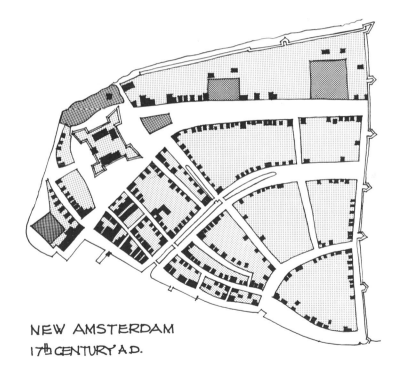

NEW AMSTERDAM
17th CENTURY A.D.

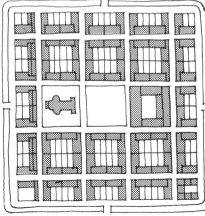

PUEBLO SAN FERNANDO
18th CENTURY A.D.

5

When the industrial revolution began in America, population growth was accelerated. Eastern and mid-western industrial cities grew very rapidly. In them, housing of all existing types, particularly row houses and tenements, continued to be built. As cities became crowded, people began to move farther away from the city center into single-family homes on individual lots. The single-unit dwellings of the village and town were severely compacted onto lots as narrow as 30 feet, complete with car and garage. But, then, more than any other housing environment, suburbia flourished. There was a similar development in southern West Coast cities, such as Los Angeles, except the influence of style was predominantly Mediterranean European rather than Northwestern European.

The age of the "skyscraper" provided the technology for the high-rise apartment. "Yankee" technological ingenuity was at work since there was no precedent for house form at this scale. Concurrently, low-rise housing was generally in the form of row-house blocks.

By the end of the first quarter of the twentieth century, the many walk-up tenements in the American city were beginning to deteriorate. Slums were developing as the exodus to suburbia, by those who could afford it, continued. However, the lifestyle of crowded suburbia was not meeting the expectations of many who had come earlier and now were trapped there. There were notions that human dignity was being compromised by both city and suburban environments and the minimal association with nature was harmful. With a movement to introduce the garden city concept that had been developing in England since the late nineteenth century, the first American garden city of Radburn, New Jersey, was begun in 1928. The amenities of earlier cluster house environments were integrated with open space and automobile circulation to provide a refreshing alternative to both block row housing and crowded suburbia.

The Radburn model was broadly interpreted to engender the garden apartment community, and it moderately liberated forms of the block organization of urban row housing and suburban single unit developments. But America was not yet ready for any large-scale development of cluster housing environments. In spite of the success of this housing environment, the automobile and yankee pioneer ethic were not to be denied and the endless expansion of suburbia accelerated at an even greater rate. The Great Depression and a world war slowed expansion only temporarily.

AMERICA WAS NOT YET READY FOR LARGE SCALE DEVELOPMENT OF CLUSTER HOUSING ENVIRONMENTS

# APPROACHING THE PRESENT

Following World War II, the decay of late nineteenth and early twentieth century urban and suburban housing, combined with the increased demand for housing by returning war veterans, created an enormous housing shortage in America. In the city the problem spawned the urban renewal programs, which, in turn, led to the socially devastating slum clearance housing programs. The planning of this "urban renewal" housing, rising to heights of over 30 stories, has been sufficiently criticized for its gross insensitivity to human needs, so that the argument will not be further labored here.

The postwar building surge partially alleviated the housing shortage for those who could afford to pay for housing. By contrast, the poor experienced, and are still experiencing, increasing difficulty in acquiring adequate housing. Partial relief came in the 1950s in the form of federally assisted housing programs (221, 235, 236 series) which were designed to create incentives for the housing industry to build for the low income and elderly. Innovation was encouraged; replacement

housing consistent with existing neighborhood scale was advocated; and high-density, high-rise housing was to be avoided if possible. All the housing industry had to do to qualify for federal funding was to build better housing for less money. The program obviously failed.

The thrust of the program was not completely wasted since out of that faint hope for a solution came numerous housing experiments and innovations. A great variety of low-rise row houses, town houses, and flats was developed, the advantages of clustering units to capture more shared open space was recognized. Several forms of contract zoning, such as Planned Unit Developments, were enacted to make this new freedom of manipulation possible.

In the 1960s the Radburn concept was elaborated in condominium communities, and high-rent cluster housing environments which are still popular. In increasing numbers, middle-age couples whose children have grown and young married couples who both work became attracted to larger-scale planned residential environments, or "new towns," such as Reston, Virginia, and Columbia, Maryland. The amenities of these environments were quickly incorporated into high-rent developments and, in modified forms, into lower priced public and private housing developments. Thus, a contemporary American cluster house environment was beginning to emerge.

NEW TOWN

## PRESENT AND FUTURE

The resurgence in the past fifteen years of development of town house garden communities is beginning to yield viable alternatives to both the single-unit housing environments that make up suburbia and the closely packed high-and medium-density apartment complexes of the city. The current popularity of town and row house cluster environments is pervasive enough to have reached most parts of America. Nor are they confined to insulated Planned Unit Developments, but are being integrated into existing urban, suburban, and even rural housing environments.

The alternatives emerge from the different scales of cluster developments, the characteristics of the site, and the increasing sophistication of site planning and building design. At the smallest scale, a single-cell cluster may be loosely connected to blend into a natural setting, or it may be organized in a compact and formal arrangement to dominate the site.

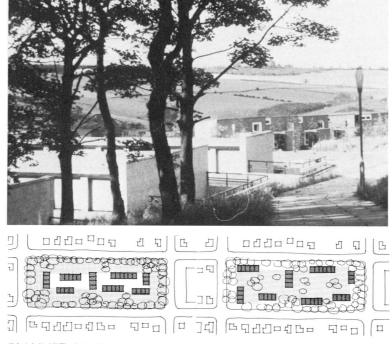
PLANNED UNIT DEVELOPMENT

The multi-celled town and row house clusters are well suited for blending into existing suburban housing environments. They may be planned to have a scale and character compatible with their immediate neighbors. By application of Planned Unit Development zoning, the clusters may be manipulated to create a generous buffer between the street and the cluster or to create more gracious internal open spaces.

The large-scale multi-celled, multi-leveled urban cluster housing is only beginning to develop. This urban cluster, usually a mixture of row and town houses and flats, forms a dynamic multi-dimensional geometry capable of growing to any size. The important distinction between the urban cluster and the traditional urban high rise is that terracing replaces vertical stacking. Early attempts to relieve the verticality and impersonality of high rises with terracing have been limited to a simple staggering of units. While this clearly enhances the individual unit with a gracious private terrace, it does little to express the hierarchy of public-private spaces that are fundamental to good cluster housing planning.

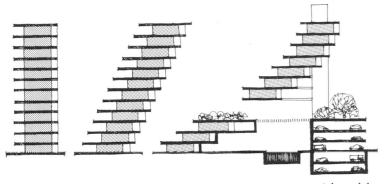

Designs for these urban cluster environments, considered by many to be the *Utopian housing environment*, have been in existence for over two decades. The actual building of them is only beginning; no doubt a long period of innovation and refinement will follow. When built they will provide an interesting comparison with clusters built thousands of years ago by civilizations with far less technological capability.

## LOW-RISE, MEDIUM-DENSITY CLUSTER HOUSING

This book addresses itself to only one scale of cluster housing. It is the scale of the multi-celled clusters associated with suburban and low-scale urban housing environments. The scale is limited to low rise and medium density. Low rise limits the height to four stories, while medium density is set at an average net density of 15 dwelling units per acre. The many reasons for this choice of focus are considered below.

LOW RISE—The four-story limit was established by several determinants, the most critical one being the problem of stair climbing. Climbing three stories of stairs is currently thought to be the maximum for healthy adults and excessive for children and elderly. In addition, behavioral studies indicate that we become disengaged from the land if we go any higher. This disengagement causes a host of human problems such as anonymity, indifference, fear of safety, loneliness, lack of community interest, and insensitivity toward natural processes in general. Some very practical determinants to the four-story limit are that the building can be constructed of most conventional building systems and still meet structural and fire safety requirements, and that unit cost compares favorably with both low-and high-density housing. And finally, four-story stacking allows for development of open spaces in medium-density housing environments.

MEDIUM DENSITY—Preestablishing human density for housing environments is, at best, an approximation. A suitable maximum density can only be determined during the site planning process, since each site, and the way it is developed, suggests its own optimum density. However, by drawing upon the long history of cluster housing environments similar in scale and by assessing the density in the community surrounding the site, we can establish a *density range*. The density will also be influenced by physical limitations of low-rise cluster housing. Once again, this does not fix density, but does set some broad limits.

By examining many examples of low-rise, medium-density housing throughout the world—America and Western Europe in particular—the average density of 15 D.U./acre was established. This far exceeds the existing single-unit suburban den-

sity of 4.5 D.U./acre, but falls well below the hundred D.U./acre density in urban high-rise housing environments. We should bear in mind that it is possible to cram over 40 two-story row houses on an acre if there is absolutely no open space except for *very* small private gardens.

The distinction between gross and net density is important. *Gross density* usually covers a large area, and includes all land, roads, parking, services, and nonresidential uses, while *net density* usually refers to a smaller segment within the gross area. Net density is usually higher than gross density since it covers a smaller land area and includes few nonresidential uses.

In cluster housing, the gross (overall) density may be 10 D.U./acre (dwelling units per acre) while the net density of each cluster may vary from 2 D.U./acre to 20 D.U./acre. Thus, variable density within a development has the advantage of responding to different physical conditions and household types.

All land has some allowable density recorded in the zoning ordinance. Because increasing density increases land value, most developers evaluate the problems associated with increasing density before assigning a final density figure. For instance, as density increases, the cost of services (parking, water, gas, fire protection, etc.) increases to a point where adding one more unit may throw off the budget balance.

We will use the term Planned Unit Development from time to time. A Planned Unit Development (also known as PUD, Planned Unit, Planned Development, Planned Community) is a parcel of land planned as a single unit rather than as an aggregate of individual lots, with design flexibility from traditional siting regulations (setbacks, height restrictions) or land use restrictions (such as mixing land uses). The greater flexibility in locating buildings and combining land uses often makes it possible to achieve an economy of construction as well as to preserve open space and to maintain a reasonably high density.

THE AMERICAN DREAM?

THE AMERICAN DREAM?

# THE AMERICAN HOUSING PROBLEM

## THE NEED FOR QUALITY HOUSING

This book is being written at a time in American history when the housing problem is particularly severe. In general, our standard of living has risen in the past two decades, but the quality of our housing has declined in many aspects. We have a plentiful supply of food, clothing, automobiles, and television sets, but there is an increasing shortage of decent housing and land to build it on. Gross national production continues to rise and luxuries are being accumulated at an accelerating rate, but an increasing proportion of American families cannot afford to purchase or rent decent housing.

Americans, including families and single people, the young and elderly, the fully able and the physically and mentally disabled, expect to live in quality housing environments. For many reasons this expectation is not being realized. In fact, it is actually becoming increasingly remote for millions of Americans.

Is the expectation well founded or built upon collective fantasy? The Housing Acts of 1949 and 1968 expressed the noble mandate *A decent home and a suitable living environment for every American family*. Yet, millions of low and moderate income families are "housing deprived"; that is, they live in "substandard housing." Today 11 million homes, approximately one sixth of America's housing, are classified as "substandard," and this is a conservatively low estimate. Qualitatively the expectation has become a real need since basic human values are being compromised in many existing housing environments. Human values do not change as rapidly as technology and economics. Indeed, many values remain unchanged: the desire to live with dignity; the need for privacy, safety, accessibility, and convenience; the need to maintain individual identity and define personal territory; and the need to live with sunlight, plants, and fresh air and water.

WHAT IS A *DECENT HOME?* Delineation of the basic qualities of "A decent home and a suitable living environment" is still very sketchy. In the 1960 census, criteria for evaluating housing omitted factors such as room size, access to natural light, ventilation, provisions of heat, dependability of services, noise, odors, neighborhood decay, and the many other obvious indicators of an adequate quality of life. Since that time several important sources of quality control, with statutory power, have begun to satisfy this critical omission. Qualitative criteria established in the Minimum Property Standards for federally assisted housing programs are very useful. Even though these standards are becoming increasingly articulate, they do not affect the quality of existing housing stock or new housing built without federal assistance. The American Public Health Associations have developed systems of rating housing quality that account for many of the omitted factors mentioned above. Furthermore, Environmental Impact Assessment begins to introduce some criteria for a "suitable living environment." While the form of the Assessment is still in an early stage of development, its importance and potential cannot be overestimated. It is the first statutory instrument that accounts for the effect that change, such as the construction of a new housing development, has on the quality of life of the entire community. Undoubtedly, if all these new qualitative criteria were to be used in evaluating existing housing stock, millions more units would be classified Substandard.

## THE SHORTAGE OF HOUSING

What is the magnitude of the housing problem? Congress in 1968 set a national housing target of 26 million new or rehabilitated units by 1978, including 6 million low and moderate income family units. In a report of their two-year survey, the Joint Center for Urban Studies of the Massachusetts Institute of Technology and Harvard University indicated that 13.1 million low and moderate income families were "housing deprived" in 1970. This means that one out of every five American households was suffering some sort of housing deprivation.

As defined by the report, this deprivation means one of three things. (1) The family may live in a physically inadequate home (one without plumbing, etc.); (2) it may be overcrowded (more than 1.5 persons per room); or (3) it may carry an excessive rent burden (over 25 to 35 percent of total income). The total U.S. housing stock at that time was approxi-

mately 69 million units. (A housing unit is a single family home, an apartment in a multi-family building, or a furnished room in a boarding house.) Of that total approximately 6 million were vacant (2 million inhabitable, 4 million uninhabitable). An additional 6.9 million were physically inadequate, 700,000 were overcrowded, and 5.5 million had excessive rents.

Some perspective is necessary. Despite its shortcomings, American housing is better today than in the past. Americans have more luxuries and amenities than people in most other countries: 9 out of 10 homes have bathrooms, 99 percent have electricity, 93 percent have running water. Most other countries, developed or undeveloped, also have severe housing problems. For example, the cost of housing in England, Japan, Germany for middle income families is very high, waiting lists (often with a bribe necessary) long, and overcrowding a standard condition. Societies with socialized government housing have long waits for apartments, and then housing is only slightly above minimum standards. For the poor, it is a toss-up as to which country, America, England, or Japan, has the worst slums.

The third world housing situation can only be considered a disaster. Large-scale urbanization coupled with population explosion makes it necessary to double the existing housing stock just to meet the recent population increases. This doesn't include any of the new units necessary to replace the minimal shacks in which most people live. These world-wide views, although interesting, are of limited worth, since we must measure our housing problem against our own ability to conquer complex problems. We cannot hide behind the excuse that our poor people are better off than some other nation's poor.

## THE COST OF HOUSING

The only valid assessment of the cost of housing is a long-range one that accounts for the direct and indirect cost to both the user and the community over the lifetime of the housing. In a break with past practices, only housing developments that assess the economic impact of the development on the community should be allowed to be built.

However, of immediate importance is the capability of the consumer to meet the direct costs of housing. Though our discussion has focused on housing problems of lower income families, that doesn't mean only unemployed minority families or those unfortunate enough to live in our worst slums. Particularly in times of inflation, many others are included in ranks of those with low incomes. Young married couples with children often are on low incomes relative to their expenses, and many have difficulty finding decent housing at reasonable costs. Elderly families and those on fixed incomes often have incomes below the norm and are improperly housed. Many blue collar workers, though fully employed, spend a disproportionate percentage of income on housing. Thus, during a slight recession, when unemployment peaks above 6 percent, thousands of families are forced from their homes.

The housing shortage is beginning to affect more people within the "secure" middle income range. Countless families in certain geographic areas cannot afford the American dream of owning a single family house in the suburbs. Whether this is a sign of future conditions in other geographic areas, or just an unfortunate local condition, is hard to say. However, all signs point to high housing costs and more families in all economic ranges being unable to meet their housing needs.

The median value of new housing has of course been increasing rapidly. Increase in costs can be attributed to four basic sources. The most obvious source is the rise in labor and material costs to construct the basic building.

A related but less obvious source is the cost to provide additional amenities and higher quality products such as air conditioners, alarm systems, high performance kitchen and laundry equipment, more plumbing, better thermal and acoustical insulation, and increased overall building size. Another source is the increased cost of land in developed areas. The average value of land in all metropolitan areas has more than tripled in the past two decades, with some areas experiencing a six-fold increase and more. The fourth source is financing and closing costs where the greatest percentage cost increase can be found. Higher interest rates, professional services, larger discounts, title search, escrow fees, etc., don't affect construction costs, but they do raise the *occupancy costs*. Front-end costs,

i.e., professional services (financial, legal, design, etc.), for necessary approvals now account for approximately 10 percent of development costs and are increasing. A major land development process may have to be approved by up to 36 different agencies.

The introduction of a new housing development into a community places an obvious new burden on its existing systems. The assessment of the direct costs of this new burden are relatively simple; that is, increased demand on utility and road systems can be measured, and the number of new students in the school system can be counted. It becomes more difficult to assess the additional costs of community administration, law enforcement, fire protection, expansion of commercial, cultural, institutional, and recreational facilities throughout the community to accommodate an increased population. These costs must eventually be absorbed by the taxpayers. The family living in the new housing development will be paying part of the tax required to "connect" the development into the community network.

## SOLUTIONS TO THE HOUSING PROBLEM

The magnitude and complexity of America's housing industry has made efforts to organize it impossible. Federal, state and local governments have been increasingly thrust into the role of housing entrepreneurship and management, since the housing industry does not have the flexibility to respond to the diverse housing needs of American society. The government has made limited efforts to sponsor innovation in housing whereas the housing industry has had little success in marketing its self-sponsored innovative housing.

At the time this book is being written, the struggle to resolve the nation's housing problems is at a "stalemate." There are several distinct housing problems, each requiring alternate solutions of its own. The urban housing problem is the most critical and needs an immediate solution. Urban high and medium density housing must take advantage of mass production techniques without producing impersonal and unsafe residential environments. The suburban housing problem and its solution centers on the issue of decreasing wastefulness of every imaginable commodity: land, materials to build the

URBAN

SUBURBAN

RURAL

housing and utility networks, and the consumption of energy in general. Suburban housing environments must use open space, develop connected housing without losing privacy, and have efficient mass transit networks to urban centers. The rural housing problem involves fewer people but poses a particular problem in terms of the many low-income rural families who badly need replacement housing. As with urban poor, the rural poor require economic subsidization to cope with housing problems. But, it is likely the rural housing demand can continue to be met by conventional means.

The underlying solution to all the housing problems lies in an increased efficiency in the use of land and material resources. However, if this efficiency results in boring and impersonal environments, the solution will be worse than the problem. Thus, the site planner, in creatively developing the site, is in a unique position to contribute to the solution, not the problem.

# THE SITE PLANNING PROCESS

Site planning is a creative process requiring the manipulation of many variables. It involves the location, placement, and relationship of all site elements. Site elements include the house; private, semiprivate and public open spaces; pedestrian pathways; roadways and parking; service facilities; etc. The three basic elements—user, site, house—must be continuously interrelated.

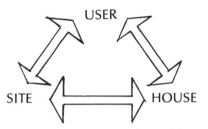

Many alternative solutions may emerge from this process. Rational judgment about which solution is the most appropriate remains the primary responsibility of the site planner. The process must not only account for existing conditions, but must also anticipate future owner expectations. Throughout this process the site planner is making *rational and creative decisions* by continuously interpreting both *quantitative and qualitative* information.

QUANTITATIVE/QUALITATIVE INFORMATION

INTERPRETIVE JUDGMENT

CREATIVE DECISIONS

This book will stress a four-part site planning process which requires the site planner to perform all functions simultaneously. The four steps are:

 PROBLEM DEFINITION

ALTERNATIVE GENERATION

IMPACT ANALYSIS

EVALUATION

All four steps operate at once, with one step dominating and being progressively refined as the process moves toward completion.

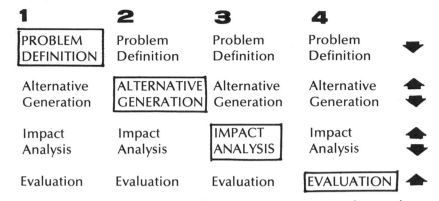

*Problem definition* involves all steps necessary to understand a design problem including site analysis. Since design is a process with many variables, many alternative solutions, and few direct answers, the "problem" will change and become clearer through analysis and testing of the many factors affecting it.

*Alternative generation* is the creative problem-solving step of the design process. Alternative approaches to the problem are developed and refined. This process can be formalized with quick design sketches and should cover a range of solutions.

*Impact assessment* is the process of discovering the effects of each alternative proposed. There are direct, indirect, and cumulative impacts, and many are not immediately obvious. However, repeated practice will increase the planner's ability to perceive the long-term impacts of each alternative.

*Evaluation* is decision making and involves judgment. After the problem has been defined, some alternative ways of solving it proposed, the probable impacts of each alternative understood, a decision must be made about which approach to take. In actual practice, the site planner makes many preliminary decisions *on his own* but is careful to record major decisions for review by the final decision makers. The final decision maker may be a client, future residents, a political body or a bureaucrat.

As an example, the problem may be defined as building some houses on a parcel of land. Initial site familiarization is part of the Problem Definition phase, and each site problem or potential identified, should be followed with alternative housing solutions. The impacts of each alternative solution can be determined, and the results evaluated for final use. Impacts should include both positive and negative results, and should consider only the most obvious at this stage. The process can initially be done quickly in one's mind, with satisfactory alternatives committed to paper. After the site has been analyzed, and alternative uses proposed and evaluated, the problem may be redefined or more sharply defined. Slowly, the process moves on to be dominated by Alternative Generation, Impact Analysis, and finally Evaluation.

This simultaneous step approach is actually a normal process; we do it subconsciously all the time. The process encourages us to make decisions rapidly, since the decision can be reconsidered and corrected later. Lastly, the problem must continually be redefined, since the problem is often too narrow or incorrectly stated and should be changed.

The process requires a knowledge and insight into all aspects of housing development—finance, marketing, user needs, building codes, architecture, construction, design impact analysis, and management. The site planner may work with other professionals in some loosely organized fashion, perhaps even as a team. He must possess insight into the roles and abilities of each team member including the architect, planner, engineer, developer, landscape architect, lawyer, banker, sociologist, interior designer as well as the eventual residents. The roles and dominance of each team member will vary from time to time, and so the process must remain flexible for testing all possible suggestions and alternatives.

## HOW DOES SITE PLANNING FIT IN?

At the largest and simplest level, planning is the correlating of human activities, architecture is the housing of these activities, and site planning establishes the environment in which both can happen. All three are conditioned by economic, social, political, technical, and physical considerations. The site planning problem becomes one of analyzing the relationships

of various subsystems (circulation, housing, open space, parking, etc.) and designing an environment in which they can function most satisfactorily.

Site planning embraces the arts of open space design, building design, and road and pathway design. Many residential environments suffer because the three are practiced independently of each other. Site planning then is the art of designing the site and all the attributes of the site as a whole.

Site planning also deals with many mini-environments— parking, private gardens, roads, houses, garbage areas, utilities, recreation facilities, etc. The creative aspect of the process involves a simultaneous design approach relating each mini-environment specifically to the total environment, instead of considering them as isolated individual elements. Any process relating individual factors to a whole will use many design techniques including systematic approaches, intuition, trial and error, sequential testing, and most importantly, repeating the process over and over.

## THE PRACTICE OF SITE PLANNING.

The title "site planner" is often used indiscriminately by professionals such as land surveyors, engineers, landscape architects, urban designers, architects, planners and others. In practice, a person with a balanced background in all aspects of environmental design is best qualified to responsibly design large-scale environments. As environmental protection and land-use legislation becomes more rigorous, it is probable that site planning will emerge as a profession in its own right.

The site planner's commissions fall into three categories. First, he may be commissioned to evaluate the potential of a site for some specific use. This "pre-stage" often requires an appraisal of the site based on limited study—a general survey to determine density, potential environments, development constraints, profitability, etc. Secondly, the site planner may participate in site selection, where the process is reversed by first establishing desirable site qualities and then trying to find a site to match. Third, the site planner may work with other specialists in developing a plan or a range of alternatives for determining the best use and arrangement of the site. This is the most typical method, and involves site analysis, development concepts, testing and evaluation, zoning change, design development, and supervision of site development. The process is complex and lengthy since it often requires interaction with a community, hearings, and reviews, all leading to the approval of an environmental impact statement.

Building and zoning ordinances often inhibit the best development of a housing complex. Thus, site planners frequently work at a disadvantage in that many local laws, rules, and regulations prohibit them from designing the best possible housing complex. For example, road widths required by county standards are set for suburban developments and prove excessive, unnecessary, expensive, and environmentally damaging for medium-density housing developments. Because of the inflexibility of engineering departments, these standards will prevail and may diminish overall site quality. The list of obstructions faced by a site planner is extensive and includes stereotyped suburban setback, density, parking, access, and room size requirements usually stated in absolute dimensions. Some of the problems are historical and based on a tradition of bureaucratic jurisdictions. Although most governments are simply not set up to effectively implement innovations, there is an increasing trend to replace the inflexible "minimum dimension" with "performance standards." Performance standards set acceptable safety, function, and environmental quality criteria which the site planner can then interpret with a considerable degree of design flexibility. Some examples of performance standards are "six hours of direct sunlight" or "no overviewing at the entrance." A good performance standard will include a means to evaluate both its quantitative and qualitative effectiveness.

## THE SITE PLANNER'S RESPONSIBILITY.

Discussion of the site planning process eventually leads to the issue of the site planner's responsibility. To whom is the site planner responsible? He has set responsibilities to the developer, but there are many other people who will be affected directly or indirectly by a site planning project including the eventual users, abutting neighbors, and the city or town. Thus, the site planner must fulfill certain responsibilities to each group and balance his proposals accordingly.

*Responsibilities to the Developer.* The time is passing when a developer can construct a shoddy development, pocket the profits, and disappear leaving unwary residents to struggle with long-term problems. However, since all developers are rightfully interested in returning a profit on their investment of resources and time, they must rely heavily on the talents of a site planner to produce an arrangement with cost efficiencies and user appeal. The developer's profit is usually dependent on speed and timing during the planning phase.

In addition, the developer's reputation is becoming increasingly important, in terms of project approvals, sales, and finance for future developments. Thus, the site planner can assist in maintaining this reputation by taking projects through the planning, approval, and construction phases as quickly and efficiently as possible. He can also assure the developer of a reasonable profit by exercising cost/quality control throughout the process.

*Responsibilities to the Users.* The needs of future residents must be considered the most important factor in the site planning process. Quality of living experience at an affordable cost is a prime consideration. The present cost of housing exceeds what many American families can afford. Furthermore, since most housing is built without subsidies, it must be paid for by the user. Good housing solutions therefore must constantly balance with should be, could be, and is. We will refer to these options throughout and develop approaches to solve each dilemma. The perfect development is of no value if people cannot afford it.

*Responsibilities to Abutting Neighbors.* Change in metropolitan areas is inevitable with new continually replacing old. The process is usually slow and not noticeable to the untrained eye. Many of our future site plans will be proposed in existing, established neighborhoods. These developments will place an indirect extra burden on neighborhood roads, open space, and shopping, as well as directly changing the relationships between adjoining neighbors.

People select neighborhoods assuming a certain stability expecting no change to occur within those bounds. At the same time developers normally are concerned primarily with their own property. As a result, most apartment complexes demonstrate a uniform disregard to the interface between new development and existing neighbors. It has become common practice to place large parking lots, or the back side of tall buildings, or garbage and service areas with little landscaping along the periphery of a development. The edges of developments, particularly inward focusing ones, are perhaps the least designed and least attractive to neighbors. This doesn't need to happen. Many corrective opportunities exist such as maintaining careful scale relationships between new and old, duplicating thematic qualities of the neighborhood, joining the street system to avoid traffic congestion, landscaping extensively, etc.

*Responsibilities to the City or Town.* Cities and towns are responsible for delivery of public services: sewer, water, recreation facilities, transportation, schools, safety, garbage, etc. Most cannot adequately deliver these services to existing residents much less to new developments. Demand for increased services created by a new development drives up local property taxes. Consequently, the impact of new development on the community must be assessed, and compensating amenities to minimize intrusion must be provided. The options are obvious: allocation of free land for future school sites and parks charged to the development; adequate roads with curb and gutters; sidewalks, lighting, utilities and landscaping; drainage solutions minimizing impact on the municipal sewer system, etc.

Overall, the site planning function must establish optimum conditions in which the present becomes the future. To do this, the relationships between human activities must be sought out, explored, and explained. Through site planning these activities must be brought together so the whole life of the neighborhood becomes richer than the sum of its parts.

## PLANNING THE HOUSING

The site planner must have the basic skills to responsibly generate fundamental planning decisions for both the site and the housing. Planning the housing for a given site is a fundamental part of the overall site planning process and includes the same four steps of problem definition, alternative genera-

tion, impact analysis, and evaluation. It involves the identification, enumeration, location, and basic design of dwelling units on the site. In this phase of the process, emphasis is placed upon the house.

The initial step in the house planning process involves the decision of what type and approximately how many dwelling units will be placed on a site. This must be preceded by an understanding of the potential users and their needs, that is, their family structure and their social, cultural, and economic background. Simultaneously, the site analysis must yield information about the site's potentials and limitations for different housing types and densities. When user needs and site potentials are correlated, the individual units and unit clusters may be designed and manipulated to adapt to the site.

# BIBLIOGRAPHY

## SITE PLANNING - GENERAL

Dubos, Rene
*A God Within*
New York: Charles Scribner's Sons, 1972

Fairbrother, Nan
*New Lives, New Landscapes*
New York: Alfred A. Knopf, 1970

Fitch, James
*American Building, Second Edition*
Boston: Hougton Mifflin, 1972

Hackett, Brian
*Landscape Planning*
Newcastle: Orifl Press Ltd., 1971

Halprin, Lawrence
*The RSVP Cycles*
New York: George Braziller, 1969

Lynch, Kevin
*Site Planning*, Second Edition
Cambridge, Mass.: M.I.T. Press, 1971

McHarg, Ian
*Design With Nature*
Garden City, New York: Natural History Press, 1969

*Design With Climate*
Olgyay, Victor
Princeton, N.J.: Princeton University Press, 1963

Rutledge, Albert J.
*Anatomy of a Park*
New York: McGraw-Hill, 1971

Reilly, William K.
*The Use of Land*
New York: Thomas Y. Cromwell, 1973

Simonds, John O.
*Landscape Architecture*
New York: McGraw-Hill, 1961

U.S. Department of Housing and Urban Development
*Barrier Free Site Design*
Washington, D.C.: Government Printing Office, 1974

## HOUSING - GENERAL

De Chiara, J. and Koppelman, Lee
*Manual of Housing*
Englewood Cliffs, N.J.: Prentice-Hall, 1975

Deilmann, H.; Kirschenmann, Jorg; and Pfeiffer, H.
*The Dwelling*
Stuttgart, Germany: Karl Kramer Verlag, 1973

Goldsmith, Selwyn
*Designing for the Disabled*, Second Edition
New York: McGraw-Hill, 1967

Hoffman, Hubert
*Row Houses and Cluster Houses*
New York: Praeger Publishers, 1967

Kennedy, Robert Woods
*The House and the Art of Its Design*
New York: Reinhold, 1953

Ministry of Housing and Local Government, Great Britain
*Housing Planning: A Guide to User Needs With a Checklist*
London: H.M.S.O., 1968

Ministry of Housing and Local Government, Great Britain
*Some Aspects of Designing for Old People*
London: H.M.S.O., 1962

Moore, Charles; Allen, Gary; and Lynon, Donlyn
*The Place of House*
New York: Holt, Reinhart and Winston, 1975

Rapoport, Amos
*House Form and Culture*
Englewood Cliffs, N.J.: Prentice-Hall, 1969

Schmidt, Karl
*Multi-Story Housing*
New York: Praeger Publishers, 1966

U.S. Department of Housing and Urban Development, Federal
Housing Administration
*Minimum Property Standards for Multi-Family Housing*
Washington, D.C.: Government Printing Office, 1971

## CLUSTER HOUSING IN AMERICA

Caminos, Horacio; John F.C. Turner; and John A. Steffian
*Urban Dwelling Environments*
Cambridge, Mass.: M.I.T. Press, 1969

Gallion, Arthur B.
*The Urban Pattern*
New York: D.Van Nostrand, 1950

Pawley, Martin
*Architecture vs Housing*
New York: Praeger Publishers, 1971

Reps, John W.
*The Making of Urban Ameica*
Princeton, N.J.: Princeton University Press, 1965

Stein, Clarence S.
*Towards New Towns for America*
Cambridge, Mass.: M.I.T. Press, 1966

President's Committee on Urban Housing
*A Decent Home*
Washington, D.C.: U.S. Government Superintendent of Documents, 1968

## EVOLUTION OF CLUSTER HOUSING ENVIRONMENTS

Allen, Edward
*Stone Shelters*
Cambridge, Mass.: M.I.T. Press, 1969

Doxiadis, Constantinos A.
*Ekistics*
New York: Oxford University Press, 1968

Fraser, Douglas
*Village Planning in the Primitive World*
New York: George Braziller, 1968

Hardoy, Jorge
*Urban Planning in Pre-Colombian America*
New York: George Braziller, 1968

Lampl, Paul
*Cities and Planning in the Ancient Near East*
New York: George Braziller, 1968

Michaelides, Constantine E.
*Hydra*
Chicago: University of Chicago Press, 1967

Moholy-Nagy, Sibyl
*Matrix of Man*
New York: Praeger Publishers, 1968

Rudofsky, Bernard
*Architecture Without Architects*
Garden City, N.Y.: Doubleday, 1964

Saalman, Howard
*Medieval Cities*
New York: George Braziller, 1968

# SITE ANALYSIS

What qualities of the land attract us? Natural qualities—lake, stream, trees, meadow—or social qualities— swimming pool, play areas, gym, meeting place. Where do we want to live? On a farm, in the suburbs, in a densely populated urban community? A purchaser's choice of house might be rather simple if the only decisions involved style, size, quality, and whether to buy or rent. What makes the housing decision complex is that the choice of a house implies the choice of a location, the site. The purchaser is likely to be concerned with the overall quality of the neighborhood, of schools and shops, amenity, and public transportation. Every location is unique and satisfies different demands, with identical houses in different neighborhoods selling at vastly different prices.

People have preferences which can be understood. Land, likewise, has potential which can be assessed and understood. This section will look at typical "site qualities or site types" and explore various ways to categorize, understand, and use them. Site analysis is more than just categorizing existing elements; the site planner must feel and understand the site completely. He must develop a sensitivity to the nature of the site and discover those site qualities which will help determine actual land use and design. An understanding of site qualities, or site analysis, informs the design process, allowing maximum aesthetic potential, reduces site development costs, and ensures adequate functioning of natural and human life processes.

## SITE ANALYSIS

Site analysis, the process of understanding existing site qualities, considers factors that determine a site's character, the purposes each factor serves, the location of each factor, the category into which each factor will fit in the design process.

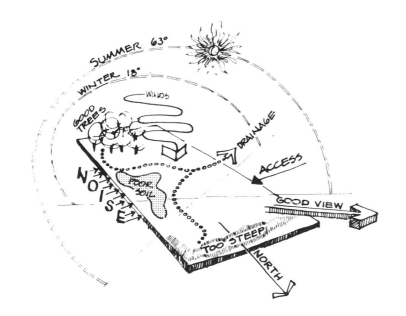

Factors which determine a site's character include:

NATURAL FACTORS      water
physiography
orientation
vegetation
view
climate, etc.

MAN-MADE FACTORS      location
cultural attraction
utilities
services
buildings
roads, etc.

These factors serve three purposes:

Functional requirements of man: moving, living, shopping, working, learning, maintaining, etc.

Pleasurable requirements: recreation, amenity, regeneration, beauty, rest, quiet, nature, etc.

Natural process requirements of the physical/biological environment: the interaction of land, plants, and animals in a self-supporting process (this will be discussed later).

Site analysis requires an understanding of on-site and off-site conditions. On-site refers to the site itself, i.e., the piece of land the client owns. Off-site is less definite, but equally important since no piece of land really ends at the property line. Off-site may refer to land forms such as valley, ridge, stream channel, or flat terrain which affect a site and which might be affected by actions taken on a site. Off-site may also refer to outside services—streets, roads, utilities, schools, playgrounds, etc. On-site factors affect the development directly and can often be controlled or manipulated by the site planner. Off-site factors usually affect the site indirectly and cannot be easily controlled by the site planner.

Site qualities can be categorized into design considerations which become the primary site analysis directions:

Site Potentials—How can the land best be used? What obvious or untapped resources exist?

Site Problems—What must we be careful of, renew, or improve?

Site Amenity—What features are unique, pleasurable, or scarce and should be reserved for all to use?

Site Danger Signals—What areas should be avoided because of excessive development costs and potential problems such as steep slopes, poor soil, creek, bog, marsh?

AMENITY. It should be obvious that urban land with any natural feature—lake, seashore, mountain, wooded stream, meadow, trees, rock outcrop is sought after and demands a high price when being sold. People like and are willing to pay dearly for natural features, as illustrated by the many shorelines, forests, and meadows that have been built upon. Additionally, lots with a view are another amenity that people seek. Land without desirable natural features or a view is less sought after and therefore less valuable.

People have always been willing to forego natural amenities to live in urban areas that provide different amenities—cultural attractions of museums, theaters, fine restaurants, symphonies, and libraries; convenience associated with nearby shopping and jobs, and minimum yard and house upkeep; and simple qualities as strolling on a boulevard or in a park, shopping for speciality items, and experiencing a diversity of life.

Unfortunately, land with natural features and areas with urban character are limited and are becoming difficult for even the wealthy to obtain. For this reason, we are suggesting that nat-

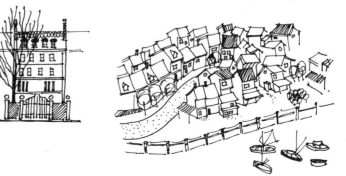

ural amenities be identified, planned to benefit all residents, and not reserved for the few who can (or are willing) to pay high prices. The correct location and careful design of new housing developments can enhance urban areas and perhaps offer desirable urban environments for those seeking them.

Site analysis involves four interrelated steps in which all readily available information is recorded:

Site visits—careful field trips over the site and through the abutting neighborhood.

Resource research—analyzing existing data sources: aerial photographs, topo maps, soil surveys, utility maps, well logs, etc.

Questioning and interviewing knowledgeable people, i.e., residents living nearby, local historians, city officials, experts, delivery men, etc.

Interrelating data—testing and comparing the information from one source with another.

The exact boundary of the site should be determined and information divided into two categories: (1) on-site and (2) off-site. Information can be obtained from three sources:

PROPERTY DESCRIPTION MAP showing property lines, existing easements, access, dimensions, and adjoining uses. A certified surveyor's map is best and will eventually be necessary, but often local township maps suffice initially.

TOPOGRAPHIC MAP showing land form, contours, and physical features (depression, outcrops, hills, bogs, etc.). The contour interval must be small enough to be useful—a 5-foot interval is adequate to begin with though a 2-foot interval will eventually be necessary. USGS (United States Geological Survey) maps are readily available and, though somewhat crude, can work for the initial step.

AERIAL PHOTO, preferably stereo pairs so the site can be viewed three-dimensionally, and an aerial photo enlargement of the site and its surroundings. The size of enlargement will depend on the size of the site. For small urban areas, 50-or 100-scale is best; for large rural sites, a smaller scale of 200 or 400 may prove more useful. Aerials are important in relating on-site land patterns to off-site conditions and therefore must show surrounding land. Aerials provide useful overall information, are the fastest source of vegetation information, and relate land features and patterns one to another. Though not necessary, it is helpful if all three maps are at the same scale, so information can be transferred and interrelated directly.

The question of whether we should study the maps first and then go into the field or vice versa is always perplexing, but is not worth worrying about. Maps should be examined quickly, unusual features noted, and the site walked with a xerox copy of the topo or aerial and a note pad in hand. The site should be visited at least three times, each for a minimum of ½ hour. Trips should be at different times of the day, one on a weekend with the others during the week, and if possible during different weather conditions. All in all, most site planners do not spend an adequate amount of time on the site, and so fail to capture its complete meaning.

RECORDING THE SITE'S PLEASURABLE QUALITIES. In observing first the visual character of the site, the planner can get a feeling for the landscape and the shape of the land, and can note all features worth preserving, such as natural areas, unique qualities, and anything else exploitable during design. Understanding overall site qualities can provide a positive contribution to the character of the design. Each site should be looked at as a whole, but key visual factors which may stand out include:

*Diversity*. In ecological terms, diversity indicates health. Visual diversity, unless chaotic, is generally pleasing, enjoyable, and offers greater variety.

*Individuality* or dominance of a landscape element—forest, hill, stream, meadow, shoreline. Any dominant quality should be enhanced or reserved.

*Cultural features*. Often early developers were careful in the use of the landforms they found, creating complex patterns of built and non-built which are now visually attractive.

*Density*. Most housing development will occur in built-up metropolitan areas. What is the density in general terms: rural, suburban, fringe, urban neighborhood, or urban core? Is the density uniform, scattered, or concentrated? Is there contrast between open areas and built-up areas?

*Fitness*. Do man-made elements—roads, buildings, grading, or planting—fit into the landscape, or do they create their own separate surroundings?

*Scale* is a proportional relationship measuring elements against each other. A site can have an overall small or large scale depending on how it is measured, by man or child, from a distance or nearby. Generally new developments should be "in scale" with old, that is, not appearing proportionately larger or smaller. Some designers fancy themselves capable of correct solutions *contrasting* scale, for instance a 20-story building in a 2-story neighborhood.

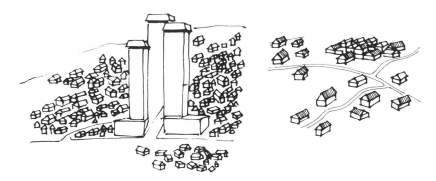

Other visual factors which should be considered include:

| | |
|---|---|
| Contrast | Impressions |
| Feeling | Variations |
| Uniformity | Connectiveness |

RECORDING FIELD TRIP DATA. Recording data as we walk the site is important. The general tendency is to "trust it to memory," but this normally isn't thorough enough. A technique of noting locations of important elements on small copies of site maps, coupled with keyed note-taking, usually works best. Some words are descriptive enough to convey an entire message and should be utilized. They include:

| | | |
|---|---|---|
| active | fresh | rapid |
| alive | friendly | refreshing |
| alpine | glacial | restful |
| beautiful | green | rich |
| bright | happy | rippled |
| brisk | high | rocky |
| clean | impressive | romantic |
| clear | inspiring | running |
| cold | invigorating | rushing |
| colorful | living | secluded |
| cool | lovely | spring-like |
| crashing | majestic | swift |
| crisp | moist | timbered |
| enclosed | mountainous | unspoiled |
| exciting | natural | vegetated |
| flowing | picturesque | watery |
| forceful | pleasant | wet |
| free | pretty | wild |
| forested | pure | wooded |

Words that describe aesthetically unappealing scenes include:

| | | |
|---|---|---|
| arid | destroyed | scraggly |
| bare | dirty | ugly |
| barren | drab | unfriendly |
| bleak | dry | uninspiring |
| brown | dull | uninviting |
| burned | eroded | weedy |
| bushy | golden | windswept |
| colorless | hot | withered |
| depressing | lifeless | worn |

If we can answer the following questions about pleasurable on-site qualities, our first site visit will be considered a success:

1. What is the general character of the site: forest, meadow, open, urban, suburban, rural, mixed second growth forest?
2. Does the site slope? In what direction? How steeply? What orientation has the site (north facing, south, east, or all)?
3. Are there any desirable or undesirable views from the site? Of what, from where, and visible from what elevation?

4. Are there any unique features: stream, rock outcrop, old buildings, forest, bog, pond, lake, or meadow?
5. Can the site be described in any other ways, i.e., as expansive, dramatic, free, undulating, enclosed, inward, outward, open closed?
6. Are there any unique detail parts of the site, i.e., a special tree, rock?
7. Are there specific problems? How noisy is the site?
8. What did we like best about the site?

## ON-SITE FUNCTIONAL CONDITIONS

All the obvious on-site functional qualities should be recorded next. These may include connections to the abutting community, i.e., auto, pedestrian and bicycle access, and utilities. Internal site functions include drainage patterns, level easily built-upon areas, orientation (where the sun is), wind direction, soil suitability, etc. The following questions should be answered during a first visit.

1. Where can auto access be located?
2. Where should auto access not be located?
3. Which areas appear too steep for construction?
4. Where are utility lines, poles, sewers, water and gas mains, etc.?
5. What property line conditions exist (fence, road, curb, gutter, sidewalk, trees)?
6. What areas are easily buildable (fairly level and with no unique features)?
7. What type of roads border the site—arterial, collector, feeder? What is the condition of the roads, and how much traffic (light, medium, heavy) do they carry?
8. What drainage pattern exists, and should it be maintained?

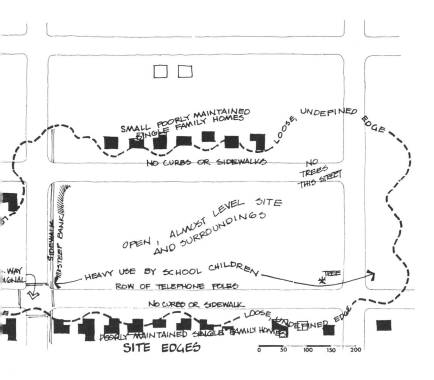

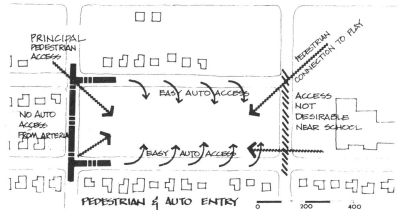

To repeat an earlier statement, it is essential to begin testing development alternatives against each analysis finding. Are any of the qualities worth saving? Could a residential community gain identity by focusing on a site feature? How much room is necessary to preserve each amenity? Do any areas within the site seem right for houses, roads, recreation, parking, or services?

## SITE DANGER SIGNALS

Site danger signals are obvious, visible warnings which indicate a probable development-related problem. A list of conditions which may present severe problems if not carefully handled during the site planning stage should be developed. Site danger signals should be considered in any design solution. Some problems may be best solved by avoiding development near or on them; others may be handled nicely through technologic innovation. Obvious signals include:

Steep slopes (over 15%)
Severe climate exposure
Earthquake danger
Slippage danger
Unstable soil
North-facing slope
Boggy areas
Noisy abutting roads

## OFF-SITE CONDITIONS

Consideration should be given to ways the site influences or affects bordering land and how the bordering community affects the site. Some off-site conditions that may directly affect the site include drainage patterns, noise from nearby roads, undesirable views, and proximity of utilities. Other conditions which may have an indirect effect and be more difficult to handle are location of the nearest primary school, park, shopping, bus stop, church, library, etc. Nearby, unused or underused land which may be used differently in the future should be noted, and some thought should be given to how future uses might affect the site.

A neighborhood profile locating the nearest community services and nearby land uses should be prepared, with emphasis on both auto and foot access. Most facilities farther than ½ mile (10 minutes walk) will not be regularly used by pedestrians, though they may be easily accessible by bicycle. Barriers such as major roads, railroad tracks, steep terrain, or hills that affect accessibility should also be noted.

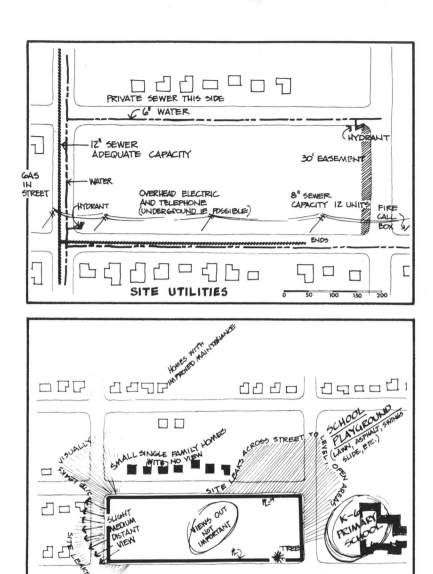

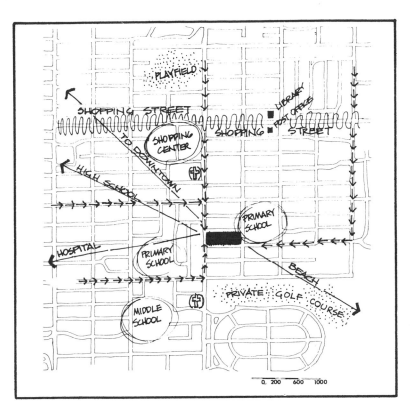

Off-site analysis is a tricky matter, for urban areas are constantly changing and conditions may be different in five years. Many of the changes needn't concern the site planner, but off-site features which the site relates to or depends on should be carefully evaluated for future changes. Such features may be an off-site row of trees, a creek, through access, vacant property, a view, or a narrow road which may not be there in the future. Additionally, new developments tend to cause a rise in nearby property values which may eventually force a change in use. Adjacent vacant, underused, or land held in absentee ownership is particularly vulnerable to change. Checks should be made of future road widening proposals, new arterials, or freeways; property ownership to determine if one owner is quietly purchasing contiguous property and plans some eventual change; and zoning to see if it is more permissive than indicated by existing uses which could allow density to be increased.

Off-site PLEASURABLE factors. Amenity is by definition a scarce resource, expensive to create and never plentiful enough to please everyone. The secret of a successful development is how much OFF-SITE open space it can borrow. Because it is off-site, the development does not pay for it. Usually this open space will be a view of the surrounding city, a lake, rugged terrain, a large estate or golf course, but sometimes a nearby public park or schoolyard can also provide recreation.

Off-site functional questions include:

1. Where are desirable community services (school, church, shopping, playgrounds, etc.)?
2. How useful are these facilities in terms of distance? Are the facilities within walking, bicycling, or driving distance, and should any connection to the site be provided for pedestrian use?
3. How are the abutting properties used—single family housing, farmland, forest, commercial, road? How do these properties affect the site? Will their use change?
4. Is there a bus stop nearby? Could buses be routed through the site?
5. How does the site drainage fit into the larger drainage pattern?
6. Do children have to cross a busy street to get to school or to a playground?

The surrounding neighborhood should be studied to determine its overall quality and any special places. Consider the visual factors discussed earlier: Diversity, Individuality, Cultural features, Density, Fitness, and Scale. Identify any special places by observation or through interviews with neighboring people. This type of analysis is subjective and interrelates accepted visual qualities with personal associations. Anything a community prizes and is known by all should be noted.

In addition to looking at the neighborhood from the site, it is important to look at the site from the neighborhood, and at the neighborhood from the road. Many people experience the landscape by passing through it in cars. What does the site look like from nearby roads? The visual quality of a neighborhood depends heavily on how the roadways look. Are they wide, curbed, uniform, and straight? Or narrow, shifting, and rural? Do they offer passing distant views? Is there a visual quality to the neighborhood as seen from the road—open, closed, varied, uniform?

Some questions related to off-site pleasurable factors include:

1. Is the overall character of the site carried to and reminiscent of the surrounding off-site area?
2. Do unique features of the site begin or continue off the site —a stream, forest, etc.? Should they be protected? What would happen if someone buys and removes them?
3. Is there any danger of a desirable view being obstructed?
4. Can access and use of a nearby park, playground, or schoolyard be assured?
5. What is the most memorable neighborhood quality?

## JURISDICTION

The city or county responsible for approving development plans and the exact existing zoning for the site should be determined, and copies of the zoning ordinances and the Planned Unit Development section obtained. Most housing developments require some administrative action—at least a variance, most likely a P.U.D. designation, and perhaps a zoning change. P.U.D. is a flexible overzone which allows considerable latitude in design standards and relies on bargaining and performance standards.

It is important to calculate the allowable density and required parking, and determine setback and height restrictions. Though it may eventually be necessary to try to change these, initial site studies should test their feasibility. Any change in zoning requirements entails a relatively long and complex bureaucratic process.

## BRINGING THE INFORMATION TOGETHER

All information should be noted as to the scale of accuracy. Is the information *accurate, an estimate, inferred, a guess, or an opinion?*Besides recording data on a base map, it is essential to draw several cross-sectional elevations through the site at a scale of at least I" = 20'. Cross-sections indicate elevational differences and relate them to site elements. Nearby buildings, vegetation, hills, etc., should also be shown at their correct elevation. Vertical elevation may be indicated as light horizontal lines at the appropriate elevation, and horizontal distance with vertical lines every 5 feet.

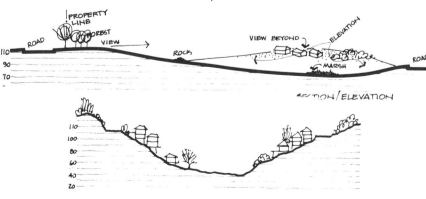

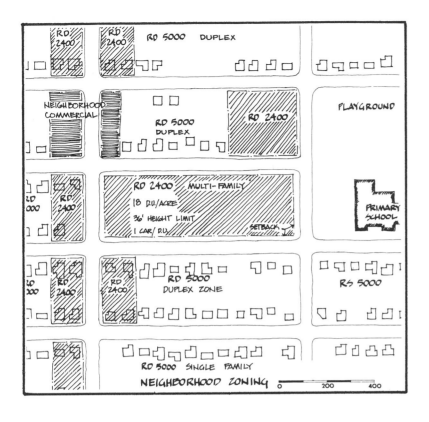

RD 2400   RD 2400   RD 5000   DUPLEX

NEIGHBORHOOD COMMERCIAL

RD 5000 DUPLEX

RD 2400

PLAYGROUND

RD 2400 MULTI-FAMILY
18 D.U./ACRE
36' HEIGHT LIMIT
1 CAR/ D.U.
SETBACK

PRIMARY SCHOOL

RD 2400   RD 2400

RD 5000 DUPLEX ZONE

RS 5000

RD 5000 SINGLE FAMILY
**NEIGHBORHOOD ZONING**    0   200   400

information which will be particularly useful in formulation of alternative site uses. We must know what we are looking for future uses, the approximate dimensions and spatial demands, and site qualities considered desirable or necessary. Evaluate through the design process to determine if more data are needed. Continue to refine the design process.

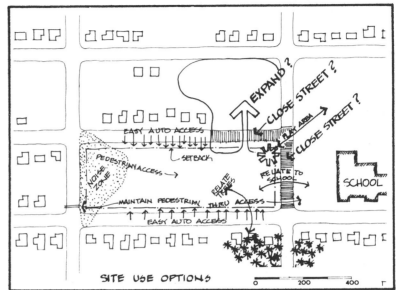

EXPAND?   CLOSE STREET?   CLOSE STREET?

EASY AUTO ACCESS

SETBACK

PEDESTRIAN ACCESS

NOISE ZONE

RELATE TO SCHOOL

RELATE TREES

MAINTAIN PEDESTRIAN THRU ACCESS

EASY AUTO ACCESS

SCHOOL

**SITE USE OPTIONS**    0   200   400

## COMBINING ANALYSIS AND DESIGN

There are a number of ways to integrate site analysis data with design to begin generating alternative housing solutions. First, we all live in a house, and have some ideas and preferences as to what works well. Thus, common sense can be a positive design input. Long-held traditional public values can be restructured to match present cultural attitudes and economic and technologic requirements. Traditional preferences include site character for house type and ways to use a site.

To discover preferred ways to use our land, study historic housing patterns. Until very recently, world-wide housing forms have remained remarkably similar. The reasons are obvious: man has assessed and dealt with his housing problems, needs, and wants over the years. Generally, we build within our financial means to ensure personal and family safety, pro-

## INTEGRATING WITH THE PLANNING PROCESS

With these observations noted, it is time to compare or collaborate the information with various resource maps. Since it is easy to gather useless or irrelevant information, some suggestions to avoid unnecessary work and expense include:

1. Gather as *little* information initially as is necessary and only information which is *readily available*. Always gather data in relation to stated need, in our case information related to use of the site for housing.

2. Begin immediately to test the site's potential for housing. To do this, think about how the land might be used. Gather

sun sun sun sun sun sun sun sun Studies indicate that people's preference for living in California, Arizona and Florida is not because of an outstanding environment, but because of the abundance of SUNSHINE.

tection from extreme weather conditions, convenience to work and play, favored orientation, and personal identity.

In recalling the form, shape, and arrangement of memorable patterns of housing, we should note why or how each form was developed, and how site qualities or factors affected the final form. Traditional housing patterns were generated by one or more of the following:

DEFENSE—Safety and security were insured by impenetrable land form, wall, or gate. Let us recall the walled fortress of Hanseatic castles, Portuguese forts, Spanish presidios, bordered on one side by ocean, wide river, or steep cliffs. Have our needs really changed?

CLIMATE—protection from severe conditions such as cold, heat, sun, driving wind, or excessive rain. In the 1700s, houses in New England villages were located right next to the street to minimize snow removal and facilitate communication. Streets in hot tropical climates are narrow and lined with two-story houses to cast shadows and cool the streets. Homes in Los Angeles have a wide overhang to protect against the hot midday sun. Swiss farm villages cluster together to gain protection from severe winters' with woodshed attached to house, shop to woodshed, and barn to shop. Row houses prevalent in colder climates reduce heat loss through common side walls.

ACCESSIBILITY—Compact, high-density mixed land uses minimize walking distance and reduce cost. Many European communities are arranged in tight fashion with shops on the first floor and living above.

PHYSIOGRAPHY/ORIENTATION opposites seem to prevail with some communities avoiding steep and difficult sites and saving them as open space, while other communities maximize and develop slopes to save level land for other uses. Many farm communities built living units on steep cliffs to save precious level farmland, namely, the Italian hillside village, compact, dense with intertwined path system, borrowed roof garden, distant views, and much sunlight. In most cases, desirable orientations were selected with proper sun exposure, wind protection, or wind cooling as prime design determinants.

Accidental placement of the GRID pattern roadway over steep hills in San Francisco forced houses to be arranged both parallel and perpendicular to the contours causing striking complexes. (It is easiest to build and service houses placed parallel to the contours, but not as interesting either visually or communally.)

COMMUNITY FOCUS—Towns have been laid out for centuries around a common facility such as the water well, commons, or a marketplace. As a town grew, individual neighborhoods adopted a smaller version common focus and developed around it. These patterns are still visible in European, New England, and Southern towns and villages. For instance, Boston and Cambridge are subdivided and related to common squares or greens. Residents describe the location of their home as being at Porter Square, Central Square, Tubman Plaza, Hyde Park, The North End, Brighton, etc. Each name identifies not only where they live but probably indicates something about their ethnic, economic, educational, or religious background.

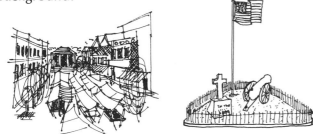

When the stranger says, "What is the meaning of this city? Do you huddle close together because you love each other?" What will you answer, "We all dwell together to make money from each other"? or "This is a community."

T. S. Eliot "The Rock"

HISTORIC ties to our past and pride in our heritage still prevail. Many popular house types draw from early American or English styles, cosmetically treating the exterior of a residence to resemble a Cape Cod salt box, stately Colonial, free-form Ranch house, or English Tudor. While the end result is always a compromise with the cosmetic approach neglecting most site planning concerns, they remain popular.

Recently, because of the automobile and other technologies in heating, air conditioning, weather protection, and communications, we have found different ways to develop, spreading freely over the land, separating work from house and house from neighboring house. In spite of new technology, our homes still need circulation and communication throughout the community, open space, shelter from the elements, safety, security, privacy and orientation to sun and view.

SITE CHARACTER. There is usually an overall character of a site memorable to most people which if missing would diminish the quality of the site. We all have mental pictures of the typical landscape character of New England, New Mexico, or the Rocky Mountains, or the Pacific Northwest. This image probably varies little from person to person. What are these qualities and can they be understood?

COMMON AND UNIQUE LANDSCAPES. Site characteristics usually can be categorized into two groups: the *Common Landscape* which is everywhere and runs ad infinitum and *Unique Landscapes* comprised of unusual isolated elements which stand out at the largest scale from the rest of the landscape. In practice, no one really recognizes, protects, or is much concerned with the Common Landscape, while many, especially conservation groups, avidly seek to protect our Unique Landscape.

Since our Common Landscape forms the predominant character of most areas, it must be understood and maintained. Common Landscapes are the typical, repetitive land forms: long valleys, endless forests, rolling foothills, expanses of flat land, etc. Unique Landscapes include rivers and streams, steep cliffs, rock outcrops, marsh and bogs, isolated elements atypical to the Common Landscape. It may be important to point out that Common Landscapes are often as rich and varied as Unique Landscapes, but since they are plentiful, we tend to overlook them.

Generally Unique Landscapes have fragile qualities which limit the amount of man-made change possible without destroying the landform. On the other hand, the Common Landscape is more abundant and easier to manipulate without losing its overall quality, if it is understood.

Characteristics of the Common Landscape—the vegetation types and arrangements, steepness of hillsides, openings and enclosures in the woods, drainage patterns—should be studied carefully to determine which characteristics should be maintained or replaced to insure continuity following development. In areas where the natural landscape has been altered, an overview of what is natural can help in reconstructing the most appropriate type of landscape.

Urban areas also consist of Common and Unique Landscapes. Neighborhoods with interesting qualities, i.e., Unique Landscapes, are often stable and because of citizen support diffi-

cult to change. Unique urban landscapes usually include natural features: rugged terrain, lush vegetation, outcrop or distant views. Common Landscapes rely more heavily on manmade character and lack vivid distinguishing elements. The normal developer's approach would be to tackle the common areas and do a minimal job. However, almost exactly the opposite should happen. We must find ways to carefully develop in areas of Unique Landscapes and to develop in Common Landscape areas as though they were Unique.

SENSE OF PLACE. So far we have been taking the landscape apart, breaking it into individual problems and potentials. Now it is time to begin putting it back together, relating individual elements to an overall structure.

Each site has a special character creating a "sense of place" which is derived from natural and cultural qualities and places it properly within the whole landscape. Sense of place can be better understood by examining the site at three scales:

1. In relation to the region
2. In relation to its drainage basin
3. In relation to itself and nearby land

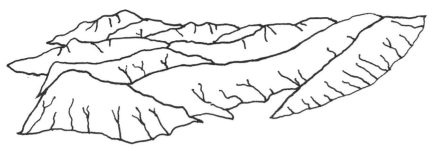

In reading the landscape, we should first look at the larger regional landscape. This ensures an understanding of our landscape as a logical system without becoming bogged down in specific details. If we can grasp this overview, we will find that each smaller landscape unit within it will operate almost exactly the same way. At the large regional scale, bold natural qualities dominate:

Major landforms
Predominant vegetation
Steepness of terrain
Climate

At the largest scale we are interested first in the continuous, common everyday landscapes. Where are the mountain ranges, what are their orientations, and generally how steep are they? What are the drainage patterns? Where are the rivers? What are the general patterns of vegetation and the dominant species? What general patterns of climate exist? Where does it rain? What areas receive morning sun? What wildlife is associated with different vegetation communities? All of these questions can be answered by reading and observing the *landscape physiography* and by drawing diagrammatic cross-sections through inference, interrelate each factor into a comprehensive whole.

We may ask why we should know about 10,000 square miles, when all we are concerned with is a two-acre site? The answer is we will know it better if we understand how it fits into the larger landscape. Once we've learned about a region we can apply that knowledge to each project. As our knowledge increases over time, our understanding of each individual site will grow.

MACRO CLIMATE—Climate is perhaps the most difficult natural quality to include in the design process. In another section we will consider the effects of climate on natural processes, but for now our concern is primarily man-related.

User climate preference varies, but generally most people prefer some sunlight in the garden during a portion of the day. In temperate areas, east-facing kitchens and bedrooms

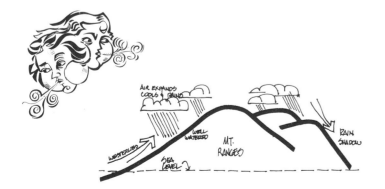

with morning sun are desirable. South, southeast or southwest sun is sought in living areas and main gardens. Western sun is generally undesirable because of its low angle.

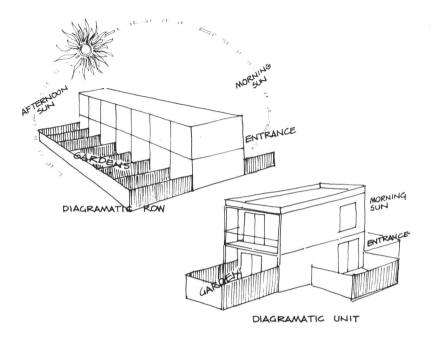

DIAGRAMATIC ROW

DIAGRAMATIC UNIT

In summary, at the largest scale the site planner places his site in the context of natural and cultural patterns of the regional landscape. Where are the hills, the mountains, rivers, valleys, etc., and does the site fit comfortably into this broad pattern? What orientation, steepness of terrain, and vegetation patterns exist? What geologic and hydrologic forces formed the landscape? This overview informs us of many natural characteristics: climatic patterns and vegetation types are a measure of site stability; soil characteristics can be inferred from vegetation patterns and aspect (orientation) from steepness of slope. Most information can be derived from aerial photos, particularly ERTS photos. Two key words here are *pattern* and *inference*. Inference, learning something about one topic through associations and by understanding another topic, is an inexpensive, efficient manner to inform ourselves about a site at this scale.

Moving from the regional landscape to drainage basin and

specific site, interest in general patterns diminishes and specific qualities become important. Emphasis changes as:

Climate shifts to orientation
Aspect shifts to prospect
Landform shifts to slope
Pattern shifts to detail

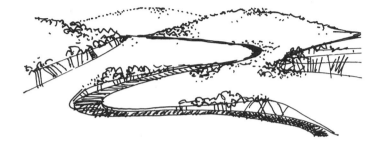

The distinction between Common Landscape and Unique Landscape still holds, with an understanding of both being absolutely necessary. Initially we will assume that Unique Landscape should not be disturbed, while Common Landscapes should be understood so they can be developed without being destroyed.

In analyzing the climate on a site, we need to understand sun angles and wind directions as they relate to the site. It is helpful to superimpose an orientation rose on a site plan to indicate where the summer and winter sun rises and sets and the highest sun angle above the horizon for both periods. Summer and winter wind directions should also be indicated.

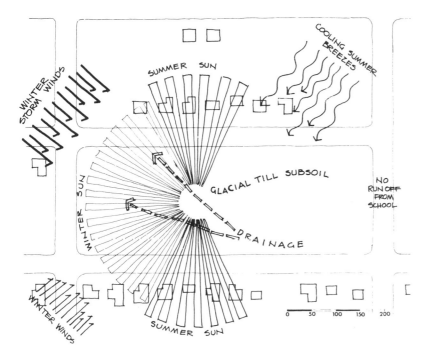

Several other climatological factors are important:

Temperature change with elevation with a 3° loss per 1000-foot rise.

Warm air rises, whereas cold air sinks (called air drainage) leaving cold pockets in low lying areas such as the bottom of valleys or depressions. Bulky buildings on a slope can block air drainage, trapping cold air behind them.

Sloping land inclined toward the sun collects more heat than level land since it is more perpendicular to the sun.

The crest and top of a hill are more windy than half-way down.

Outdoor living areas should be shielded from cold winter winds, but cooling summer breezes should be encouraged to flow in.

## SITE ANALYSIS SUMMARY

Analysis should proceed with site use in mind. It is important to reexamine patterns of the site—the major slopes and land forms, orientation, vegetation patterns, site drainage and unique features as rock outcrops, etc. Areas obviously suitable for housing such as level or slightly sloping land should be blocked out. Access points should be noted, as well as land-scape features of high amenity or recreation value. Problem areas such as poor views, abutting undesirable land uses, over-viewing, etc., should be noted. Site danger signals and areas of high potential should be recorded, i.e., slopes steeper than 15%, natural habitat areas, places of high wildlife potential, soil subject to slippage, unique landscape qualities, sensitive hydrologic features, etc. The process links analysis with use and should begin to indicate a range of site use potentials and clarify or describe the site character. Site character is a useful determinant in developing generic housing.

# HOUSE ANALYSIS AND CONCEPT DEVELOPMENT

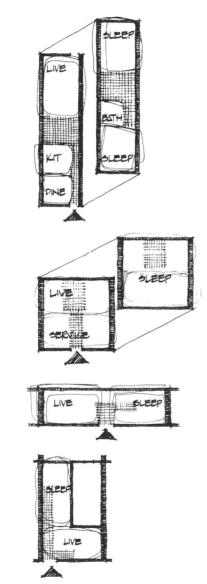

The process of planning the housing for a given site is a fundamental part of the overall site planning process. In most cases the development process begins with the search for a site that can accept a preconceived housing type. A sophisticated development program will include an economic feasibility study based on an analysis of market demand and an array of cost-benefit trade-offs. Even though this study is generally done by others, the site planner may be called upon initially to exercise a broad *qualitative* judgment of the type and quantity of dwelling units a given parcel of land may accommodate. Less frequently the development process may begin with an analysis of the site to determine the type and quantity of housing most suitable for it. In each approach the site planner must possess considerable knowledge of the house analysis and design process in order to develop a complete site plan. This chapter, then, will consider the process of house analysis and concept development.

## HOUSE ANALYSIS

The house analysis process may be organized into sequential parts:

Determinants of house quality and suitability

Identification of household type

Identification of house type

Correlation of household/house type

## HOUSE QUALITY AND SUITABILITY

The basic quality and suitability of the housing for a given site must emerge from an expression of the socio-cultural background of the users, the potentials and limitations of the site, and the material and technological resources of the region. In the study of human settlement and house form it is demonstrated time and again that man, site, and material resources become an inseparable triad. Without considerable knowledge of a given culture, it is difficult to determine to what degree man has adapted to the natural condition of the site and the materials resources of the region, and to what degree the site and materials have been modified to accommodate man's needs. The present condition in American housing is less than clear, since the quality and suitability of housing is established primarily by popular taste. Technology has the capability of changing a site's configuration and transforming raw material into composite material. The analysis that follows is structured with certain positive beliefs and expectations built in:

Basic human needs cannot be compromised; the house must establish an equilibrium between function and amenity without being wasteful.

The house must "fit" the site; the house must express a compatibility with, and respect for, the natural amenities of the site.

## HUMAN NEEDS AS DETERMINANTS OF HOUSE QUALITY AND SUITABILITY

Early man, preoccupied with survival, was satisfied with an unadorned shelter that was dry, warm, and protected from his

predators. It soon became necessary for the shelter to be defensible from the attacks of other men. The Agricultural Revolution saw the house relocated near the crop and sources of water and fuel. Even though the Iron Age, Industrial Revolution, and Technological Revolution witnessed the development of the city, the basic dwelling has not changed much except for the addition of some mechanical attributes. In the Renaissance, when the concept of "firmness, commodity, and delight" became commonplace, "delight" began to relate to those additional qualities that make the house more than a shelter for survival. The house became an enjoyable living environment. As different cultures flourished, another quality emerged—the symbolic quality of the person's dwelling. More recent study of human behavior has articulated the need for the individual to experience privacy and to feel safe in his identifiable territory. The human needs listed in this analysis are a very simple summation from contemporary behavioral studies on the subject.

TERRITORY

ORIENTATION

PRIVACY

IDENTITY

CONVENIENCE

ACCESSIBILITY

SAFETY

## WHAT ARE THE HOUSE QUALITIES THAT ACCOMMODATE THESE NEEDS?

In most cases the qualities can be carefully described. To the extent that cultural norms apply, some of the qualities may also be quantified; for example, territory is usually bounded by one's property line; the maximum decibel rating that constitutes aural privacy is a given number. Research in human behavior is just beginning to yield quantitative data on all aspects of perception. In time there may be standards for measuring visual privacy, convenience, safety, etc. A measure-

ment of the effectiveness of house quality to accommodate people's needs may also be made by evaluating existing house environments. The seven needs mentioned above take equal measure of any house environment such as the primitive vernacular house, the modern high-rise apartment, the traditional suburban house. Let us test the latter since it is the genesis of several of the house types being considered.

The suburban house and lot, with its well-defined boundaries, clearly identifies the occupants' *territory*. The house sits neatly near dead center on the lot (as building codes would have it) and is buffered from the adjacent neighbor's territory by outdoor recreation areas for children and adults. With some good fortune the house and lot will have an *orientation* allowing for favorable daylighting, enough sun for growing plants, but some shade to avoid excessive heat build-up or sun glare, a territorial view, openess to summer breezes but protection from cold winter wind and driving rain. Yard, entrance, and interior spaces are *private* so that neighbors and passersby cannot easily perceive what is happening inside. The house is probably compact enough to be *convenient*, the car is parked as close as possible to the kitchen, the garbage can is nearby (too often by the entry), and children at play in the yard can be easily supervised. The house is probably not *accessible;* there are steps up to the entrances. With luck there may be a garage floor or patio that is level with the house floor, allowing a disabled person to enter unassisted. The house and lot are sufficiently different from the neighbors' to be unique and have *identity*. The color of the house, the fencing, and the maturing shade trees all contribute to identifying this house as someone's "home." And finally, it is *safe;* the residents have a sense of security from outside intruders. There are adequate exits in case of fire. Rooms are adequately heated, illuminated, and ventilated. The structure is stable, built with durable materials on firm soil.

Let's take a closer look at each of these needs and describe some of the house qualities required to satisfy them.

## TERRITORY

We can perceive our territory and judge whether it is being violated through our senses of sight, hearing, smell, and touch. In medium-density housing, territory is primarily private outdoor space clearly belonging to the family, that is, a garden, balcony, terrace, etc. Usually territory is defined by fencing, planting screen, berm, change of level, party wall, or the house forms themselves. On a smaller scale, interior space such as a bedroom, study, a corner of the living room may clearly be the territory of the individual. Behavioral studies support the common sense judgment that some specific indoor and outdoor space is necessary for a combination of personal psychological and physiological reasons. In over-crowded housing, the lack of definition of personal space—individual territory—is the source of many social problems.

The authors stress maximum ground orientation and recommend striving for private outdoor spaces for all units, particularly those occupied by families with young children. The outdoor spaces are smaller than those of a single family house lot but are still adequate to satisfy all defined needs. *Visually*, territory is constant by day. In planning we must orient units so that sun glare from one neighbor's windows will not keep another neighbor from using his terrace. At night, visual barriers must be positioned to block out harsh night lighting from neighbors, street lights, and vehicle headlights.

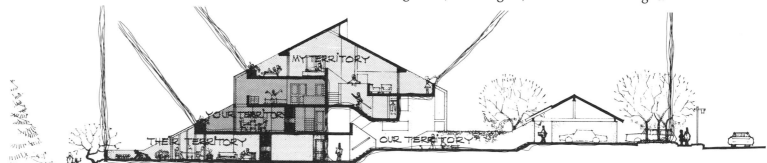

TERRITORY

It is most difficult to control *noise* violation of territory (sound pollution) from distant sources such as aircraft, passing trucks, trains. We can exercise some control in not recommending sites adjacent to airports, highways, or railroads as building sites. However, it is possible to dampen local noises such as children at play and loud rock music, by placing very dense barriers between one's territory and the likely source of the noise. Sound transmission through interior common walls can be a very serious violation of territory and can only be solved by initially building in a high quality sound barrier.

Like noise, *odor* from distant sources (air pollution) is difficult to control. If a site has a constant prevailing breeze, open space territory could well lie windward. By the way a building is sited and shaped it is possible to create interior ventilation to eliminate indoor odors. Exhaust fans can ventilate interior spaces, but their exhaust outlets should be placed high on a wall or roof, not near the neighbor's window.

## ORIENTATION

We all enjoy sunlight most of the time, and value it both inside and outside the house. The orientation affording the most sunlight is south facing. The garden and main living areas should receive maximum sunlight. Slight rotation to the east or west may further improve orientation, with southwest being ideal for absorbing maximum afternoon light. Sleeping rooms and kitchens work best with east-facing windows which receive morning sunlight.

There are different demands for sun energy based on the climate of the site location. *Sun Insolation*—absorption of the sun's thermal energy—is desirable in most climates as a means to warm spaces and, of course, make plants grow. In almost any climate *sun insulation*—the suppression of the

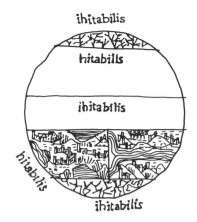

sun's thermal energy—is also needed when there is an excessive thermal buildup. This is accomplished by installing thermal insulation in the roof and wall systems and by shading devices such as properly placed shade trees, screens, roof overhangs, etc.

*Daylighting* is another aspect of sun orientation. Even in locations with limited sunlight it is possible to site a house, position its windows, overhangs, in order to capture optimum amounts of daylight. While direct sunlight is appealing, there are situations requiring reduction of its brightness and glare when it can be best handled by adjustable filters or screens such as blinds, shades, special glazing, etc. We should remember that reflected light is equally intense; window glazing must be positioned so as not to violate a neighbor's territory.

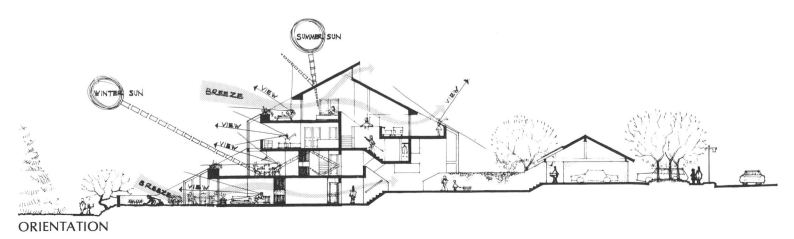

ORIENTATION

*Air movement* in the form of *wind and breeze* can influence orientation, particularly on sites that have a history of high wind speeds from a constant direction. Breeze is a gentle and positive force. Wind is an excessive and destructive force. In either case, breezes and winds are carriers of a host of climate modifiers such as rain and snow, sweet fragrances, and foul odors, and even serve to amplify or dampen sound transmission. We should remember that facing into the source of hurricanes and tornadoes will require building houses strong enough to withstand such force.

The amenity of *view* is perhaps the most important determinant for orientation of the house. As such, it must remain an ever-present concern throughout the site planning process. Several subsequent chapters will deal with view in detail. For purposes of orientation, view is both qualitative and scalar; that is, the view into one's private garden court is intimate where the view to the horizon is distant, broad, and shared with many others.

It is very important to work with sun, wind, and view as dynamic forces; daytime differs from nightime; and winter differs from spring, summer, and autumn; winter winds generally come from one direction and summer breezes from another. Both site and house plan must demonstrate sensitive response to these dynamic qualities to guarantee the users a viable living environment.

## PRIVACY

As house density increases, the importance of designing for privacy also increases. Privacy can no longer be created by open space isolation such as one experienced living in a nineteenth century American farmhouse on 160 acres of land. In medium-density housing, privacy is created primarily by *shared barriers* such as opaque sound-proof party walls, floors and ceilings, fences, shrubbery, etc. (see previous section on Territory).

Internal privacy is accomplished conventionally by constructing rooms with doors and windows that cannot be easily looked into. External privacy—privacy on entering and leaving one's house, and privacy in one's garden, terrace, or balcony—is more difficult to achieve. Each unit entrance should be afforded maximum privacy by minimizing the number of other unit entrances close by and eliminating side-by-side entrance doors. Overviewing is even more complex in that privacy is needed from adjoining neighbors in the garden and from neighboring units.

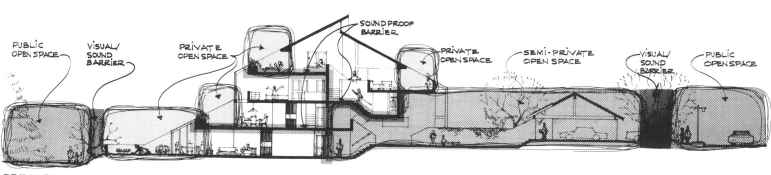

PRIVACY

## IDENTITY

We all seek to maintain our individual identity. Our choice of housing and the way we maintain it is an important means of expressing our identity. There is increasing evidence that the primary factor in housing and settlement form is *socio-cultural* not climate, material resource, or construction technology related. In analyzing historical models for their symbolic qualities and "practical" qualities, it is surprising to find how much man will physically inconvenience himself in order to maintain a symbolic identity.

We tend to seek identity through selection of a house style, e.g., Northwest, Ranch, Cape Cod. In medium-density housing a house style generally is consistent throughout the development. In traditional row housing, identity can be developed through decoration and other applied effects as has been done in good taste for centuries in cities throughout the world.

Recently, with more sophisticated technology, diverse and "acrobatic" house forms have emerged that allow for greater individual identity. We are using the generic term *cluster* for such housing and will be looking at the approaches for its efficient design and siting. It is important to acknowledge that, while the cluster housing form is appealing in diversity and allows for many opportunities to create *privacy and identity*, it is generally considered more costly to build and maintain than the simple row house form. There are, however, some attractive cost/benefit trade-offs which will be developed in subsequent chapters.

## CONVENIENCE

For our purposes, convenience is the degree of physical ease or lack of difficulty encountered in progressing through daily household activities. The history of the house indicates that convenience is an *attitude;* our ancestors were greatly inconvenienced compared with contemporary house dwellers. Our culture's performance record for converting yesterday's luxury into today's necessity is unsurpassed. However, it is difficult to judge whether contemporary environments are too convenient, just right, or not convenient enough.

Convenience is in the eye of the beholder. A shelf or window sill may be at the right height for an adult but out of reach for a child. One housekeeper may prefer a small, compact kitchen, while another may find it necessary to have a large, open kitchen. Some users may even want to trade convenience for some other amenities such as high windows that let in lots of light but are difficult to wash.

CONVENIENCE/ACCESSIBILITY

## ACCESSIBILITY

Accessibility to all parts of the housing environment by all members of the family may be considered a basic human need, but there are many qualifying conditions. It is apparent that an adult, whether able-bodied or disabled, should have access to the entire housing environment. This requires on-grade access to houses and single-level living units or vertical lift systems in multilevel houses. Conversely, there are parts of the house that should be made inaccessible to children for reasons of safety.

Accessibility cannot be generalized. The degree of accessibility must be carefully adjusted to the needs of the intended user group. Furthermore, some aspects of accessibility are easy to accomplish and can be of benefit to everybody. For example, level access into units simply makes good sense. Providing ground-level units for the elderly and physically disabled can be achieved easily. On a detail scale, accessibility can be made more convenient by use of simple items like lever handles rather than hard-to-turn door knobs making doors easier to open for the able bodied as well as for little children and arthritic elderly people.

## SAFETY

Safety is a sense of security in one's house and garden, day and night, season after season, and year after year. This means protection from the many things that threaten human safety and cause property damage.

People create most safety and security problems, either directly through vandalism, assault, theft, arson, etc., or indirectly through pollution of air and water. Destruction by natural forces, although less frequent, is vastly more severe and damaging. Floods, slides, hurricanes, earthquakes, volcanic eruptions, forest fires, among others, can annihilate entire communities.

The way houses are sited and the size, configuration, and access of open space can determine the users, therefore effecting a designed-in security. The house must be as strong and durable as possible (a direct function of cost) to endure the natural forces. And, the house must be reasonably fireproof and/or provide adequate fire escape routes.

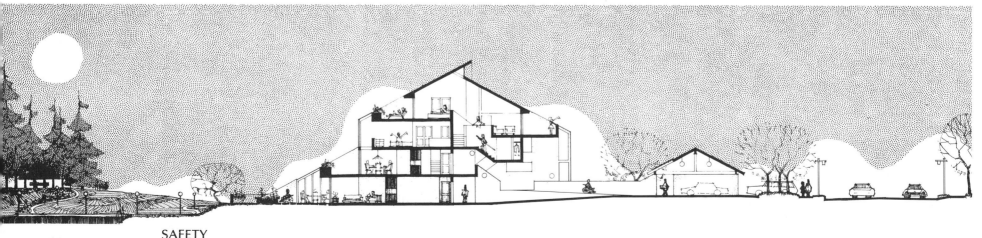

SAFETY

## SITE POTENTIALS AND LIMITATIONS AS DETERMINANTS OF HOUSE QUALITY AND SUITABILITY

What characteristics of the site directly influence the quality and suitability of the house? How can the house be designed to enhance the natural amenities of the site? The previous chapter on Site Qualities and Site Analysis established a basis for determining characteristics and amenities of the site. Extrapolating from these factors, we develop information for the design of the houses themselves. The organization of the interior spaces, both horizontal and vertical, and the interior/exterior spaces such as entries, decks, gardens, and terraces, depends on the basic site characteristics discussed in the previous chapter. They are important enough to repeat here;

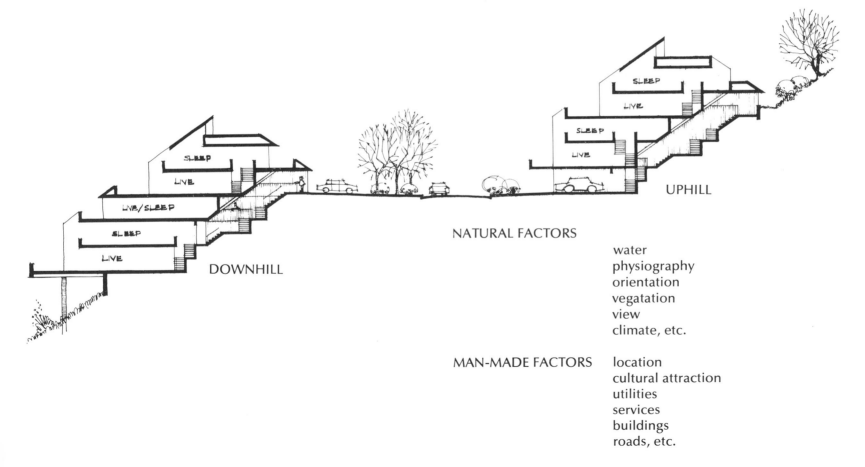

DOWNHILL

UPHILL

NATURAL FACTORS

water
physiography
orientation
vegatation
view
climate, etc.

MAN-MADE FACTORS

location
cultural attraction
utilities
services
buildings
roads, etc.

*Climate and orientation* influence the size and position of doors and windows. *View* into a garden or to the distant horizon is also controlled by window size and position. Orientation to the street influences the position of the entry; that is, spaces requiring more privacy are positioned away from the street. The *slope* of the land form influences the configurations and positioning of the house more than by any other site characteristic. The typical two-story structure, on a site with sufficient slope to call it a "partial daylight basement" type, fits less graciously above ground on a level site. Whether the house sits *uphill or downhill* from the access road may well cause the interior spaces to reverse with respect to entry, service, and view orientation. Other site factors that influence the organization of housing are amenities and utilities. The amenity of a distinctive land or vegetative form such as an existing shade tree may well become the major "furnishing" of a

patio that serves living room, dining room, and kitchen alike, as well as the focal point for many interior spaces. Consequently, this amenity may be the major determinant in organizing the interior spaces. Moreover, housing must be organized to relate to existing man-made networks of utility services such as water, electricity, gas, telephone, television cable, and storm and sanitary sewer. Some or all of these will influence where and how deep and high buildings can be constructed.

## MATERIALS AND TECHNOLOGY AS DETERMINANTS OF HOUSE QUALITY AND SUITABILITY

We have the capability to build any style of housing with a vast assortment of materials just about any place in America. It is commonplace to find the New England Colonial style in Southern California or Southwest Adobe style in Northern Minnesota. There are no rules; individual taste combined with sufficient dollars knows no constraint. If this is so, how does the site planner contribute to the analysis of the quality and suitability of the housing type for a given site? The site planner must proceed with considerable objectivity. His primary role is to use his understanding of the site, both qualitative and quantitative, in recommending a house character that is complementary to the site.

Several material and technological determinants to which the site planner must give direction are:

CONSTRUCTION METHOD   The ways the housing is initially constructed can vary considerably. Each approach will impact the quality of the housing and the site itself. First, the on-site "stick built" house is the most lengthy approach but yields a greater design flexibility and adaptability to site configuration. Second, the on-site assembly of factory-built components is moderately flexible, and fairly rapid and efficient. Third, the on-site installation of factory-built units is extremely rapid, not very flexible, and potentially disruptive in that heavy equipment is needed to place the units.

**TRANSITION OF HOUSE FORM TO LAND FORM** The most structurally and ecologically efficient foundations systems may not enhance quality in terms of human use. A pole foundation may make on-grade access impractical' whereas a flat slab, on-grade unit may provide a choice of access.

**CHOICE OF BUILDING MATERIALS** It is recommended that building materials be visually compatible with natural on-site materials. Indigenous building materials "weather" naturally, generally fit well with the surroundings, and are durable. Materials may be chosen to reinforce the house form as it relates to the land form. For instance, a house cluster in a rocky setting may be firmly anchored with a strong concrete or masonry base. Or a house cluster on a wooded site may be most compatible if sided with wood.

**CONSTRUCTON COST** Cost is always a determinant of house quality. The choice of materials, the complexity of the detail and configuration of the house form, and the degree of craftsmanship are all cost/quality related. Because of his "overview" of the design of the entire site, the site planner has a unique advantage and responsibility to judge the best value for the amount of money invested.

## IDENTIFYING HOUSEHOLD TYPE

This phase of the planning process requires special input from the developer, or his market consultant, on the projected user population. The developer, in reviewing alternatives, will be able to determine who the projected users will be by providing fewer, bigger units to attract wealthy clientele or by increasing the density and building smaller units, if the development is to provide federally-assisted, low-income housing.

However, since alternative solutions are not likely to yield the same profit, the user population may well be identified as a component of the plan that is projected to yield the highest profit. It is not possible at this point to explore trade-offs with other variables that would allow any user population to be accommodated on any given site, but it is worth considering that such a condition would be socially ideal. Our stated goal of developing medium-density, low-rise housing moves towards that goal by reducing the land cost per unit below that of the single-unit residence.

### WHAT IS HOUSEHOLD TYPE?

It is a basic classification of the various social units that make up the traditional "family." The description of each type is based on the following determinants:

- Identification of members who make up a household— single, young couple, couple with young children, couple with teen age children, couple with grown children, elderly couple, elderly single

- The socio-cultural and economic background of the members

- The physical condition of the members

In this early phase of the planning process the identification of the projected user population is by household type, which is simplistically described in terms of family size and income level. A sample matrix for correlating family size and income level follows:

| SIZE \ INCOME | Low | Moderate | Middle | High |
|---|---|---|---|---|
| Young Single | ◯ | ◯ | | |
| Young Couple | ◯ | ◯ | ◯ | |
| Young Couple, Young Children | | ◯ | ◯ | |
| Middle Age Couple Teen Age Children | | ◯ | ◯ | ◯ |
| Middle Age Couple, Grown Children | | ◯ | ◯ | ◯ |
| Elderly Couple | | ◯ | ◯ | |
| Elderly Single | ◯ | ◯ | ◯ | |

The family size follows the traditional life cycle, but in its simplicity it excludes, for example, middle-age singles, grandparents, other relatives, extended families, etc. The income levels are reasonably direct. Since the distinction between moderate and middle is fine, they can be combined at this phase.

The present demand for housing is fairly well scattered in terms of family size. In terms of income level, there is no doubt that housing demand comes from the 13 million American families who are "housing deprived," and who are almost entirely in the low-to-moderate income level.

## WHAT SPACES ARE REQUIRED FOR EACH HOUSEHOLD TYPE?

A thorough development of space requirements for each type could reasonably be the next step. Referring back to *House Qualities*, user needs (i.e., territory, orientation, privacy, identity, convenience, accessibility, safety) would be developed for each type. These in turn would be translated into *activities*, and finally into *spaces*. However, another shorthand step we will take is to make some basic assumptions about household activity and space requirements in order to quickly match household type with house type.

Here is a sample matrix for correlating household activities and spaces for a couple with young children:

| SPACE \ ACTIVITY | Sleeping | Living | Eating | Cooking | Hygiene | Study | Play |
|---|---|---|---|---|---|---|---|
| Bedroom | ◯ | | | | | ◯ | |
| Living Room | | ◯ | | | | ◯ | ◯ |
| Dining Room | | | ◯ | | | | |
| Kitchen | | | | ◯ | | | |
| Bath | | | | | ◯ | | |
| Study | ◯ | | | | | ◯ | |
| Family Room | ◯ | ◯ | ◯ | | | ◯ | ◯ |

In terms of household type (and housing type), there are two basic types of spaces—*interior* spaces and *interior/exterior* spaces. We should remember there is also exterior space on-site and off-site in the form of open space.

The basic *interior spaces* are familiar to us all; they are living, dining, kitchen, bedroom, and bathroom. A secondary set of spaces that are less basic include "study," "utility room," "family" and/or "recreation" room, storage, and garage or carport (attached or detached). And, there are the circulation spaces of entry, hall, and stairway,

*Interior/exterior* spaces are "outside" spaces that are contiguous with "inside" spaces, including decks, patios, terraces, entries, pathways, enclosed garden courts, and even fenced-in yards. They must be regarded as living spaces equal in importance to interior spaces.

In identifying the kind and number of spaces for each household type, the number of bedrooms required is the established base since it directly reflects the number of people in a family. A good rule-of-thumb is two people per bedroom up to eight people and four bedrooms; beyond that it is difficult to use standards. As the number of bedrooms grows, other spaces grow proportionately in size and certain new spaces are added.

Here is another matrix for correlating bedroom spaces to other interior spaces. The unit is identified by number of bedrooms, the spaces by activity.

| ACTIVITY | UNIT (BEDROOM COUNT) | | | | | | |
|---|---|---|---|---|---|---|---|
| | EFFICIENCY | ONE | TWO | TWO | THREE | THREE | FOUR |
| Sleeping | alcove | bedroom | 2 bedroom | 2 bedroom | 3 bedroom | 3 bedroom | 4 bedroom |
| Living | combined | combined | combined | living | living | living | living |
| Eating | | | | alcove | alcove | dining | dining & alcove |
| Cooking | alcove | alcove | kitchen | kitchen | kitchen | kitchen | kitchen |
| Hygiene | bath | bath | bath | 1-½ bath | 1-½ bath | 1-½ bath | 2 bath |
| Study | | | | study | study | study | study |
| Play | | | | | | family | family |

## IDENTIFYING HOUSE TYPE

There are several basic types of contemporary cluster housing the site planner must become familiar with in order to quickly manipulate house form in the early phases of the site planning process. They are:

ROW HOUSE

TOWN HOUSE

FLAT

PATIO HOUSE

MAISONETTE

TERRACE

## ORIGINS OF THE HOUSE TYPES

We can trace the *form* of the basic types to origins in traditional American (and European) single-unit dwellings. As the single units merge together in a cluster, sidewalls become party walls and side yards cease to exist.

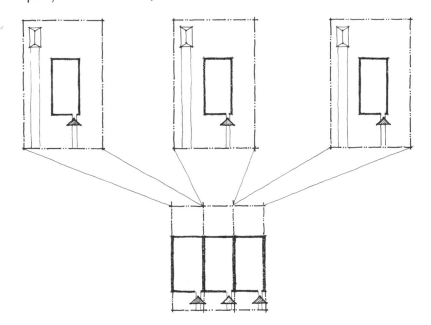

The traditional progression of entering on the public side (front yard), moving through the unit, going out into the private garden (back yard) is retained.

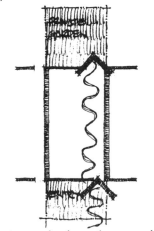

The now disproportionately deep front and back yards may be foreshortened. During the past 50 years the purpose of the front yard has been shifting from the traditional semi-private open space to an anonymous public open space. While the front yard may be decreased in size, it may also be redefined as a semi-private space by various screening devices.

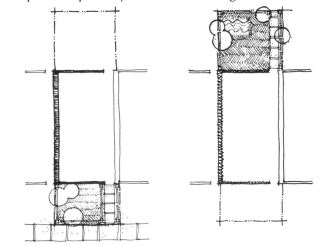

The traditional "back yard" once served many large-scale utilitarian functions, many of which have ceased to exist. In recent years, the back yard has become more a passive recreation space for the family. In cluster housing it becomes a well-tended, not-so-large private garden.

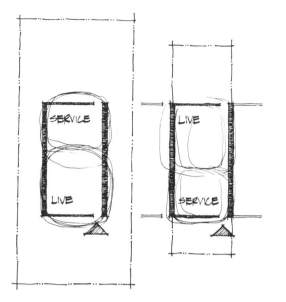

THE ORGANIZATION OF INTERNAL
SPACES IS SHIFTED

The organization of internal spaces is also shifted in cluster housing. The rural tradition of viewing the road from the front porch or the living room window directly behind it, has been inverted by fronting the living room and other "private" spaces on the private garden side. To allow for this inversion, the kitchen and other service functions move to the entry side and thus must be by-passed by the formal entry.

ROW HOUSE—The row house originated in the traditional two-story house situated on a narrow or medium width lot. The basic "living" functions are at ground level; these include living, dining, kitchen, half bath, and possibly a study. The upper level is devoted to bedrooms and bathroom facilities. Since the row house is flanked on both sides of the long axis by party walls, access, view, daylighting, and natural ventilation must all come from the two narrow ends. Entry is at one end, north side if possible, while the private garden is at the opposite end, south side if possible.

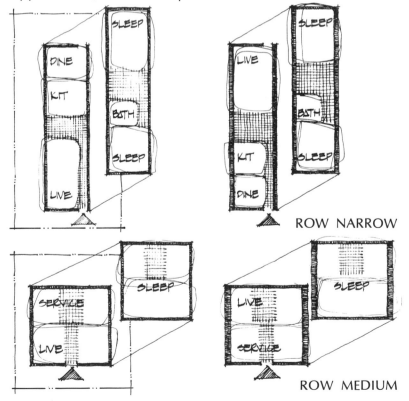

ROW NARROW

ROW MEDIUM

The frontage may vary from narrow, 12 feet, to wide, 40 feet
The depth will adjust accordingly: 24 feet to 40 feet.

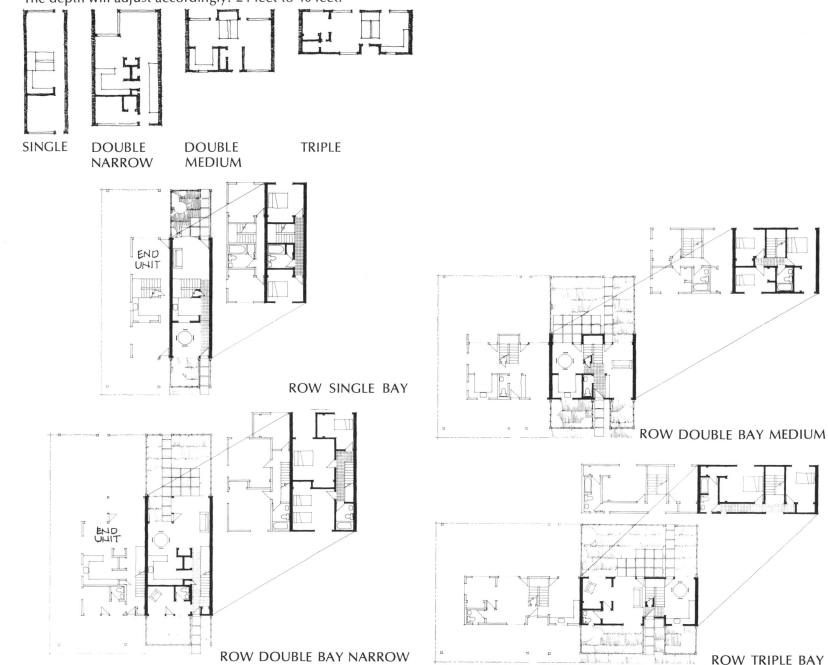

SINGLE    DOUBLE    DOUBLE    TRIPLE
          NARROW    MEDIUM

ROW SINGLE BAY

ROW DOUBLE BAY MEDIUM

ROW DOUBLE BAY NARROW

ROW TRIPLE BAY

As the unit grows in width, more private spaces shift to the private garden side; the living room is the first, followed by dining, then possibly a small study. Entry and kitchen remain on entry side, sometimes joined by bath, dining, and study/bedroom. Stairs and bath, not requiring daylighting and natural ventilation, can remain in the middle. On the upper level bedrooms occupy the ends, with stair and bath in the middle. The primary, or master bedroom will usually front on the private garden side. Parking is in adjacent lots.

TOWN HOUSE—The town house is the same as the Row House with the addition of parking inside the building. Inside parking requires a wider frontage (to accommodate the drive plus entrance and useful interior space) and sometimes a depth in excess of 40 feet. The town house offers the full convenience of a single family house except without side yards.

FLAT—Its origin is virtually worldwide. As a one-story unit it relates most to the country home which faces the road and has a center entry hall flanked on one side by the "living" spaces and on the other side by the "sleeping" spaces. This same concept characterizes the popular contemporary "ranch" house. The actual arrangement of the space in a flat is quite adaptable. Of all the house forms, the flat is the most

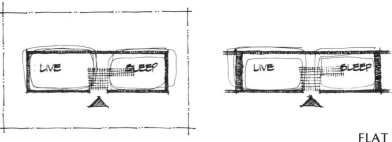

FLAT

flexible, capable of assuming many configurations. It is also the most convenient and accessible. Its primary disadvantage is its large ground coverage, which minimizes the number of units that can be ground oriented. Flats are usually double-sided, meaning that they have outside rooms on both *long* sides of the unit. The narrow sides then become the party walls. Entry remains approximately in the middle of the long side and usually shares this side with the kitchen, bathroom, and secondary bedrooms. The "private" side is usually shared by the living, dining, and primary bedroom. Thus again the formal spaces have moved to the private side and the service spaces to the entry side.

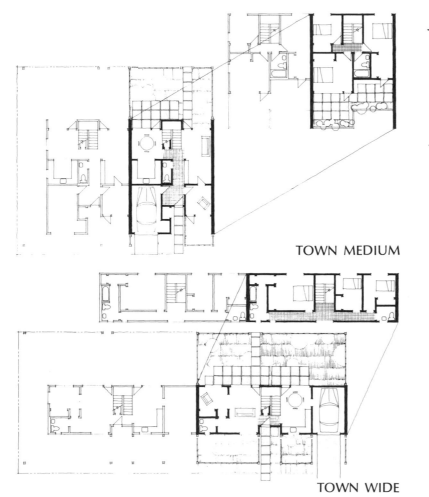

TOWN MEDIUM

TOWN WIDE

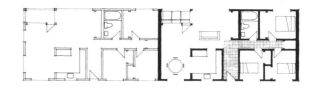

FLAT

PATIO HOUSE—This form, used primarily in warm dry climates, has begun to emerge in American housing as a variation on the traditional one-story ranch house. With the entry in the middle, living spaces are on one side and bedrooms on the other. To fit on a narrower lot, the form is "bent" and the private space fenced in. With the elimination of side and front yards, the ranch house becomes the patio house.

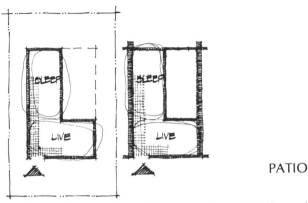

PATIO

Thus, the patio house in pure form is a one-story "L" shaped house on a square lot. The unit is 40 to 50 feet square with living in one direction, sleeping in the other, and service (cooking, washing, eating) at the intersection. The space enclosed by these two legs becomes the garden which should be oriented south or southwest. In certain areas two-story portions can be added as long as they don't cause overshadow or overviewing problems. Entrances are usually arranged to serve four units in a cluster court arrangement, necessitating a main walkway or road every four rows of patio houses. Furthermore, parking can occur within the unit in a garage or in a separate lot nearby.

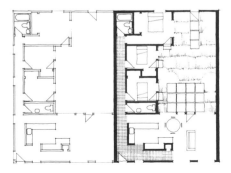

PATIO

MAISONETTE—A standard type of "high density" low rise used extensively throughout the world. It is considered high density for a maximum vertical stacking of one two-story unit on top of another, with two flights of stairs to the main level of the upper unit. The trade-off for the higher density is primarily loss of ground orientation for the upper unit and some stair climbing. The maisonette can be manipulated to gain some qualities of the terrace house but is still more challenging to organize without compromising privacy, orientation, and convenience.

TERRACE HOUSES—Row or patio houses can be terraced up or down a hill to enhance the view, provide proper orientation, etc, allowing gardens or terraces on the roof of the unit below (hence the name). Terrace houses conserve space while providing desirable amenities, but require extreme care in layout to assure successful circulation and entry.

The six house types make up the basic components of cluster housing.

Without a description of the *individual household* a match with house type cannot be accurately made. Matching will occur later in the overall process when many other particulars of each unit are known, such as location, access, orientation, etc. At this early phase in the process a shorthand method is required to make fundamental choices (that will be rechecked as the process goes through its continuous recycling). For instance, we may sketch scenarios, or user profiles, on each household type responding to the human needs of territory, orientation, identity, privacy, convenience, accessibility, safety. Combining this with the bedroom/activity matrix helps determine the appropriate house type. We should remember that as the overall site plan evolves other criteria may reduce the choice still further. User profiles of individual households are presented in the following paragraphs.

Here is a matrix of correlated types:

| HOUSEHOLD | BEDROOM | HOUSE TYPE | | | | | |
|---|---|---|---|---|---|---|---|
| | | ROW | TOWN | FLAT | PATIO | MAISONETTE | TERRACE |
| Young Single | Efficiency | | | O | | | |
| | One | | | O | | | |
| Young Couple | One | | | O | | | |
| | Two | O | O | O | O | O | O |
| Young Couple, Young Children | Two | O | O | O | O | O | O |
| | Three | O | O | | O | O | O |
| Middle Age Couple, Teenage Children | Three | O | O | | O | O | O |
| | Four | O | O | | O | O | O |
| Middle Age Couple, Grown Children | Two | O | O | O | O | O | O |
| | Three | O | O | O | O | O | O |
| Elderly Couple | One | | | O | | | |
| | Two | O | O | O | O | O | O |
| Elderly Single | Efficiency | | | O | | | |
| | One | | | O | | | |
| Disabled | | | | O | O | | O |

YOUNG SINGLE. People in this group generally are only moderately concerned with *territory.* They tend to be more gregarious and seek maximum social interaction with their peer group. Being away from units during workdays and fairly mobile on weekends, they benefit less from *orientation* amenities. They seek *privacy* in an environment that enhances social interaction, mostly privacy *inside* their unit. *Identity* is generally not a great concern since young, single people are fairly mobile moving a lot and are not able to pay for the more unique physical amenities that give a housing environment strong identity. *Inconvenience* is generally acceptable if the trade-offs in the form of lower rent, more interesting setting, and neighbors are there; they tend to walk farther and climb more stairs to their unit; they have less personal property to pack in and out. They require a full measure of *safety* from theft during their extended absence, and being in an age bracket that is highly vulnerable to physical harm, they need security and protection.

Young single best fit into *efficiency or one-bedroom units* which can either be integrated into interesting locations or clusters of larger house types—tops, corners, above garages, etc.—or in their own clusters tucked in inaccessible (usually interesting) site locations that could not accommodate clusters of larger house types.

YOUNG COUPLE. If both are working, the description of young single generally applies. However, if one person remains at home, there is an increase in several of the human needs. For the person at home the amenities of a good orientation—daylighting, sunshine, view—are essential. Privacy

increases in importance. While peer socialization is still very important, young couples need more time to be by themselves. For the most part young couples get along quite well in one-bedroom units, and if they can afford it, may have a two-bedroom unit for the option of having a guest room or study. The one-bedroom unit, which need not be a ground-oriented one, has the same location adaptability as the young single unit. A two-bedroom unit may also have a full kitchen rather than a kitchenette. It may be a small row house, town house, or maisonette, probably with the sleeping rooms upstairs.

YOUNG COUPLE, WITH CHILDREN. With the transition to a two-generation family, attention is focused on the development and well being of young children, so that the emphasis of human needs shifts.

The children's territory must be limited and well defined with physical barriers such as fences, railings, doors, gates, etc. *Safety* and territory become synonymous; barriers must be made secure with locking devices and spaces made free of hazards. Young children instinctively seek out good *orientation;* they quickly find the bright warm places on a cold winter day or the cool shady places on a hot summer day. Although they are affected by their perceptual world, they do not yet value view amenity or identity. Children require little *privacy* since they live in a "world of their own." With their limited motor skills, they experience considerable *inconvenience* which is further compounded if they must live in an adult world where everything is too big, too high, and too heavy.

Couples with young children may find their personal privacy and territory severely encroached upon by the children and thus require a minimum amount of "adults only" space, at least during evening hours.

Couples with young children should be provided with optimal

ground orientation and private outdoor play space. If the site allows a percentage of single-level housing, two or three-bedroom patio houses would ideally accommodate these families. If not, they can also manage well in medium-sized row houses or town houses, again provided ground-oriented amenities are accessible.

MIDDLE AGE COUPLE, TEENAGE CHILDREN. The basic difference between couples with young children and grown children is usually the number of bedrooms needed. A private bedroom for each grown child is desirable, allowing *privacy* for all members of the family. Other space requirements increase in proportion to the number and size of members; for example, group spaces like the dining and living rooms must allow for more chairs, bigger tables, etc. In response to the demand for diversity of spaces for socializing a new space, the play or family room, must be added.

Consequently units may require as many as four bedrooms, a separate dining room, a play or family room, a utility room, and possibly a two-car garage.

The row house, town house, and patio house have to be large to accommodate so many spaces. If land area is tight, the patio house might have to be eliminated and stacking variations of the row house and town house encouraged. And, since the family is at its largest size more private outdoor space is necessary.

MIDDLE AGE COUPLE, GROWN CHILDREN. Middle and late middle age is considered by many as the best time of life.

Children are gone, housework and expenses are less, and free time is more plentiful. People are generally still physically active.

Since *territory* does not have to be shared with children, couples can spread out a bit and have more *privacy*. *Convenience* is desirable so that leisure time can be enjoyed. With fewer family members less outdoor space is required. Most house types work well. Two bedrooms are about right: one for sleeping and one for a bedroom/study. A third bedroom is a nice luxury for overnight visitors. A separate dining room is important because people in this household group tend to entertain more frequently. The town house is the most efficient choice, but row, maisonette, or terrace would also be appropriate.

ELDERLY COUPLE    ELDERLY SINGLE.    This group is at a time of life when a more restful and passive lifestyle can be enjoyed. *Privacy* becomes more important; the option of having total visual and acoustical separation is essential. Since our physical systems become less tolerant of extremes as they age, housing plans for the elderly should provide an even *orientation*—even temperature, very little air movement (chill factor), even daylighting such as north light. Because of their limited strength and stamina, *convenience* is essential for the elderly. For instance, units should be planned for minimum maintenance. In addition, the elderly require a greater sense of *safety* since they feel, and generally are, less able to protect themselves from harm. Good security with locks, night lighting, surveillance, and easy egress in case of fire are all necessary.

The elderly require efficiently organized space, less than before but enough to hold selected cherished possessions. Since stairs are difficult for the elderly to climb, they must be ground oriented. It takes particular care to integrate the smaller one or two-bedroom unit—ground oriented—into a cluster and still mainain privacy. A position in a cluster that allows for privacy on an optional basis is ideal. If a site can allow for some lower rise units, the elderly can cluster with their peers, but their units must be reasonably close to other household types, so they can enjoy the experience of watching children at play, people passing by, or doing simple outdoor activities, etc. Many elderly people love to garden so that enough daylight must be available. Therefore, the site planner must make a special effort to integrate into a plan as many ideal mini-environments for the elderly as possible.

DISABLED. The disabled are not considered a separate household type because the 10 percent of us who have physical, mental, or physical/mental disability now aspire to live nearly normal lives in normal living environments. More and more disabled individuals live in the community, either individually or as a family member. The special physical needs of a disabled person vary with the nature of his disability; that is, the person confined to a wheelchair has quite different needs than the blind person. To accommodate the disabled, we are now beginning to establish design standards which are gradually being legislated into law. We, as site planners, have a major responsibility to see that the design standards are sensitively applied.

While the disabled desire to maintain a "normal" lifestyle, they have special human needs which cannot be generalized. However, accessibility (the convenience of independently gaining access and use of facilities) is a particular problem for many disabled. Some obvious examples of their accessibility-related needs are 5 percent sloping ramps for wheelchairs (though 8 percent is often recommended)and braille identification on buildings, doors, and objects for the blind. Because the disabled are usually less mobile, the amenity of a good *orientation* is extremely important. To have an interesting, ever-changing *view* could be the most important physical attribute of a house to an immobilized human being.

Any of the house types are capable of accommodating the handicapped provided all their facilities are on the ground floor. The disabled receive maximum benefit from ground orientation and horizontal planning, meaning easy and continuous horizontal flow of floor surfaces.

## HOUSE CONCEPT DEVELOPMENT

The material in the section of house type identification has given the site planner some basic components to begin a simple massing of housing units into clusters. As the site concept begins to develop, the individual house and cluster concept must *simultaneously* develop. At the same time, the site planner can no longer depend on the limits of the given house type inventory but must begin to generate variations of these, or completely new house concepts, that appropriately fit the developing site concept. The site planner needs a quick, simple approach to developing house concepts. This may be taken in four basic steps as follows:

TERRITORIAL SPACE

MINI SITE ANALYSIS

SPATIAL ORGANIZATION

SCHEMATIC DESIGN

TERRITORIAL SPACE. The basic objective is to efficiently organize a set of programmed interior and exterior spaces into one overall territorial space envelope. This is most easily done by drawing a simple plan and section of the territorial space at a scale of one inch equals ten feet. In addition to showing what is inside the space, we need to show elements immediately adjacent such as sidewalks, streets, open space, attached units. The example of space used by one unit is quite a simple one; its spatial organization is easily developed. As cluster configurations become more complex, so will the territorial space of each unit. The spatial organization of an L-shaped, tri-level town house on the end of a cluster, for example, would require much greater thought and ingenuity to develop.

MINI-SITE ANALYSIS. Now a mini-site analysis can be made to inventory the natural and man-made factors affecting the territorial space. This can be done on an overlay of previous diagrams. Simple notations - words, arrows, shading, texturing all help to quickly record the information.

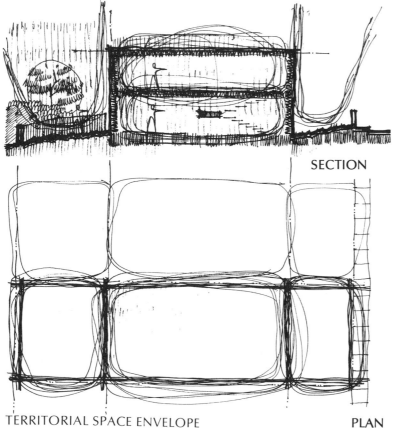

SECTION

TERRITORIAL SPACE ENVELOPE                                   PLAN

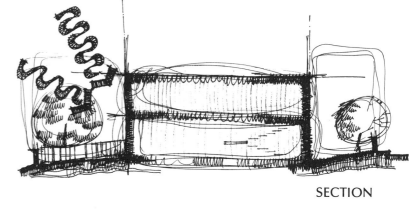

SECTION

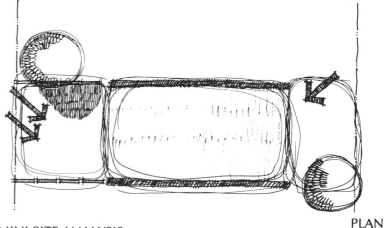

MINI SITE ANALYSIS                                          PLAN

60

SPATIAL ORGANIZATION. Another overlay can now be made to designate the preferred location of each space. The spaces can be defined by a series of "soft" overlapping rectangles that should completely fill the territorial space envelope. We should develop several alternative arrangements, compare them, combine the best parts of several and recycle the best ones until we feel confident that all reasonable alternatives have been explored and the final organization is the most suitable. In making this judgment it is important to review the human needs inventory (i.e., territory, orientation, privacy, identity, convenience, accessibility, safety) and to correlate it with information from the mini site analysis. The most formative phase of the concept development is in progress.

Before beginning the diagram, we should list all the spaces required. For review, here is an outline of the spaces. There are two basic types of spaces—*interior spaces and interior/exterior* spaces. In addition, exterior space also exists on-site and off-site in the form of open space.

The basic *interior spaces* are familiar to us all; they are living, dining, kitchen, bedroom, and bathroom. A secondary set of spaces that are less common includes "study," "utility" room, "family" and/or "recreation" room, storage space, and garage or carport (attached or detached). Circulation spaces which include entry, hall, and stairway are a third set of interior spaces.

*Interior/exterior* spaces are "outside" spaces that are contiguous with "inside" spaces, such as decks, patios, terraces, entries, pathways, enclosed garden courts, and even fenced-in yards. These must be thought of as living spaces equal in importance to interior spaces.

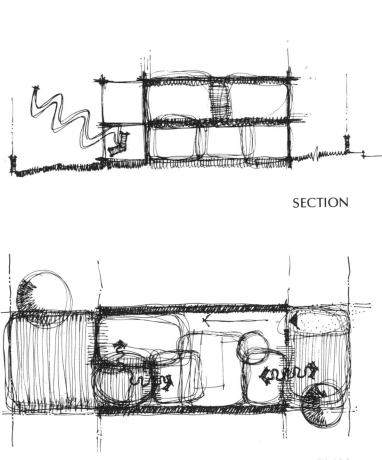

SECTION

SPATIAL ORGANIZATION      PLAN

SCHEMATIC DESIGN. The house concept has been set and the site planner has the minimum amount of information to use in the development of the cluster concept. At this time the planner has the option of making the concept more complete by refining the diagrams into simple architectural schematic drawings. It is usually a matter of timing; if there aren't too many unit variations in a housing development, it is feasible to go ahead. In an architectural schematic the spaces now assume their final size and shape. The very important decision of window location and configuration is made to maximize view, daylighting, and ventilation without compromising privacy. Doorways are carefully positioned for convenience and accessibility. The section drawing can show heights of windows, balcony railings, and fences, depth of roof overhang, change in level of patios and decks, adjusted grading in outside spaces, and many of the *vertical relationships* that cannot be shown on a plan. To give a section a sense of scale figures of adults and children should be drawn. Trees also help to establish scale when drawn to a correct form and dimension. In the plan view window and door locations should be shown. To give scale to the plan it is very useful to sketch in major furnishings such as beds, couches, and dining room tables.

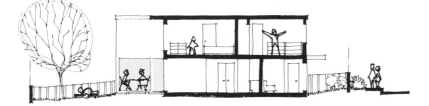

SECTION

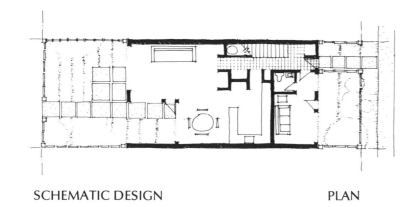

SCHEMATIC DESIGN          PLAN

SIZE OF INTERIOR SPACES. The floor area, smallest horizontal dimension, and ceiling height of each space are established through the ingenuity of the designer and the minimum standards of the building code in force. The ingenuity of the designer varies with skill and experience; therefore the site planner who may not have the skill and experience should be guided by existing standards. Fortunately, the F.H.A. *Minimum Property Standards* for multifamily Housing, published by H.U.D., is an excellent source of information on the size of spaces and many other aspects of site and house planning. The authors refer particularly to Chapter III—Site Planning and Chapter IV— Building Planning. The following information on room size is excerpted from Chapter IV.

MINIMUM ROOM SIZES. Table 4-1 set forth minimum room sizes and the smallest (least) dimensions for each room. Areas and dimensions shown are minimum and do not necessarily indicate optimal space for required living functions or placement of furniture. In a specific project, larger rooms may be necessary to assure continued market acceptance. In addition to minimum areas and least dimensions, rooms should have an appropriate functional relationship with other rooms within the living unit and should be suitable for their intended use.

Ceiling Heights—The standards recommend a 7'-6'' minimum ceiling height in all habitable rooms in cluster house types. Hallways, bathrooms, and garages may drop the ceilings to a 7'-0'' minimum.

Storage—The standards recommend that primary bedrooms should have a minimum of 5'-0'' linear feet of closet while secondary bedrooms should have a minimum of 3'-0'' linear feet of closet. There should be a minimum of 3'-0'' linear feet of coat closet near the entry, and a minimum of 1'-6'' linear feet of linen closet near the bedrooms. In addition, there should be a minimum of general storage within each unit as follows: 0–1 BR = 150 cu. ft., 2 BR = 200 cu. ft., 3 BR = 250 cu. ft., 4 BR = 300 cu. ft.

With the completion of the schematic design, the house concept development is set in terms of basic planning; there still are many decisions to be made about the actual appearance, or character, of the unit. Decisions about appearances are often preconceived by imposing some given style. This must be avoided because it denies the purpose of a thoughtful site analysis which may very well influence the character of the units and clusters. The underlying thesis of this book is that each site has its own character that should be positively reinforced through the design of the units and clusters.

Table 4-1 MINIMUM ROOM SIZES FOR SEPARATE ROOMS

| Name of Space | Minimum Area (Sq.Ft.) | | | | | Least Dimension |
| | LU with 0-BR | LU with 1-BR | LU with 2-BR | LU with 3-BR | LU with 4-BR | |
|---|---|---|---|---|---|---|
| LR | NA | 160 | 160 | 170 | 180 | 12'-0'' |
| DR | NA | 100 | 100 | 110 | 120 | 8'-4'' |
| K | NA | 60 | 60 | 70 | 80 | 5'-4'' |
| Kette | 30 | 40 | NA | NA | NA | 3'-6'' |
| BR (primary) | NA | 120 | 120 | 120 | 120 | 9'-4'' |
| BR (secondary) | NA | NA | 80 | 80 | 80 | 8'-0'' |
| Total area, BR's | NA | 120 | 200 | 280 | 380 | |

*Abbreviations:*    BR — Bedroom    DR — Dining Room
LU — Living Unit    LR — Living Room    Kette — Kitchenette

## HOUSE ANALYSIS SUMMARY

House analysis is an integral part of site analysis. The analysis should result in an inventory of the house types most appropriate for the site. The process begins by establishing performance requirements in terms of human needs, site potentials and limitations, and materials and technology. A profile of likely users is established by household type, and the space requirements of each household type are determined. Then, identification of house types that might be appropriate is made. Finally, a correlation is made between the household types and the house types. This provides the site planner with a basic set of "building blocks" to manipulate in the following site concept development phase.

## HOUSE CONCEPT DEVELOPMENT SUMMARY

The house concept development is an integral part of the site concept development. As the basic "building blocks" find their place in the site concept, they must be individually studied to confirm the "fit" is appropriate. If the fit is imperfect, the unit must be adapted or replaced by another house type. The fitting process requires a clarification of each unit design. The process begins with a definition of territorial space and progresses through a mini site analysis of the territorial space. Then the spaces inside the territorial spaces are organized in response to the mini site analysis, and very simple schematic designs are developed. The site planner can now cycle the schematic designs through the site concept and cluster concept.

## BIBLIOGRAPHY

### HUMAN BEHAVIOR IN HOUSING

Barker, Roger G.
*Ecological Psychology*
Stanford, Calif.: Stanford University Press, 1968

Cooper, Clare, C.
*Easter Hill Village*
New York: The Free Press, 1975

Hall, Edward T.
*The Hidden Dimension*
Garden City, N.Y.: Doubleday, 1966

Lynch, Kevin
*The Image of the City*
Cambridge, Mass.: M.I.T. Press, 1960

Maslow, Abraham
*Toward a Psychology of Being*
New York, Van Nostrand, 1968

Perin, Constance
*With Man in Mind*
Cambridge, Mass.: M.I.T. Press, 1970

Proshansky, Harold M.
*Environmental Psychology*
New York: Holt, Rinehart and Winston, 1970

Skolnick, Arlene
*The Intimate Environment* Boston: Little, Brown, 1973

Sommers, Robert
*Personal Space*
Englewood Cliffs, N.J.: Prentice-Hall, 1969

### HOUSING SYSTEMS

Cutler, Stephan L. and Cutler, Sherrie S.
*Handbook of Housing Systems for Designers and Developers*
New York: Van Nostrand Reinhold, 1974

Dietz, A. and Cutler, L.
*Industrialized Building Systems for Housing*
Cambridge, Mass.: M.I.T. Press, 1971

Habraken, N.J.
*Supports: An Alternative to Mass Housing*
New York: Praeger, 1972

Safdie, Moshe
*Beyond Habitat*
Cambridge, Mass.: M.I.T. Press, 1970

# HOUSE PLANNING CHECKLIST

The checklist is a useful tool to use both during the concept development phase and immediately following it to verify the unit meets the basic needs of the intended users. The list includes only very basic requirements for all household/ house types. In a site development large enough to have many different types, the site planner would have to develop checklists for each.

Most of the checklist questions have at least one answer in the form of minimum standards set forth in the local building code and/or F.H.A. housing standards. These standards are, in themselves, a well developed checklist. The outline form presented here is intended to augment them and to allow for the inclusion of other constraints that naturally emerge out of a thoughtful site, household and house type analysis.

The checklist follows the hierarchy of spaces established earlier in this chapter.

## LIVING

- Is its form flexible enough to allow for alternate furniture arrangements?
- Can it be separated from the main circulation pattern of the house?
- Can it be visually and acoustically separated from the other interior spaces?
- Can it accommodate a secondary study area?
- Is it connected to the private outdoor space so the living function can be easily extended outdoors?
- Can it function as a temporary extension of the dining area?
- Are doors and windows placed to enhance view, daylighting and ventilation without violating privacy?

## DINING

- Is the space large enough to seat family and guests at a table?
- Is it directly connected to the kitchen?
- Can it function as a secondary living or study space?
- Is it connected to the private outdoor space so the dining function can easily be extended outdoor?
- Are doors and windows placed to enhance view, daylighting and ventilation without violating privacy?

## KITCHEN

- Is the equipment and counter arrangement efficient for food preparation?
- Is prepared food easily transferred from kitchen to dining space?
- Is it directly accessible to entry for ease of bringing in groceries, etc.?
- Does it have adequate view and daylighting amenity?
  Does it have adequate natural and/or mechanical ventilation to exhaust cooking odors?
- Is there space for informal eating?

## PRIMARY BEDROOM

- Is the space flexible enough to have different furniture arrangements? Double bed or twin beds?
- Is there space for secondary furnishings? Chest of drawers, desk, chairs, bedside table, T.V.?
- Is there adequate closet storage?
- Can a baby crib and infant supplies fit in?
- Is there adequate view, daylighting and ventilation?
- Can it be made dark and quiet?
- Does it have easy access to a bathroom?

## SECONDARY BEDROOMS

- Can it accommodate twin beds?
- Is there space for a chest of drawers, desk, chair, and night table?
- Is there adequate closet storage?
- Is there adequate view, daylighting and ventilation?
- Is there easy access to a bathroom?
- Can it be made quiet for private activities? Studying, sleeping?

## STUDY

- Is there adequate space for study furnishings such as a desk, drawing table, large musical instrument, etc.?

•Can it be used by more than one person at a time?
•Can it serve as a guest sleeping space?
•Is there adequate storage space and shelving for books equipment, etc.?
•Is it acoustically separated from general house noise?

## UTILITY

•Is there adequate space for equipment and working surfaces?
•Can sewing and ironing be done in the space?
•Is there adequate equipment and supply storage?
•Is it adequately illuminated and ventilated
•Is it easily accessible from an entry?

## FAMILY/RECREATION

•Is its form flexible enough to allow for alternate furniture arrangements?
•Is it large enough for activities such as ping-pong, billiards, or group dancing?
•Does it have direct access to private outdoor space?
•Is it adequately illuminated and ventilated?
•Is it acoustically isolated to contain high noise level?
•Does it have easy access to a bathroom?

## STORAGE

•Is there adequate general storage for off-season clothing and equipment, automotive and garden tools, baby carriages, trunks, extra furniture, etc.?
•Is the storage properly located throughout the house to minimize the distance objects must be moved?

## GARAGE/CARPORT

•Is it large enough to fully open car doors?
•Is there storage for automotive equipment, tools, etc.?
•Is there direct access into the unit?
•Is it well illuminated at night?

## ENTRY

•Is it directly accessible to living/dining/kitchen?
•Does it have a clothing closet nearby?

•Is it possible to view a person outside the door without being seen?
•Is it well illuminated at night?

## HALLWAYS/STAIRWAYS

•Are they wide enough for people to by-pass?
•Are they well illuminated?
•Are they acoustically dampened?

## PATIO/DECKS/TERRACES

•Are they large enough to accommodate outdoor furniture?
•Chairs, chaise lounge, tables, umbrella, barbeque?
•Are they easily accessible from living/dining/kitchen spaces?
•Are they level with interior spaces?
•Can they be observed from other units or public spaces?

# SITE SYSTEMS

A housing complex can be divided into many individual parts —play spaces, lawns, laundries, bedrooms, garages, garbage cans, lights, sidewalks, etc. But individual parts are difficult to piece together and one can easily become involved in details and never grasp the essence of total community. We prefer to begin conceptually, organizing the site into three simple, basic but comprehensive site systems. The three site systems —open space, housing, and circulation—are flexible enough to encompass a variety of changing activity. As each system is manipulated, the results can be tested through detail site studies and evaluated for approval or elimination.

## RADBURN GARDEN COMMUNITY

Many of the concepts referred to were first developed in America in 1928 in Radburn, New Jersey. The Radburn style of layout was designed by Clarence Stein and Henry Wright, integrating British garden city concepts with the automobile. The design included complete separation of cars from pedestrians, green-belt pedestrian areas, superblock layout, cul-de-sac residential streets, reverse house plans, and neighborhood units focused around a school.

The Radburn superblock combined several typical rectangular grid blocks into a larger, more flexible planning size. Green belts formed the backbone of the neighborhood with large

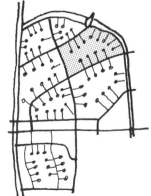

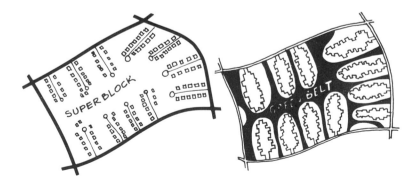

open areas in the center of the superblock joined together in a continuous park. A hierarchy of roads, each specialized type planned to serve one traffic purpose minimized auto intrusion to the neighborhood. Culs-de-sac were extensively used for quiet, safe access for a small number of homes. Two other types of roads were developed—local roads linking traffic from culs-de-sac and major roads surrounding several super-blocks. Pedestrian circulation was separated from cars, with walks primarily located away from roads and at different levels

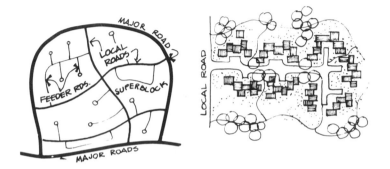

where they cross. House plans were reversed placing the living room away from the road, facing the garden and community park. Service rooms such as kitchens and porches faced toward the cul-de-sac.

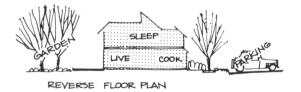

REVERSE FLOOR PLAN

Radburn was never completed because of the 1930s depression. However, its form has been duplicated the world over, and little improvement seems necessary. It has considerable flexibility and can vary from low-density detached units to high-density attached units, with gardens possible on both sides, with parking arrangements varying according to topography and budget, and with different unit types including patio, town, and row houses.

Overall, the Radburn plan provides a quieter, safer environment for family life than the traditional suburban layout. Criticism usually focuses on the fact that children prefer to play in the road rather than in the open space in front of the houses. This is to be expected—kids look for and enjoy certain risks associated with roadways, and the grassed open space does not always satisfy their needs. Additionally, in approaching the rear of the house by auto, the view is of cars and clotheslines which sometimes appears untidy. In some instances, the pedestrian system has failed because residents have found that the roads lead more directly to shops and community services. However, a better relationship of shops to pedestrian systems would solve this problem.

The Radburn plan should not be considered a rubber stamp and applied as if it's an end-all answer; instead, its positive qualities should be understood. Where necessary, more organic and flexible layouts using other housing types or varied auto access patterns should be developed. In each case the principles discussed above should remain valid.

# HOUSE TYPE

We will be stressing the variability of four basic house types:

ROW HOUSE. A two-story attached unit with living accommodations on the first floor, and sleeping above. Typical units have cooking and eating on the access side, with living rooms on the garden side. The auto is parked nearby in a lot or parking court.

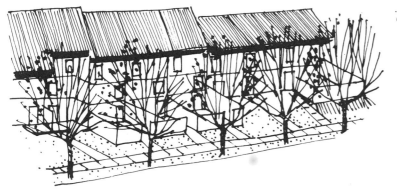

TOWN HOUSE. The closest approximation of our suburban living condition. In most respects, it is the same as a row house except parking is provided within the unit.

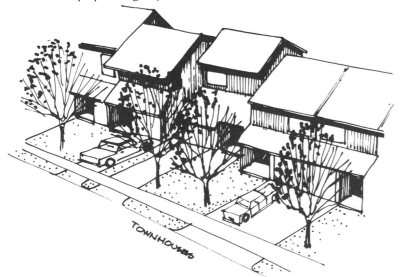

PATIO HOUSE. Like a carpet of uniform, one-story attached homes spread over the land. Each unit has an enclosed patio oriented to the sun and potentially serving all rooms of the house. Parking is in grouped arrangement away from the units. This small house is perfect as a starter home or for families without children.

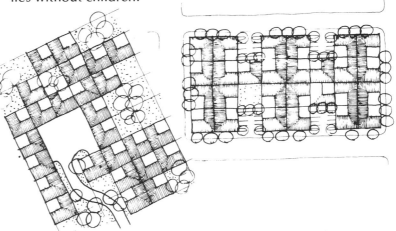

FLAT. Units with living all on one floor, which can be stacked up to four floors high. Parking is in carports or open lots

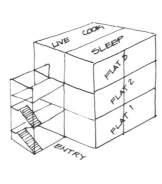

nearby. Two main variations of these house types may prove useful. Row or town houses stacked atop one another to create a four-story block are called maisonettes. Two or three-

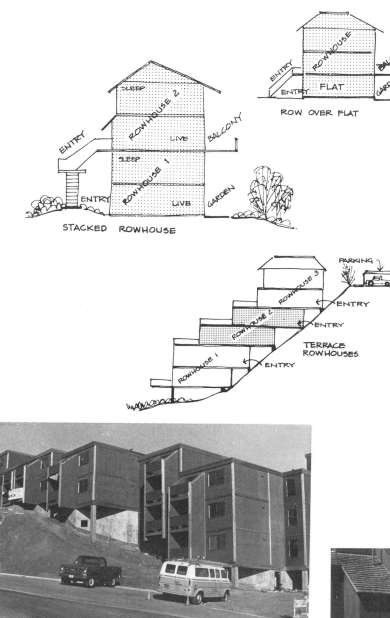

STACKED ROWHOUSE

ROW OVER FLAT

TERRACE ROWHOUSES

By low rise housing, we mean dwellings not over four stories tall which are served directly from the ground. GROUND ORIENTATION is really the key, with private entries and private gardens the symbol.

story combinations are also possible using flats. Terrace units step up or down a grade, with the higher unit using the roof of the unit below as a garden. Maximum orientation and view to all units is provided.

These house types are generated in part from the suburban, single-family model idealized by so many Americans. The conversion involves eliminating unnecessary space while saving qualities deemed necessary for a full life. Further, a second floor is added for sleeping, and the living room reversed to place it away from the road and near the garden. Side yards and side windows are eliminated since they are too small for any real use. The rear yard is reduced to a manageable size, providing enough space for necessary activities, but not so much as to require expensive landscaping and maintenance. Medium-density housing must capture this unused private open space and return it as useful public open space.

## GETTING STARTED

At this stage, buildings play a small part in the site planning process. A site planner must know the internal arrangements of each house type and rough unit dimensions to generate various arrangements on the site. Moreover, the planner needs to understand how houses are attached, what orientation and site conditions are favorable to each house type, and how clusters are formed.

Row and town houses are attached in a lineal fashion with side walls abutting one another. Two units together form a duplex, three a triplex, etc. For cost efficiency, four units together is about the minimum while more than 10 begins to be

too long. To start with, we may assume each row house unit to be 20 feet wide and 35 feet deep. This means a four-unit row would be 80 feet long by 35 feet wide, and six-unit, 120 feet long, etc. The exact width need not be determined at this stage, since 20 feet wide is an average workable width, and measurements can be refigured later to accommodate exact designs. Town house width and depth should be greater to allow garage space for a car, with 24 feet by 40 feet deep being acceptable starting dimensions.

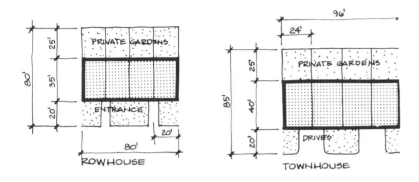

ROWHOUSE

TOWNHOUSE

Patio houses are in concept more uniform and easier to arrange. Dimensionally, assume a grid of 40 feet square. This allows for an L-shaped living space, shared access, and private garden. Orientation should follow the principles discussed above, with garden and living spaces receiving sunlight from the south quadrant. Entrance can be from the north, east, or west. Once the original 40-foot grid has been established, auto circulation, unit access, trees, open space, parking, and service areas can be located, and variations developed within the confines of the property.

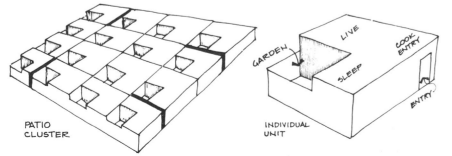

PATIO CLUSTER

INDIVIDUAL UNIT

At this preliminary stage, rough dimensions for individual row and town houses can be combined to form blocks 4 to 10 units long. Each block can be identified as having an entrance side and a garden side, and an ideal orientation. Each unit block should have a bubble of space front and rear for use and privacy. There are many architectural and landscape methods to minimize the size of this space (to be discussed later), but for now we may assume that the garden side requires a 30-foot deep arc and a 20-foot deep space at the entrance. It is helpful to draw template units to the scale of our plan drawing including, 4, 6, and 8 and 10-unit combinations for town and row houses. The privacy bubble, dimension, ideal orientation should also be indicated. This sheet of information should be kept available for reference. The authors do not recommend locating units on the site until the circulation and open space systems are understood, then all three systems can be integrated and manipulated together.

## UNIT ORIENTATION

Unit orientation is never simple or clearcut. There are ideal orientations for each room or outdoor space, but few sites are situated so all houses can have a perfect orientation. Both row and town houses should ideally have the entrance in the north quadrant, that is, facing north, northeast, or northwest. Conversely, the garden side should face south, southeast or southwest. With this arrangement building length would run somewhat east and west with the entrance side on the north and the garden on the south.

## SINGLE VERSUS DOUBLE LOADED

The cost and convenience differences between single-and double-loaded arrangements must be fully understood. Loading usually refers to service from a lineal space—a road, corridor, or path. Single loaded means only one side of the road is used for access to one row of houses. Double loaded means both sides of the road serve as access for units. Double loading is less expensive, since the cost of the road is shared by houses on both sides. Units located away from a road are

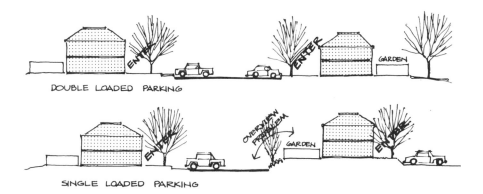

DOUBLE LOADED PARKING

SINGLE LOADED PARKING

not as affected by the single/double-loading cost problem. We can observe that most existing urban and suburban developments are double loaded. The cost factor aside, double loading can be monotonous, and in some places the added cost of single loading is justifiable for aesthetic purposes. Additionally, some sites are too narrow for double loading, leaving only the possibility of single loading.

Ideal morning and afternoon sun orientation is possible only in single-loaded arrangements. Traditionally, morning (east) sun is preferred in bedrooms and kitchens, with afternoon (west ) sun shining into living and family rooms. Aligning double-loaded roads north/south is the best orientation solution, with one side's garden and the other side's entrance in morning sun, and vice versa for afternoon sun. This is fairer than one row of units with north facing gardens and no sun all day.

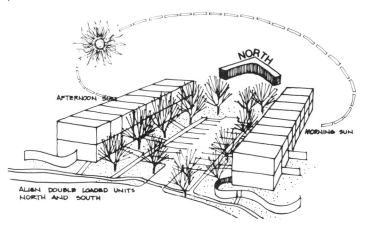

ALIGN DOUBLE LOADED UNITS NORTH AND SOUTH

## CLUSTER AND COMMUNITY

Individual units seldom create a "community." The designer must refine and revise his plan until there is overall coherence, until the total environment of each unit is optimal, until the complex relates positively to the neighborhood, and most importantly, until the physical design creates a potential "sense of community."

SENSE OF COMMUNITY. What is sense of community? Residents of any neighborhood want to feel part of the develop-

ment in which they live, be proud of it, and identify with it. Feeling part of a neighborhood requires knowing one's neighbors and being able to meet friends easily while on foot. By its very nature, cluster housing suggests a greater sense of community than suburban-type single-family housing, as demonstrated when the two are contrasted: cluster versus linear, compact versus sprawl, public versus private, pedestrian versus auto, community versus individual.

CONVERSION—LINEAR TO CLUSTER. Most of the arrangements we will be discussing are clustered or concentrated around a node or point. Nodal in cluster housing means space, image, identity, and pedestrian usage. Site planning elements creating community are: cluster, amenity, pedestrian, sharing, compactness, focus, and privacy.

*Walking* replaces auto travel as prime means of movement in and around the cluster. Walking increases the apparent size of a neighborhood and the chance of meeting people.

*Amenity*, natural or man-made, should be available for communal use and enjoyment, rather than incorporated into the private gardens of a few houses.

*Sharing of resources.* Many facilities are becoming too expensive for people to own individually or are used too infrequently to justify ownership. Such facilities may include parking, laundry, swimming pool, tennis courts, auto wash area, shop, gym, football field, etc.

*Compactness* creates group focusing units whereas sprawl develops individual focusing units, not allowing the bonding together of neighbors. In cluster developments the individual family continues to be the key social unit, but additionally it is part of a neighborhood social unit. Compactness also means many necessities of daily life are within walking distance, strengthening this tie to the neighborhood.

*Focus* is identity, something which makes a neighborhood memorable and different from others, a place we want to return to.

*Privacy* is essential in any community even though contacts with neighbors may be pleasant. Every household must have real privacy at the entrance, the private garden, and inside the house.

*Clustering* removes some units from direct street access and places them in various arrangements around open space. There are two conceptual cluster arrangements: <u>around an entrance court</u> and <u>around a garden space.</u>

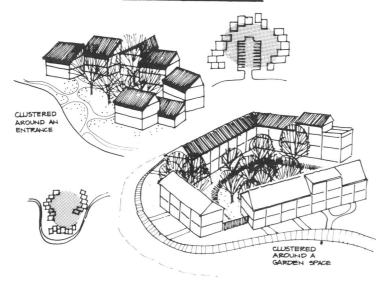

When units are arranged around a garden space, entrances are on the other side. Or, with a private garden on the entrance court side, neighbors are able to use the common area with relative privacy. Or, when three or four buildings are arranged around a small "urban" court, the private garden falls on the opposite side. Residents living with this arrangement are likely to meet neighbors at the entrance, the space becoming a common place for 1-to 20 families. The three schemes, though appearing similar, cause vastly different feelings and experiences for residents.

## OPEN SPACE—KEY TO "STAY AT HOME COMMUNITIES"

Open space includes all land which is not occupied by building. Open space includes traditional spaces like parkland and play areas, but also roads, walks, private gardens, service space, parking areas, etc. Moreover, open space is not just

unbuilt-upon land; it is meant to be used and enjoyed. Every inch of outdoor space can enhance the development if it is considered in the site planning process.

For most housing complexes we will try to *maximize the pedestrian precinct*. This means providing for safe walking, playing bicycling, and freedom from intrusion by the automobile. Open space can include a pedestrian movement system, which is significantly different from vehicular circulation to warrant special consideration. First, it relates to the slowest and technically least demanding mode of movement, walking. Open space is bounded and crossed by the vehicular network but may require separate spaces safe from auto intrusion. Lastly, it is more than a circulation system in that it contributes to imageability and livability throughout the neighborhood.

Open space affords the visual amenity provided by earth, grass, flowers, trees, as well as by such landscape elements as streams, ponds, mounds and depressions, paths and resting places. Over and above this, it provides the means of preserving and enhancing existing natural amenities. Green open space buffers against environmental nuisances and has an important role in the maintenance of a favorable ecological balance providing a habitat for desirable flora and fauna. Open space can beneficially influence the microclimate by improving heat reradiation conditions and by providing channels for air drainage and favorable air flows. The system operates as more than just open space; it provides a readily accessible place for informal recreation.

There are three broad, overlapping ways of looking at open space:

SIZE—The size of usable open land allocated into large or small spaces.

HIERARCHY—A system of spaces throughout the community (long, linear) connecting to and serving all housing clusters directly.

OWNERSHIP—Responsibility for use and maintenance of open space.

Let us consider first Ownership. Open space can be classified broadly into three forms of ownership: PUBLIC, SEMI-PUBLIC, PRIVATE

Public Open Space is owned by every one. It is maintained at public expense and is usable by all. Examples of this type of open space would be public parks, playgrounds, roads, and sidewalks. Public open space boundaries must be readily understood by all people; for instance, a gate or fence may signal that the public space ends and that private space begins. Within many developments, public open space is not publically owned but controlled by community residents. However, the same rights for public access and circulation should be possible, with routes made clear to the general public.

Semi-Public Open Space is space owned by the residents and set aside for their communal use. Nonresident use is limited to guests, with general public barred. There are also many examples of semi-public open space in exterior portions of commercial establishments, such as gas stations, shopping centers, office buildings, etc. A user knows the limited right of use and acts accordingly lest he be asked to leave. Typically people have some business or reason for being there, and are not just passing time.

Semi-public can be divided into more and less private access. For instance, semi-public space used for unit access would have to be less private to allow visitors to reach the units; or recreation areas more private by barring all nonresidents.

Semi-Public Space as Security Barrier. Traditionally, it has been possible for visitors to reach the front door of most houses directly from the public space, but higher density solutions and security concerns are changing that assumed freedom. In medium-density housing open space ownership has shifted from predominantly public to semi-public. Access is limited to residents, friends, or those who have some specific business to complete. Many lobbies, parking areas, and halls of apartments are locked and arranged so access can be controlled by a gate. This space is becoming important as a screen for eliminating unwanted visitors.

It is common for much of a development's recreation space—play areas, swim pool and gardens—to be semi-public space and protected from unauthorized use. This assures privacy to resident users and may encourage them to take an active part in policing and maintaining the space.

Private Open Space. All units should have some private outdoor space, whether a yard, a balcony, or a terrace. (A terrace is usually over some living space, in effect a roof garden.) The size of private gardens depends on who lives there, what outdoor needs they have, and what open space facilities are nearby. As we might expect, families, especially those with children under five, need more space than couples without children, or elderly and unmarried people. With adequate community recreation space for active play, private gardens need serve only for outdoor cooking, eating, gardening, tinkering with equipment, garbage and tool storage, and general outdoor enjoyment. All in all, this should be far less space than found on a ¼-acre suburban lot.

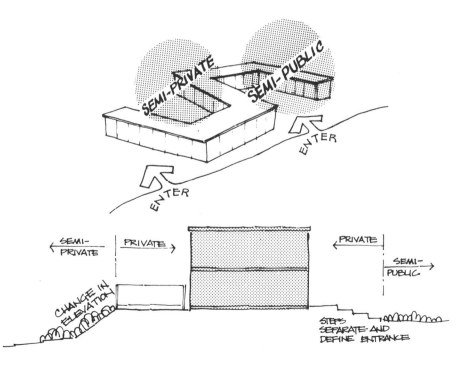

Assuring proper orientation is the main problem. Private suburban gardens are large enough to allow some sunshine regardless of the yard orientation. On the other hand, since the garden in a medium-density housing development is smaller and shadowed by two- to four-story buildings nearby, it must be perfectly oriented.

A garden should be clearly private, protected from over-viewing. It should have direct access to the house, although it may connect to the semi-public or public portions of the open space system. Privacy and territory requirements should be obvious and similar to those inside the house.

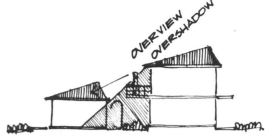

The three types of ownership fit together in hierarchical order — *Public to Semi-public to Private*. Public portions of a development usually meet public portions of the larger neighborhood (the street, a city park, schoolyard, large open space, etc.) on one side and semi-public spaces on the other. Finally, private spaces connect to the semi-public system which acts as a buffer to assure maximum privacy. It is possible to vary the arrangement of spaces, connecting private spaces to public spaces or eliminating one or two systems completely, as long as the end results are clearly understood by the designer.

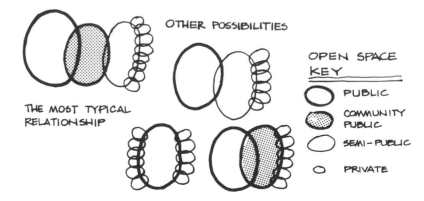

## OPEN SPACE HIERARCHY

Another way to look at open space is as a hierarchy of spaces, each serving specific functions, yet interrelated to satisfy community needs. Most large housing developments can be broken into three distinct parts:

The _Community System_ analogous to public ownership

The _Neighborhood System_ analogous to semi-public ownership

The _Development System_ analogous to private or semiprivate ownership

Community Open Space is the main and largest open space of any development. This open space should be determined by the positive character of the land, i.e., by physiography, drainage, orientation, views, amenity and an understanding of ecological processes. It should express the genius loci— fundamental essence of the land—and be capable of guiding and controlling the form of development.

Community open space is meant primarily for passive use: walking, resting, viewing, bicycling, going somewhere (or nowhere). Active recreational facilities are usually located slightly away from this system but are visible and accessible from it. Paths and walkways should be carefully sited to facilitate circulation without destroying the natural landscape. Planting should be long lived and environmentally advantageous; maintenance should be minimum after two years' initial adjustment.

Small housing development may or may not include an open space system. Small developments should relate, if possible, to an off-site green belt system. Mini-landscapes might have to be created for sites that do not have natural amenities. Sites bordered by undesirable land uses (industrial or commercial land or arterials) should be buffered by planting then can become part of the community open space system.

Neighborhood Open Space is the most used network, connecting the pedestrian from home to all major public facilities —tennis courts, swimming pools, community centers, golf courses, etc. Most neighborhood recreational facilities—tot lots, sitting areas, play areas, play courts. etc—are located in neighborhood open space. This system of space becomes an extended garden for flat dwellers proving safe play for tots, meeting space for mothers, and informal gathering area for teens.

The neighborhood system must be *continuous*, and long enough to reach all residents to extend their private garden into the larger public garden. providing public use facilities at pedestrian intersections. These include play areas, tot lots, and meeting and rest areas tailored to fit resident requirements.

The neighborhood system must make available a variety of pedestrian routes—some along roadways in widened, planted pedestrian areas safe at all hours of the day and others as internal landscaped footpaths offering alternate connections. Since surveillance is important to ensure safety, many heavily used pedestrian routes are related to roads where there are large numbers of passersby.

Development Open Space refers to the land right around a cluster of housing units, and may be privately owned. This space must be carefully planned with the other two systems to ensure privacy and pleasure to the residents of each unit. Thus, the site planner has to advocate both for the privacy of individual residents and for the benefits of common facilities. It may be necessary to fence or buffer public areas from private, or to use different levels separating activities by elevation. Programming the location of noisy activities such as play areas, swimming pool, or tennis courts away from housing units is desirable but often there is not enough space. In addition, development open space can visually "borrow space" from adjacent neighborhood open space, and vice versa, as it is seemingly larger.

Ambiguous Open Space. One reason for categorizing open space is to avoid what we call ambiguous open space, space that seems to belong to no one. In suburban developments this problem does not exist because the land is either private yards or public roads. Individual home owners care for the yards, and the city maintains and polices the roadway. But in areas with more common space, ownership and maintenance responsibilities become unclear, and land may fall prey to increased vandalism and crime.

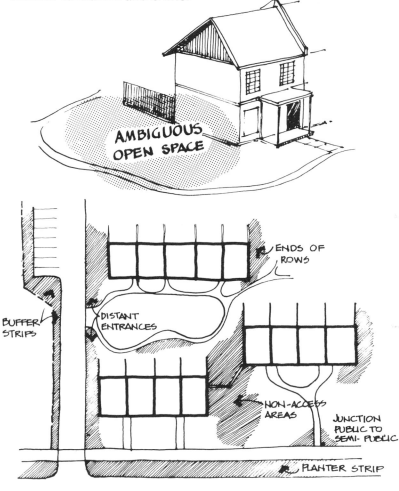

AREAS LIKELY TO BECOME AMBIGUOUS OPEN SPACE

All spaces should appear to belong to somebody or to a cluster of residents. All areas should be well planted and maintained. Lack of maintenance is a sure sign of ambiguous open space.

## DETAIL LANDSCAPE DESIGN

Regardless of how well the open space system is conceptualized and laid out, if the final detail landscape design is poorly conceived, the development will never achieve its full potential. Detail design determines the way open space facilities are developed and go together. Garret Eckbo has stated, "the quality of landscape is determined by the quality of relations between it and the users—the more involved and participating man is with his out-of-door environment, the more successful the development." Open space gains this involving quality through treatment of its details.

Describing how to properly design the final landscape will not be undertaken at this time. For large projects a set of Performance Standards for detail landscape treatment should be developed.

## SIZE OF OPEN SPACE

If we assume that some percentage of the development, say 20 percent for a round figure, must be green space usable for recreation and pleasure, the site planner must choose how it will be divided, where it is to be located, and the size of each space. Open space is an expensive element in any community. It is essentially land the developer can't directly sell and can't make an accountable profit on. Someone must pay for it and should receive maximum benefit in return.

Traditionally, single-family developments have allocated a majority of open space for private use, i.e., back yards, front yards, and side yards. This allocation is fair in a sense that one pays for the exact amount received. Thus, in suburban communities, open space amounts to small, undevelopable, and virtually useless leftover spaces. Few suburban communities boast large fields for random play, or natural amenities such as a creek or marsh. This disadvantage is subtle but important. Most single family yards are too large for actual family use, too expensive to landscape and maintain, and yet are actually limited by size as to what activities can be carried on.

Higher density developments must shift the balance, allocating small, carefully designed private yards to each unit, and grouping the remainder into common open space, accessible to all and serving purposes not possible on the prized quarter-acre plot, such as football games, tennis, swimming, and forest walking.

To ensure a quality environment, each housing unit should be allocated a small private garden. (This rule may be relaxed as the design process proceeds and will be discussed later.) The garden should be closely related to the unit's living space, be it kitchen, family, breakfast, or living room. It must catch some sunlight and be private without overviewing. Once every unit has some small private space, the remaining open space can be allocated into:

*All Private Spaces.* The simplest, and perhaps most democratic, method of allocating open space could be to divide it equally and attach it to each unit, that is, make it all private. In certain instances, such as when there is an adjoining public park or playground, it may be desirable to increase the density, relate the development to the public space, and allocate the remaining spaces privately.

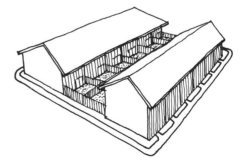

_Public Space in Large Amounts_. Sites with natural amenity, steep topography, a lake, forest, meadow, etc., may choose to save the natural area for common use, and cluster dwellings advantageously around it. This preserves the amenity, provides a communal space for everyone to use, and becomes a strong design determinant. Allocation of some private space to each unit is still important. The size of large green space can vary from one acre to 500, the more the better.

_Many Small Public Spaces_. Lands with undistinguished natural amenities can develop identity by grouping a number of units (say, 10 to 20) around a small common open space. Three or four clusters comprise a neighborhood and should be designed for the specific needs of those residents (i.e., for children's play, swimming, or gardening). Each neighborhood could be landscaped to ensure individuality. Several problems arise with this type of space allocation. Do visitors enter a unit through the green space, or from some other side? Are the spaces public or semi-public? Who maintains and polices them? Should abutting private gardens be fenced or not fenced? This last consideration must be weighed in all cases—and will be discussed more fully later.

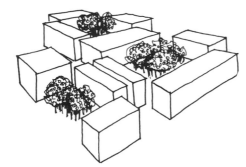

Three factors may help us decide which form of allocation is best.

_User Needs_. In all cases, resident use of green space should be a prime determinant of the shape and size of the land. Young children aged one through five need simple, flexible spaces that are easily supervised and close to home (the private garden is perfect), while older children may require level areas for specialized activities plus adequate room to roam. Older people may enjoy the quiet beauty of a long continuous forest walk. Thus, user needs can be roughly categorized by age, and will be more fully discussed later.

_Borrowed Open Space_. Existing public open space in the neighborhood is an important determinant of what facilities are planned for the development. If there are tennis courts or football field nearby, there is probably no need to duplicate them in the development. A good technique is to inventory nearby public facilities, determine access from the site, and check on availability for use and permanence. If the public facilities are appropriate, the development could be linked to them with a path, some trees, or an opening in an existing fence.

_Existing Land Patterns_. The site may have qualities that signal a proper or best use of the open space. For instance, land rich in natural amenity suggests preservation. This is critical site planning matter because the tendency is to develop too close to and out of scale with most natural amenities. For instance, if we try to locate structures close to a river, stream or lake, we might actually diminish its value. We should consider the best way to enhance the amenity, i.e., how much setback is needed, how should community access be provided, and how should circulation work around or along it. By all means, we shouldn't shy away from trying to save all site amenities (e.g., a fine old tree).

## GETTING ON WITH IT

How does one get started? The process is a guided trial and error testing of various patterns for arranging open space in terms of ownership, hierarchy, and size. Since these relate closely to the siting of the Housing and Circulation systems, we will not discuss the entire process now. For now, let us consider several logical steps which should be taken.

1. Analyze amenities of the neighborhood. Locate available off-site recreation and open space resources. Evaluate usefulness, access, permanence, etc. Relate these to the site as desirable views, points of access, and potential use facilities.
2. Analyze amenities on the site, e.g., stream, forest, hillside, meadow, or other unique natural feature, that should be worth preserving. Is there anything of cultural value? Are there any distant views? Locate each amenity and assess the size of land required to preserve it. Rate or prioritize each feature; consider the possibility of linking them.
3. Provide an open space buffer where necessary, along a busy street or between the housing development and an incongruous land use. Hypothesize how a buffer might be used, namely, for walking, bicycle riding, or recreation. Link the buffer where possible to on-site and off-site amenities.
4. Relate the size of the specific site to the open space systems we discussed. Does the community system appear unnecessary? Are adjacent public parks adequate, perhaps eliminating the need for some on-site public spaces? Generally, the smaller the project (one to two acres), the smaller the public portion with a greater proportion of land allocated to semipublic and private open space. Large projects have a more balanced allocation of open space, possibly tending toward grander public spaces.

Typical recreation and landscape facilities

| | |
|---|---|
| Children's play area | Allotment gardens |
| Swim complex | Greenhouse |
| Open lawn | Game tables |
| Decorative fountain | Sculpture |
| Benches | Basketball hoop |
| Bocci | Tennis court |
| Horseshoes | Volleyball court |
| Wading pool | Barbeque |
| Spray pool | Speciality garden |
| Climbing tower | Viewing platform |
| Fish pond | Car repair |
| Patio | Orchard |
| Car wash area | |

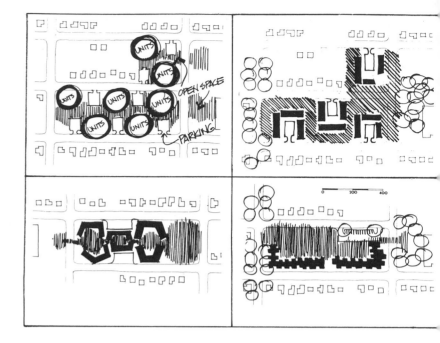

Several conceptual arrangements that we should consider are:

1. Developing a preliminary program of open space user needs by categorizing user groups as elderly people, young married people, teenagers, and families. User needs should be related to size and location of facility. Are large, level fields needed for active sport? Are long, narrow walkways needed for passive use? Or will small courtyards serve the needs of residents?
2. Proposing opposite solutions, that is, all private versus all public spaces, all in large plots versus all in small plots. Considering opposites helps define and clarify the extreme positions, so through evaluation an intermediate choice can be made.
3. Developing conceptual bubble diagram relationships between open space elements. This is the time to experiment with alternative relationships, for instance linking public to private spaces and public to semi-public, and developing hierarchies of space. This policy-making stage can then serve as a base for testing the suitability of each alternative scheme.

4. Combining the three Open Space ownership possibilities discussed earlier and diagramming the results, perhaps in a matrix. This provides an opportunity to examine alternatives and determine responsibilities. For instance, who should be responsible for maintenance, policing, and lighting?

5. Developing patterns of open space distribution (as illustrated):

6. Hypothesizing sequences of pedestrian movement through the site's open space. Where should it connect to the existing community? How close should it come to nearby houses? To trees? To roads?

7. Integrating open space with other two-site systems, Housing and Circulation.

## CIRCULATION

Public roadways consume approximate 30 percent of our total metropolitan land. They serve important movement functions in getting us to work, play, school, etc., but, if not properly planned, they can also be disruptive, noisy, and dangerous.

Most towns and counties have roadway standards and specifications designed primarily to serve auto efficiency. Minimum concern is shown for environmental quality (noise reduction, amenity, and dust removal) or for the safety and pleasure of the pedestrian, bicyclist or nearby resident. Standards developed for conventional subdivision layouts include large front yards to serve as buffers against automobile intrusion. Additional roadway width is required so cars can back out safely from driveways. Lastly, most road standards have been developed for low-density development, where long distances must be traveled to reach home and high speeds are an asset to the driver.

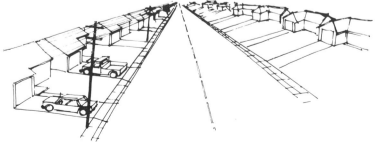

Medium-density housing requires almost exactly the opposite road standards. First, the distance to home is reduced in length, so one doesn't (theoretically) have to travel fast to get home. Second, open space is at a premium and cannot be used extensively to buffer the adverse effects of automobiles. Wide front-yard setbacks simply cannot be afforded. Third, auto parking can be grouped to minimize backing out into major streets, reducing the need for wider streets. Lastly, the prime requirement for medium-density living is to provide a quality environment for its residents, which necessitates minimizing auto intrusion.

This does not mean the automobile is going to be eliminated. Even if we completely changed our land use patterns to include school, shops, and work within walking or public transport distance, we would continue to depend on the private auto for pleasure trips, speciality shopping ,visiting, and many other needs. The authors do make two suggestions: First, that the auto can travel at slower speeds when inside a medium-density residential community, since distances are not great; and second, that medium-density communities can eliminate the need for the second or third car, since recreation, schools, and shopping are nearby. Often a higher-density community is large enough to warrant its own stop for buses in the mu-

nicipal system or even for its own small public transportation system.

It is impossible to relate one system of circulation to all site types or development sizes. For instance, a small development may need only one road, not really a complete system, but it must relate to the existing public road system. New towns and large developments require a complete network of roads, serving various speeds and volumes of traffic. Regardless of the size of development, it is important to understand how traffic moves as a total system.

## HIERARCHY OF ROADS

Roads are classified according to their ability to handle volumes of auto traffic at specific speeds. Generally, high speed and high volume mean low environmental quality and low pedestrian use of adjacent lands. As traffic speed and volume decrease, environmental conditions improve and pedestrian use is enhanced.

From a conceptual point of view, two transportation dispersal schemes are possible:

1. One that uniformly distributes traffic loads on all streets. Thus, all streets are meant to carry an equal share of traffic and are the same width.
2. One that has a hierarchy of roads. Roads are of different widths and sections so that each road is scheduled to carry a specific quantity of traffic, with abutting land uses tailored to fit the environmental condition.

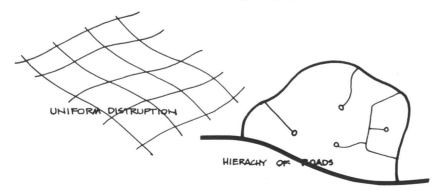

UNIFORM DISTRUPTION

HIERACHY OF ROADS

Most American cities began with a uniform distribution system with streets of equal width. As traffic pressures grew, a hierarchical order was imposed and certain streets were widened to carry greater volumes of traffic. Compromises such as non-limited access, improper abutting uses, and inadequate rights-of-way, as well as more cars has overcrowded the widened streets and forced more cars back on the narrower streets. The result is heavy traffic everywhere, with streets carrying more autos than originally intended and a lower overall environmental condition.

The authors suggest adherence to a hierarchical classification system, coupled with carefully considered abutting land uses. For a housing development, three types of roads are adequate: *major, local, and access.*

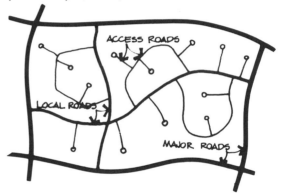

Major Roads are efficient distributors of vehicular traffic, providing optimal routes from any point on the site to any other point that is more than a short distance away. They tend to equalize travel time; that is, the longer the distance that must be traveled, the easier and therefore quicker the actual traveling. They form a large-scale network with a minimum of intersections. The net of major roads does not shift or bend to accommodate residential development, and no residential development is served directly from it. In principle the major network is in the form of a rectangular grid; in practice the grid is warped and reorganized in response to the topography and configuration of the site and to existing roads.

Major Roads are not to be considered freeways. In practice, Major Roads may become boulevards with a wide section,

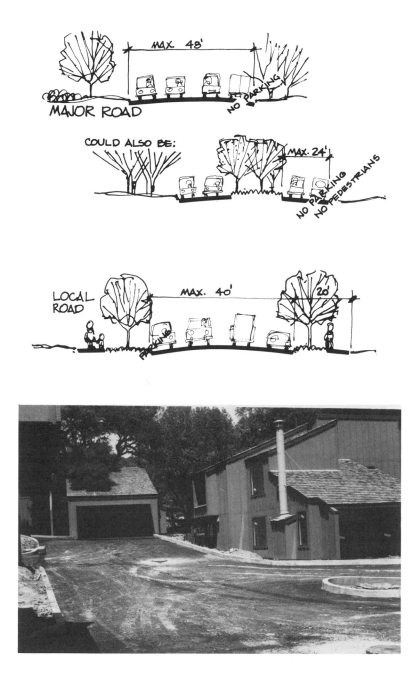

median strip, and planting with two lanes in each direction, and with no parking, no foot traffic, and buffer planting along each edge. No access to abutting uses should be permitted, and abutting uses should be protected from intrusion. Commercial, industrial, or shopping developments or units for people without children would be appropriate. Speeds of up to 35 mph assure minimum environmental impact, which can be further reduced by depressing the roadway slightly and planting heavily.

Local Roads are distributors within the network, connecting with major roads but taking on forms responding to the physical layout of development. They should not attract traffic desiring to move quickly through the site and need not be used exclusively for vehicles.

Local roads serve both the auto and pedestrian. Parking is normally allowed, sidewalks are provided, and dwelling units can be located along them. Roads should be wide enough for adequate planting, pedestrian safety, comfort, and perhaps a bicycle path. One 12 foot wide lane in each direction plus parking on both sides adds to 40 feet of roadway. An additional 15 to 20 feet on each side for walks, planters, bike routes, etc., brings the total right-of-way to 80 feet wide. Elimination of parking on one side or portions of the sidewalk could reduce the right-of-way somewhat, but not without compromise.

Access Roads connect with the local roads (never directly with major roads) to provide access to individual buildings or to integrated groups of buildings. They are planned so that motor vehicles using them have to be driven slowly, thus making conditions safe for a variety of casual neighborhood activities.

Locating Access Roads. Access roads should be located after all buildings are sited. This is the opposite of the traditional American way of siting roads. The authors are proposing that environmental conditions, i.e., sun, winds, view, privacy, etc., determine the siting of open space and buildings and that building location determines the route of the access road. This means that access roads may bend, and curve, and become very narrow, often violating good traffic planning procedures.

However, by the time a resident is on the access road, he is within two minutes of home and can well afford to travel at 5 to 10 mph.

Access roads, often without a sidewalk, are the shared domain of pedestrians and autos. They should vary in width, and may even be one lane wide serving two directions. This would force one car to wait while another passed. They should be aligned with good viewing so kids can play comfortably, adventurously and without danger. Since these roads are substandard by most engineering criteria, the site planner often has to battle for their approval. However, to eliminate this problem, many developments have designated access roads as PRIVATELY OWNED. (Private roads do not have to be built to public standards, are installed by the developers, and are maintained by future residents.)

Most road systems are too organized and are related too directly to the dimensions of the automobile. Local and feeder roads could, in violation of existing engineering standards, be far more interesting, exciting, and safe if they:

- Followed irregular alignments, except where there is a real danger. (Frequent turns keep a driver alert and also reduce driving speed.)

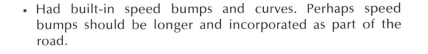

- Had built-in speed bumps and curves. Perhaps speed bumps should be longer and incorporated as part of the road.

- Followed the lay of the land, e.g., over a hillock or into a swale. Views to assure sight distance could be opened by removing selected vegetation. It would be desirable to eliminate curbs where possible, vary road widths, and alternate sidewalk location alignment and width.

- Provided no access at all. Some places don't need a roadway or can be reached on foot or from a golfcart or mini-car. Removing the auto, without diminishing resident convenience, is an easy way to improve a site plan.

OPEN SPACE FOR MOVEMENT. To understand the movement system as a whole, it is essential to realize that open space is in itself a fully operative circulation subsystem assuming a variety of important functions. Although it is restricted to pedestrians and bicycles (as well as by service and emergency vehicles), it has all the attributes of a system. It has continuity; the entire site can be traversed without leaving the system. It has nodality; the pathways converge on points of amenity, commercial and community centers, and schools. It has its own internal hierarchy of use from fully public through semi-public to private. It represents an attempt to revolve the conflicting demands for safety (through surveillance and intensive use) and privacy.

> The size of a park is directly related to the manner in which you use it. If you are in a canoe traveling at three miles an hour, the lake on which you are paddling is ten times as long and ten times as broad as it is to the man in the speedboat going thirty.—Every road that replaces a footpath, every outboard motor that replaces a canoe paddle shrinks the area of the park.
>
> Paul Brooks
> The Atlantic Monthly

## HOW TO LAY OUT A ROAD SYSTEM

As with all other aspects of design, there are no procedures that will work in all cases. The four-part design approach in which all facets are considered at once is appropriate here.

Our primary site planning concern will be:

A  To minimize auto intrusion into the neighborhood unit.

B  To separate roads carrying higher volumes at higher speeds from residential units.

C  To maximize convenience and auto access to each dwelling unit.

In determining how a development fits into the existing roadway system, we should use the three-part road hierarchy discussed earlier. Large developments (say, over 50 acres) may have all three systems. Medium-sized developments probably require only local and access roads relying on existing roads as Major roads, while small developments may use only ac-

cess roads. In all cases forget for now about the Access system, as it relates to buildings, and will be determined almost automatically at a later stage.

An understanding of the Road hierarchy should suggest the most appropriate access points from existing roads as well as points of no access. (Often the local traffic planner can suggest points of no access which pose the greatest constraints.) Access points should be back from an intersection (100 feet if possible to allow stacking room for traffic waiting at the intersection), should not be from a major road, and should avoid three-way intersections as drivers sometimes mistakenly drive right into the development.

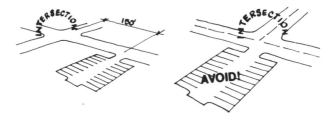

The road system should be related to open space amenities. It is important to designate places where roads should or should not go. For instance, steep topography (7% in snow country, 15% for other areas) should be avoided as well as natural areas such as bogs, creeks, forests, meadows, etc. Where the road system would be enhanced by paralleling the green space should be considered. This is the beginning of a blocking-out process, which eliminates places where roads should not go and defines where they could go.

We are looking for road arrangements which maximize the pedestrian precinct, allowing long uninterrupted walks and large areas for free play and enjoyment. We might get some ideas by examining a Superblock where major or local roads encircle an area, with dead-end streets serving housing units, leaving the center for pedestrian use.

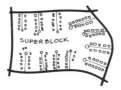

SUPER BLOCK

# THE SITE AS A SYSTEM

In conclusion, the use of a site for cluster housing can be best understood by considering the elements of the three interrelated parts. These parts together make the cluster housing site a system.

| HOUSE | OPEN SPACE | CIRCULATION |
|---|---|---|
| Town house | Ownership | Major roads |
| Row house | Hierarchy | Local road |
| Patio house | Size | Feeder roads |
| Flats | | Open space |
| Combinations | | |

The number of considerations in designing a housing development may seem endless, but if organized into a workable outline they are manageable. First, a list should be made of elements necessary for a livable development:

| | | |
|---|---|---|
| Sun/orientation | Garbage | Ventilation |
| View | Identity | Guest Parking |
| Privacy | Accessibility | Play |
| Quiet | Private gardens | Storage |
| Amenity | Parking | Utilities |

Next, the site analysis should be reviewed for the normal existing site conditions

| On-site | Off-site |
|---|---|
| size/shape of site | roads |
| trees | utilities |
| topography | parks/playgrounds |
| orientation | amenity |
| views | shopping |
| amenity | services/utilities |

Then, certain aspects handled as follows:

SUBTRACT (remove diagramatically from the plan)

1. Areas of desirable amenity
2. Danger-signal areas
3. Necessary buffer zones

ADD:

1. Buildable areas
2. Potential road locations
3. Site access points (auto and pedestrian)

# SITE CONCEPT DEVELOPMENT

The basic ground rules have been set out and it is time to begin. For simplification we will start with a small site in an established neighborhood where most roads, services, and neighbors already exist. The site will be small (½ to 3 acres) with a unit count totaling 7 to 45 units. (Beginning with Chapter 8 we will extend the process to larger undeveloped tracts of land.) All in all, an urban site with existing roads and nearby buildings is an easy design setting because we can relate the new development to existing features.

We should work at two scales, the largest comfortable site scale (20 scale if possible) and a smaller scale (perhaps 100) so the site can be related to nearby features. Sheet size should fit the table easily and not exceed 42 inches in one direction. If the site has been carefully chosen, it will probably front on local roads, making development easy and living pleasant. If there are any arterials adjacent to the site, note that living next to the arterial will be noisy and buffers necessary.

The search for form in site planning is a thinking process of problem solving and rationalization with a number of factors to consider. Factors which affect the form of a housing development include:

- physical characteristics of the site and neighborhood
- human needs
- technology
- cost

There are many approaches to the design stage of site planning. Some designers can intuitively feel the way a site should be used, while others draw from experience or are reminded of other similar developments. Still others are able to construct analogies which stimulate creative processes. A more recent design approach stems from technology and is guided by repetitive forms generated by a system. The approach advocated here is a free-wheeling process which uses elements of the intuitive and structural system approaches to create approaches that more accurately express the vitality of our society. These are formalized, cyclical processes allowing one to consider the complete problem in total environment terms. The simultaneous, four-step site planning method described

PROBLEM DEFINITION
ALTERNATIVE GENERATION
IMPACT ASSESSMENT
EVALUATION

in Chapter 1 is an example. All similar approaches possess the following characteristics:

- they must be freewheeling processes, unhampered by conventional attitudes of what is good design, how we have done it before, or with what forms
- they must interpret performance criteria rather than specifying standard solutions; this requires a broad problem definition.
- they are primarily decision-making processes considering all alternative approaches and utilizing rational and objective decisions.

HUMAN NEEDS. The Development Program, the next step, will describe human needs in the broadest sense, and more specifically what cost framework the developer is anticipating. We should consider these questions: For whom are we designing? How many and what type units? How many bedrooms? How many cars? What resident income level? How much and what kinds of open space? Other on-site facilities? Any special user requirements?

These questions are part of the Development Program, a set of directions from the developer pertaining to his requirements for use of the property. The program is a judgmental evaluation based on:

1. Marketability and income levels of anticipated residents.
2. Zoning and other existing neighborhood uses.
3. Existing site potentials or constraints.
4. The developer's profit requirements.

In later chapters we will discuss how to formulate a Development Program; for now we will assume that one will be furnished with the following information:

- number type and size of units (bedroom count)
- anticipated household type (categorized by family size and type)
- number and type of parking (covered, uncovered)
- development cost (low, medium, or luxury category)
- any special requirements to be met.

Most Development Programs are inadequate, so user needs must be interpreted to adequately inform the design process. In determining user needs, we must discover what physical forms best serve the motions, actions, events, interactions and forces related to residents of the development and the neighborhood.

## WHAT IS A GOOD SITE PLAN?

A site planner of cluster housing must struggle with two key dilemmas. Ultimately, all planning decisions must attempt to reconcile these two dilemmas.

1. The first dilemma is finding the proper balance between individuality and collectiveness. Individuality is expressed at the unit entrance, in the private garden, and by the way a unit is visibly distinct from its neighbors. Collective environments are the shared areas surrounding individual units, i.e., roads, parking, open space, landscaping, buffers, and service areas. Typically, individual areas are extensively developed, while collective areas are not. However, collective environments affect the quality of living for individual units and represent one of the real site planning challenges. The dilemma here is achieving a balance between the individual and collective areas in the allocation of amenities and degree of development.

2. The second dilemma deals with choice and also contrasts individual and collective good. It can be expressed by the question: How can we provide the greatest opportunity for individual choice within the framework of a complete housing environment? The dilemma is the tension between

# DEVELOPMENT PROGRAM CHECKLIST

| User Needs \ Household Type | YOUNG SINGLES | YOUNG COUPLES | YOUNG FAMILY | COUPLES WITH TEEN AGERS | COUPLES WITH GROWN CHILDREN | ELDERLY COUPLES | ELDERLY SINGLES |
|---|---|---|---|---|---|---|---|
| Income level<br>*low, middle, high* | | | | | | | |
| Number of units<br>*One bedroom, two, three, four* | | | | | | | |
| Size<br>*square footage* | | | | | | | |
| Parking Spaces<br>*Resident*<br>*Guest*<br>*Total* | | | | | | | |
| Unit Type<br>*Flat, Row, Town, Patio, other* | | | | | | | |
| Open Space<br>*Private*<br>*Communal* | | | | | | | |
| Circulation<br>*Dominant auto*<br>*Dominant pedestrian*<br>*Combination* | | | | | | | |
| Special<br>*Handicapped*<br>*Children*<br>*Elderly*<br>*Other* | | | | | | | |

opposite poles; on the one hand, maximum freedom of choice implies total absence of environmental constraints, while full environmental effectiveness entails a highly organized system imposing many constraints on people.

The site analysis should describe a site's physical attributes and may even suggest alternative use arrangements. Site analysis information should include build/no-build zones, site access/no-access locations, unique areas, steep topography, views, desirable sun orientation, and a feeling of the surrounding neighborhood's character.

We will begin the search for form with a quick, broad-brush study of several obvious cluster arrangements. This will familiarize us with the spatial and physical features of the site and their limitations. We can quickly eliminate a number of undesirable options and perhaps develop a feasible conceptual approach. Site planning involves first finding a direction, then eliminating the problems through design.

Let us begin by drawing to scale several Row, Town and Patio house combinations (four to ten units) and several parking lots, leaving adequate room for entrance and garden. The authors do not recommend template cutouts, but prefer drawing freehand block forms to match.

CLUSTER IDENTITY—A principal site planning objective is to "cluster" units around an open space. Open space or semi-defined outdoor rooms create territory, identity, and lead to social interaction. Cluster space can be created:

- at the entrance, by arranging the entrances to several units around the same space.
- off the private garden with a shared interior garden court-yard.

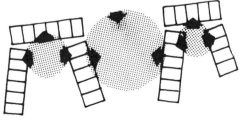

Both approaches produce quite different results. Units relating to each other at the entrance are easily identified as a cluster, providing opportunities for social contacts as residents enter or leave home. The public image is high, as the entrance court is a semi-public space. Conversely, in a shared interior-garden space residents meet socially during their leisure time, when they are enjoying their garden or are using the common space.

## DEFINING CLUSTER SPACES

Space can be defined by both buildings and landscaping, and should be visibly the territory of a cluster of units. The simplest way to create a space is to arrange two buildings at 90°

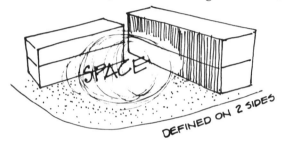

to each other. The back side of the corner (a 270 degree angle) is not a definable space because it doesn't encircle ter-

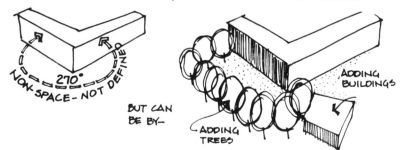

ritory. Placing buildings opposite one another creates a space, even though it is open at both ends. The space can be more defined and territory further increased by adding a third or

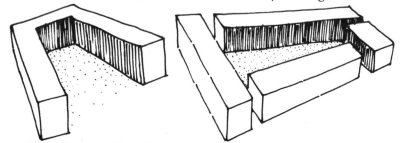

fourth building. Space can be created in one linear building by stepping units inward, with the building enclosing a small space. Usually two units are stepped back at a time to minimize costs.

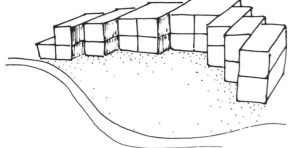

Trees and landscape features are effective space definers and can be interchanged with architectural elements. Think of trees as volumes capable of creating an edge. The only disadvantage is that trees may not provide space definitions for a

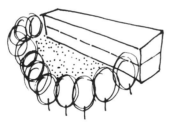

number of years. Garages, carports, fences, trellises and retaining walls are flexible space definers which can be used with success.

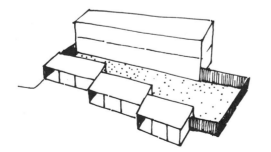

Angles between two buildings greater than 90° and up to 135° create and enclose space yet allow visual continuity to continue past. Angled space, typical of many European plazas, is easy to work with but for some unknown reason has been all but overlooked in America.

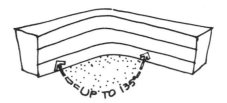

Space is defined if it is enclosed in some understandable fashion. Space can be enlarged by overlapping the defining elements, allowing it to "leak" beyond.

Let's look at a standard city block. Assume it to be 200 feet deep and 400 feet long, with the north arrow allowing an ideal sun orientation as shown. For temperate climates the ideal sun orientation will probably be with the garden facing the sun—south, southeast or southwest. For hot southern climates it may be advisable to use a southeast garden orientation, that is, with the garden facing southeast.

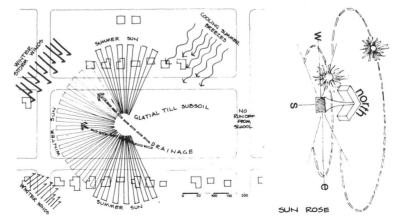

For urban sites, with existing streets and good public transportation, two questions must be addressed:

1.  Should the dominant street access be on foot or via car?

2.  Should individual units relate directly to the street, or should residents first enter a common court, then enter each unit?

Both questions are related to the future role automobiles will play in our lives. We have come to rely totally on auto access as the connection between home and daily chores. With better public transportation, a pedestrian entry may be preferable. The car would be stored some distance from the house, and strong pedestrian routes developed to connect existing streets to each unit. There are obvious compromises; for instance, auto and pedestrians can share a common entry corridor, or some units can relate to the street, while others in the same development relate to interior courtyards.

TOWN HOUSE. Let us try first the standard American approach by lining the street with units. A section should be drawn through the narrowest portion and the width measured. Now let us try a town house scheme with parking inside the unit. The town house is the logical unit to line roadways since it requires driveway access to serve parking. Town houses can be spaced several feet back of the sidewalk allowing for small planting, or placed 20 feet back with an entrance garden plus extra car parking in the driveway. Let us allow 40 feet of depth for the unit, and assume 20 feet of rear garden depth as a trial start. When added up the 20, 40, 20 feet total 80 feet, with 40 feet left over from our 200-foot deep block. Town houses should be 25 to 30 feet wide so we can divide the space in the other direction all the way around. With this arrangement we have public open space around the units in the form of street and sidewalks, a semi-public strip just inside the sidewalk joining the entrance garden, a private garden in the rear, and small shared semi-private interior space.

CORNERS ARE ALWAYS A PROBLEM. There are several solutions:

- putting a row of town houses along both long sides without turning the corner.
- Turning the corner with town houses perpendicular to each other at the corner. Starting at the street, we move in 20 feet for parking (or 5 feet for only entrance planting), 40 feet for the unit itself and 20 feet for garden space for a total of 80 feet. By overlapping buildings we should be able to squeeze six to seven units in this direction, equal to the number lost in the other direction.

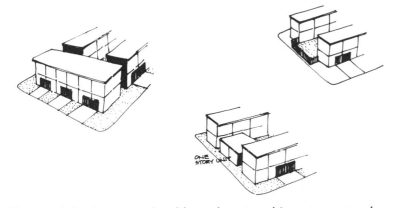

The result looks somewhat like a donut and is not spectacular, but most of the qualities of a single-family house are duplicated. The car is garaged inside the house and each unit has a private entrance, private garden, and individual identity. This scheme does offer a 40 foot strip of common land between the units and room for site planning adjustments.

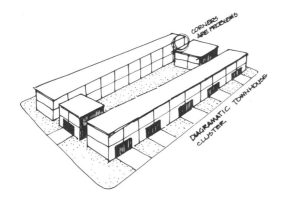

PATIO HOUSE. The patio house is the easiest unit type to site. We just divide the land into 40 foot squares on a grid, and provide entrances and parking. It is almost that simple and the results are usually worthwhile.

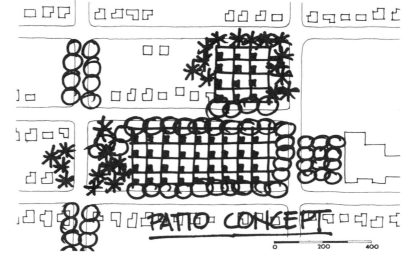

A 200 foot deep block will accommodate five rows of units. Patios should face south, southeast, or southwest. The entrance to interior units is via a passageway which feeds two rows or four units. These narrow passages can be designed in a variety of ways to make them attractive.

Parking can be in open lots at one end of the development, inside units fronting the road, or scattered throughout the development by eliminating some units.

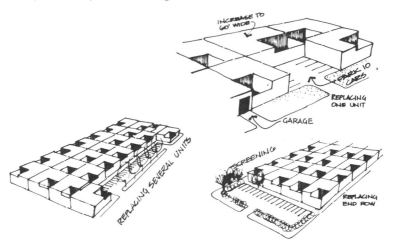

ROW HOUSE. Row houses are more complex to site since they need no road access and can be accommodated in many ways. Therefore, the number of possible arrangements is large. Row houses are located either <u>parallel</u> or <u>perpendicular</u> to the street. Locating buildings *parallel* to a road lengthens the amount of roadway required and exposes all residents to the environmental problems of the automobile. Placing buildings *perpendicular* or at some angle to the road exposes only the end unit to the road, but allows units to be easily served by it.

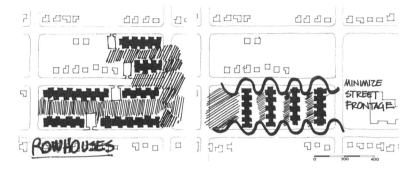

Row houses should be a minimum of 16 feet wide and can range up to about 24 feet. Unit depth can vary from 30 feet to 40 feet with 32 feet working well. The units are typically two story with living and cooking on the ground floor and sleeping upstairs.

<u>Units with Adjacent Parking</u>—This arrangement introduces the access road, which usually works perpendicular to the local road in cul-de-sac fashion. Because it is relatively quiet and free from excessive traffic and because of its strong form and identity, the cul-de-sac has become one of the most popular street types.

Single-loaded parking courts serve one set of row houses from a 40 foot wide parking area. At least ten feet between parking and units is needed for a walkway and planting. Fifteen feet would be better allowing enough room for a small entrance garden. This arrangement is typical of many of the German layouts of the l930s with entrances facing the north quadrant and gardens facing south. Unfortunately, gardens are next to the parking lot. However, if the land slopes slightly, elevation can be taken up between the garden and parking, leaving the garden higher and assuring privacy. One positive feature is there is no overviewing into a neighbor's garden across the court.

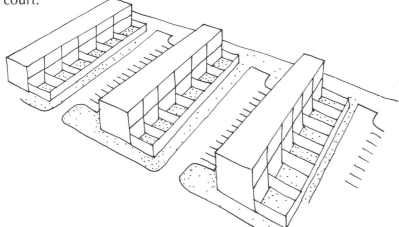

Double-loaded parking works in a similar fashion, but with two rows of units facing the parking. For even sun distribution, parking and units should be oriented in a north/south direction, with the east-facing row receiving morning sun in the garden and the west-facing row afternoon sun.

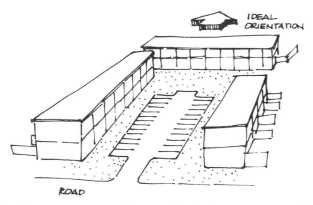

The real advantage of the double-loaded arrangement is the garden space located behind the unit and away from roads.

This courtyard can be attractive if it is large enough, has private gardens next to each unit, and tree planting for privacy between opposite units.

## CATCHING UP

The arrangements we have been talking about are straightforward and are meant primarily for small tracts of level land within built-up areas. The exercise of testing typical arrangements of town, row and patio houses on a site will help familiarize us with the size, configuration, and problems of the site. This exercise should take an hour, be done in bold fashion with feltpens and without detail design. Even though we may have a particular solution in mind, it is best to stay flexible.

DEVELOPING A CONCEPT. Having been quickly through site manipulation, we should reassess the potential of the site as a whole. Is a strong concept emerging? What is the basic character of the concept? Does the concept enhance cluster housing? Does the concept enhance the "fit" of the surrounding environment? How can the concept be diagramed? Many developments have been designed without a concept.

In general site design suffers if:

1. It is an amalgamation of solutions to a series of individual problems, or
2. It is designed as one would paint a wall, starting in one corner and working across until it has all been covered.

There is little chance that a strong concept can emerge from these approaches. What if no strong concept emerges? If a site is totally without character, it is more important for a designer to develop a concept.

WHAT IS A CONCEPT? A concept is an abstract idea or way to satisfy a developer's program, develop a memorable housing environment, and satisfy user needs for a specific site. Concepts are based upon particular impressions and information that can be expressed graphically and from which a design can be developed. Concepts are the product of understanding and interpreting the site's potentials and limitations (through analysis), user needs (embodied in the program), and combining them into an overall idea. There are many subtleties; for instance, the overall idea isn't drawn directly from site or user needs but from a designer's impressions of these. Impressions are a generalized sense of what is right; they stem from real life experiences built upon years of cultural heritage. Developing a concept is a probing, thinking process which is usually time consuming, although it can sometimes happen in an instant.

CONCEPT DEVELOPMENT. Many sites have obvious attributes which literally beg for concept adoption. If there is a view of the sea, or 200 foot tall trees, (or even 40 foot tall trees), rock outcrops or any amenity, it should become a strong part of the concept. Less directly, concepts can provide something people want, but which isn't available naturally:

- rural feeling in the city
- recreational opportunities
- choice of living environments
- view from each unit
- peace and quiet
- safety for children at play

In general, concepts relate to four factors:

Amenity
Identity
Land use organization
Functional activity patterns

Natural amenities may be scarce, or absent on urban sites and may have to be created. In this case, the concept becomes what is possible:

- intensifying urban qualities
- creating a small forest or orchard
- using traditional layouts and materials
- giving every resident a private garden
- developing a leisurely atmosphere

The development program, covering anticipated household needs, is another consideration. There is no purpose in thinking about a swimming pool if the principal tenants are elderly and don't want to swim; or of an Oriental garden if all the families are going to have active children. What the residents can afford, how they will spend their time, and what values they hold must become part of the concept.

Concepts are far more than a wish list of desirable features. Private gardens for all units, good sun orientations, parking for l.5 cars per unit, and reasonable rents, are program requirements within which a concept must work. The concept *inter-*

*prets* these requirements plus site realities into generalized approaches in order to accomplish them.

Qualities I would like to have near my home

| | | |
|---|---|---|
| private yard | grassy meadow | horse stable |
| basketball court | baseball diamond | game room |
| small lake | swim pool | open hillside |
| picnic area | rock outcrop | golf course |
| small forest | car repair area | bicycle trail |
| natural stream | wood shop | tennis court |

Concept development relates to the overall pattern of development and has its own intrinsic requirements. These requirements include that dwelling units be private; that they be oriented to insure plentiful air, light, and sun; that they be properly related to amenities such as green space and view; that they be conveniently related to function patterns such as parking; and that they be properly related to each other.

OTHER CONCEPT DEVELOPMENT AIDS. Experience is a common tool for synthesizing a concept. What we have seen, how we have lived, and how we think create impressions which are reflected in concepts we develop. This does not mean copying exactly what seems to succeed elsewhere, but rather keeping it in mind and adapting elements to the needs of a particular site and set of residents. We should not hesitate to draw ideas from other projects. If we approach the design process honestly, no two designs will be exactly the same.

Unique character sets the image for many residents. Any memorable quality which is unusual enough to be remembered can serve as a basis for a concept.

OPPOSITES SHOULD BE TESTED DURING CONCEPT DEVELOPMENT, AND EACH STUDIED UNTIL A FULL RANGE OF "IN BETWEEN" CONCEPTS EMERGES.

Opposites can be:

- low rise versus high rise
- all public open space versus all private open space
- inward focus versus external focus
- street oriented versus open space oriented
- individual versus collective

Access. The system of access from public to private offers many opportunities for concept development. The strategic location of access points governs intensity of use, suggests the type of use, can produce or stop growth, and can create or destroy areas of calm.

Unity. The use of a single basic building material or shape creates unity which is often noted and remembered. All developers struggle with the problem, searching for some "theme" to make their development look distinguished or different. The usual solution is a superficial "theme" (Cape Cod, Ranch, or Colonial) or cosmetic exterior treatment, with the result that most newer developments look essentially the same and lack variety and identity.

The whole should be divided into the three site systems— Open Space, Housing, and Circulation and a concept developed for each. The authors recommend against incrementalism in concept development, if the subdivisions exceed these three.

Tradeoffs. If some units do not benefit from the concept, they may be given something else (such as rent reduction, larger garden, view, larger apartment) as compensation.

The balance of this chapter will look at a number of site planning concerns from a concept-forming point of view. We should keep loose, work in broad-brush, diagramatic plan

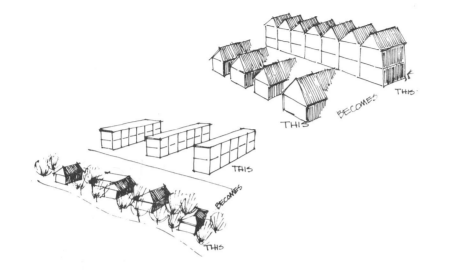

## FITTING THE DEVELOPMENT INTO THE NEIGHBORHOOD

Local setback and height restrictions, as well as the setback, size, and bulk of adjacent buildings should be checked. It is important to study carefully nearby architecture and its relation to the street to determine if any of our early test solutions are compatible.

In general, buildings define streets in one of two ways. First, buildings either joined or spaced closely together define the street space and create a distinct linear character. Town or patio house arrangements lining the road complement this street pattern.

Second, buildings spaced farther apart or staggered tend to give the street a less restricted, less linear character, with trees becoming the principal street space definers. Row houses located perpendicular to the roadway complement this type of street, with spaces opening up between the ends of rows of units.

The fear most abutting residents have is that a new development will overpower their own homes. These fears are real, especially when large apartment buildings are constructed in single-family neighborhoods. The safe approach is conceptually to match new buildings with existing buildings, duplicating bulk, materials, and disposition of buildings on the lot. The match is essential where there is visual contact, with change possible in other areas. Contrast is permissible only if good reasons can be articulated.

## UNIT ENTRANCES

It is essential for units to have privacy and identity at the entrance. That does not mean total isolation; it means a compact design with architectural elements or planting as screening devices. Each entrance, or entrance court, must also have an obvious connection to a public street since Americans relate well to streets and depend on them for orientation.

There are several conceptual entrance arrangements.

1. Direct street access. For first floor entrances to row and town houses, a small walk may be connected from the road or sidewalk to each unit. Units should be set back at least 10 feet from the street, and planting or fences added to screen noise and prevent overviewing from the main walk. A small "front porch" may be included. Where possible, entrance doors should be separated from one another, though this requires more individual walkways. An arrangements with two doors side by side, separated by a wall or planter, is acceptable.

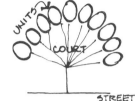

2. Courtyard entrances. In this scheme, residents leave the street or sidewalk, enter a small courtyard shared by a number of units, and then move to their own individual entrance. There are many possible court arrangements, with the preferred entrance being a separate, short walkway to each unit's front porch.

3. Path-related entrance. In this scheme, a major path runs perpendicular to the street or sidewalk, and connects rows of units in single or double-loaded fashion, or connects units in a courtyard cluster. Small individual walks serve each entrance from the row or courtyard, and fences or planting assure privacy and identity.

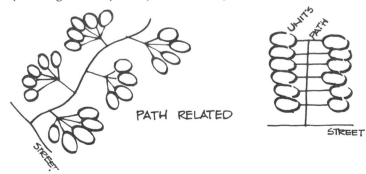

4. Parking-lot-related entrance. Parking lots, as extensions of streets, can make good entrance courts. Typically, a walk surrounds the parking lot and connects to the street. Individual entrance walks 10 to 15 feet long lead from this walk to each unit, achieving identity and privacy. The arrangement is popular with residents who need their cars nearby.

Conceptually, first floor entrances require a main walk some distance from the unit - say eight feet, with a smaller walk leading to each unit. Planting or fences can screen noise and views of the main walk. Each entrance achieves some privacy and identity if there is a small raised front porch. Meander the path, vary its width and separate unit entrance doors where possible, even though additional walkways are required. Two doors, side by side separated by a solid wall or planter is usually acceptable where cost must be minimized.

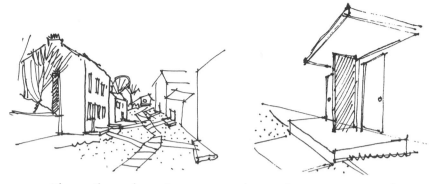

The authors do not recommend use of two entrance schemes which are favored by developers because of their low construction costs.

1. Double-loaded interior corridors serving two rows of units from a common interior hallway have disadvantages. This hallway is usually narrow, dark, and dreary; does not allow through ventilation in the unit; is noisy because of the proximity of entrance doors and echoing caused by the enclosed linear space; lacks space belonging to each unit (territory) and lacks privacy at each entrance. The result is an insensitive, impersonal entrance which works against developing a sense of community. There is one exception: double-loaded corridors can function well for small housing developments, especially for elderly people,

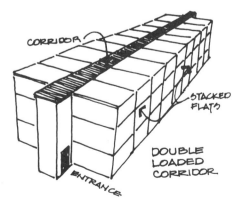

where all residents are quiet and appreciate the warmth and protection of an interior hallway. To accomplish this, it must be at least 6 feet wide, well illuminated and ventilated.

2. Exterior balcony, an exterior deck attached to and running the length of the building on the entrance side, has disadvantages because the deck is usually noisy and privacy at the entrance is minimum. However, this arrangement is better than the double-loaded type, in that it is open to the elements and allows through ventilation to each unit.

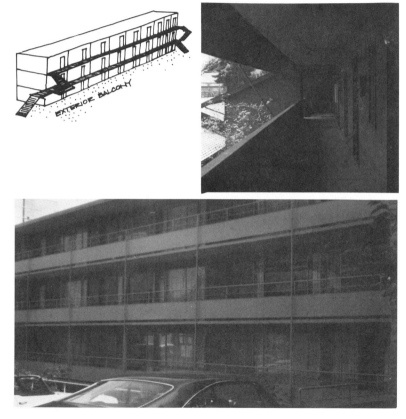

Upper Story Access is more difficult because of the need to cover *vertical* distance (i.e., going upstairs) and because of the high cost of constructing decks and aerial walkways. The preferred arrangement is similar to ground floor access: separate, identifiable entrance areas, protected and private, with stairs shared by a minimum number of units. Ideally a stair unit should serve no more than four families.

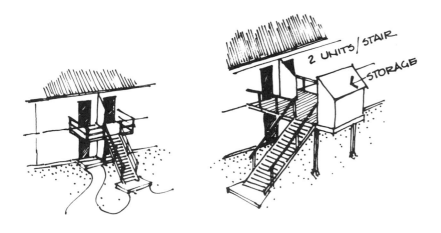

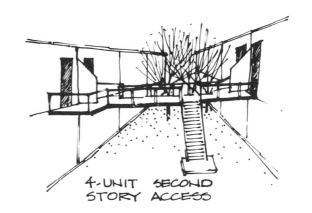

4-UNIT SECOND STORY ACCESS

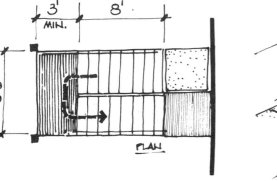

PLAN

PLATFORM COULD BE LARGER

3' — 17' (17 RISERS) — 3'

SECTION

3' MIN. — 8'

PLAN

A stairway shared by two or four units is acceptable provided no one has to walk directly past another unit. Serving two upper units is relatively easy since the stair can be located between the doors and each entrance screened with a fence or planter. Serving four units is more tricky. The stair can lead to an aerial walkway, set about eight feet out from the units and connected appropriately with bridges, or the stair can be located between rows of units with a bridge connecting each building and serving two units.

Second story access requires considerable space which must be allowed for early in the site planning process. In calculating the amount of space to reserve, a 6-inch stair rise and 12-inch tread is suggested. The final dimension may change slightly, but this allows adequate room and is easy to figure and measure. Consider a story to be 9 feet high—8 feet of headroom plus one foot of structure. That means the length of a one-story stair would be 18 feet plus at least 3 feet of landing top and bottom. Stairs can run straight or they can reverse and return. Both configurations require approximately the same amount of overall room.

Entry stairs must be 3 feet wide and include a handrail. Ideally they should be roofed for rain protection. In addition they may be open or closed at the sides, and may be integrated into the building or stand free.

VIEWS. Are there any desirable views from the site? Generally, since views are cherished and sought after, the more units with a view, the better. The individual/collective dilemma should be addressed: is the view sufficiently available so most residents can enjoy it from individual units, or is it limited and best shared from a common outdoor space?

The best locations to view from and the exact elevation the view becomes visible should be determined. A section should be drawn through each location, carefully locating sight lines and view blockage. The section can then be used to test the placement of buildings in determining the most advantageous arrangement. Some conceptual view-oriented arrangements include:

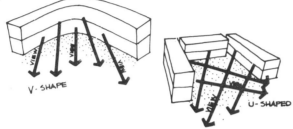

- V-shaped or U-shaped court opens the view to units on one side.

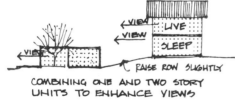

- Terraced units open the view to many units. Level land may be terraced by depressing a one-story unit slightly, placing a two-story row behind with living on the second floor and utilizing the roof of the unit in front as a roof garden. The next row behind may be on top of a parking garage and separated by a courtyard for light and air. The court becomes a pleasant common yard entrance space.
- sometimes a penthouse can be added atop an interior unit, when it may not be possible to give all units a view.
- a front row of units can be broken at two, four or six-unit intervals, with other units placed behind the opening

gaining a framed view. Although the panoramic view is touted as being most desirable, the framed view is often more interesting and should not be overlooked.

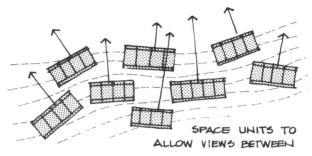

Let us avoid placing a parking lot immediately in front of a view. On the other hand, a parking lot or any other undesirable visual elements may have to be masked by using planted earth mounds, fences, trees and shrubs.

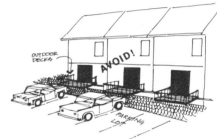

## OPEN SPACE MANIPULATION

Natural Amenities. Any full-grown tree, stream, rock outcropping, meadow, or varied topography should provide focus for part of the development. Focus is an important principle in formulating a site planning approach because it suggests "cluster," with a group of units relating to the object of focus.

If a site has any natural qualities, we should assess whether they should become part of the common entrance or part of the garden space. For instance, a fine old tree carefully integrated into a parking court can make the area seem as though

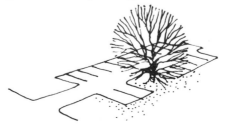

it is well established. Conversely, a full-grown tree in a communal garden can make the setting seem complete and can offer visual privacy between opposite units. With any natural amenity, it is important to allow adequate room for continued functioning and growth.

## BUFFERS AND SCREENING

The site should be assessed for undesirable abutting land uses, such as a busy arterial, industrial activity, an adjacent unscreened parking lot, and a buffer designed. Buffers can be:

1. A tall fence or earth mound to completely eliminate the undesirable view. Fences, though expensive, offer immediate relief for the first floor; however, floors above seldom receive any visual protection from a fence.
2. Planting trees and shrubs provides a buffer for everyone, in time. Most trees require five to ten years to reach reasonable size, but then do a good job. A reasonable amount of space should be allocated for tree planting: a 5-foot width won't do; 15 feet to 20 feet is a better minimum. In determining if trees should be evergreen or deciduous, we should consider that evergreens block the view all year long but also block or filter sunlight.
3. Separating living units from undesirable neighbors with a buffer of space, possibly a parking or recreation area, is sometimes necessary. Noise is reduced somewhat over distance by trees and fences.

When units must abut an undesirable view, it is best to face the entrance side rather than the garden side to it. This is a compromise decision which can be justified as follows: entrances are used for shorter periods of time, don't need as much sunshine, can be small, and are easier to screen from undesirable views. Gardens, on the other hand, are larger, need sunshine, and can't be easily screened. If, however, the buffer is to be a wide, planted open space, it may be advantageous to abut the private garden to it. Whenever possible, buffers should perform multiple uses, serving also as parking, open space, gardens, play areas, etc. The secret of medium-density living is efficient and overlapping use of all land.

## PRIVATE GARDENS

We have mentioned the need for every unit to have a sunny outdoor garden. A garden works best if it is on grade, that is, on "good old mother earth"; however, a roof deck or balcony is almost as good for many users. In order to receive optimal amounts of sunshine, gardens must face southeast, south, or

southwest and be unobstructed by tall trees or adjacent buildings. The most desirable garden space is away from the roadway, preferably adjoining a larger common open space.

The *minimum* usable garden size is about 10 feet square allowing room for a small table and chairs, a chaise lounge, or children's play. This 100 square feet is usable surface and does not include planting or buffer area. A more comfortable size is about 500 square feet with 200 square feet of paved or usable surface. However, standards vary with household types: families with children need more space, young couples need less, and so on.

Private gardens typically relate to the main living area, such as a family room, living room, or dining room. It is sometimes possible to connect the garden to two rooms, doubling its usefulness. Private gardens off bedrooms are a luxury which serve little purpose and should be avoided unless there is no other option, a unique view exists, or the units are for upper income residents who can afford the garden space.

BACK TO BACK GARDENS

Back to Back Gardens. Double-loaded access usually results in back-to-back gardens in the rear. Most suburban gardens are laid out in this fashion and work with some measure of success, primarily because they are large enough to ensure privacy and allow proper sunlighting. When garden sizes are reduced in depth and flanked by two or three-story buildings, privacy becomes a real problem. Fences and tree planting can help, but they do reduce sunlight. To provide a balance of sunlight to all units, double-loaded arrangements should run north/south affording morning sun to one row of units and afternoon sun to the other. Variations in unit height reduce back-to-back garden problems. A one-story row on the sun side lets light in, reduces overviewing, and diminishes the scale of the building.

Single-loaded units are most satisfactory with access from the north quadrant and the garden in the south. Regardless of climate, gardens should always face the sun.

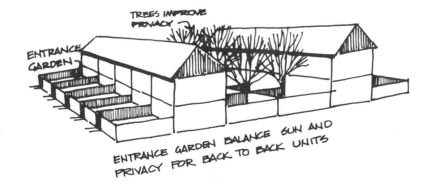

ENTRANCE GARDEN

TREES IMPROVE PRIVACY

ENTRANCE GARDEN BALANCE SUN AND PRIVACY FOR BACK TO BACK UNITS

Most row, town and patio houses are flexible enough to accept an enclosed garden on the entry side opening from the kitchen or dining area. This may assure sunshine to each unit, or simply give all units two gardens. End units can open to a garden off the end of the building using the corner space which would otherwise be amiguous open space.

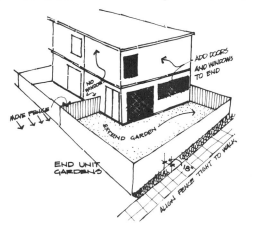

## PARKING

Movement and storage of the automobile is the biggest site planning problem. Each automobile requires approximately 350 square feet for parking including room for maneuvering. As a comparison, 350 square feet is roughly equivalent to one-half the ground space occupied by each house. In other words, a two-story unit with 1400 square feet of total living space occupies 700 square feet of ground space equivalent to twice the 350 square feet parking area for one car. A family with two cars requires ground floor space for parking equivalent to 100 percent of its own ground living area. Obviously this cuts deeply into usable recreational open space, but loss of open space is not the only problem. Getting the auto to each house usually interrupts open space, limits the continuity of pedestrian walks, and causes noise and safety problems.

Auto parking must be provided for family cars, guest cars, and recreational vehicles such as boats, trailers, and campers. Parking ratios, normally expressed as cars per unit, vary from .25 (one car per four units) to 3 (three cars per unit) depending on marketability of the unit, ordinance requirements, and urban or suburban setting. Developments in urban areas with good public transportation, convenient shopping, and public facilities require fewer parking spaces than suburban developments where residents are dependent entirely on the auto for daily family functioning.

Cars may be grouped in open lot arrangements, inside or under buildings in separate shared parking garages, or along the street. Each solution has cost and convenience advantages or disadvantages to different users.

107

The all-American convenience solution is a garage attached to each house, with a direct link between street, parking, and house. In principle this is possible even at densities up to 14 d/u (dwelling units) per acre. In practice, the number of roads required to service this solution eliminates most meaningful community open space, leaving only a standard single-family suburban development. Some users, particularly families with children and disabled persons, find attached garage convenience essential. A compromise may be to provide attached garages for all three or four-bedroom units, with more efficient parking arrangements for all other units.

The ordinary open parking lot is by far the most efficient, least costly, and least damaging to open space and overall environmental quality. With decreased reliance on the car, it can work advantageously at densities up to 20 d/u acre. Because open lot parking is inexpensive, most developers overuse it, creating lots that are too large, not relating them comfortably to units, and ignoring landscaping and other buffering devices. With care in site planning, the open parking lot can be a positive auto storage method. We should:

- minimize the number of cars in each unit: 10 to 12 cars is a comfortable number.

- orient the parking lot to the houses it will serve. The connection should be obvious and the parking should feel like part of the cluster. Pedestrians should be able to walk in front of cars toward their houses.

- orient single-loaded parking lots parallel to a row of houses running roughly east to west to satisfy most orientation requirements.

- orient double-loaded court parking in a north/south fashion.

- make the most efficient use of space with perpendicular parking. Plant each parking court to soften and buffer it. Trees screen best, with one tree for two to three cars producing overall visual protection. Shrubs provide extra buffer and may be necessary in certain locations.

Front yard parking mars the landscape, reduces the on street parking and causes safety problems (backout over sidewalk) for the pedestrian.

Size Requirements for Parking Areas—Even though the average size of automobiles continues to become smaller, with compact and sports models replacing large luxury ones, a space 9 feet by 20 feet is still required for storage of each car with a backout space of equal size. This totals 40-feet wide for single-loaded lots and 60-feet wide for double loading. For large cars, where space is not a premium or where garages are to be built, a 10-foot or 12-foot by 20-foot size is better. Perpendicular parking is preferred since it uses the least amount of space and operates with two-way traffic allowing for dead-end parking areas. Although angle parking consumes more total space, it is useful where the width is tight. For instance, a single-loaded 45° angle lot can be constructed in areas only 30 feet wide; double-loaded in 47-foot wide spaces. The angle arrangement is *one way* requiring a separate entrance and exit.

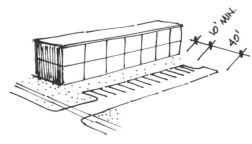

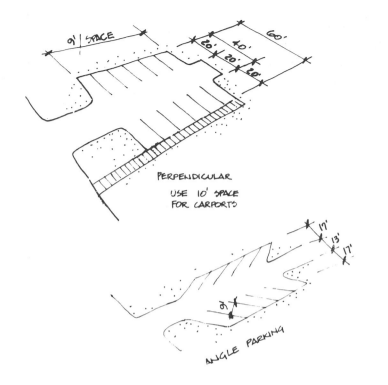

PERPENDICULAR
USE 10' SPACE
FOR CARPORTS

ANGLE PARKING

Parallel parking along a street requires smaller parking space size: 7 feet by 18 feet with an extra 5 feet between every two cars for maneuvering. Parallel parking spaces can be designated with sidewalk or planter spaces extended out from the curb to define spaces.

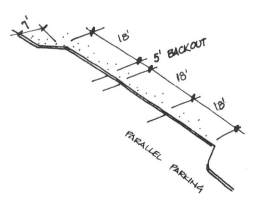

5' BACKOUT

PARALLEL PARKING

## HOW CLOSE CAN BUILDINGS BE?

Row, patio, and town houses touch each other in one direction where two blank walls abut. Beyond that units can be farther apart or close together, depending on the design. However, the following factors must be considered in designing:

- overshadowing—Every building throws a shadow in one quadrant, which may overshadow another building, garden, or window. Some overshadowing is inevitable, but gardens or windows in complete shade are undesirable.

- overviewing—Unit windows facing other unit windows create overviewing situations which diminish individual privacy and limit window use. Private gardens are also subject to overviewing from units alongside, above, or straight across.

Several design opportunities for dealing with overshadowing and overviewing are as follows.

*Window Wall to Blank Wall.* These can be very close, say, 5 feet apart, with no loss of privacy. The most important private areas are the living room, dining room, kitchen and garden. Bedroom and bath fall into another category where privacy is desirable but not essential.

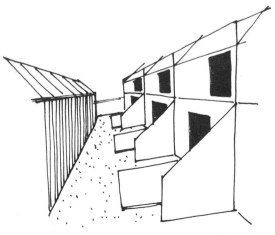

BLANK WALL TO WINDOW WALL

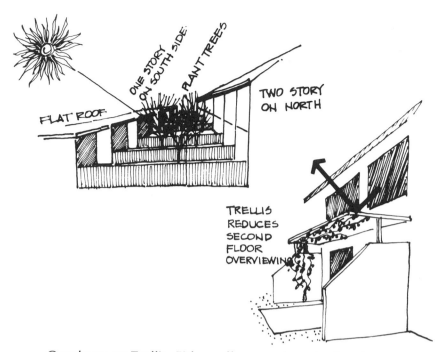

*Overhang or Trellis.* Either offers good protection from overviewing. To test their effectiveness, we may draw a section. Vines trailing from the trellis provide extra privacy.

*Tall Fences* between units and at the rear garden edge can sometimes create complete privacy from passersby, but do not block views from above. Fences can be constructed after buildings are completed or can extend as a part of the architecture using the same material. Planting hedges or vines on a trellis creates the same, but a subtler, effect over time.

*End Units* do not have as much of a problem with overviewing, since large windows may be moved from the rear wall to the end wall.

*Bedroom Window Facing Living Window.* This doesn't eliminate overview, but so the theory goes, people should not be using one room while their neighbors are using the other. Obviously this is not true 24 hours a day, but it does work during the most used portions of the day. The trick is to avoid directly opposite living room windows. Any form of staggering or alternating of buildings or windows will also help.

## COMBINING BUILDING TYPES

So far we have considered the use of one type of building over the entire site, which may work well for small sites requiring only one or two buildings. For larger sites, combinations of row, town and patio houses and flats may be desirable. Combinations of unit types should be based on matching particular design problems with characteristics of each unit type. A number of examples follow.

Town houses require street access and therefore function best around the perimeter of a site. Conversely, row and patio houses do not require direct street access. Therefore, combinations of town at the perimeter and row or patio in the interior should be considered for sites bordered by roads but with large interior spaces.

Patio houses are usually one story and may be combined with row or town house units to vary heights. A patio house on the end of a row of two-story units reduces the visual scale. Interior courts seem larger when flanked by low one-story patio houses.

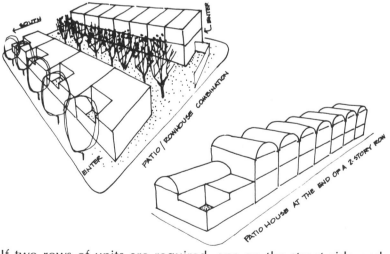

If two rows of units are required, one on the street side and the other on the inside, a combination of low patio houses on the perimeter, and taller row houses in the interior assures sunlight, ventilation, and views to all units. If a view is spectacular, the interior row house plan might be reversed, placing living and cooking on the top floor.

On sloping sites, combinations of one-story patio houses and two-story row or town houses can be arranged alternately up the slope to assure views and sunlight to all units. A section drawn through the slope becomes the design tool; finish floor elevations are adjusted until all units have a view.

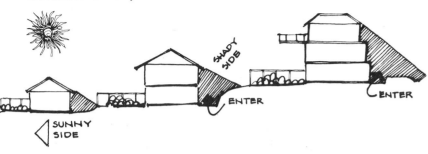

Row and town houses can be combined together on the same row by eliminating a driveway and providing parking elsewhere. This may be appropriate on the end of a row of units close to the corner, where a driveway may conflict with cars on the street.

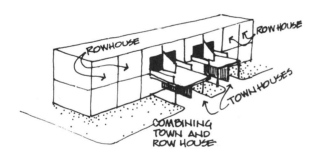

FLATS can be inserted in a variety of ways. They can replace patio houses in all the variations discussed above. They can be inserted in a row of row or town houses, varying the width and window pattern to avoid monotony and balancing the housing selection. Moreover, they can be located above carports. Finally, flats can be added above or under a town or row house, creating a three-story maisonette. Placing flats under means residents in the unit over need walk up only one floor. Extra height on the north side causes little overshadowing problem and allows height to be reduced elsewhere without losing density.

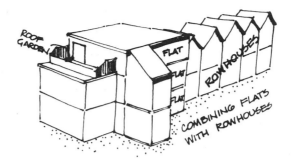

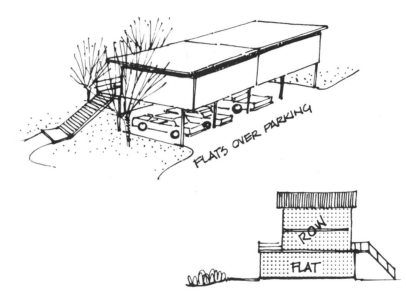

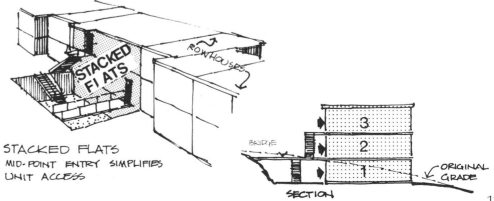

111

KEY LOTS are two lots, one placed behind the other without normal street frontage. This arrangement reduces street development costs yet allows for privacy and other desirable housing concerns. Typically, four units are clustered around a common entry court, with quiet interior lots away from the street being ideal for families with young children.

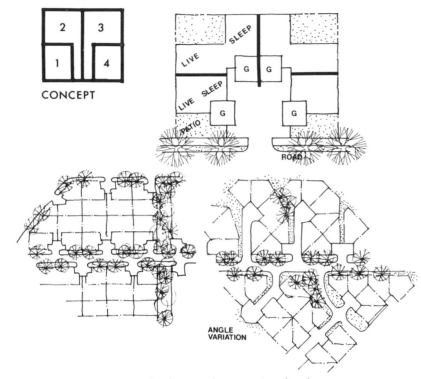

DUPLEXES: Two attached units form a simple cluster arrangement which conforms to existing lot lines and usually requires a minimum number of approvals before construction. They should be used when:

- Left-over spaces are not large enough for row, town, or patio houses.
- Approvals for zone change or variance is difficult to acquire.
- Existing single family neighborhoods desire to increase density over a period of time.

Duplexes have many advantages for urban development and may be constructed on lots as small as 40' X 100', still pro-

viding ground orientation, parking, individual gardens, privacy and identity.

Three duplex arrangements are suggested:

- Side by side units, ideally located with the garden facing south and to the rear, and the entrance and road opposite in the north quadrant. Locate a private entry on each side, sharing the outdoor space with its adjacent unit.

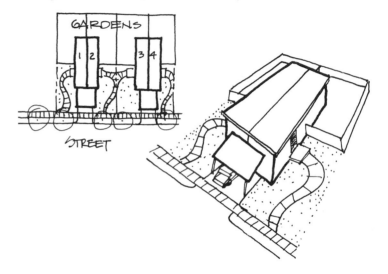

- Back to back configurations work best for east/west orientations, with entrance along the north side and private gardens on the south. Back to back duplexes sharing a common entry court should be oriented north/south to guarantee some sunlight to each garden. Parking may be located at either end or in grouped lots nearby.

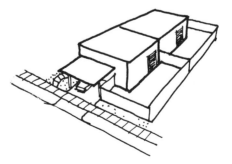

- Stacked duplexes are the easiest to arrange because of their efficient lot coverage. Typically the lower unit entrance is along one side near the street, with second story stairs on the same side to the rear. This arrangement allows for one garden on the opposite side with a second garden in the rear.

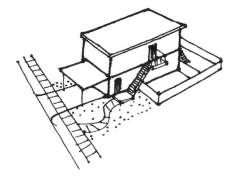

As a caution, rows of duplexes lined up in soldier fashion with stereotyped setbacks, heights and side yards produces a monotonous character and lacks sense of community. The same street takes on a different character if setbacks, side yards, unit widths, and landscaping are varied, or units are clustered.

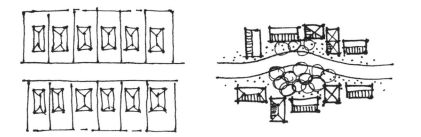

## EVALUATION

Now that we have a fair understanding of what may be possible or desirable for a site, how do we determine which solution is best? Through evaluation we can assess a scheme, using set values. The simplest procedure is to define our values in the form of development goals or principles. Some examples include:

*Privacy*—Does each unit have privacy from overviewing at the entrance and private garden?

*Private Garden*—Does each unit have a south-facing outdoor space of at least a certain number of square feet? (The number of square feet varies. It may be 100, 200, 400 or 1,000 feet, and may also be 50 percent of the space occupied by units.

*Quiet*—Is noise intrusion to the living spaces of each unit minimized? Do units face away from street noise? Is there an adequate buffer, as well as careful arrangement of noisy recreation activities such as tennis, swimming and children's play areas?

*Pedestrian Safety*—Does a common semi-public walk, free from auto intrusion connect to all private gardens?

*View*—Do 50 percent of the units (the figure may vary) have a view with some "substitute" amenity for those units without a view?

*Access/Identity*—Does each unit have clear, direct pedestrian and auto access for residents? Is parking within 300 feet of the unit? The distance will vary with the type of development; for instance, suburban residents usually demand much shorter walks, say, 100 feet, while urban dwellers are willing to walk farther. In general, the tradeoff between "car at your door' and "car at some distance" is more open space, and people are beginning to find it a worthwhile trade.

# LEGEND

| KEY | NO. | DESCRIPTION |
|---|---|---|
| | 23 | ROWHOUSE |
| | 37 | FLATS |
| | 41 | TOWNHOUSE |
| | 20 | PATIO HOUSE |
| | 13 | MAISONETTE |
| | | TREES TO REMAIN |
| | | NEW TREES |
| | | CONTOURS |

## SUMMARY SITE PLANNING PROCESS

Following analysis and program development, it is important to:

- Determine all the site functions—the approximate architectural plans and their shape, general shape for parking, service area, outdoor areas, roads, etc.
- Outline on the site plan usable and nonusable area (based on earlier site analysis).
- Match the "use areas" to site functions and look for working relationships between site and function.
- Reanalyze the entire process. We must verify the logic of our proposal, refine details, and design the entire site.

Graphic Checklist. To communicate our site planning intent, we should make sure the following information is clearly displayed.

A. Overall Site Plan—at the largest scale possible to fit comfortably on a drafting table (but not wider than 42") Include:

Legible title information (project name, address, designer's name)

Legend (building types, open space types, vegetation to be saved, etc.)

Scale plus north arrow and other reference points

Roads and parking to scale

Building types to scale and graphically distinct. Communal facilities if required

Private yards

Existing and proposed vegetation

Adequate and legible labeling

Buffer zones

B. On separate drawing (same scale, legend, title, etc.)

1. Open Space Concept—public, private, and semipublic spaces—amenity provisions, recreation
2. Circulation Plan—types of roadways (major, local, access), pedestrian/bicycle routes, parking areas
3. Housing Concept— types and location— relation to roads and open space (include detail drawings to clarify)

C. Sections, Perspectives, and Detail Blowups to clarify important points

D. A Summary of uses to include:

1. Total area in acres (or square feet)
2. Area of public parkland in acres
3. Area of private ownership (buildings and logical abutting space)
4. Area of semi-private ownership (include roads, communal areas, etc.)
5. Housing types—and number of each

   single family
   attached
   apartments
   other
6. Total number of units
7. Gross density $\dfrac{\text{total number of units}}{\text{all areas except public parks}}$
8. Parking
   total
   covered
   uncovered

ADDITIONAL READINGS

Cullen, Gordon
*Townscape*
London, The Architectural Press, 1961

Cutler, L.S. and S.S.
*Handbook of Housing Systems*
New York, Van Nostrand-Reinhold, 1972

Ministry of Housing and Local Government
*Desgining a Low-Rise Housing System*
London, H.M.S.O., 1970

Ministry of Housing and Local Government
*Cars in Housing*
London, H.M.S.O., 1966

Ministry of Housing and Local Government
*Planning for Daylite*
London, H.M.S.O., l968

Urban Land Institute
*The Home Association Handbook*

Urban Land Institute
*Density Zoning*

# FITTING IN - CLUSTER CONCEPT DEVELOPMENT

As part of site concept development, the cluster concept has been given a basic form. Approximations concerning the cluster design have been made as follows:

- Total number of units to be placed on the site
- Total number of each house type to be placed on the site
- Location, size, and house mix of each cluster
- Basic configuration of each cluster

Concepts for individual clusters may now be developed. The assumptions made about the housing earlier in the process must now be further developed as design concepts made to fit each designated cluster location.

## FITTING IN

Compatibly fitting the cluster to the site is a fundamental requirement in designing housing environment. The fundamental idea of fit — to develop a compatability between what is man-made and what is not — has been part of every civilization. And yet, one of the great distinctions between civilizations has been their individual expression of compatible fit, the ways in which they have built their settlements into the landscape.

Each civilization has developed its own unique interpretation of fit; a fit attuned to the time, place, culture, and technology of that civilization. It seems that truly compatible fitness emerges only when a civilization has had sufficient time to develop. Thus, by studying the housing environments of different times, places and civilizations, the serious student of site planning for housing environments will be rewarded with insights which will help to balance the potpourri of directives on fitness with which he is being bombarded today. This historical perspective will help him overcome the difficulty of responding to the capricious and sentimental character of popular taste in American housing.

The increasing awareness of ecological and conservation issues is beginning to influence our assessment of the fitness of housing in America. The ecological movement that exploded in the early 1960's was characterized by the question of its most eloquent spokesman, Loren Eisley, "Is man but a planetary disease?" John Simonds wrote in his very important book, Landscape Architecture, that, "In the natural landscape man is the intruder." After a half decade of massive self-recriminations, the beginnings of positive thinking were dramatized in Ian McHarg's book, Design with Nature, in which he instructs us to design in the context of "ecological fitness." He indicates that if man can become reattuned to natural processes, he can become the "good shepherd of the planet earth." All the writings of Rene Dubos build a positive philosophy for the concept that man has the unique and exciting role of further enhancing natural systems — actually causing lifeless regions of the earth to come to life.

The advances in scientific technology are very slowly filtering down into the housing industry. We could soon experience such dramatic technological changes within the industry that any traditional attitudes about fitness would be swept aside. However, long-term projections indicate that the image of traditional styles will dominate for some time. The potentials of the new technology will be limited to the mass replication of traditional forms and to one-of-a-kind experiments.

Our immediate and near-future concerns are based on the realities of the need to conserve land and natural resources. This tends to favor man fitting in at the highest density that is ecologically, socially, and technologically acceptable.

The ideal condition sought here is to introduce man into natural systems in numbers that will allow the systems to perpetuate themselves and perhaps be even further enhanced. An operative natural system, whether it be a rocky plateau or a verdant river valley, presents a place undisturbed by man. With the inclusion of any new life form, — i.e., man — the system further evolves, as all dynamic systems must to exist. The new condition and the new natural system of the site then include man. Although we cannot expect to go on a site without modifying it, we are only beginning to understand how to become part of the site's natural system without destroying the attributes that attracted us to it.

# CLUSTER FIT AND SITE CHARACTER

There are several basic approaches to fitting the cluster form to the land. Throughout the book the authors emphasize the importance of developing methods for modifying the cluster form and the land form to *accommodate each other*. However, the book clearly presents a bias towards preserving the character of the site by retaining as much natural amenity as possible. There are three basic approaches to preserving the character of the site; they vary primarily in degree of site modification.

SITE CHARACTER REINFORCED. Housing may be organized to reinforce dominant site characteristics. The house clusters themselves become landscape elements. By their massing, configuration, and location they can make a dynamic site more dramatic, or a passive site more tranquil.

SITE CHARACTER PRESERVED. After analyzing a site, the site planner may judge the housing at any density would destroy the site and therefore recommend against using the site for this purpose. This is rarely the case since there is usually an appropriate place to fit in a cluster or two.

SITE CHARACTER MODIFIED. Many sites can be modified in a manner that both enhances their character and makes them more suitable for housing. We all share a dissatisfaction with thoughtless destruction of sites and natural systems by heavy-handed site development practices. Conversely, there is also a danger that a too-protective approach to site development may compromise a good design concept. We cannot feasibly transplant a climax forest, but we can selectively remove existing vegetation and introduce new vegetation. We cannot feasibly build a new mountain, but we can prudently reshape land forms to further enhance site amenities.

## FIT OF CLUSTER FORM TO LAND FORM

There are numerous fit relationships between cluster form and land form.

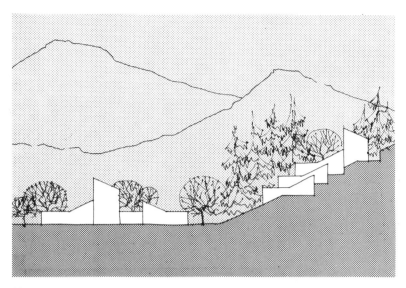

CLUSTER FORM/LAND FORM MEETING. The cluster form interfaces with the natural surface of the earth.

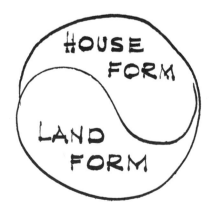

CLUSTER FORM RISING. The cluster form may disengage from the land form and rise above the earth.

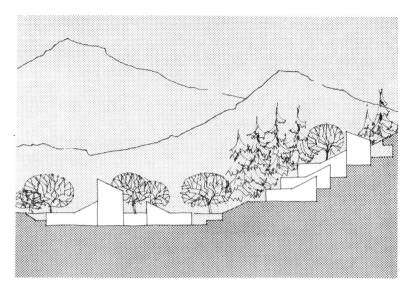

CLUSTER FORM DESCENDING. The cluster form may be integrated with the land form and become recessed into the earth.

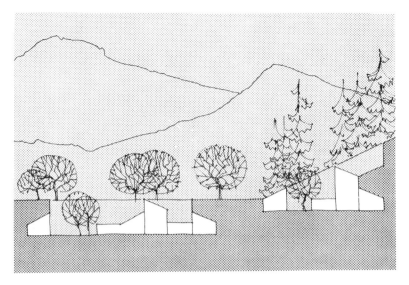

LAND FORM DESCENDING. The land form may be depressed to obscure the cluster form.

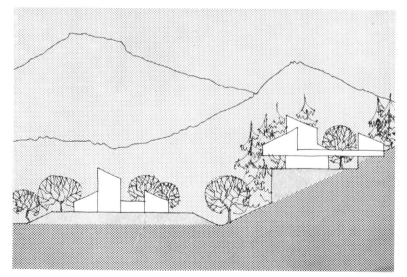

LAND FORM RISING. The land form may be raised to accentuate the cluster form.

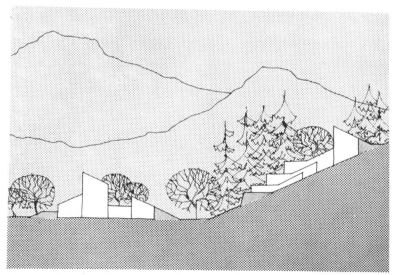

LAND FORM BERMING. The land form may be bermed to absorb cluster form.

## DETERMINANTS OF FITTING IN

The determinants of fit may be grouped into functional, psychological, and technological categories. *Functional fit* requires the cluster to be integrated with the least amount of disruption to the site's natural processes. *Psychological fit* requires that the cluster be considered to fit by both the users and adjacent neighbors. *Technological fit* requires the cluster to be built into the site systems as efficiently as possible.

While the site planner must work simultaneously with all the determinants of fit, development of functional fit is the major task. This does not mean it is always the most difficult task since there are numerous situations in which the determinants of psychological or technological fit are unique enough to dominate. Following a brief description of psychological and technological fit, the remainder of the section will focus on the process of functional fit.

### PSYCHOLOGICAL FIT

Each individual perceives the environment differently from other individuals and cultures. By interview and observation of users it is possible for the site planner to gain insights into their perception of the housing environment. The interpretation of these insights requires the site planner to make judgments about many intangible and unmeasurable aspects of the physical environment, especially those related to psychological fit, which are sense of place and expression of identity through image, style, symbol, and ritual.

PERCEPTION OF SENSE OF PLACE. There are many settlements in the world that seem to fit graciously into their natural setting. They are said to possess a sense of place. The perception of this fit is immediately apparent, not just to the culture that built the place, but to people from cultures with quite different values as well. Knowledgeable people from the many arts and sciences disciplines give various accounts of what underlies this "sense", but no one explanation can satisfy all people. It is fairly certain that "sense of place" is a consequence of more than just the arrangement of physical

things. In time the culture of a people becomes built into the physical setting in ways that defy rational analysis.

It remains that sense of place cannot be planned for specifically. It presents itself only after the settlement reaches a maturity. Like the fine English lawn, however, there is a point of true beginning; "Plant a few well-chosen seeds and wait one hundred years or so."

IDENTITY - IMAGE, STYLE, SYMBOL AND RITUAL. Identity distinguishes from sense of place because it can be built into a new housing environment by the intentional development of image. A new housing environment may be built to replicate the image of fine housing environments of the past by the use of style, symbol, and ritual. The users of the new housing may pursue a contemporary lifestyle or, when it pleases them, participate in rituals of the lifestyles of the past.

However, symbol and ritual can become an end in themselves. In many civilizations they have become so highly developed that they dramatically affect the physical organization of housing environments. Many symbolic objects and house forms originally grew out of the solution of simple pragmatic problems. Then, following a long period of time, the original purpose was forgotten and only the form-symbol remained. Many other symbols and rituals that emerged directly from spiritual and theological origins have also been built into house form.

The contemporary American housing environment is a potpourri of experiments in psychological fitting. Many mistakes are being made by attempting to manufacture housing environments that appear to "have always been there." There are indications that popular taste in housing is shifting from this sentimental image to forms of contemporary design that make the most of site amenities. It is far more appropriate and enduring to build new housing environments that utilize *underlying design principles* of fine housing environments of the past, not their image superficially rendered in polyurethane. There are many examples of excellent contemporary American housing environments that tastefully combine these principles with a sensitive interpretation of contemporary American lifestyle.

TECHNOLOGICAL FIT

There must be compatible technological fit between house cluster, site, and utility systems.

HOUSE CLUSTER-TO-SITE. Technological fit of house cluster-to-site is influenced by the form and location of the house cluster, the type of foundation and structure of the house cluster, the stability and bearing capacity of the soils, and the intensity of climatic forces such as temperature, moisture, wind and water erosion. For instance, the one-story wood frame house built on gently sloping land (0-6%) with a high soil bearing capacity is the simplest expression of technological fit. Because the structure is lightweight and its mass is evenly distributed, it will require a minimal foundation system. Its low profile is minimally vulnerable to wind forces. Diversion of natural drainage around the structure on a gentle slope is easily accomplished.

123

By contrast, to accomplish a compatible technological fit between a high mass heavyweight structure and a steeply sloping site with poor soil, drainage, and climate conditions requires a more elaborate and sophisticated foundation, structure, and building methodology. It requires a much larger foundation to distribute a highly concentrated load on soil that can carry very little load. It requires a much stronger structure to maintain stability and survive greater wind forces. Moreover, it requires very careful drainage to avoid the risk of soil erosion and slides. Higher mass requires a more fire-safe building system which increases the weight of the structure.

HOUSE CLUSTER-TO-UTILITY SYSTEM. Technological fit of house cluster-to-utility system is influenced by the utility requirements of the cluster, the form and location of the cluster, and the adaptability of the utility distribution system.

The utility requirements for housing continue to increase, while the utility distribution system is reasonably stable. The television cable has joined the water, gas, electricity, and telephone supply lines. In addition to these off-site linkages, there

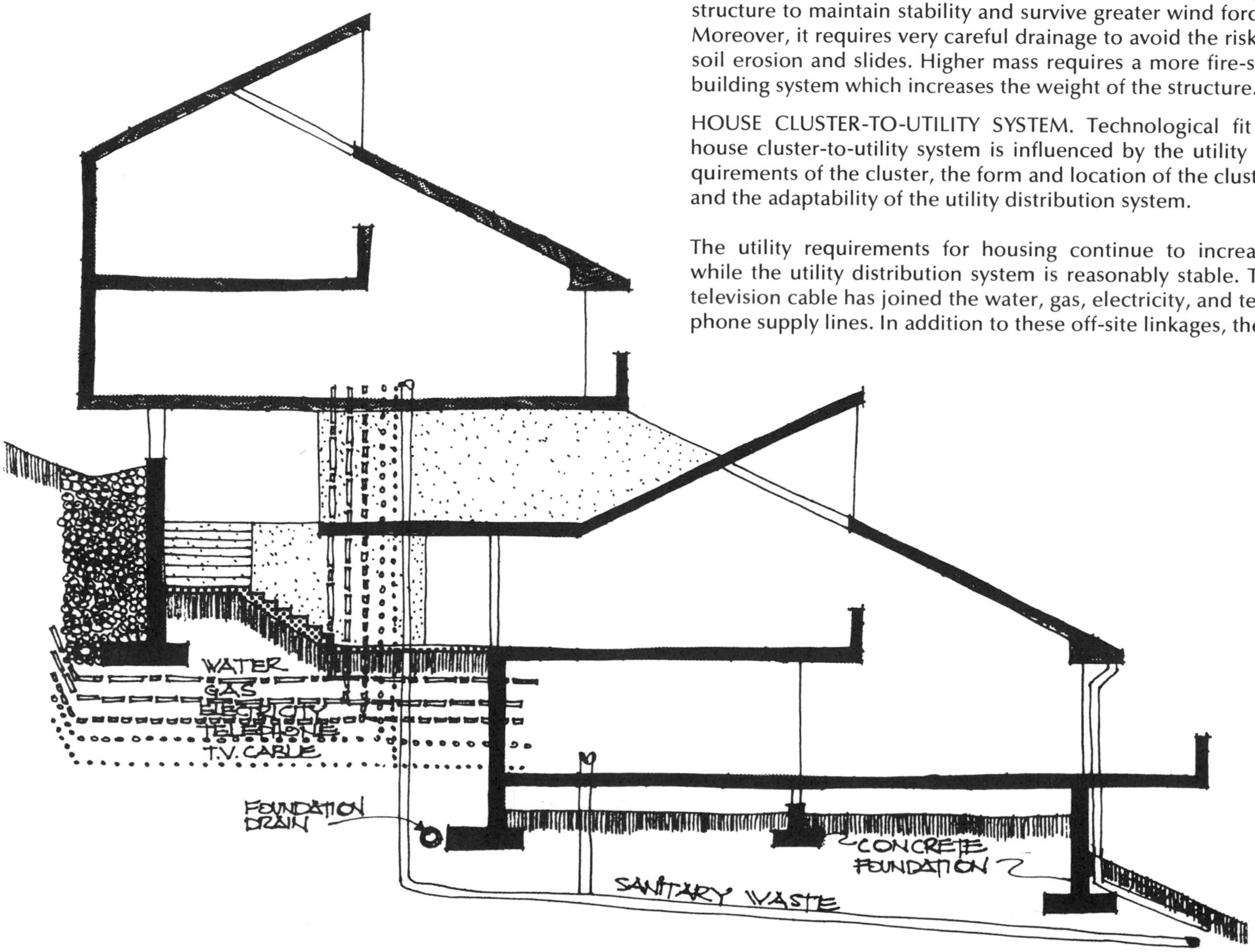

WATER
GAS
ELECTRICITY
TELEPHONE
T.V. CABLE

FOUNDATION
DRAIN

CONCRETE
FOUNDATION

SANITARY WASTE

124

may also be on-site utility facilities such as storage tanks, sewage treatment plants, incinerators, power generators, and pumping station. The sanitary sewer line is the only formal discharge system; exhaust fumes, smoke, and excess heat continue to be uncontrollably discharged from housing developments into the atmosphere.

A highly compact cluster may be designed to allow for an efficient utility distribution system within the structure and for an efficient connection to the site's utility distribution system. Gravity flow requirements of sewer lines may require that a cluster rise above a sewer main, or that sewage be pumped uphill at considerable expense. Excessive lengths of wiring and piping required to connect into the site utility distribution system may cause a line loss of energy and pressure. To solve these problems, technology is developing more sophisticated and accessible utility distribution "packages" that allow for more flexibility and future adaptability.

UTILITY SYSTEM-TO-SITE SYSTEM. Technological fit of the utility system-to-site system is influenced by the capability of the site to receive the utility distribution system with the minimum interruption of its natural systems. To fit into the natural site systems, the efficiency of both underground and overhead utility distribution systems may be compromised by the need to be routed around natural amenities rather than through them. Overhead wiring has many maintenance advantages over below-grade wiring, but their removal from view is considered an amenity that far outweighs the disadvantages.

THE COST OF TECHNOLOGICAL FIT

Optimum technological fit may be measured in terms of efficiency, even though many cost-benefit trade-offs lead to a reduction of that efficiency. The real cost of technical efficiency is best measured in terms of the amount of land rendered non-productive when it is used for housing; the amounts of materials and energy consumed in preparing the site, building the housing, and then maintaining both; and the amounts of human energy and time consumed in the process.

When we attempt to total the real costs of today's housing, the sum is incredibly high. Even though building methods have shifted from the pre-industrial, labor-intensive emphasis on handcraftsmanship to the high-energy, high-technology emphasis on the automated production of easy-to-assemble components, the building of housing continues to account for a major part of world-wide consumption of land, materials, energy and time.

Land for housing is becoming further removed from the off-site resources required for building and maintenance. This land is often difficult to build upon since the topography is irregular and steeply sloped, and the soils have poor bearing capacity.

MATERIALS are becoming increasingly unavailable, and in some cases scarce. This is particularly the case with materials made by high-energy reduction processes such as metals, glass, and plastics.

ENERGY demand to fabricate high technology materials is enormous. The production of one square foot of polished plate insulating glass consumes 15 KWH (Kilo Watt Hours) of energy. By comparison, one square foot of two inch thick wood plank consumes 1/3 KWH of energy. Thus, the total energy required to deliver the materials and fabricate a 1,000 square foot house may vary from 12,000 KWH to 60,000 KWH.

OPERATING ENERGY required to maintain the service systems in housing is increasing steadily. We are only beginning to develop the technology that might reverse this trend. Certainly voluntary reduction of consumption has been regarded with indifference by the American public.

HUMAN ENERGY AND TIME required to build housing with high technology materials and tools is less than in pre-industrial times. However, this time advantage is lost if the resultant product has a short life span. Although contemporary housing is more durable in some respects and less in others when compared with pre-industrial housing, the net result is that new housing does not last as long and therefore must be replaced more often. American housing stock is barely increasing because of rapid deterioration of existing housing. The time gained in rapid production is lost to the need for more time to build new units.

## FUNCTIONAL FIT

To achieve functional fit, the house cluster must be completely accessible and have the most favorable orientation the site will allow.

### ACCESSIBILITY

A large amount of energy is expended by men and machines in gaining access to relatively "inaccessible places." If accessibility were the only determinant for fitting the cluster, then single-level house types on flat sites would be ideal. But for many reasons already discussed, there is need to develop other site types. Since site development costs usually rise in direct proportion to the degree of accessibility in difficult sites, compensating amenities must be provided to offset the greater expenditure of materials and energy required to build there.

There is need to develop access for people and a great variety of mechanical conveyances and utility distribution systems. A distinction is made here between *pathways* for people and *roadways* for vehicles and distribution systems. Access is also necessary for development and maintenance.

PEOPLE PATHWAYS. The free flow of people through the cluster environment is the most important access determinant. The form must be situated on the site so as to afford the occupant the maximum number of options to conveniently flow into and out of the house form. The pathway itself may be many things; a paved walk through an entry court, steps up or down to the entry level of a house, interior stairs to upper or lower levels of a house, a doorway to a balcony or terrace. A terrace or patio serves as the pathway to the garden, the lawn as the pathway to the border planting surrounding it. All these pathways are important attributes and linkages for fitting in the cluster.

On flat sites nearly all exterior space may be used as an unarticulated pathway; for initial construction and longterm maintenance this is an ideal way to conveniently circumvent the cluster. Since on sloped sites a continuity of pathway around the cluster is difficult to develop, steeply sloping pathways and/or a series of retained terraces are required with steps built in. Steps, however, prohibit the use of wheeled vehicles like wheelchairs, bicycles, baby carriages, and wheelbarrows.

There is great merit in articulating outside flat places on sloped sites for people to use. This is a costly process, but well worth the expense in terms of amenities gained. There is an important bonus provided by terracing: the meeting of the cluster form may be nicely articulated with the terraced land form and many of the awkward structure-to-ground transitions eliminated.

ROADWAYS. It may be necessary to bring a roadway directly into the cluster form as an attached garage or carport. This requires the cluster form and the road alignment to be close to the same elevation; the form can no longer find its own

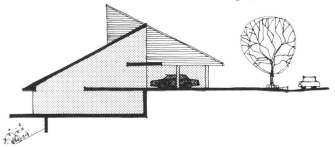

elevation. A pedestrian pathway from parking to the cluster becomes a highly versatile linkage between the inflexible roadway and the not-too-flexible cluster form. The main advantage of disengaging the cluster form and roadway is that the two systems are basically incompatible, particularly on

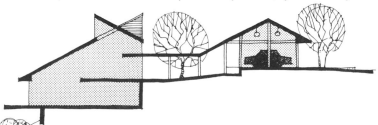

sloping sites. Through thoughtful planning, the degree of inconvenience to people in terms of distance traveled on foot usually can be minimized or the experience made a pleasant and meaningful one.

Very often a roadway serves also as an entry pathway Depending upon alignment, width, and surface treatment, this can be a pleasant as well as efficient relationship. Access by other vehicles may influence the fit of cluster form and roadway to land form. Service vehicles such as delivery trucks and fire trucks must get close enough to the cluster to do their jobs.

Access during the initial development of the site and construction of the cluster is highly demanding. The fit of the cluster must be technologically reasonable; if the natural systems of the site are destroyed in the process, the effort is self-defeating. The final fit may be influenced by the ability to build adjacent to natural amenities such as tree, rock outcroppings, interesting physiography or a natural drainage system without destroying form. The same problem persists through the life of the cluster since it must be maintained. As plants increase in size, some parts of the cluster exterior may become inaccessible.

ORIENTATION

Not only must the cluster form fit the land form of the site, but it must also respond to the environmental condition of the site.

SOL-AIR ORIENTATION. Sun and wind are the two main influences in physically orienting the cluster on the site. These two basic forces have the capability of combining in a variety of ways to create climate. In some climates their forces combine to reinforce a condition; for instance, a hot, dry wind is no comfort on the desert. In some climates the forces tend to cancel each other; the cool ocean breeze reduces the sun's radiant heat build-up on a Pacific island.

With the scarcity of land it is not always possible to seek the best site based on its micro-climate. The cluster may often be required to adapt to an adverse sol-air orientation; for instance, a north-facing slope in a cloudy, temperate climate. However, cluster housing, compared with single-family housing does offer the site planner some flexibility to mass the units in locations having the most favorable orientation.

## ORIENTATION AS A DETERMINANT OF CLUSTER FORM

One of the most important determinants of cluster form is its response to the sol-air force set. We can learn a great deal about the *morphology of cluster form* by studying both forms in nature and vernacular cluster form. In that study we find structures that are both efficient and responsive to sol-air forces: like the wind-swept Monterey Pine or the thick-walled adobe pueblos of the Southwest.

ARCTIC

TEMPERATE

HOT-HUMID    HOT-ARID

The cluster form also has to adapt to change. One way to deal with excessive heat gain or loss is for residents to turn on an air conditioner or furnace; another way is to minimize the load by drawing drapes to reduce heat loss, or opening doors and windows to allow cooling breezes to flow through. Doors, windows, storm windows, awnings, drapes, screens, shutters, and other adjustable elements allow the house form to adjust as the orientation changes.

SUN. To gather heat energy, the cluster form should be oriented to maximize exposure to the south. To avoid heat gain from the sun, the cluster form should have a long north-south axis to minimize south-facing wall space; it will also have generous overhangs on east, south, and west to shade walls. Cluster form usually has a "shady" side for every "sunny" side; with proper orientation and thoughtful interior space planning, both can be developed as amenities. Landscaping too can provide an efficient sun-shade relationship, i.e., deciduous shade tree provides shade in summer and sunlight in winter.

DAYLIGHT. There are many ways to adapt cluster form either to bring daylight in or keep excessive light out. The form itself can be shaped to funnel, bend, reflect, or block out daylight.

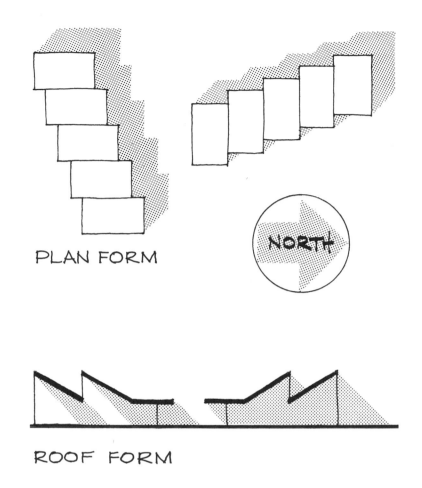

PLAN FORM

NORTH

ROOF FORM

BUILDING FORM

Orienting the main windows to the south maximizes daylighting but makes control of it complex. By comparison, daylight on the north side provides a more even and controllable light source. The cluster form must be shaped and oriented to allow as much direct sunlight as possible in garden areas. A sunlit garden is at a premium in housing of this density; yet it is often compromised to favor other amenities. An optimal daylighting design cannot just happen; it requires a special measure of concentration on the part of the designer to understand what happens to daylight through both its daily and annual cycles.

WIND. To prevent damage by very strong winds, the cluster form may assume an airfoil form so that winds will "slide over it." To invite breezes to pass through the cluster, its form may assume a funnel shape that induces air movement.

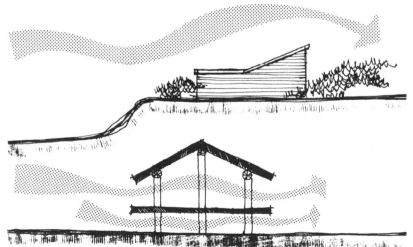

PRECIPITATION. In a location that frequently has excessive amounts of precipitation in the form of rain, snow, dust, or sand, the cluster form may be oriented to minimize infiltration to the interior or the piling up at exterior passageways.

SOUND. Orienting for sound is appealing to consider but is rarely consciously done. Noise can best be handled by controlling it at the source.

# CLUSTER CONCEPT DEVELOPMENT

The cluster, like the house, is an entity made of many parts. It is a larger and more complex entity of which the individual house, with its private open space, is a part. The clustered units form a mini-community in which these parts are shared: semi-private open spaces, paths and stairways, parking facilities, mailboxes, trash containers, and childrens' play areas.

This section deals with the process of manipulating and organizing these parts into a cluster design. Emphasis is on the manipulation of the cluster itself, and how it can be adapted to a variety of site conditions. Because this is a complex process, the site planner must begin by manipulating only the basic functional determinants; as the concept begins to emerge, other determinants will automatically be included at the proper point in time. However, as the process moves toward completion, the site planner must confirm that all determinants have been considered.

The basic functional determinants are the following:

ACCESS

ORIENTATION

SLOPE

CLUSTER TYPE

CLUSTER CONFIGURATION

PARKING

ACCESS.

The basic elements of accessibility are path ways, roadways, and utility distribution systems. Access is annotated by the alignment of the three elements with reference to the cluster entry, parking, and site topography.

ORIENTATION.

The 6 basic elements of orientation are sun insolation, sun insulation, day lighting, view, wind, and precipitation. Orientation is annotated by north arrow, altitude of summer and winter solstice, view angle bearing, and mean velocity of prevailing wind.

SLOPE

The basic elements of slope are amount and direction. Slope amount is annotated by percentage in relation to level. Slope direction is annotated by the relative elevation of the on-grade access to the main level of the cluster.

CLUSTER TYPE

The basic elements of cluster type are its size and the dominant housetype, or housetypes. While it is likely that a cluster is composed primarily of one housetype, it is also possible to mix several housetypes. Cluster type is annotated by the total number of units in the cluster and the dominant housetype.

CLUSTER CONFIGURATION

The basic elements of cluster configuration are its basic geometrical form and relative position on the topography. Cluster configuration is annotated by its geometry and the angle it creates in relation to the dominant topographical lines.

PARKING

The basic elements of parking are garages built into the cluster, open parking lots, or separate parking structures. Parking is annotated by area designation.

## ACCESS

Stairs
Ramps
Roadway
Overhead utility
Underground utility

## ORIENTATION

North arrow
Summer solstice altitude
Winter solstice altitude
View Angle
Wind speed and bearings

## SLOPE

Level
Uphill
Downhill
Irregular
North facing
West facing
South facing
East facing

## CLUSTER TYPE

Row house
Town house
Patio house
Flat
Terrace
Maisonette
Mixed

## CLUSTER CONFIGURATION

Parallel
Perpendicular
Diagonal
Irregular

## PARKING

In the cluster
Open lot
Covered
Dispersed

PROCESS

The approach to developing cluster concepts is the same as described in Chapter 3 for house concepts. The four basic steps are as follows:

TERRITORIAL SPACE

MINI—SITE ANALYSIS

SPATIAL ORGANIZATION

SCHEMATIC DESIGN

131

TERRITORIAL SPACE. The basic objective is to efficiently organize a set of interior and exterior spaces into one overall territorial space envelope. The envelope contains the *mini—community* composed of the cluster form and the shared open spaces. In a very simple diagram the territorial space envelopes of each unit are gathered together to become the "interior" space of the cluster form. The designer should draw a simple plan and section at a scale of 1" = 20'. The unit space envelopes should be simple and fluid, allowing emphasis on the designation of the shared open spaces. The edge of the cluster space envelope should be fully annotated with descriptions of its interfaces with other parts; for example, does it interface with other cluster space envelopes, public open space, roadway, edge of development, etc.

MINI—SITE ANALYSIS. An overlay of the previous diagrams should be drawn, with notation of all the Access, Orientation, and Slope determinants, as well as site amenities and danger signals such as natural drainage, major vegetation, etc. Simple notations— -words, arrows, shading, texturing— all help to quickly record the information.

SPATIAL ORGANIZATION. In this phase the configuration of each unit may be manipulated to respond to a desired configuration of the overall cluster form. *Simultaneously*, the cluster form must remain fluid enough to respond to the requirements of each unit. Since this manipulation sets the design, it must be done very thoroughly. Now all determinants must be accounted for. Another overlay should be drawn and spaces refined with soft overlapping forms that *completely fill* the territorial space envelope. The designer should develop many alternatives, compare them, combine the best parts, and recycle the best schemes until all reasonable alternatives have been explored, before a final diagram is made.

SCHEMATIC DESIGN. A final set of overlays should be drawn. While plans and sections are essential, it is desirable to add elevations to study the fit of the cluster form to the land form, and to determine whether accessibility around the perimeter of the cluster is adequate. As architectural schematics, the drawings must show spaces at their proper size and configuration, and show sufficient detail to establish human scale, such as stair treads, retaining walls, plant forms, windows, doors, terraces, fences, etc.

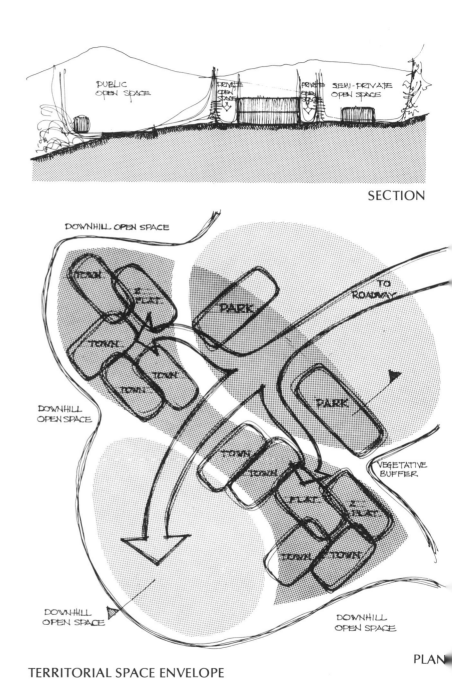

SECTION

PLAN

TERRITORIAL SPACE ENVELOPE

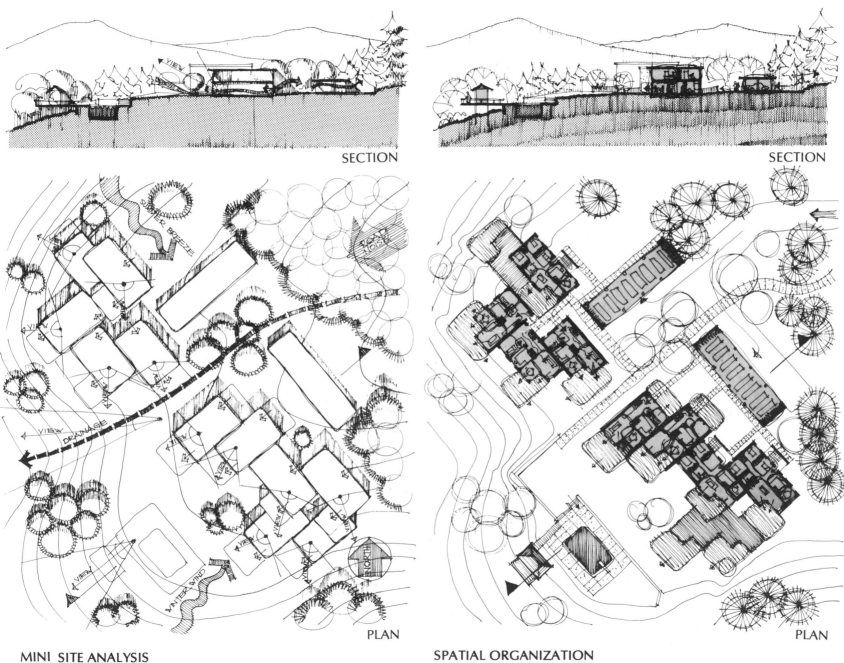

SECTION

SECTION

SUMMER BREEZE

ROAD NOISE

VIEW

VIEW DRAINAGE

VIEW

VIEW

VIEW

VIEW

VIEW

VIEW

WINTER WIND

NORTH

PLAN

PLAN

MINI SITE ANALYSIS

SPATIAL ORGANIZATION

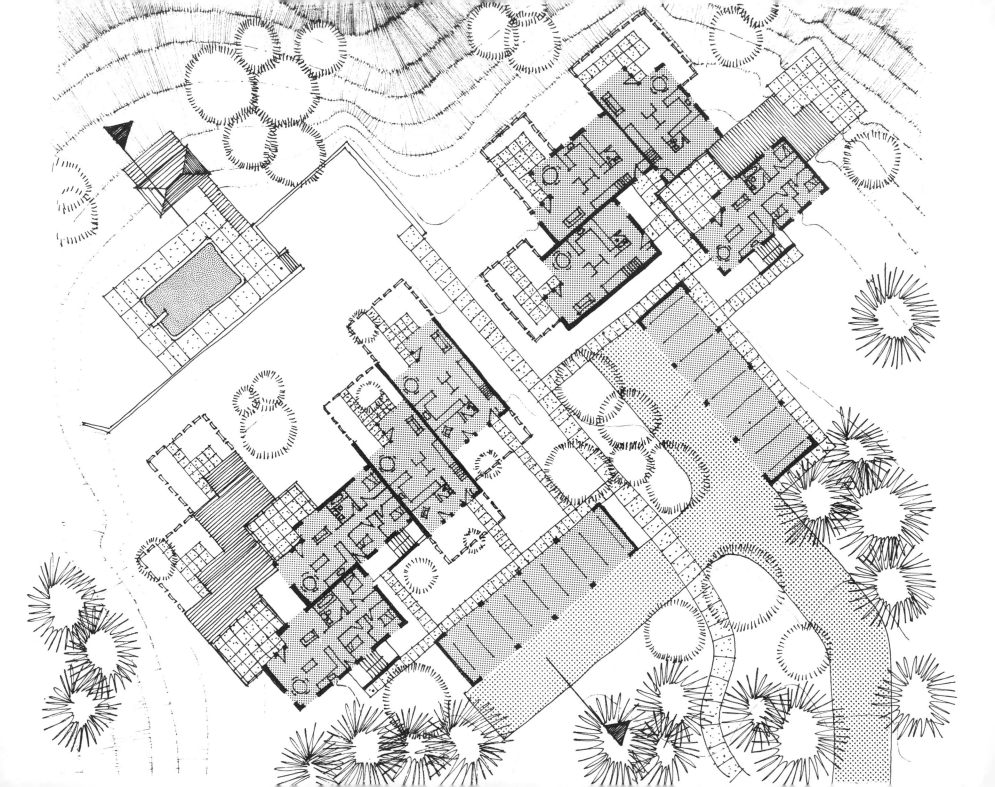

# MANIPULATING CLUSTER CONFIGURATION

The preceding example of cluster concept development showed the evolution of a single alternative. In actual practice the site planner must rapidly develop many alternative configurations. As the planner gains experience, thus mentally inventorying an increasing number of configurations and manipulative techniques, the speed of generating alternatives increases. The following material is intended to provide the beginning site planner with some of the basic configurations and techniques to begin with.

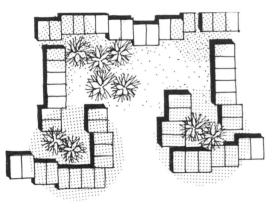

Create sub-clusters to define cluster form and cluster open space.

Stagger alignments of units both horizontally and vertically to create unit identity, privacy at entry and in private outdoor space, and to shape cluster open space.

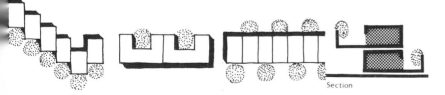

Section

Alter axial alignment of some units to respond to different access and orientation potentials.

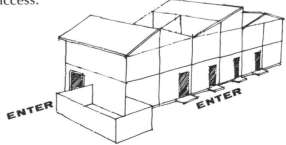

Position car shelters to complement cluster form, create privacy at entry, and shape cluster open space.

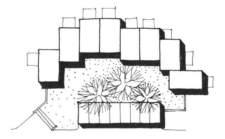

In linear clusters, make distinction between "outside" units (end units) and "inside" units by altering axial alignment, orientation and access.

ENTER     ENTER

Use vertical circulation elements (stairs, elevators) as "universal joints" in connecting sub-clusters.

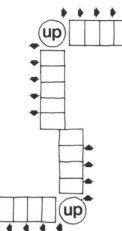

EACH CLUSTER TYPE, identified by its dominant house type, has a unique potential for being manipulated.

ROW HOUSES can be easily adapted to many configurations since they do <u>not</u> have to relate directly to auto access. Whereas the geometry of row houses surround a parking court or roadway is greatly influenced by the dimensions and configurations of the road/parking arrangements, the geometry of isolated clusters is more flexible and adaptable to more site conditions since it is not predetermined by road/parking alignments.

The simplest way to arrange cluster forms is to locate two sub-clusters at right angles to the parking. By closing off the parking court this configuration creates cluster open space and defines cluster territory.

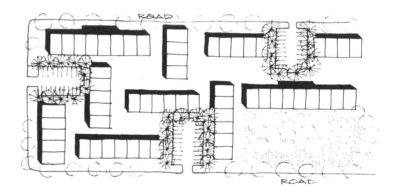

Height variety adds interest and scales down adjacent open space. Some units on the north or east side might be two story, while end units might be one story, although flats might be used as one-story end units.

Other possible cluster arrangements can be created by: eliminating one story from the end of the row so that units adjacent to the sidewalk are lower. This configuration adds variety to the cluster and makes the scale more human. To compensate for the loss in density, a story or two may be added toward the center of the row. This additional unit may be another two-story rowhouse, or a three-story arrangement of two units with one floor each of living space and one-half floor each of sleeping space.

Staggering several units creates individuality and forms small spaces. This can be done most effectively by moving two or three center units back so the space is defined by the end units.

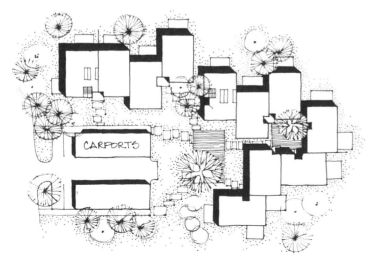

Shifting the alignment of one sub-cluster so it is not at a right angle to the parking area. Since one subcluster is turned away from the other, an informal entry court is created, the box effect of parallel/perpendicular development is eliminated, and direct rear yard overviewing is reduced.

When units are placed at right angles to the street, end elevations stand out and may be worth developing as dominant features of the composition. For instance, if a wall links the end units, visual emphasis is shifted from the garden spaces between the parallel blocks to the road itself, and the layout begins to take on the characteristic appearance of a street.

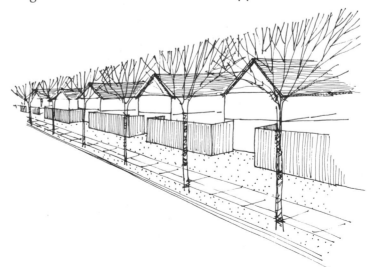

TOWN HOUSES which must be linear to provide individual auto access are more difficult to adapt to cluster arrangements. At best it may be possible to relate several units around a common entry court, or to tie a larger number together architecturally and visually.

Long facades may be subdivided into smaller elements. For mechanical efficiency it is wise to adjust two units together, either forward or backward. Moving two interior units back creates a small private space at the entrance. The pattern may be extended to create a highly imageable V-shape.

Several units may be stepped forward, eliminating the 20-foot parking strip, thus enlarging the rear yard.

Heights may be varied by making end units or one complete side only one story high, or conversely, some units are three floors high (by adding flats above the townhouse).

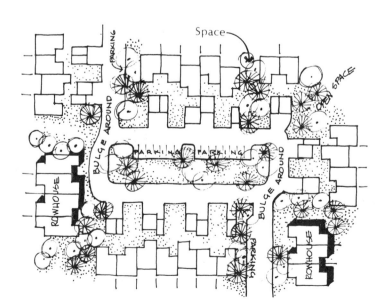

Space

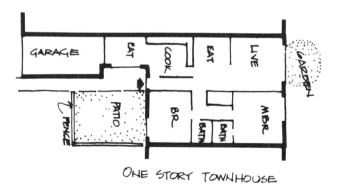

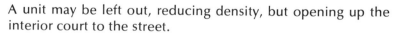

ONE STORY TOWNHOUSE

A unit may be left out, reducing density, but opening up the interior court to the street.

Carports, garages and parking stalls may be combined for variety. Driveway locations should be considered carefully because every two-car driveway eliminates one on-street parallel parking space.

Private gardens may be constructed on the front side of east and south facing buildings, assuring a sun pocket. To ensure privacy, fences, some planting and design care are needed.

Planting a row of trees around the entire block at the sidewalk and trees between the units in the interior space provides privacy between units. The units shown in these diagrams are approximately 80 feet apart, a comfortable distance for privacy between units. With careful planning, units can be as close as five feet apart.

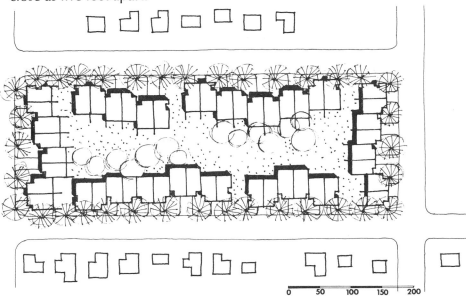

Units may be removed and replaced as stacked maisonettes on the north or east side for a total of four stories. This enlarges the open space and creates no serious overshadow problems since the tall units on the north cast their shadow on the street.

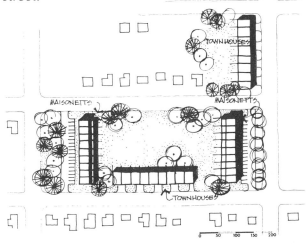

## PATIO HOUSES

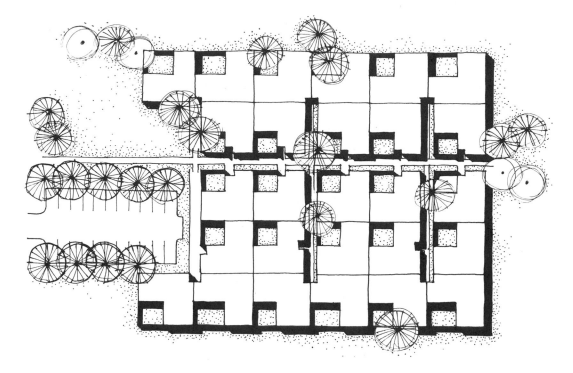

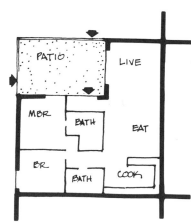

PATIO HOUSES may be staggered to relieve the monotony of grid geometry. The basic rectangle can also be adapted to a variety of interlocking L-shaped configurations. Units of 2,000 square feet are large enough to accommodate a garage, two to three bedrooms, and staggered sections. The spaces created by the staggering may be planted areas adjacent to the street or individual patios for interior rooms.

To improve the entrance sequence, the plan may be reversed, placing the patio on the street or public walk so the entry is the patio area. A fence with gate is essential to maintain some degree of privacy.

A unit might be eliminated to provide a small community space for play, sitting, gardens or swimming pool. Depending on its proposed use, the space could be located on the periphery or within a court.

Varying the roof peak, hip, gable instead of flat roofs usually built on patio houses.

Other variations include:

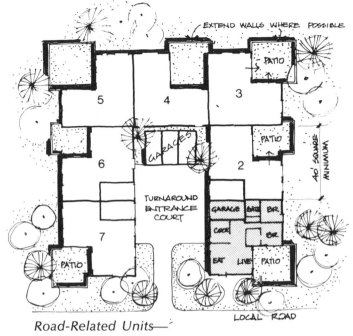

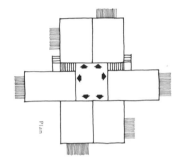

*Road-Related Units—*

Adding windows to the end elevation.

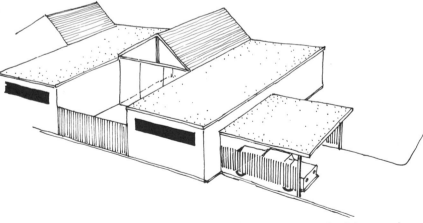

A second story to some units on the east or north side may be added to minimize overshadow to interior units.

Using the wall as a carport wall when it faces a street.

FLATS, being internally flexible, allow for considerable variation of cluster configuration. Like the patio house, they may be arranged in variety of interlocking configurations. In a cluster of stacked flats, many variations of overall configuration, circulation, and balconies and terraces are possible.

By clustering unit entries around shared stairways, corridors can be minimized or completely eliminated. Primary daylight orientation can be saved for interior "living" spaces by placing the stair system on the "shady" side.

Flats may be stacked to terrace down toward a view and daylight, enhancing privacy on balconies and terraces.

Privacy of ground-level outdoor space can be enhanced by rotating units above.

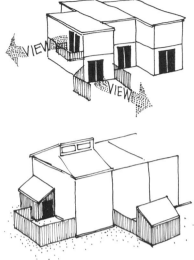

Adding dining room, greenhouse, bedroom, den or extension to the living room. The room should be one story, perhaps defining a small garden and used as a roof garden for rooms above.

Moving the garden from the rear to the end and adjusting windows and doors to fit.

TERRACE HOUSE clusters are the most rewarding but challenging to manipulate because of the difficulty of aligning vertical elements such as structural columns, stairways, and mechanical systems. These problems are more difficult to solve with man-made terracing that occurs above grade than with on-grade terracing that follows the natural slope of the land.

Generous openings should be provided to allow light and air to penetrate into the lower covered entry areas created by the upper terrace house rear overhang. Enlarging the vertical circulation space to upper units creates view, light, and ventilation wells.

Terraces should be set back far enough to prevent overviewing and to guarantee privacy of terrace below.

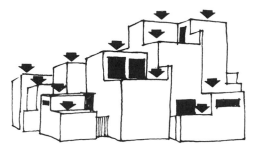

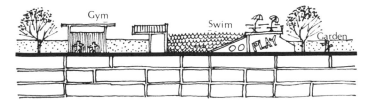

For variety, terraces should both extend beyond and be set into the basic form of the unit.

The end unit may have its terrace thrust out to the side or to create a unique corner terrace.

Mini terraces on the "shady" side may be used to complement the entry or an interior room.

Upper units may have the grandest terrace of, all, their roof tops. This should be attractive to young people who would not mind climbing additional stairs.

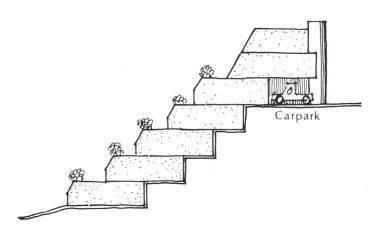

Terrace walls may be oriented to serve as light catchers reflecting light into interior spaces.

The rear overhangs of a terrace house may be utilized as a built-in car shelter. Extra care should be taken to provide for acoustical and visual separation between car and entry of interior spaces.

143

## CLUSTER ENTRANCE CONFIGURATION

The cluster entrance, as the primary connector of the cluster open space with the rest of the development, must be manipulated to give identity to the cluster and to articulate its territory. More importantly, the treatment of the entrance must reflect the degree of privacy the residents desire. Entrances may therefore be very open, inviting passerby to stroll in, or they may be very closed and intimate, discouraging entry by anyone who does not "belong there."

To create an intimate scale at the cluster entrance, several units may be stepped inward to reduce the size of the entry "portal." End-unit entrances may be shifted to provide access directly from the cluster entrance pathway. The portal may be further defined by landscape treatment such as a trellis, fencing, and special paving. A gracious, easily identifiable pathway should link the parking facility to the entrance.

Providing carports helps define the entrance space of sub-clusters. Planting and pedestrian access should be provided between carports at intervals.

Adding a sub-cluster at the end of the parking court defines the whole space as an entrance court. Angling the subclusters defines an additional space at the end of the parking. Moreover, setting the end unit back from the parking a distance

and formally planting the space creates a unified cluster entrance. Sub-clusters at the end of the parking courts may be lower than the others.

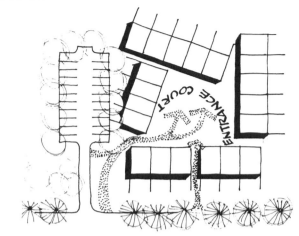

On linear clusters several identations may be made to create entrances for four to six unit sub-clusters.

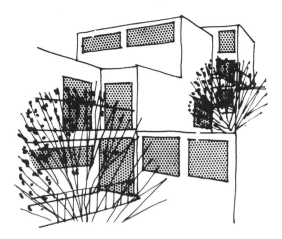

## WINDOW MANIPULATION

The location, size and type of windows influence the interior view, daylighting and ventilation of individual units, as well as the exterior character of the cluster. The site planner need not design the exterior of the cluster but should make basic decisions about visual privacy both in private spaces and in semi-public and public spaces.

VIEW windows should be provided wherever possible without compromising privacy. Windows should be placed to provide view options from as many interior rooms as possible. In medium density housing it is necessary to frame miniviews in small courts, intermediate views in shared open spaces, and distant overviews in public open spaces.

Different window shapes can be used to frame different types of views: a tall, narrow window is appropriate for a view of tree form and sky; a high horizontal window allows sky viewing with complete privacy; a full "picture" window allows uninterrupted viewing of an intimate private garden court. A door with glass is an important view window provided it does not compromise privacy.

DAYLIGHT windows should be placed to capture light without violating privacy. A high window, a skylight, or a window of translucent glass can be located to capture lights of different quality at different times of the day and seasons of the year.

VENTILATION windows usually serve for daylighting as well and they must be thoughtfully located to induce natural ventilation, without creating uncomfortable drafts.

Windows should be located high to release hot-air buildup. To induce a cooling breeze, opening windows (or doors) should be provided on the cool, shady side of the unit.

## CLUSTER HEIGHT MANIPULATION

The manipulation of the vertical scale of a cluster — its height relative to surrounding buildings and landforms — provides the site planner with many options for refining both cluster form and cluster open space.

Vertical scale may be varied to create interest and diversity, and to relate to the pattern of surrounding buildings.

Cluster height should be increased to the north and terrace downward to the south to avoid overshadowing.

Height may be increased at the center of the cluster, then terrace downward to the edges to match neighborhood scale.

An increase in cluster height at the high end of a sloping site can minimize blockage of view from downhill units.

Cluster height should be modified to shield as many units as possible from external disturbances such as cold winds, traffic noise and bright night lights.

SUMMARY

FITTING the cluster into the site is a fundamental requirement in designing housing environments. The three basic approaches to fitting in the cluster without destroying the character of the site are preservation, reinforcement, and modification. While the cluster form may be modified to adapt to the site, the site form may also be modified to adapt to the cluster. The determinants of fit may be grouped into functional, psychological, and technological categories. Although the site planner must work simultaneously with all three, the development of functional fit is the major task.

CLUSTER CONCEPT DEVELOPMENT is similar in approach to house concept development. The cluster, like the house, is an entity made of many parts which form a mini-community. The basic parts are the clustered units and the shared open spaces, circulation systems, and site amenities. In developing the cluster concept, the site planner must begin with the very basic determinants: access, orientation, slope, cluster type, cluster configuration, parking. Then the manipulation process begins with a definition of territorial space and progresses through mini site analysis of the territorial space. Finally, the spaces within the territorial space are organized in response to the mini site analysis, and very simple schematic designs are developed. The site planner may introduce these as components in the site refinement phase which immediately follows.

MANIPULATING CLUSTER CONFIGURATION can be done at scales ranging from moving entire sub-clusters to adjusting the location of a particular window. The primary purposes of manipulation are to refine the fit of the cluster to the site; to give the cluster identity and establish its territory; to carefully shape cluster open spaces; and to achieve an equilibrium between private open space and cluster open space. Each house type's unique potentials for being manipulated, coupled with manipulation of cluster height, entrance, and window location can increase the site planner's inventory of alternative configurations and manipulative techniques.

# REFINING THE SITE PLAN

By now several alternative conceptual site plans should have been developed and evaluated. The next steps involve refining, reorganizing, or recycling concepts.

- REFINING—If one concept is clearly better than the others, it should be refined and individual elements designed more precisely.
- REORGANIZING—If no one concept is best but several have good points, a new scheme may be developed by combining and manipulating the best of all the concepts.
- RECYCLING—If none of the concepts works well and good parts are few, a fresh start is recommended so new alternative site concepts may be developed.

## CLUSTER DESIGN

The design of building groups and clusters continues to be a weak point in American architecture. What makes a cluster distinct from either individual units or a continuous carpet? Some distinguishing characteristics of clusters are mentioned below:

- A focus or focal point serves a group of houses, rather than an individual house
- There is a measure of similarity among buildings, giving the whole design a unified appearance
- Each cluster is articulated, that is, groups of buildings are made identifiable through the use of planting, material, design, color, or open space.
- There is definable space relating to a group of units, i.e., territory.
- A trellised walkway, covered bus stop, sign, or special planting, identifies cluster entrances. Although clusters need several entrances and exits, the primary entrance should be clearly identified.

OPEN SPACE FOCUS. Focus for a group of houses may be provided by open space. This open space may be used either communally or privately; the choice depends on amounts of available space and the needs of prospective residents. In developing open space, it is necessary to determine if the open space should be "external" (more public) or "internal" (more private). Common internal open space abutting private gardens is preferred for these reasons: the garden is made to seem larger; access to common open space during leisure time is direct; and individual gardens are quite private. Raising private gardens slightly allows views out to the open space and clearly distinguishes private from public space. On the other hand, common open space at the front door has certain advantages: entrance identity is created; children's play can't disturb the quiet of private rear gardens; parents can supervise from kitchen windows that face the front; and lastly, access between kitchen and common open space may be appropriate for our relaxed ways of living.

A compromise is to allocate some open space at the cluster entrance and divide the remaining open space for communal use off the rear gardens. In any case, the planner should make a commitment to an open space layout. He should evaluate and refine it until it works well.

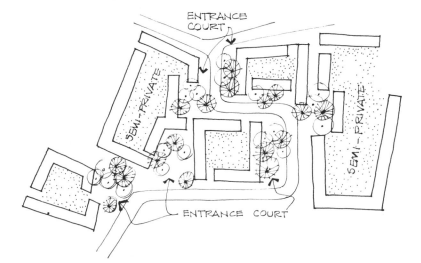

How do residents move from parking into their homes?'
How do guests move from parking into their friend's house?
How does a resident move when emptying his garbage?
How do kids move from home to play spaces?
Where are bicycles and prams stored?
What doors do neighbors use when visiting?
How are deliveries made?
Where do you pick up your mail?
Where do you wash your car?
Where can a resident walk his animal?
gardens?/ Are there community gardens? allotment
Are there individual storage areas?
How does a resident move to the laundry room?
How do residents move to a community center?
How do guests on foot or bicycle move to your house?

At this point in the design process, it is necessary to consider if there is an emerging order of Public, Private and Semi-Public, space in any schemes. In Chapter 4 three open-space arrangements were discussed: *all private*, with the space divided among units; *shared in small, identifiable portions* related to specific clusters of units; and *shared, in large parcels* by the total community and not recognized as belonging to any particular group of residents. How open space is allocated depends on amounts of available land as well as on needs of residents. If land for open space is limited but if there is a park or playground nearby, the illusion of open space may be created by facing units toward it and securing access for residents. If there is not much land the open space may be divided into private gardens (the width of each unit by at least 15 feet deep). Or if community identity is desired, the open space may be used for entrance courtyards.

How Many Units Form a Cluster? This depends on many variables: the residents, their shared interests, their housing expectations and needs, site configuration, amenities, and a host of other intangibles. Four or five units is about the minimum while twenty is about the maximum number of units able to identify with the cluster. Twenty units provide enough diversity to allow people to meet others with compatible interests while creating a large enough group so individuals may have privacy. When we speak of 4 to 20 units we are talking about the smallest identifiable cluster (except for the family) within the development. Like other systems, residential developments are hierarchial. The 4 to 20 unit cluster will probably be known only to those who live there, is where most personal exchanges will take place, and will be the most important unit to its residents. A development or neighborhood may include many small clusters until it becomes recognizable to outsiders. Beyond the cluster and neighborhood classifications there are other categories such as district, town, city, county and state.

ARRIVAL—It is important to consider how a future resident might reach his home. What is the sequence in his journey from street to home? Does he walk through a parking lot? Is there a sidewalk? Does he walk through a garden? Are parking lots screened from view? Does he pass too close to a neighbor's window? Is he likely to meet his neighbors? Does his door stand out? Is it next to a neighbor's? How much privacy does he have at his door? Is the entrance inside or outside, covered or open? Does the sequence from street to door work? Arrival, probably the most important sequence to be considered, must provide a satisfactory approach for family and guests on foot and via car. Arrival implies access, or connection to the road system. Four basic road relationships exist in cluster housing and are considered below.

1. Direct Street Access. This means resident parking in garage, carport, or parking stall is directly adjacent to the house. Access for residents and guests is clear, direct, and popular with most people, but with the disadvantages that living is adjacent to a road.

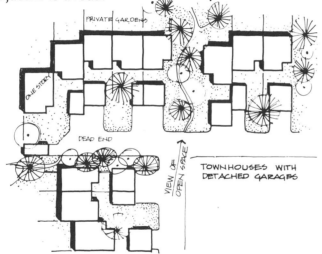

Where possible, the driveways of two adjacent units should be combined, leaving more space on the street between drives for parking and eliminating curb cuts. With an 18-foot setback, a second or visitor car can park in front of the garage.

A slightly more efficient arrangement involves grouping parking at 90 degrees off the street, serving units directly behind. This is really a cross between individual garage parking and court parking with clear direct unit access. But, it won't work on busy roads. All units facing a roadway should have their main entrance from that road. However, to deemphasize the importance of the road and to create a quality living environment, units facing the road should be limited. Resident types that need easy access to roads and automobiles are large families, families with handicapped members, and elderly residents. Also, luxury developments may have to provide direct, easy auto access to each unit to satisfy residents.

2. Court Parking. Units placed parallel to a parking court can be easily identified as one arrives. A sidewalk in front of the parked car directs people to the units.

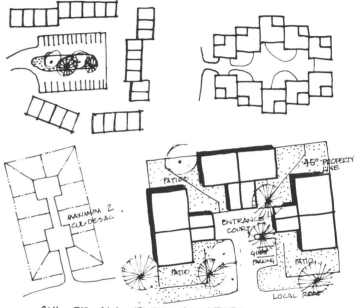

CUL-DE-SAC PATIO CLUSTERS

3. Separate Parking Lots. Separation of cars from units costs less and creates higher environmental quality with the loss of some convenience and easy identification of units. A pedestrian route clearly marked with signs becomes necessary. This parking arrangement may not be acceptable to residents who prefer direct access.

Walks connect parking lots or bays to housing units. A different paving material may be used to separate walks from roads. If some units are located on steep, inaccessible slopes, access to parking may be via a funicular railway (diagonal elevator). Installation and maintenance costs are high, so its use should be restricted to luxury units or where it would serve a large number of units reducing the per-unit costs.

4. Separate Parking Structures. At higher densities, where cost is not a prime consideration or where fragile land limits development, central garages may become reasonable. A prime site planning consideration is whether guests should park in the garage; probably not since garages are disorienting to people unfamiliar with them. Outdoor guest parking should be provided elsewhere.

Each garage must have a clear connection to the road system and to units. Covered access is desirable, circuitous routes through building basements to an elevator should be discouraged. If basement access is necessary, natural light, ventilation, and a short, well-marked route should be provided.

Since one approach probably won't work for all units in a development, combinations are in order. In fact, a solution relying solely on one parking access configuration would provide little choice for future residents and would probably be monotonous.

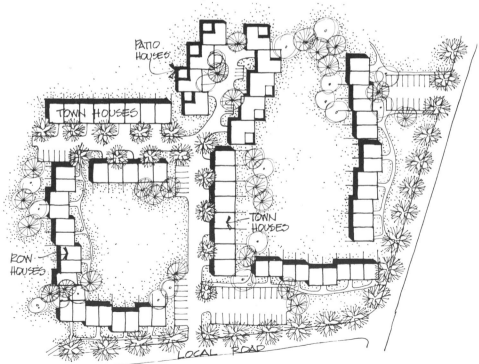

GRADING PLAN: The planner should prepare a diagrammatic grading plan to be sure the proposal will work. Existing and proposed contours should be shown as well as the location of: 1. level areas for buildings, parking, recreation or other uses, and; 2. slopes necessary to take up grade. The finish floor elevation of each unit or row of units should be determined. (Generally at least two units should be the same elevation.) Once the grading scheme works diagrammatically, the planner should refine it, adding drainage, and adjusting level areas to the proper slope. Some grading necessities for site planning include:

1. Where possible, locate buildings on level pads to avoid costly retaining walls. (Sloping land, foundation retaining walls, and low rock walls are less expensive than free-standing retaining walls.)

2. Make sure handicapped people can circulate freely throughout the development. This entails maximum 8% ramped access around all stairs and curb cuts everywhere.

3. Stay flexible, and be willing to make adjustments to building locations, the width of parking or roads. Many designers assume the plan is fixed and feel obligated to solve each problem through grading, rather than by shifting elements within the plan.

4. Do a refined grading plan of the final site plan to make sure it really works. Do *cut and fill* balance reasonably? Can *zero percent increase runoff* be accomplished? Is there room to stockpile topsoil for reuse? Can grading be reduced by pole or long foundations, half-levels, or stepping? Is there adequate room to grade and save existing trees?

# CIRCULATION

Refining the roadway involves three activities:

1. Shortening each road to reduce its impact on individual units and clusters, and to reduce costs.
2. Organizing parking to relate most directly to each unit without compromising environmental quality.
3. Designing the road to assure buffering and integration with the other plan elements.

The road pattern should be cohesive. A dominant auto or pedestrian entry clearly should identify a development from the outside. On the other hand, secondary circulation patterns may be internal with all culs-de-sac connecting to·the local road and then to the city road. Through-roads should be clearly more important than other roads so guests don't wander needlessly or get lost. However, through streets should be minimized and culs-de-sac used more often. To reduce traffic in the internal area of a development, high-density areas should be located near the auto entrance. It is essential that the road have a turnaround just beyond the high-density area.

*Revising Existing Street Patterns*—In existing neighborhoods, converting some roadways to parking streets creates a super-block which improves pedestrian circulation while still maintaining through traffic. Every other street could be converted to parking, leaving intermediate streets for through traffic. Double loaded-parking requires 60 feet of width plus five feet of sidewalk and additional planting space on each side. Since this may be wider than the existing street, space may have to be borrowed from adjacent property.

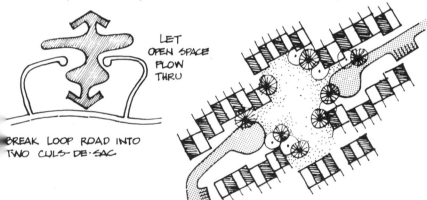

LET OPEN SPACE FLOW THRU

BREAK LOOP ROAD INTO TWO CULS-DE-SAC

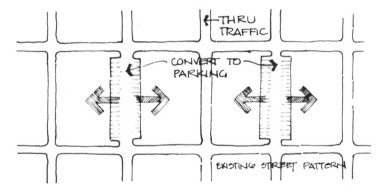

In most urban areas, the grid roadway pattern is dominant, and should be followed. The grid pattern can be varied and adjusted in many ways to provide a high quality living environment. Some examples are shown below:

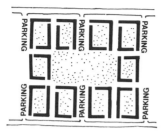

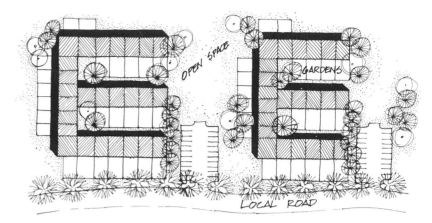

Vary private garden locations to fit individual needs, either:

1. Adjacent to common open spaces.
2. Backing on to busy streets.
3. At the entrance - in single loaded fashion.

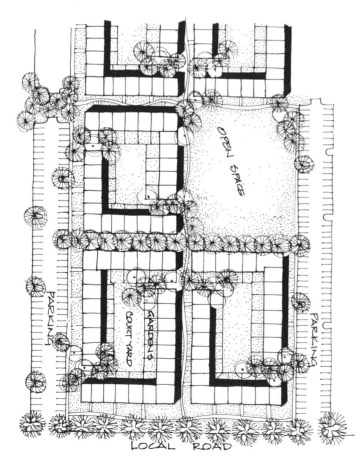

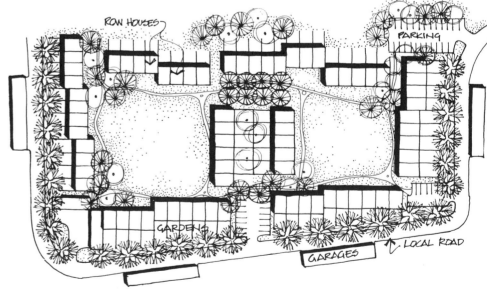

Internalize cluster and individual units adjacent to busy roads.

INWARD FOCUSING DEVELOPMENT: To create an intimate entrance, invert the standard plan, creating a private narrow loop drive, and focusing row house entrances to it. Private gardens and garages are on the public road side, and the entrance becomes a common play space for the development. Densities up to 20 D.U./acre are possible.

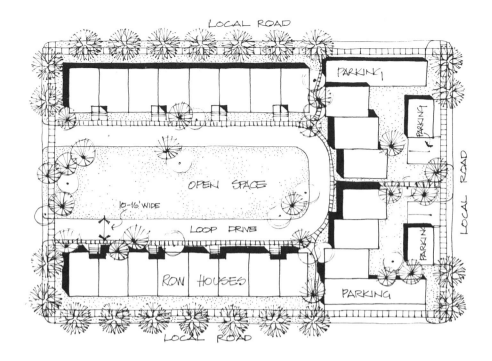

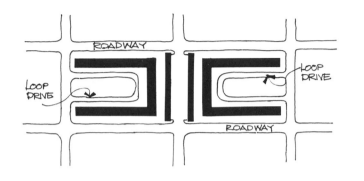

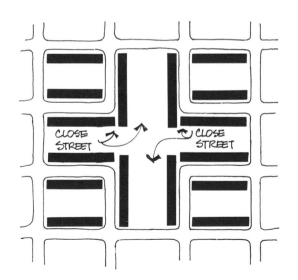

Streets can be closed to create large, continuous open space areas.

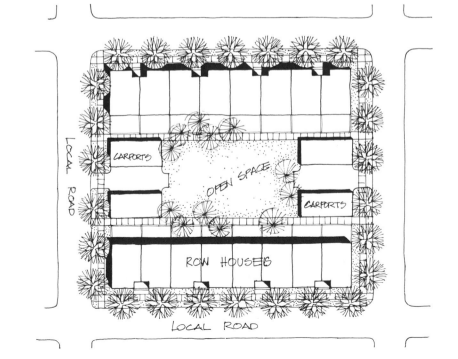

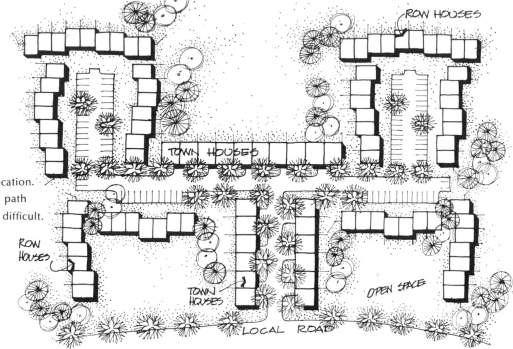

Let the grid pattern determine the court size and location. Vary the size, and establish a network of pedestrian path ways. Auto access and parking should be just a little difficult.

BOULEVARDS. Some of America's most fashionable housing is located on wide roads, for instance, Park Avenue in New York, Commonwealth Avenue in Boston, and the Jackson Street in San Francisco. These grand old boulevards remain popular despite increased traffic and a seemingly lower environmental quality. Although the reasons for continued prestige and demand are unclear, they may relate to the strong *imageability* of the avenue.

Boulevards generally have wide sidewalk space with plantings, a center median, and formal buildings lining both sides. Units along boulevards have small, formal entrance gardens with steps separating the private entrance from the public street. Setbacks are uniform, sideyards are missing, and parking is serviced from an alley *behind* the building. Buildings are at least four stories, and are often constructed of the same material, with individuality expressed through architectural detailing.

Living along a boulevard is permissible for all household types *except* families with children. Though boulevard traffic needn't travel at high speeds, conditions are usually less than ideal for raising children.

*Rear-Access Schemes*—Dwellings may be laid out so they are approached by guests from the main road directly to the front entrance, with vehicular parking in small culs-de-sac at the rear. Front and rear entrances are always confusing. The front entrance is ceremonial; it is the main entrance serving guests as well as family members. The front door usually leads to living quarters without passing through sleeping or service

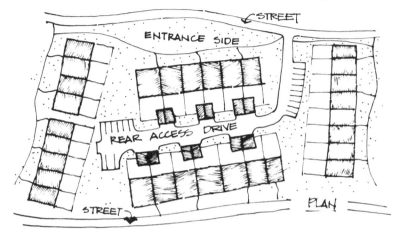

rooms. The rear entry, meant for deliveries and everyday use, leads into the kitchen, den, or service porch. Two hundred feet from the road is about the maximum distance for units not facing it. The problem with the rear-access scheme is difficulty in naming streets and numbering houses since one rear service road may serve two or three main streets.

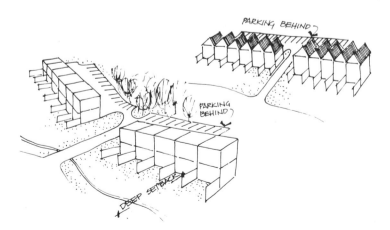

*Units Along Busy Roads*—Every development seems to have one busy road, which is a site planning problem. Space along the road would be wasted if not built on, yet it isn't the most desirable place to live. There are several common-sense solutions to the problem:

1. Locating a row of single-family units with large deep yards backing up to road and with service from another road.

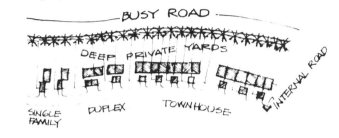

2. Making a fenced buffer strip. The area may be mounded and planted, and a trail or bike path run through it.

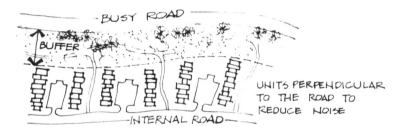

3. Designing an access road parallel to the busy road to serve units. This adds space between units and the busy road, reducing impacts. In any case units should not be located on the busy road.

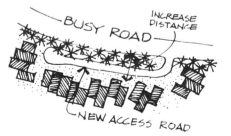

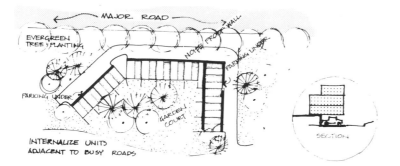

4. Using the space for parking or active sport facilities.

For busy streets, rear-access garages off an alley work well. Guest and service vehicles park on the street, while residents park behind units off the alley.

PARKING—A major problem with medium-density housing is providing parking space that does not dominate the scene.

Three obvious solutions to reduce the visual impact of parking on a housing community are:

1. Clustering parking in manageable units.
2. Removing parking from the cluster.
3. Screening parking area.

*Clustering parking* into manageable units requires small groupings of cars, say, 10 to 12, organized in a compact arrangement. Clustering can minimize the length of drive and is efficient economically.

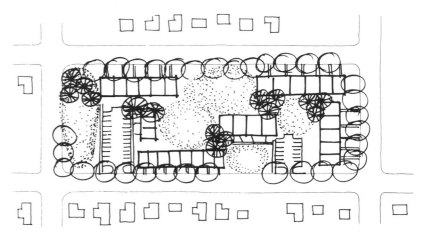

The road may serve up to four patio houses directly, allowing each unit to be easily reached from the street. Row houses may be served by a parking court treated as quiet, deadend street extension. Three or four bedroom units may have attached garages.

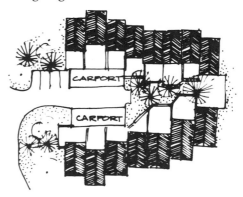

*Removing parking* from the cluster means residents may be somewhat inconvenienced, surveillance of autos will be harder, and service for guests and deliveries will be difficult. Some residents, particularly young single people or families without children, may like living farther from their cars if desirable amenities such as trees, quiet, or a view are provided.

Separate fenced lots away from units are acceptable for storing boats, trailers, campers, and recreational vehicles, which may be parked in tandem to maximize use of the space. Closed circuit television may be used to provide security.

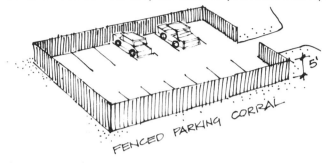

FENCED PARKING CORRAL

*Hiding Parking* areas is the simplest method. Trees spaced as close as 10 feet apart reduce the visual impact from both above and alongside, and shade the car during hot days. At least 30 inches of space should be allowed for car overhang. Paving area may be reduced 24 inches if bumpers are used, and trees may be planted between cars by widening the parking bay to 11 feet. Generally two trees per three cars is adequate for most buffering.

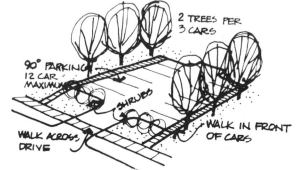

*Berms* or earth mounds which physically (and often gracefully) block views of cars are useful where there is adequate room.

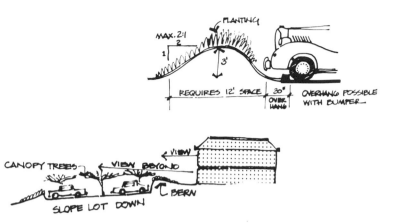

Architectural solutions such as *fences or retaining walls* are immediate, effective methods to screen unwanted views. Even though they require little room and can be designed to solve difficult problems, they are often deleted during construction because of budget overruns.

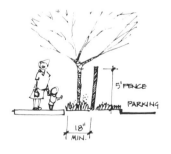

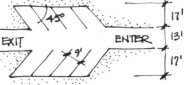

Angled *parking* arrangements should be considered on one-way loops and narrow roads. They require 10 fewer feet of width than single-loaded perpendicular parking.

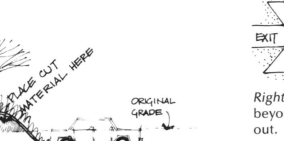

*Right-angle, dead-end* parking courts require an extra 8 feet beyond the last parking space to enable the end car to back out.

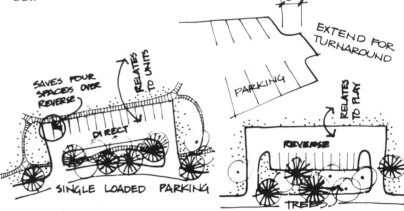

*Depressed parking lot* is an expensive but effective technique for reducing the visual impact of cars. Since cars are approximately 4 feet-6 inches tall, depressing a lot three feet screens most of their height. By mounding around the edge of the lot, it is possible to completely eliminate views of the cars.

*Grassed parking areas* are lots paved with cobbles or bricks spaced so grass can grow between them. These lots have a softer appearance than fully paved areas but they cannot support heavy use.

OTHER PARKING ARRANGEMENTS— *Parallel parking* is acceptable where topography or tightness of the site prevents roads from being wide. Typically, a road leading from a row of units to their parking court beyond has parallel parking for guest and service vehicles. Parallel parking opposite perpendicular parking is not recommended because of the potential for collisions.

*Tandem Parking* is an efficient space user, because cars are parked close together. However, cars on the outside must be moved before cars on the inside can be moved. This parking arrangement works well for vehicles that are not used frequently such as a second car, boat, or trailer. Two spaces in tandem might be allocated per unit.

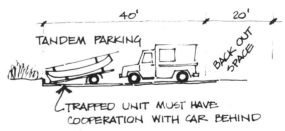

*Carports* eliminate the need to use interior space for parking in such units as town houses. They are constructed adjacent to a building and may include storage areas for garden tools and toys. They may also help define exterior garden spaces.

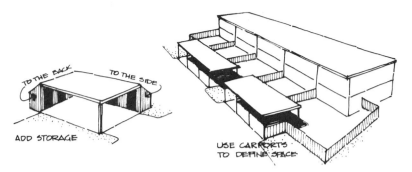

ADD STORAGE

TO THE BACK

TO THE SIDE

USE CARPORTS TO DEFINE SPACE

Roofs of carports, if flat, may be used as open space; for instance as a roof garden for upstairs units or rooms. The carport roof might even become space for future additions, say, for a third or fourth bedroom. Bedrooms over carports fall under a stricter fire code regulation, but this problem can be easily solved.

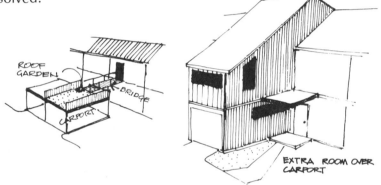

ROOF GARDEN

BRIDGE

CARPORT

EXTRA ROOM OVER CARPORT

If carports are desirable but the budget is tight, concrete or gravel parking space might be constructed initially and the carport later when it becomes affordable. If carports are to be added in the future, extra width should be provided for columns. Ten feet of width works if the column is set back at least five feet from the driveway, otherwise eleven feet would be better.

EXTEND ROOF OVER WALK

ADD WALLS OR FENCES

WALK

20'

10' OR 11'

SET POSTS BACK 5'

UNCOVERED PARKING

LINK CARPORT AND UNITS ARCHITECTURALLY

WALK — RAIN PROTECTION

Double-loaded parking courts are more attractive with covered parking on only one side. Carports over both rows enclose the space excessively, creating a dark, oppressive area. Roof profiles should be kept low for scale.

Sidewalks should be located in front of parked cars, between parking and the units. Ten to fifteen feet of separation between parking and units allows for a small entry garden and assures privacy and identity at the entry. A change of level—up or down—further defines the unit.

Use carports as design elements to create space, take upgrade, extend buildings or channel traffic. Some carports may be enclosed as a private garage, though the apparent size of space is reduced.

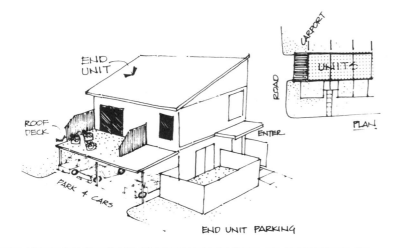

END UNIT

ROOF DECK

PARK 4 CARS

ENTER

CARPORT

UNITS

ROAD

PLAN

END UNIT PARKING

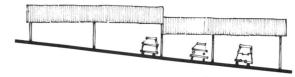

SLOPE CARPORTS MAXIMUM 8%

*Parking Garage*—Parking under buildings is costly but preserves open space, eliminates the visual impact of cars, and becomes more feasible at higher densities or where land costs are high. Because of structural supports, larger storage and maneuvering space is usually required. Requirements of space, ventilation, and fire protection are major cost factors. Moreover, a principal disadvantage is the loss of open space access at ground level since units are one floor above the ground (except for sloping sites). Parking facilities under buildings can be divided roughly into two types:

1. The complete garage with storage and maneuvering spaces inside the building. This solution requires 45 feet width for single-loaded and 65 feet for double-loaded parking plus an entrance/egress route. Ventilation must be handled mechanically, and a concrete roof may be required under

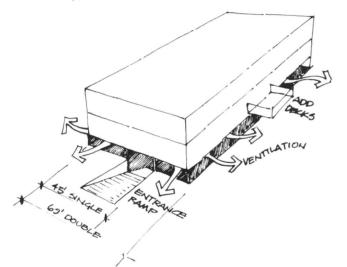

fire regulations. Large buildings with more than one floor of parking require ramps, and if parking is wider than one bay, a connecting circular route at the end. The solutions are endless, complex, and expensive.

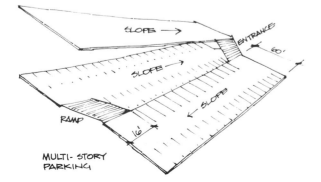

2. Half-In/Half-Out arrangements with parking under the building, and maneuvering space outside the building. This protects the auto, saves some open space, and minimizes fire and ventilation problems. However, on-grade gardens are not possible from this side. Two rows of units may be placed back-to-back with an open area between serving as backout space for both rows. While efficient, this arrangement must be designed carefully to avoid orientation, privacy, and noise problems between the rows of units.

Access between garage and unit is often complex. An interior stair leading directly to the unit may serve town houses. For stacked units, access from car to the upper unit requires walking around the end of the building. Since parking garages are confusing for guests, separate well-marked, on-grade parking should be provided for them.

DESIGN. The easiest approach to designing a parking garage is to first lay out the parking arrangement, place a roof over it, and then site units on top of the roof. Utilities and structural design may be adjusted at a later time, though a check with the structural engineer during the design process is advisable. Parking should utilize the perpendicular pattern with 10-foot wide bays and a 65-foot wide double-loaded dimension. The entrance/egress road should be 16 to 18 feet wide with a 16-foot-wide circulation path skirting the end if two bays are necessary. Angled parking is possible in a narrow building, but one-way traffic requires a separate entrance and exit.

Sloping terrain is a natural for parking structures, since each floor can be entered directly from a different level of the slope. This minimizes interior ramps and separates parking into smaller units of 10 to 20 cars.

Depressing the garage 3 to 4 feet reduces cost and improves looks. However, a two-foot-wide opening is necessary around the garage perimeter for ventilation, so portions of the garage must be above grade. Grading spoils may be used for mounding around the structure. Bridges and steps for unit access should be located after the building arrangement is developed.

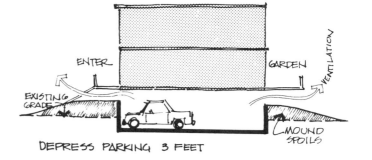

DEPRESS PARKING 3 FEET

Forty-foot-wide single-loaded parking bays work under most row houses. A 30-foot-wide row house with 10-foot entry and 20-foot garden is an alternative over double loaded garages, but an expensive one since construction costs for outdoor space over parking structures is high. Other combinations are possible. A 100-foot-wide parking structure (one double-loaded and one single-loaded bay) allows 20-foot shared en-

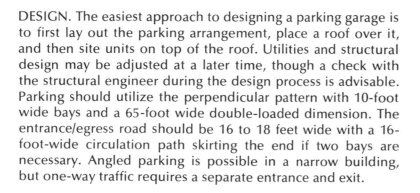

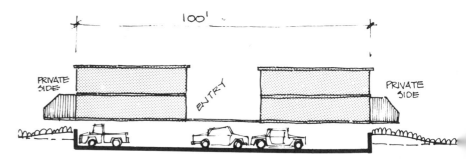

trance space, serving two 30-foot-wide rows of units with small gardens on each side. Developing units half on, half off the parking structure is also possible.

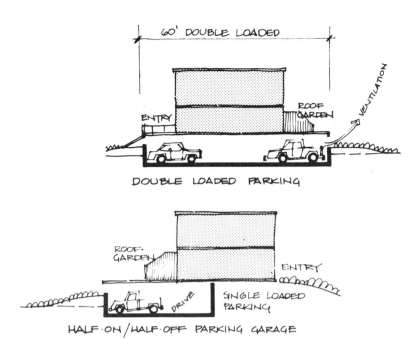

60' DOUBLE LOADED

ENTRY

ROOF GARDEN

VENTILATION

DOUBLE LOADED PARKING

ROOF GARDEN

ENTRY

DRIVE

SINGLE LOADED PARKING

HALF·ON/HALF·OFF PARKING GARAGE

## OPEN SPACE

ELEMENTS OF URBAN OPEN SPACE are courtyards, streets, public yards, etc. Urban implies these spaces are small and overused, serve many residents, and create noise and privacy problems for adjacent units. One programming approach is to limit resident access and provide only views into the space.

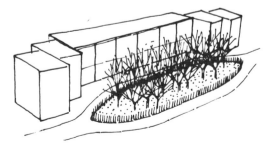

This has been done with many urban spaces in London and New England which are planted with trees and fenced, with no yards opening onto them but with many rooms viewing them. The approach has validity for some users and for steep or fragile sites, but not for people who need accessible outdoor spaces at home such as families with small children.

A more realistic approach is to think of each urban outdoor space as an outdoor room. Outdoor spaces can be: *circulation channels* or hallways for moving through, and *nodal areas* or rooms for doing things. Nodal spaces become living rooms, play rooms, service rooms, bedrooms, dining rooms, etc.

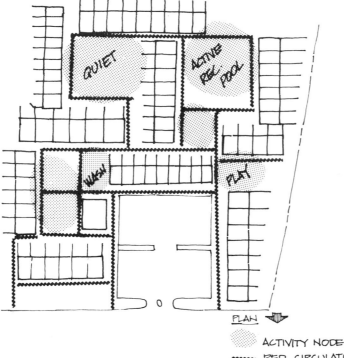

PLAN

▒▒▒ ACTIVITY NODE
∿∿∿ PED. CIRCULATION

Some rooms serve several activities—as dining and resting. Once the potential functions of each outdoor room have been determined, details such as including special paving, lighting, and planting may be developed. The planner's task is to anticipate how a given space will be used and who the users will be. Each user category has some particular requirements and a larger number of general requirements common to all users. The authors' preference is a mixed resident population with some young unmarried, some elderly, and some families—a typical small town mix with a varied open space system.

## TYPICAL USER RECREATIONAL NEEDS

This simple list of user recreational needs must be expanded by the designer to gain a more precise idea of various resident needs. Although user needs are grouped here according to age for ease of understanding, in practice facilities must often have multiple uses, serving mixed age groups as well as active and passive pursuits.

*Tots:* Children one to four years old must be under almost constant surveillance by an adult supervisor. However, they can roam and play in private yards, balconies, or enclosed areas, which though simple, must provide a diversity of experiences.

*Five to Eleven-year-olds:* Children in this age group are able to supervise themselves to a greater degree. With bicycles these children can explore a larger area. Organized sports are generally not yet important, and play requirements are easily satisfied. Play activities include:

| | | |
|---|---|---|
| Ball playing | Wading | Playing School |
| Playing with toys | Kite flying | Playing with dolls |
| Digging | Acrobatics | Tag |
| Wrestling | Imaginative games | Follow the leader |
| Swinging | Boxing | Climbing |
| Tree climbing | Stringing beads | Dressing up |
| Skipping | Playing soldiers | Racing |
| Hopscotch | Sword fighting | Handspringing |
| Playing catch | Playing shop | Sitting |
| Sliding | Playing house | Crafts |

*Eleven to Thirteen-year-olds:* Children at these ages are beginning to outgrow previous play patterns, yet are not quite old enough to participate in teenage activities.

*Teenagers:* This is the most difficult age group to plan for. Teenagers participate in organized sports and semiorganized social gatherings. They have considerable mobility and are not content to conform to planned facilities. Teenage recreation activities generally include:

| | | |
|---|---|---|
| Listening to records | Sitting | Cooking |
| Telephoning | Driving | Story telling |
| Teasing | Crafts | Sewing |
| Joke telling | Dating | Role playing |
| Tape recording | Reading | Organized sports |
| Listening to radio | Dancing | Car repairing |
| Talking | Partying | Studying |
| Eating | | |

*Young adults, twenty to thirty years old*: This group is more concerned with social organizations, is easily satisfied and highly mobile, and doesn't require elaborate systems of recreation. However, young adults like a focus such as club with facilities for tennis, swimming, riding. Social involvement tends to be somewhat passive.

*Older Adults:* This group's recreational needs are similar to those of the previous age group but tend to be more passive. Activities typically include occasional sports, walking, gardening, etc., and enjoyment of family and supervision of children.

*Elderly*: This group uses outdoor spaces passively for walking, sitting, viewing, education, small game playing, and gardening. Recreational activities include:

| | | |
|---|---|---|
| Conversing | Story telling | Sitting |
| Chess | Bowling | Radio listening |
| Crossword puzzle | Letter writing | Gardening |
| Checkers | Sewing, knitting | Reading |
| Dominoes | Painting and drawing | Crafts |

To summarize, the recreational needs of children until about 11 to 12 years old, adults, and elderly can be predicted and satisfied, causing no specific site planning problem. But it is difficult to plan for the recreational and leisure time needs of preteens and teenagers. Additionally, girls are more difficult to serve than boys. It is therefore important when reviewing any recreation scheme to ask: How does this serve teenagers? How does this serve teenage girls?

REFINING OPEN SPACE. At this point the open space system should be refined. Are there any distant views which should be preserved, opened up, or designed to become part of the open space focus? Should any units be eliminated or adjusted to open up the view? How can communal space be extended visually? Should any units be adjusted to save a tree or natural amenity?

The pedestrian circulation system should also be evaluated and refined. Is there easy access between units and the street, pedestrian path, or bike trail? Major path alignments and minor routes such as unit entrance walks should be designated in a diagram. Important movement directions should be indicated; a recommendation might be made that the same paving material be used on all major through-paths in the development.

The distinction between public and semipublic spaces should be considered. This may be accomplished through use of level changes, steps, retaining walls, or baffles. A distinct pavement change between public and semi-public areas may reinforce the difference between these spaces. Routes from public sidewalks to the main doors of all dwelling units should be direct and obvious.

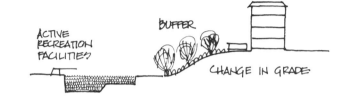

Contrast. The juxtaposition of narrow, enclosed spaces and unrestricted open spaces creates visual contrast which makes the open space seem larger than it actually is. This provides variety of visual experiences for those using the spaces.

170

To create contrast all minor circulation spaces may be tightened. For instance, blank walls may be as close together as four feet with a path between. Whereas light and ventilation windows may face onto a narrow space, view windows obviously should not. View windows can sometimes be shifted to a wall not facing a narrow space. In general, circulation and setback may be made smaller if:

- They lead for a short (25 to 30 foot) distance to a larger space.
- Two blank walls face each other.
- One blank wall faces a window wall.
- Units overlook an adjacent public park or borrowed open space.
- Planting will be done to ensure privacy.
- They are used for entry.

Economizing open space. Locating open space behind all units is a basic cluster housing principle, which in some cases may result in a thin, meaningless network of spaces. If this happens units should be sited closer together with back-to-back gardens separated by a narrow walkway. Group the remaining open space in a meaningful amount at the ends of buildings where circulation routes converge.

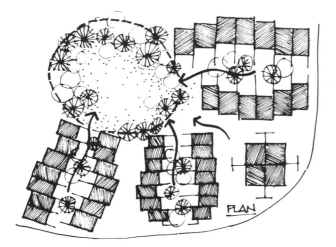

PLAN

Eliminating ambiguous open space. Ambiguous open space is land which visually and functionally doesn't seem to belong to any cluster. Large planting beds along walkways fall into this category, as do poorly developed areas and space between public and private zones. Ambiguous space may be eliminated by:

1. Assigning a use to all open space, which must be developed and maintained for this use.
2. Making ambiguous open space relate to nearby cluster as part of its private gardens, entrances, or parking area.
3. Placing this space in an "unusable" condition, such as taking up grade or buffering with careful planting.

## DETAIL SITE DESIGN

Once buildings and other program elements are fitted to the site so that the whole functions properly and achieves an expressive form, the scale shifts to detail design. In the case of a cluster housing, detail design is the articulation, shaping, and forming of the exterior spaces around buildings, including vertical and horizontal adjustment of buildings where necessary. It involves grading, definition of paved and planted areas, selection of broad categories of plants (trees, shrubs, ground covers) and full use of all form, compositional, and design elements.

CORNER TREATMENT. The basic space-defining technique is placing rows of units at 90 degrees to one another, creating a corner which is always a problem for the designer. Suggestions for eliminating the problems of corners follow.
- Units may end but not overlap or touch, creating a small defined space. This allows through passage, and provides a pleasant setting for both adjacent units. The space must be large enough to have an identity and to be maintained.

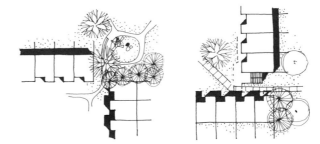

- Units may pass one another, creating a tight passage leading to the last unit entrance and beyond. This arrangement provides space for inserting a stairwell, changing unit types, lowering to single story, or creating laundry or club facilities.
- Units may run past each other and overlap in T fashion. The effect is similar to that above.

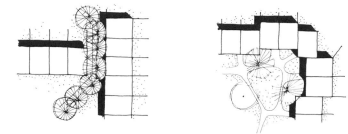

- Units may join completely, eliminating through passages and using corner space for living or service. Access is difficult, and requires borrowing internal space from an adjacent unit.
- Units may touch, but not pass, eliminating through passage, while leaving the space beyond.

## BUILDING VARIATIONS

Row, Town or Patio house clusters should be varied to increase individual identity and to reduce the monotony of repetitive units. Generally each variation increases the total cost, so the site planner must weigh the advantage/disadvantage of each variation to achieve a necessary balance. Variation options available to the site planner include:

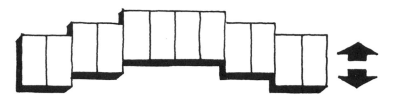

Stagger units

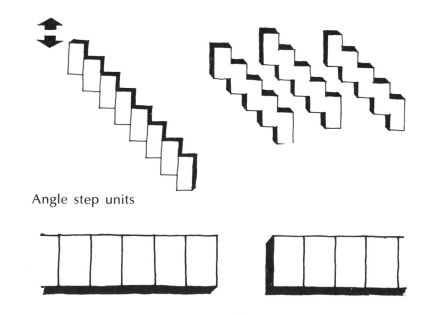

Angle step units

Break the row

Mix unit types

Vary architectural treatment

Adjust building height

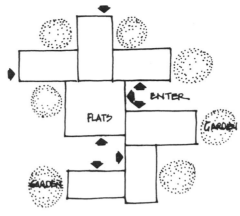

Turn units

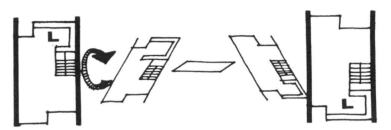

Reverse units

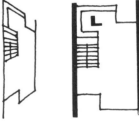

Flip-flop units

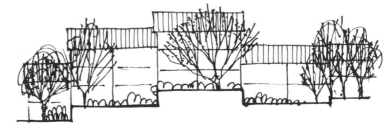

Plant with variety

173

"Strive to create a community subdivided into a hierarchy of increasingly more private zones."

S. Chermayeff

PRIVATE GARDEN 'WING WALLS'

FENCING. People like to fence their gardens to maintain privacy, to define their territory, and to protect and restrict their children. The effect of fencing can be achieved with fences or plantings. If well planned fencing may enhance garden spaces without making them seem confined.

Adjust each private garden for size, privacy and sun orientation. The objective is to make them as large as possible without jeopardizing communal open space. Wing wall fences should be installed to ensure privacy between adjacent units. Each fence should be 5 foot-4 inches tall and extend to block views of the active use area. Units not facing common open space should have slightly larger rear yards and be totally fenced. Fences should be kept low to make the yard seem larger.

Shrubbery near the end of each garden provides visual protection without disrupting the view. Trees and shrubs may be planted within the common open area, if its primary use is passive recreation and sunlight isn't severely blocked. Raising gardens several feet higher than the common open space and planting a low shrub buffer makes them quite private. Treeless land may be contoured inexpensively with mounds to create interest and insure privacy.

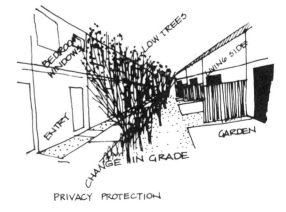

PRIVACY PROTECTION

Gardens located along roadways and entrance gardens should probably be fenced. Entrance gardens can serve both entrance and private activity if a baffle gate is used. Gardens facing each other have no privacy unless fenced. While a fence across *one yard* may provide privacy for both gardens, it blocks the view from the fenced garden and reduces the apparent garden size. Another alternative is to align one row of gardens at a 45-degree angle, lengthening the garden depth and eliminating some overviewing. Forty-five degree angles have not been extensively used in housing, primarily because the remaining acute angle is difficult to handle. However, the addition of a dog-leg fence section perpendicular to the building before the 45-degree fence, can overcome the problem.

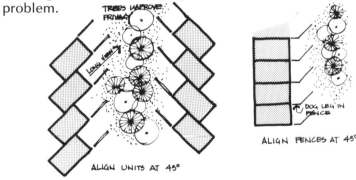

ALIGN UNITS AT 45°

ALIGN FENCES AT 45°

SERVICE ACCESS TO PRIVATE GARDENS. Attached houses do not have side yards even though access to rear entrances is needed. Units abutting a common open space have access.

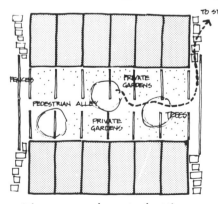

Units with rear yards not abutting common open space can gain access by a narrow walkway from the street around the end unit connecting all gardens in the row. Privacy may be increased by planting, depressing the walkway, or installing a rear fence. The path should bend and return toward the street forming a blind entrance; a gate ensures additional privacy.

Back-to-back private gardens may use a 6 foot-wide fenced walkway with gates to each yard though this is difficult to maintain. Two units may share a side yard tunnel access to the rear garden, either entirely within one unit or straddling the property line, and covered with the second floor. Many New England row houses have this type of rear yard entry.

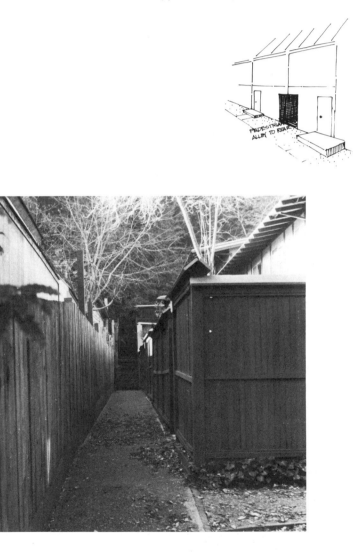

CLUSTER ENTRANCE. Each cluster entrance must be designed to ensure identity and privacy. There are many design possibilities, each defining the private entry within the cluster courtyard.

*Pavement Change* between "cluster" and "individual" entry. The cluster entry might be brick and the individual entry exposed concrete, for example.

*Indented Entrances.* Entry porches that are indented define entry space by surrounding it with walls and a roof. The roof shields users from rain and overviewing.

*Change in level.* Changes in level either up or down defines and separates each entrance from the common courtyard. Several steps with walls, sloping planting, or a rockery create a small entrance garden.

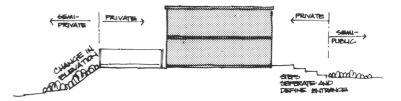

*Fencing or planting* where spaces are tight ensures privacy and identity for each unit.

STREETSCAPE ENTRANCES—Most successful row houses have either a communal interior open space shared by residents, or special landscaped roadway treatment at the entrance such as:

*Traffic Island*—Roadway traffic is diverted into two one-way lanes moving around a small median park. The arrangement can occupy a complete block with symmetrical row houses on both sides staggered back where the park space begins. The median park should be at lesst 12 feet wide, but preferably 20 feet. It should be planted with trees and grass or ground cover. It may be fenced and have a gate for entry. Depending on user requirements, a fountain, bench, or play equipment may be included. Even if a median park is not used for active recreation, the island of green may be enjoyed visually and may provide an identifiable focus for the street.

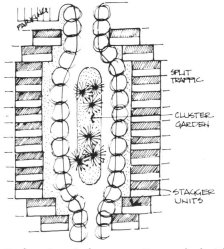

*Pedestrian Safecross*—Expanded sidewalks at the corners define the block, slow auto speed, and reduce through auto traffic. Trees may be planted in the safecross, and street furniture such as kiosk, mail box, bus bench added according to user needs.

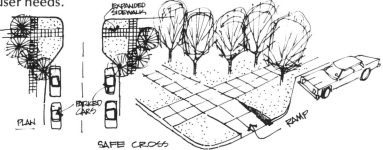

*Expanded Sidewalks*—Setting one row of buildings back 12 to 20 feet allows room for development of a linear park. Landscape treatment should make it imageable and serve user needs. It might be landscaped or fenced to prevent improper parking by cars.

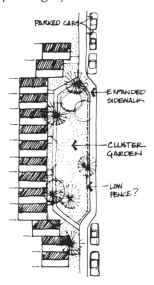

177

Cul-de-sac turnarounds with little traffic can become part of the open space with kids playing safely in both the street and the park.

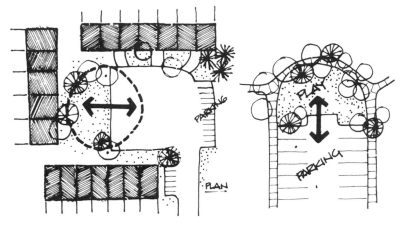

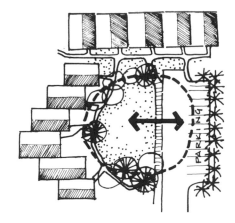

PLAN

PARKING

PLAY

PARKING

PARKING

Other cul-de-sac arrangements

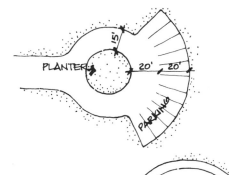

PLANTER

15'

20' 20'

PARKING

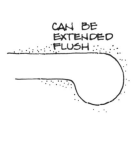

CAN BE
EXTENDED
FLUSH

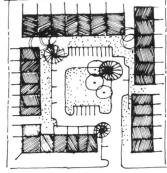

ENLARGE AND RESHAPE CUL-DE-SAC
TRAFFIC ISLAND

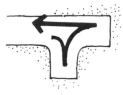

HAMMER HEAD
TURN-AROUND

20'

40'

45'

MINIMUM RADIUS FOR
MANY CARS W/ NO PARKING

40'R   FOR ALL CARS AND
MOST SMALL TRUCKS

45'R   MEETS MOST CODES
BUT IS TOO WIDE

TURN AROUND RADIUS

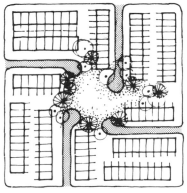

DEAD HEAD CUL-DE-SAC INTO
COMMON OPEN SPACE

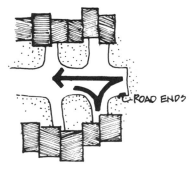

ROAD ENDS

TURNAROUND
IN PRIVATE DRIVES

# DIAGRAMMATIC PLANTING PLAN

Don't skimp on the landscape. Landscaping is an essential element to create a good environment. Good environment sells or rents a completed development faster than any other factor. Sprinkling a few trees around won't do—landscape development starts with the first conceptual design and becomes a permanent integral part of the project.

Develop a DIAGRAMMATIC PLANTING PLAN consisting of *trees, ground cover and lawn*. Determine the purpose of each tree arrangement - such as to define space, create an image, give direction, provide climate protection or assure privacy. Describe trees as evergreen or deciduous, by height (low to 20 feet, medium to 40 feet, and tall above 40 feet) and by desired shape (round, oval, weeping, conical, upright, etc.). Consider separately and as an integrated whole the space around each cluster, the open space, and the roadway. Trees should reinforce the original design concept.

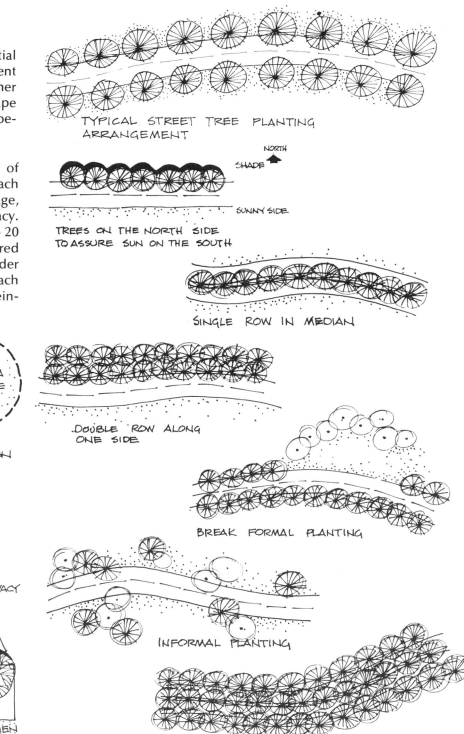

TYPICAL STREET TREE PLANTING ARRANGEMENT

NORTH

SHADE

SUNNY SIDE

TREES ON THE NORTH SIDE TO ASSURE SUN ON THE SOUTH

SINGLE ROW IN MEDIAN

DOUBLE ROW ALONG ONE SIDE

BREAK FORMAL PLANTING

INFORMAL PLANTING

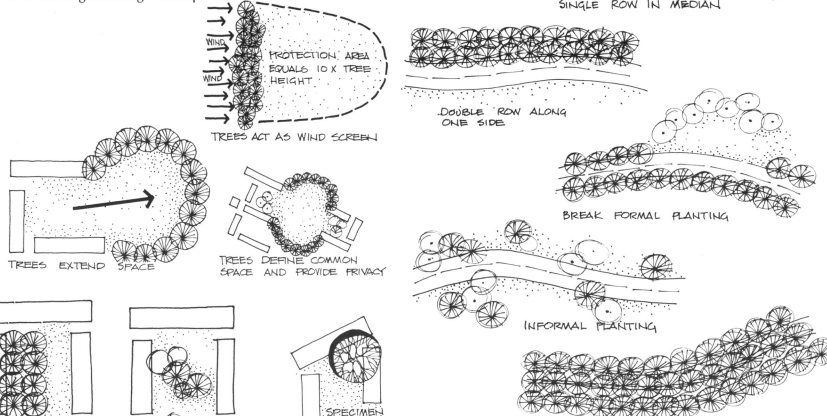

WIND

WIND

PROTECTION AREA EQUALS 10 X TREE HEIGHT

TREES ACT AS WIND SCREEN

TREES EXTEND SPACE

TREES DEFINE COMMON SPACE AND PROVIDE PRIVACY

FORMAL

INFORMAL

SPECIMEN TREE

179

## DIAGRAMATIC TREE PLANTING

| ARRANGEMENT | PURPOSE |
|---|---|
| • FORMAL | • BUFFER |
| • INFORMAL | • SPACE DEFINER |
| • EVERGREEN | • PRIVACY |
| • DECIDUOUS | • SHADE |
| • ORCHARD | • CIRCULATION |
| • FOREST | |

TREES
SEPERATE CLUSTERS

TO ASSURE PRIVACY
WITHIN A CLUSTER

INDUSTRIAL LANDS

TREES ACT AS A BUFFER

TREES SCREEN
PARKING

PLANT CLUMPS
WHERE POSSIBLE

TO DESIGNATE
CIRCULATION

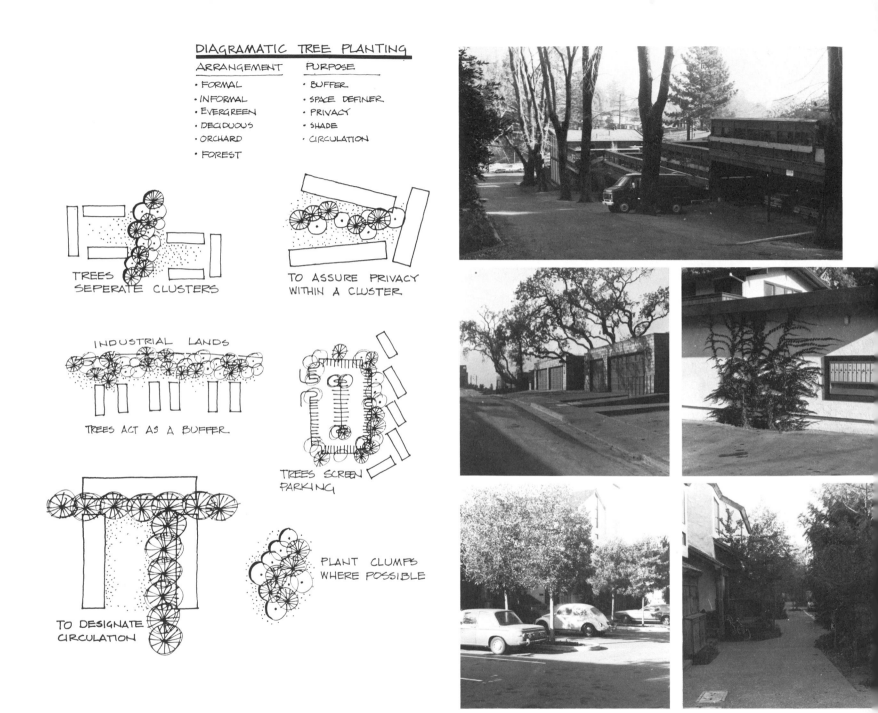

# PART TWO-LARGE SITES

The art of Site Planning relies on determining satisfactory relationships between existing and proposed conditions. In urban areas, where an infrastructure already exists with roads, open spaces, and buildings to relate to, it is relatively easy to develop site use concepts. In sparsely developed areas, with few roads or buildings to relate to, the design possibilities are seemingly endless. Deciding which is the best solution is almost impossible. In this section, we will discuss how a site planner determines guiding *constraints* and uses each constraint through *rationalizations* to guide site organization.

Material in the previous section dealt principally with housing located on small land parcels within built-up areas. In this section, the information is extended to include larger parcels of land in less developed areas. At this scale, there are few man-made site determinants on which to rationalize design decisions. Decisions will be based in large part on natural process factors, that is, how site use affects and is affected by geology, soils, climate, hydrology, vegetation, and wildlife.

In addition to natural process determinants, visual, functional, and user needs factors must inform the site planning process. Since each site is different, each must be assessed individually; thus, in some instances, natural process data are the principal guiding factors, while in others, that information may not be as relevant.

# LARGE-SCALE SITE ANALYSIS:
# NATURAL PROCESSES AS DESIGN DETERMINANTS

In earlier chapters we have discussed natural site qualities as amenity which is sought by residents and is worthwhile preserving. Destroying natural qualities and later replacing them as landscaping adds unnecessary extra costs to a development. This may disrupt natural processes and systems, destroying their value as part of the natural landscape and creating future problems and costs.

In the past, many natural processes were considered problems to be engineered and corrected by building retaining walls, grading extensively, creating elaborate drainage systems, or even developing management programs. In many cases we have succeeded, but only temporarily and at high costs, because over the long run, natural processes eventually wear out our attempts at modification.

Let us consider what natural processes are. They are, quite simply, the natural forces at work when man does not intervene: geology, soils, climate, hydrology, vegetation, and wildlife. These natural processes are all interrelated; for instance, soil combined with water and sunlight creates an environment in which plants can grow. Vegetation modifies soils and water supply, provides food and cover for wildlife and is itself eventually modified by these processes. Natural processes working together form a natural system. Thus, the term ecosystem has come to mean physical and biological processes working together in a self-sustaining system.

Geology
Soils
Climate
Hydrology
Vegetation
Wildlife

Time is an important ecological factor. Man's impact is often very great in a short period of time. After being impacted by man's actions, an ecosystem may continue to exist and function, but some desired plants and animals may be unable to compete or adjust, and may be replaced by less desirable species; for instance, carp and catfish may replace salmon; alders and bay trees may replace oaks, fir, and hemlock; and rats may replace squirrels, chipmunks, and other desirable ground animals.

Incorporation of natural process data into the site planning process can reduce initial development costs if critical areas are avoided, and can reduce long-term maintenance costs by eliminating the need to continually counteract natural processes. Furthermore, it can add to a site's amenities since critical natural processes usually involve forests, streams, meadows, and other prized, diverse, and visually attractive landscapes.

## SCALE OF APPLICATION

We assume that proposed development occurs in a metropolitan area, where some intrusion by man has already taken place. But, in practice, sites for major housing developments must also fit into a regional growth program, with transportation, utilities, services, work, play, school, and shopping facilities organized. This minimizes questions of growth/no growth and development/nondevelopment of virgin lands. However, when large-scale developments of virgin lands are contemplated, the site planner should refer to the extensive literature on the growth issue and apply sound ecological principles in site planning.

For our purposes, we may assume that man can interact and develop properly within a framework of natural constraints. We may also assume that the most sensitive wildlife has probably been displaced from the site, that areas of high natural value *will* be retained intact or developed with restraint, and that areas of low natural value (from a process point of view) can be manipulated, changed, and developed more freely.

This point of view will be disputed by many environmentalists, and perhaps rightly so, but the fact remains that within our metropolitan areas, we must attempt to deliver a positive environment for various household types at the lowest possible cost. Compromise seems to be the best answer.

"The landscape and its natural processes offer opportunities and constraints for land utilization. By identifying and interpreting explicit natural phenomena which contribute to a balanced ecosystem, the planner is able to specify the most and least suitable land use for a particular landscape."

Ian McHarg

## NATURAL PROCESSES AS COST FACTORS

Natural processes affect development costs in three ways:

INSTANTANEOUS NATURAL HAZARD such as landslide, flooding, earthquake, avalanche, hurricane, tidal wave, fire, or volcano. Each occurrence of these hazards results in severe property damage. Highly susceptible areas are usually known or can be predicted during the site planning process.

CUMULATIVE NATURAL HAZARDS, which over the long term add to maintenance and management costs, include erosion, sedimentation, slippage, and standing water.

INTANGIBLE COSTS involved in maintenance of the balance of life between man, animals, and plants. This balance requires that birds, small mammals, insects, microorganisms, and plants be assured of food, water, shelter, and protection. Dollar values for "balance of life" are difficult to calculate since the values themselves are somewhat abstract. What is the value of clean air, of a child's being able to observe wildlife, of preserving nature for unborn generations, or of preserving natural areas near the city?

Once natural hazards are recognized, they can be addressed by:

- <u>Avoiding</u> the problem area by not building there.

- Correcting the problem by applying technology (at extra cost) to overcome known conditions. Special foundations, retaining walls, or extensive drainage systems are typical solutions.

- Deferring or transferring the problem. This is the "ostrich approach," typically used by developers who gamble that a natural disaster will not occur until legal responsibilities are over and transfer long-term costs to unwary future residents.

## GETTING STARTED

An ecosystem may be viewed as a black box of natural process subsystems (geology, soils, climate, hydrology, vegetation, and wildlife) with *inputs* and *outputs*. Inputs are our proposed modifications of the land and their effects—impervious surfaces, noise, changed drainage patterns, erosion, noise and air pollution, heat buildup, etc. On the other hand, outputs are the emerging qualities of the landscape following development— what it is like and how it functions.

We must identify those emerging qualities which are important to society and assume their presence following development. For instance, what vegetation and wildlife do we value? How should our streams and creeks function? What water quality is important?

Determining societal values isn't really difficult since we have adopted many national and state laws describing sought after levels of environmental quality. We have laws regulating our potential impact on endangered species, unique vegetation, wetlands, shorelines, estuaries, scenic highways, rivers, water quality, wildlands, and farmland. We have some laws concerning floodplains, and earthquake and landslide prone areas. Currently, many cities are creating drainage utility districts and are stressing zero percent increase runoff and other ecologically sound drainage methods. Even noise pollution and contributing factors are being analyzed, as are dozens of other quality of life factors. But, just because there are laws and community interest in environmental quality, we shouldn't assume that all is ok. Only the ground work is laid thus far, but we do have a base to build on.

With a clear understanding of *desired values*, it is not necessary to understand all the workings of an ecosystem. We need only know the changes in output caused by changes in inputs. If these changes are adverse to the things we value, then it may be necessary to examine some or all of the processes that comprise the ecosystem.

The analysis process begins at a regional scale and progresses down to site scale until every portion of the site is understood in relation to the region. Work progresses with interpretation of maps, diagrams, and charts, and verification or reinterpretation through site visits.

Ecological site planning at this scale involves four steps.

1. Determining the site's most significant natural process limitations, and prioritizing the remaining processes. Typically, one or two processes surface as key limiting factors, requiring in-depth study.
2. Inventoring and mapping existing natural process data. While some data may be obvious from field visits, other data may be gathered efficiently and inexpensively from existing maps or studies. Occasionally when data are not available, intensive and expensive field studies may be required.
3. Interpreting the findings for limitations to development. This usually involves a scale of possible actions from *build* to *no-build*, with a *build-with-restraints* category.
4. Developing site planning guidelines, including valued features, drainage concepts, road widths, parking arrangements, unit access conditions, foundation types, and so on.

To begin, we should gather the following materials:

- A USGS map at 1:62500 showing the site and its surroundings.
- A site topography map with five-foot contour intervals and property lines. (USGS scale is acceptable for nondetailed study.)

# MATRIX: POTENTIAL IMPACTS, CONFLICTS AND CONSEQUENCES OF DEVELOPMENT

**GENERIC FIRST IMPACTS** (column legend)

1. Deliberate or gradual understory & litter buildup
2. Partial tree canopy removal
3. Partial understory or grass cropping or removal
4. Canopy and/or undergrowth destruction or removal
5. Complete cover, grass, debris removal
6. Shallow soil exposure
7. Deep soil exposure
8. Unloading slopes (excavation)
9. Weighting slopes (buildings, fill, etc.)
10. Surface areal compaction
11. Surface linear compaction
12. Bedrock exposure
13. Rigid structures (buildings, utility lines, paving)
14. Transitory stress (shaking by blasting, vehicular movement)
15. Subsurface water reduction and/or interruption
16. Subsurface water concentration
17. Surface water sheet flow reduction and or interruption
18. Surface water sheet flow concentration
19. Unseasonal surface water addition and or concentration
20. Reduced stream flow
21. Chemical alteration, surface, subsurface soil and water
22. Creation of airborne particulates
23. Foreign soil layers
24. Introduction of exotic plants
25. Impervious surfaces (buildings, paving, compacted fill)

**COMMON DEVELOPMENT ASPECTS — Selected Residential**

| Development Aspect | 1 | 2 | 3 | 4 | 5 | 6 | 7 | 8 | 9 | 10 | 11 | 12 | 13 | 14 | 15 | 16 | 17 | 18 | 19 | 20 | 21 | 22 | 23 | 24 | 25 |
|---|---|---|---|---|---|---|---|---|---|---|---|---|---|---|---|---|---|---|---|---|---|---|---|---|---|
| Fire suppression and fencing | ■ | | | | | | | | | | | | | | | | | | | | | | | | |
| Tree thinning, trimming for views | | ■ | ■ | | | | | | | | | | | | | | | | | | | | | | |
| Mechanical clearing trees &/or undergrowth | ■ | ■ | ■ | | | | | | | ■ | | | | | ■ | | | | | | | | | | |
| Chemical spray of poison oak or weeds | ■ | | ■ | | | | | | | | | | | | | | | | | | ■ | | | | |
| Off road truck & dozer pre-constr movemt | | | | ■ | ■ | | | | | ■ | | | | ■ | | | ■ | ■ | | | | ■ | | | |
| Site stripping for construction, roads, grading | | | | | ■ | ■ | | | | ■ | | | | | | | ■ | ■ | | | | | | | |
| Deep trenchg, compacted backfill for utilities | | | | | | | ■ | ■ | | ■ | ■ | | | | ■ | ■ | ■ | ■ | | | | | ■ | | |
| Blast, rip, excavate for rds, bldgs, garden | | | | ■ | ■ | ■ | | | ■ | | | ■ | | | | | ■ | ■ | | | | | ■ | | |
| Compacted fill for roads, buildings, patios | | | | | | | | ■ | ■ | ■ | | | ■ | | | | ■ | ■ | | | | | ■ | | ■ |
| Uncontrolled, uncompacted downhill & piled fill | | | | | | | | ■ | ■ | | | | | | | ■ | | | | | | | ■ | ■ | |
| Gradg & planing for drainage swales or control | | | | ■ | | ■ | ■ | | ■ | | | ■ | | ■ | ■ | | ■ | ■ | | | | | ■ | | |
| Undrgrnd drain lines, subsurface grvl blankets | | | | | | | ■ | | | | | | | | ■ | | | | | | | | | | |
| Dp footgs, retaing walls, concrt encased utils | | | | | | | | | | | | ■ | ■ | | | | | | | | | | | | |
| Shallow trenched foundations, curbs | | | | | | | | | | | | ■ | ■ | | | | ■ | | | | | | | | |
| Stockpiled soil, sand, buildings materials | | | | | ■ | | | | ■ | ■ | | | | | | | ■ | | | ■ | ■ | ■ | ■ | | |
| Dump concrete & plaster wash, thinner, ash etc. | | | | | | | | | | | | | | | | | | | | | ■ | ■ | | | |
| Curbs & gutters, paved or compactd dvrsn ditch | | | | | | | | | | | | | ■ | | ■ | | ■ | | | | | | | | ■ |
| House, paved roads, drives, patios, swimg pool | | | | | | | | | ■ | ■ | | | ■ | | | | | | | | | | | | ■ |
| Slope erosion control seeding and planting | | | | | | | ■ | | | | | | | | | | ■ | ■ | ■ | | | | ■ | ■ | |
| Garden preparation & planting of nursery stock | | | | | | | ■ | ■ | | | | | | | ■ | | ■ | ■ | | | | | ■ | ■ | |
| Lawn area preparation and planting | | | | | | | ■ | ■ | | | | | | | | | ■ | ■ | | | | | ■ | ■ | |
| Garden and lawn sprinkler irrigation | | | | | | | | | | | | | | | | | | ■ | ■ | | | | | | |
| Spray or granular, insecticide or fert | | | | | | | | | | | | | | | | | | | | | ■ | | | | |
| Septic system & leaching fields | | | | | | | | | | | | | | | | ■ | | | | | | | | | |

Patri, Tito, David C. Streatfield, and Thomas J. Ingmire, *Early Warning System: The Santa Cruz Mountains Regional Pilot Study*, Berkeley, California. Department of Landscape Architecture. University of California.

- A soils map and interpretation guide from U.S. Soil Conservation Service.
- An aerial photo of the site, at a scale not exceeding a desk top and preferably at the same scale as the topo map.

These four maps should be sufficient to begin with, although we may eventually need: (1) a geology map with cross sections and historical perspectives; (2) a water resources diagram, well logs, or location of aquifer discharge or intake; (3) climatological data from the nearest weather station, as well as macro climate information for the region; and (4) insights of the value and role of plant and animal life found on the site.

The bulk of material gathered during this initial stage is *second source* data, generated by someone else for some other purpose. Second source data are usually inexpensive to gather and interpret, although somtimes not as specific as required. In time, on-site investigations and primary source data may be required. At that point, the ecological planning effort is best served in a cross-disciplinary effort between the site planner and geologist, ecologist, soils scientist, hydrologist, and other specialized natural scientists.

Since ecosystems are complex, a site planner can never hope to fully describe or understand but a few of the simplest interactions. But he should collect and display data describing major interactions and dependencies of each site, and ignore interactions that are obviously "weak."

There are two important points:

1. The system should be examined from the standpoint of the output, or emerging qualities important to society at a given time.
2. Systems may be reduced to subsystems (soils, geology, etc.) in order to understand the change in output caused by changes in input relevant to the proposed development.

# SITE LIMITATIONS

SITE DANGER SIGNALS. The landscape can usually be read and interpreted through the use of site danger signals—visible indications or warnings of potential natural process trouble. Site danger signals can warn of a potential functional problem as flooding or slippage, or a condition which may upset the balance of life. On a first site visit, we should look for the following, noting the location and describing carefully. Each marked area should later be evaluated to verify the accuracy of the first impression, and to determine if the area is usable or usable with certain management development procedures.

Though the principles of ecologic planning do not vary, specific site danger signals are often regional in character and vary across the United States. A site planner must beome familiar with those phenomena typical of the region. He can then supplement this knowledge with evidence visible on a first field trip indicating which processes are likely to cause problems.

Some common signals are:

GEOLOGY
- Steep slopes
- Presence of past landslides
- Presence of volcanos
- Evidence of creep (slippage)
- Known earthquake faults
- Clay layers (best seen in slopes around road excavations or sheer cliffs)
- Rare or unique physiography

SOILS
- Peat
- Beach dunes
- Erosion
- Underlayers of impermeable material such as clay or till
- Water absorbability relating to shrinkage and swell in clays or shale
- Standing water
- Bald areas indicating infertile soils

CLIMATE
- Flagging or stunted growth of trees indicating strong winds or extreme cold
- Lack of vegetation
- Extremes in temperature, wind, rain

HYDROLOGY
- Aquifers
- Aquifer recharge areas
- Flood plains
- Springs
- Shorelines
- Wild rivers
- Estuaries • Wetlands • Marshes
- Rerouted surface drainage
- Erosion
- Standing water in late winter or early spring
- Horizontal seepage lines on a hillside

VEGETATION
- Rare or unique flora
- Forest or woodland
- Bent trees indicating slippage
- National Parks or Forests
- Unhealthy communities (detected through infrared aerial photos)
- Community's extent—i.e., is it contained exclusively on the site
- Habitat for wildlife

WILDLIFE
- Rare or unique fauna
- Spawning or breeding grounds
- Migratory rest stops
- Forage areas

## WHO DOES WHAT?

Site planning based on principles of ecology may require the input of natural science specialists—ecologist, soils scientist, botanist or zoologist. The partnership of natural scientist and site planner is new, and in instances uneasy. Difficulties sometimes occur because of differences in training. A natural scientist is trained to investigate thoroughly, often taking years, whereas a site planner must use the best available information and make a decision quickly.

To begin, the site planner should ask the natural scientist specific questions or pose several alternative solutions and seek a response. Joint field trips over the site, where factors and conditions can be observed and analyzed, are perhaps the most rewarding.

Once the most sensitive processes or areas have been determined, ecological data can be gathered. The following are suggestions of concerns a site planner may have at this scale of work.

## ECOLOGICAL INTEGRITY

Ecological integrity is the way all individual natural processes relate together on a site to produce overall stability. This is achieved through a diversity of site elements, because with many different forms of life the overall structure is complex, producing many interdependencies which serve to buffer the system from sudden change. (Although all land is continually changing, it must be protected from certain types of rapid change.) Thus, diversity indicates the health of an ecosystem. Sites that lack natural diversity such as the dune grass areas, meadows, tundra, and swamps are more sensitive to man's impact.

Size and biological productivity of the site determine its ability to support a diversity of wildlife. Larger sites, long natural edges, water, and a variety of vegetation are condusive to wildlife habitat.

Diversity, in a larger sense, then suggests the interdependency and interrelatedness of each natural system to the other systems. While some natural process factors can stand together, others become meaningful only when several systems verify and compound the same problem. For instance, the presence of Horse Tails, steep slopes, bowed trees, and soils with known clay layers is a good indication of slippage.

## GEOLOGY

Geology is perhaps the most difficult natural process to "see" and describe. This is the case because geologic elements are often covered by soils (although sometimes soils and geology are the same), because the geologic process is so slow we cannot grasp the time frame, and because the science of describing geologic structure is more of an art and not really very precise.

The underlying structure of a site allows us to predict the way a site has and is likely to behave over a period of time. Even though precise data is difficult to obtain, we should be able to determine base geology, surficial geology, nearby geologic cross sections, and the site's geologic history. This information should be related to information about soils, and also about hydrology and vegetation.

Site geology can be verified where it has been exposed by road cuts, landslides, erosion, or other disturbances. Are the soils underlaid with an impervious layer preventing percolation? Knowledge of groundwater percolation can form the basis of a drainage scheme which relies on subsurface percolation in areas where geologic bedding allows good drainage.

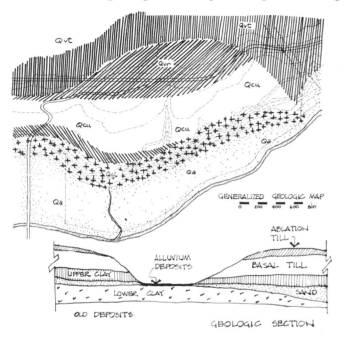

SLIPPAGE POTENTIAL. Certain geologic structures, combined with *steep topography*, excessive rainfall, earthquake, or man-induced modification can cause a landslide or creep.

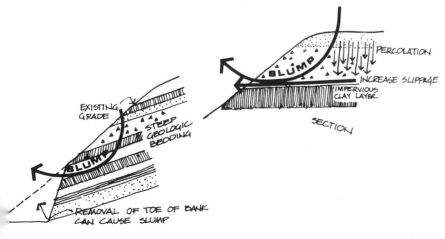

- Impervious clay layers can trap water, which eventually acts as a lubricant causing soil on top to slip away.
- Slopes with steep geologic bedding can slide if man removes a supporting portion.
- Changed drainage patterns can divert excessive water onto a slope, increasing the weight of soils which may slip under the force of gravity.

FLOODING. Level areas are prone to flooding if:
- They contain level or pocketed areas which collect rainwater. (These same soils would not normally cause flooding on sloping land.)
- They include impervious geologic or soil layers near the surface, causing groundwater to rise, essentially a very high water table.

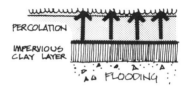

BEARING CAPACITY. Each geologic structure or soil type has a bearing capacity which relates to foundation costs. In theory, a foundation for almost any building could be located on almost any site, but at tremendous costs. However, in actuality soil or geologic structures not capable of readily supporting proposed buildings should be eliminated.

## SOILS

Soils are a major determinant of existing and potential plant communities and are associated with the following natural hazards:
- Slippage or landslide
- Danger of flooding
- Earthquake instability

Soil types vary from region to region, and are usually classified by the Soil Conservation Service as to characteristics and use

189

potential. In the past, descriptions dealt primarily with the capability of soils to produce crops. However, newer classifications describe urban use limiting factors including:

1. Septic tank suitability
2. Frost heave potential
3. Shrink/SWELL CHARACTERISTICS
4. Slippage potential
5. Flooding danger
6. Corrosion potential
7. Permeability
8. Subsurface drainage
9. Erosion potential

We should try to obtain the most recent soil survey, and a description of urban use soil limitations from the Soil Conservation Service (USDA). The most recent survey is desirable since, though soils don't change much over the years, our methods of classifying and mapping them have improved. Soil maps are only an approximation of soil types with exact boundaries being impossible to determine. Any extreme soil condition should be verified through cross reference with another natural process (vegetation, for instance) and actual field inspection.

GROUNDWATER PERCOLATION. It is important to determine areas which absorb water well and areas which don't. Generally, gravelly or sandy soils drain well, while clay or silty loams don't.

- High density development is appropriate over impermeable soils, since both result in a high amount of surface runoff and generally have a well-developed stream system capable of supporting intensive runoff.
- Surface runoff should be encouraged over permeable soils which have adequate underground storage capacity. Berms and swales may be used to guide and collect runoff from impermeable areas.

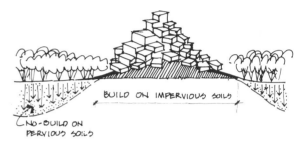

OTHER PROBLEMS. Septic tank suitability, frost heave, shrink/swell, corrosive action, and erosion are all mechanical problems related to soil which should be understood as problems and technologic systems designed to solve them. Common sense should prevail. If septic tanks can never work, the site planner or developer should not try to subvert the system by running a perk test in mid-September (the driest month). Instead, he should try to connect to a small community sewer-treatment system, or to the existing system. He might also scale down or abandon the project. With a heaving soil it is essential to determine what, if any, foundation system can overcome the problem and at what cost? Can plastic pipes be substituted for concrete or iron pipes in a prime corrosive area? If soils subject to erosion are found on steep topography, erosion is likely.

There are exceptions—subsurface drainage may work on sites with sharp drainage—gravelly or sandy soil that can absorb large quantities of water. Sites adjacent to a large lake or body of water may, without problems, discharge surface drainage into it. (It may be desirable to trap dirt and oil particles before discharging into the lake.)

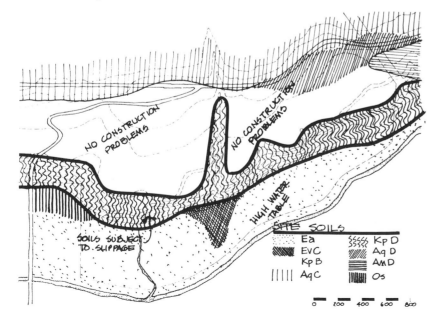

# HYDROLOGY

Water passes over and through the site in a complex cycle of percolation, interception, surface runoff, evaporation, transpiration, and groundwater flow. This complex process involves cloud formation, rainfall, a watershed of rivers, lakes, and streams all interwoven into a dynamic, balanced phenomenon. The word balanced is important, because an undisturbed watershed has achieved over the years a balance among the amount of precipitation, the amount removed by evaporation, transpiration and runoff and the amount stored. Any change of flow within the cycle, be it increase or decrease in runoff, groundwater storage, evaporation, etc., alters some other portion of the cycle, and the change may not be desirable.

Precipitation is removed naturally from a watershed in a combination of four ways. Each must be studied in order to assess the change of flow caused by a proposed development.

1. By surface runoff. This is the most common way, accounting for up to 50 percent of rainwater removal.
2. By subsurface runoff. This is underground drainage moving slowly.
3. Through evaporation. Water is evaporated from all types of surfaces.
4. By transpiration. This is evaporation from the leaves of plants, as part of their respiration cycle.

Most undisturbed watersheds are dynamically balanced, that is, they are able to accommodate precisely the amount of rainfall normally received within their systems of rivers, lakes, streams, and subsurface drainage. Any land use change, such as coverage by houses, parking, and streets affects the soil's ability to absorb and carry away runoff. Additionally, sealed surfaces such as roads and roofs cause water to run off the site quickly, instead of traveling slowly through vegetation as on an undeveloped site. This rapid removal causes a surge in runoff, placing heavy demand on nearby streams and creeks immediately following rainfall. With light rain, there may be no trouble, but with heavy rainfall or continued storms, the surge of rainwater can cause stream erosion, flooding, and environmental degradation of the watercourse. Eventually, there may be pressure from local government to divert stream water to a system of culverts, thus destroying a natural stream where people walk and kids play and where small animals live.

Traditional methods of site drainage demand extensive mechanical systems to trap, guide, and carry some water away. This method drastically upsets the hydrologic cycle, causing decrease in groundwater, increase in peak flow, downstream erosion, potential flooding, low stream flow in summer, etc.

However, working with the natural hydrologic cycle is possible even though it means changes in traditional methods of urbanization. Using a series of swales, permeable soils, and holding ponds, excess storm water runoff can be stored and released slowly, in effect duplicating the natural hydrologic process.

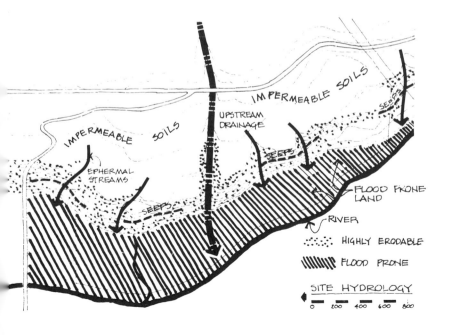

IMPERMEABLE SOILS

IMPERMEABLE SOILS

UPSTREAM DRAINAGE

SEEPS

SEEPS

SEEPS

EPHERMAL STREAMS

SEEPS

FLOOD PRONE LAND

RIVER

⋰⋰ HIGHLY ERODABLE

▨▨ FLOOD PRONE

SITE HYDROLOGY

0   200   400   600   800

HOLDING RUNOFF ONSITE UNTIL AFTER THE STORM. The site planner can choose from several possible methods to insure against unnecessary runoff. With some exceptions, the principle for drainage of larger sites is to keep runoff onsite until after the storm. When rains have subsided and stream flow is reduced, the runoff can be added to the stream. In effect this more uniformly distributes the runoff, reduces flash impact on the stream, and may save it from "culvert treatment." Keeping runoff onsite requires devising holding areas, for example, impoundment basins, underground tanks, or built-up storage areas on roof tops.

Test to see if the drainage system can be used as a backbone for green space. Modern drainage concepts minimize the use of underground pipes, instead of relying on surface drainage. Take advantage of this by making drainage do double duty.

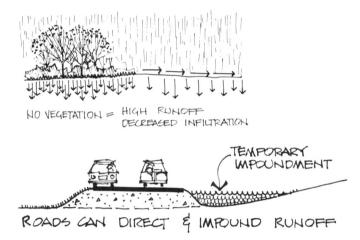

NO VEGETATION = HIGH RUNOFF DECREASED INFILTRATION

TEMPORARY IMPOUNDMENT

ROADS CAN DIRECT & IMPOUND RUNOFF

IMPOUNDMENT BASINS are earth-formed areas, usually on the lowest portion of the site, to which all runoff is directed for temporary storage. A slow release mechanism, perhaps a small diameter pipe in the bottom of the pond, allows water to escape at a rate duplicating natural flow. (Overflow spill-

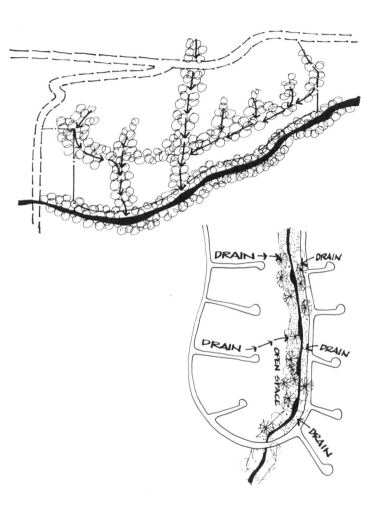

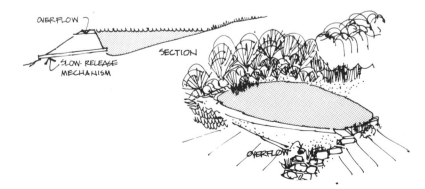

OVERFLOW

SLOW-RELEASE MECHANISM

SECTION

OVERFLOW

The advantages of keeping rainwater on the site lies in maintaining a balanced hydrologic system: replenishing the underground water table and keeping the level high, wells full, trees in the watershed healthy; and avoiding excessive runoff which may degrade the stream channel.

ways are necessary for emergencies.) The holding basin may be used when dry as a grassed play area or may perhaps be maintained year round as swamp or bog.

UNDERGROUND STORAGE TANKS may be necessary in dense urban areas with excessive pavement where provision of an impoundment basin is impossible. The tank should be located on the lowest portion of the site, perhaps in a basement, with runoff directed toward it, and should have a slow release mechanism to feed runoff back into the natural drainage system. This method is expensive, but may be necessary in situations where flooding is severe.

FLAT ROOFTOPS may be used for rainwater storage provided a suitable built-up edge is installed. The edge (about three or four inches high) contains the water which is stored until after the storm when it is released slowly. Two downspouts are necessary: a slow release one to duplicate the rate of natural runoff, and an emergency drain for overflow purposes. Obviously, the roof has to have enough structural strength to support the weight of water without collapsing. An energy conservation advantage of rooftop storage is that water provides a blanket of insulation.

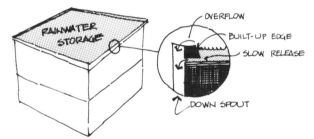

Large developments may combine all three methods, with several holding basins performing the lion's share of the storage effort.

CALCULATING THE SIZE OF A HOLDING BASIN is in principle a simple process which should eventually be verified by a qualified engineer. The process assumes that water normally removed by surface runoff *can continue* to drain following site development. In other words, the amount to be stored is the amount that exceeds normal runoff.

Three factors are important in calculating the size of a holding basin:

1. The intensity of rainfall in inches per hour
2. Proposed impervious areas in acres
3. Coefficient of runoff determined by subtracting the existing coefficient from the proposed coefficient.

These three can be multiplied together using the formula $Q = CIA$. The calculation borrows from the Rational Formula used in calculating storm water runoff for sizing drainage pipes where Q equals discharge in cfs, I equals intensity of rainfall, C equals the coefficient of runoff and A equals area in acres. Coefficients of runoff vary from .1 in forested areas to .5 for planted, impervious soil, and up to .9 for urban areas.

| Condition | c = |
|---|---|
| Roofs | .95 |
| Pavement | .95 |
| Bare Gravel | .30-.60 |
| Bare Sand | .10-.50 |
| Bare Loam | .20-.60 |
| Bare Clay | .30-.75 |
| Vegetation over sand | .05-.30 |
| Vegetation over loam | .10-.40 |
| Vegetation over clay | .15-.50 |

Steps to guard against excessive erosion include:

1. Grading erosion-prone or steep areas only during dry periods
2. Stockpiling all topsoil for reuse.
3. Devising and implementing a pregrading plan consisting of small check dams to control and catch erosion when the final plan is implemented. These areas should be constructed by hand or with a backhoe, and planted immediately.
4. Planting all disturbed areas immediately and insuring that runoff is guided away from newly planted banks.

Erosion is a problem all developers face and its implications are severe. First, our entire life is linked to topsoil — it allows plants to grow from which all life flows. Without plants life ceases. Topsoil is limited in quantity, and takes 1000's of years to manufacture. Additionally, erosion means sedimentation with topsoil landing elsewhere, perhaps in a trout or salmon spawning stream.

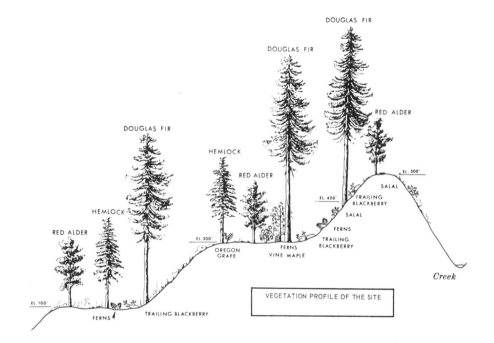

DOUGLAS FIR

DOUGLAS FIR

RED ALDER

HEMLOCK

RED ALDER

EL. 500'

DOUGLAS FIR

EL. 420'

SALAL

TRAILING
BLACKBERRY

SALAL

HEMLOCK

FERNS

EL. 300'

TRAILING
BLACKBERRY

RED ALDER

OREGON
GRAPE

FERNS
VINE MAPLE

FERNS
TRAILING
BLACKBERRY

*Creek*

EL. 100'

FERNS

TRAILING BLACKBERRY

VEGETATION PROFILE OF THE SITE

## VEGETATION

Vegetation is perhaps more important as a "balance of life" factor than as a factor providing direct cost reduction to the developer. Obviously, plants serve as amenity, visual and sound barriers, erosion control, and form givers, though these benefits are hard to calculate. From a natural process point of view, vegetation begins the flow of energy through the total ecosystem, providing food and shelter for a host of interdependent microorganisms, insects, birds, and other wildlife.

PLANTS ARE INDICATORS of soil stability, soil condition, and soil moisture level, etc. Although vegetation indicating certain

conditions varies from region to region, examples shown here are vegetation native to the Pacific Northwest.

> Plants indicating wet soil conditions: (Willows, Cottonwoods, Cedars)

> Plants indicating high groundwater table: (Horsetail, Willows, Cottonwoods)

> Plants indicating, but which can live on, poor soils: (Alders, Scotch-broom)

> Plants which indicate climax conditions: (Western Red Cedar, Western Hemlock)

> Nitrogen enriching plants which improve and build a soil: (Alders)

PLANT COMMUNITIES. One of the fundamental ecological elements used to describe an environment is its plant community. A plant community is fundamentally the product of interaction between two phenomena: *differences in environmental tolerances and the heterogenity of the environment.* In other words, a plant community is an area with a uniform environment, which when changed, changes the environment in some way. A plant community is described by identifying its location, its environment, and its dominant plant species. Classification of plants into communities is always approximate, since there often is overlap between communities because of similar soil types, climate, orientation, and moisture content.

Four factors affect plants and plant communities: <u>soil, sunlight, moisture and elevation</u>. The site planner's first task is to look for unusual conditions.

*Soil*—Is there topsoil? Is the soil highly acidic, or alkaline? Is it peaty? Is the soil a normal, loamy soil?

*Sunlight*—Is there too little or too much sun?

*Moisture*—Two sources of moisture become important, with consideration again focusing on extremes. First, moisture from rain, snow, or fog is captured directly on plants' leaves and

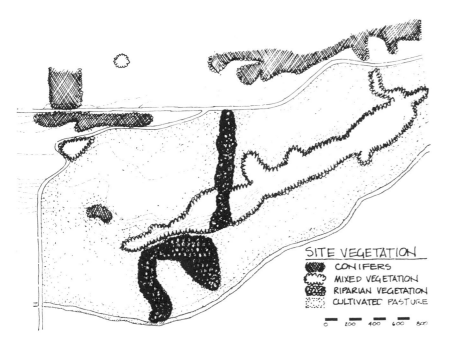

SITE VEGETATION
- CONIFERS
- MIXED VEGETATION
- RIPARIAN VEGETATION
- CULTIVATED PASTURE

0    200   400   600   800

Thinning a forest will increase the chance of trees being toppled by wind, particularly shallow rooted trees. To guard against tree toppling, a sufficient mass of forest should be left intact.

NOTE AND RESERVE
VEGETATION WITH:

- UNIQUENESS
- SPECIES DIVERSITY
- HIGH QUALITY
- STABILITY

- RESERVE OR REPLANT EDGE OF NATIVE SHRUBS

needles and is indirectly absorbed through the roots. Second, groundwater supplies water to roots of plants. We should look for extremes: heavy or light rain, frequent fog, poorly drained soil, peaty or boggy areas as indications of natural problem areas. Regarding rainfall, it is important to distinguish between the times of the year when it rains; for instance, in Seattle it rains primarily in the winter with little rainfall during summer, while on the East Coast it rains more during the summer.

*Elevation*—For areas less than 1000 feet high, elevation is not a problem. Higher areas require special consideration since elevational differences limit the species of plants capable of surviving.

PLANT SUCCESSION. As certain plant species are replaced by stronger species, plant communities change; this process is called plant succession. The process of change can be understood through classification of site vegetation into communities, and then determining the likely progressive stages of transformation from bare site to climax forest.

PIONEER communities consist of the simplest site vegetation, grasses, which invade bare ground following a severe disaster. These grasses, weeds to most of us, are highly durable, hardy, short-lived, and intolerant of shade. As they die and decay, the soil is changed. Seeds of herbaceous shrubs germinate and these shrubs replace the grasses as the dominant species. They are eventually succeeded by woody shrubs, then woody trees. In the Puget Sound lowlands, alders and big leaf maples are early successional trees which are dominant species for 40 to 60 years and are then replaced by later successional species, the conifers.

CLIMAX communities are stable and the plant species are shade tolerant. The stable (climax) plant community of the Puget Sound area is the Western Hemlock community which includes a variety of vegetation types depending on elevation, moisture, logging, fire history, and nearness to urban areas. The dominant species is Western Hemlock, with Douglas Fir, Alders, and Maples in abundant supply.

WHAT DOES IT ALL MEAN? From a site planner's point of view, knowledge of transitional plant community stages indicate how the site will appear in the future and describes the type of plants most easily grown on that site. Native plants are the most well-suited plants for the site in that they need the least maintenance. Non-native plants can be made to grow, but only with considerable assistance in the form of water and fertilizing, and pest control. Although the use of exotics should not be discouraged, plants from either the climax or succession stands are desirable if maintenance is to be minimized.

## WILDLIFE

Wildlife distribution is often determined more by the types of food and shelter afforded by vegetation than by other physical factors—hence their distribution tends to conform to plant communities. However, the mobility of many animals complicates this since one animal may inhabit different plant communities at different times.

DIVERSITY of species is again the key to a stable wildlife community. Diversity means the web of interactions will be complex, with alternate interactions possible should one link in the chain disappear. The site planner must assure adequate and proper food sources, shelter, and water for existing wildlife species.

Retaining some portion of the site for wildlife is most successful if the following suggestions are considered.

_Any water feature is maintained_. A stream, brook, lake, or spring provides a desirable habitat, particularly if natural water edge vegetation is allowed to grow and people are directed away from the edge. People can "use" the water in a cluster or concentrated manner, leaving the rest natural for wildlife.

_Natural areas are maintained_. Natural areas provide shelter for living and while many "metropolitan" animals and birds are capable of living side by side with man, they need some "natural" area for food and shelter. Often the edge between two natural features—as between forest and meadow, between meadow and lake, or lake and forest—provides a thicket for cover and food. Generally, forests do not support as many

species as its thicket edge. The important dimension of the edge is its length, the longer the better. Additionally, the edge should consist primarily of natural plant species and should not be maintained by man; pesticides and other harmful sprays should not be used.

_Special attractions_ are provided to encourage wildlife to inhabit a place. Special attractions may include a salt lick, protection from domestic animals, and adequate food supply. The holding basin, for instance, might be a suitable habitat for amphibians and birds, particularly if marsh-type plants develop.

Urban ecology is presently a scientific unknown since little is known about exact numbers or distribution of plants and animals required or the exact value of each type. Inferences and ecologic generalizations indicate that, while we can survive without native plants and wildlife, the cost may be high. Besides, many people feel the health of man's "civilized" habitat can be better understood by observing the health of surrounding plant and animal communities.

## PHYSIOGRAPHY AS THE SUM

Physiography is a total landscape unit, that is, a large-scale land form (valley, sloping plain, hogback ridge) related to all the natural processes at work there.

Physiography may be considered at different scales as follows:

*world-scale features* such as continents and oceans

*major relief features* such as mountain ranges

*formations* such as valleys and drainage basins

In order to describe physiography we should record topography plus land form orientation and obvious surface features (such rock outcrops, exaggerated forms, slide areas, drainage problem). All sites have a distinct land form type which, if valued, may suggest the best use of the land. For instance, a valley may be best developed in a manner which preserves the valley floor by developing on the ridges or slopes.

Physiography is created by the interaction of all other processes:

Parent geologic material
Upheaval of earth
Volcanic actions
Climate, including orientation
Gravity (e.g., slides and avalanches)
Erosion (wind, water, glacier)
Vegetation and wildlife

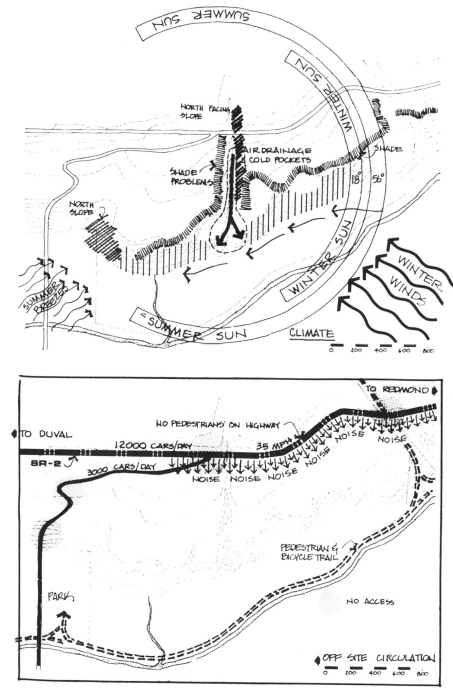

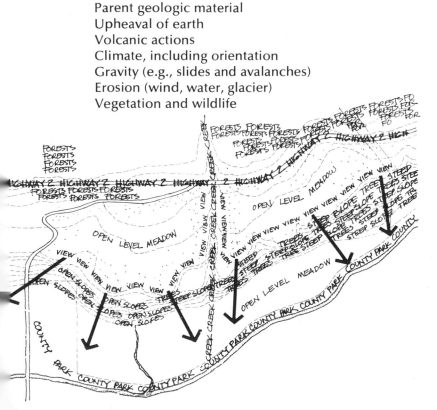

**COMBINING SEVERAL FACTORS.** Soils data, combined with other natural process data, insure a better understanding, since in theory, the pattern of vegetation types should correlate with patterns of climate, soils, and wildlife. Physical soil properties that influence the pattern and distribution of vegetation include: parent material, soil texture, water retention capabilities, soil profile, organic matter, drainage potential, acid level, and mineral content. The process is reciprocal; while soil influences the plant community, plants and animals alter the soil. For instance, plants alter soils through the weathering of rocks, entrapment of particles, organic additions through leaf litter, moisture retention, etc. Litter, duff and humus accumulation, and soil structure modification play both a helpful and detrimental role in plant growth; for instance, trees that cast heavy leaf litter may smother slow-growing tree seedlings or deprive seedling roots of a constant supply of moisture. The accumulation of thick surface layers of organic debris restricts the species that can cope with it, thereby contributing to simplification of vegetation. Animals alter soil structure by burrowing, digesting food, and increasing the soil's organic content through defecation.

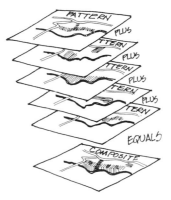

Geology
Soils
Water Resources
Vegetation
Climate
Physiography
Wildlife

Besides the cost advantage, most areas performing important natural process functions have high visual and amenity values, and may be of greater worth when preserved for residents' enjoyment.

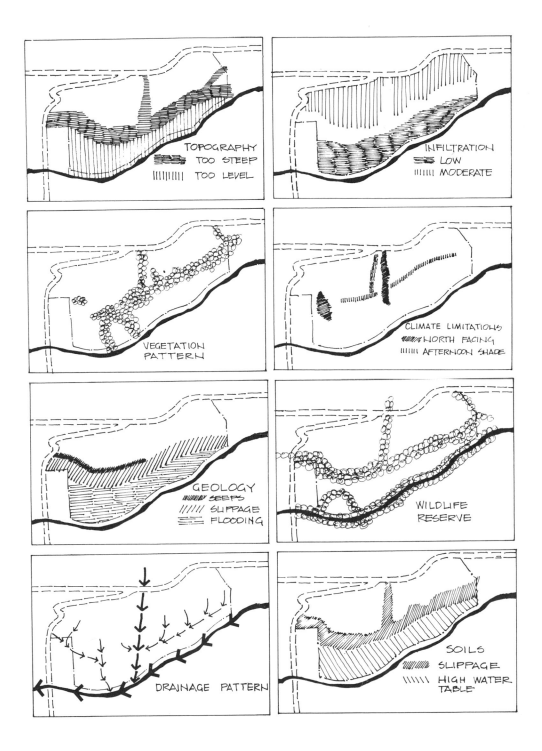

TOPOGRAPHY
≡≡≡ TOO STEEP
||||| TOO LEVEL

INFILTRATION
≡≡≡ LOW
||||| MODERATE

VEGETATION PATTERN

CLIMATE LIMITATIONS
≡≡≡ NORTH FACING
||||| AFTERNOON SHADE

GEOLOGY
≡≡≡ SEEPS
///// SLIPPAGE
≡≡≡ FLOODING

WILDLIFE RESERVE

DRAINAGE PATTERN

SOILS
≡≡≡ SLIPPAGE
||||| HIGH WATER TABLE

199

# LARGE-SCALE ANALYSIS CHECKLIST

The source and accuracy of all information should be noted. For instance, is certain information an <u>estimate</u>, <u>guess</u>, or <u>opinion</u>?

I. INFORMATION GATHERING (We should remember that information is expensive to gather)
- A. In relation to stated objectives
- B. In time to be useful
- C. Over the total design period can we postpone gathering it? Can someone else do a better job?

II. INFORMATION ON-SITE AND OFF-SITE
- A. Natural features
- B. Manmade features
- C. Visual analysis
- D. Circulation
- E. Jurisdiction

III. MEASURES TO LOOK FOR
- A. Site potentials
- B. Site problems
- C. Site amenities
- D. Danger signals

IV. INFORMATION RELATES TO
- A. Man's functional requirements
- B. Man's pleasurable requirements
- C. Nature's processes

V. RESOURCES WE SHOULD CHECK
- A. ERTS and infrared high altitude aerial photos useful for large-scale relationships
- B. USGS maps at 7½ min. 1 inch 2000 feet (useful for topo vegetation, roads, major buildings, developed/undeveloped land, landmarks, political jurisdictions)
- C. Photogrammetrics at 200'-400' scale (useful to show buildings, roads, rights of way, property lines, topo)
- D. Aerial photographs in either stereo-pairs or enlargements useful for detail relationships, inference, verification
- E. Other people's previous experience

VI. SITE DESCRIPTIONS
- A. Orientation (sun, wind, storm direction)
- B. Ownership (property lines)
- C. Topography
- D. Lay of the land (relationships)
- E. Nearby community facilities
- F. Urban design (scale, density)

VII. SITE OBSERVATION
- A. Three visits to site (minimum ½ hour each), twice on weekdays, once on a weekend, at different times of day and with different weather conditions
- B. Conversations with neighbors
- C. Visual analysis—Views, Amenity, Physiography (total physical environment)
- D. Urban design—essential urban character. Continuous scale (bulk, height, color, texture) Townscape (unity, thematic qualities) Public vs private spaces, attitude
- E. Circulation—public roads, pedestrian walks, public transportation
- F. Quality of neighborhood (We should note "hidden" signs such as maintenance, public display, and burglar alarms)
- G. Composition of neighborhood (number of children, renters versus owners, old people, public versus private lives)
- H. Soils type (foundation potential)
- I. Climate
- J. Noise problem (source, level)

VIII. AGENCY INVOLVEMENT
- A. Local agencies (county or city)

    Building Department (zoning, setback, density, parking restrictions)

    Engineering Department (public utilities such as water, sewer, storm, light; fire hydrants, road widths, conditions; property description)

    Transportation Planning (road capacity, road designation, future plans)

    Assessors (ownership, history, taxes)

    Private utilities (gas and electric; water, telephone; right-of-way locations, capacity)

    Health Department (septic requirements)

- B. State agencies (federal agencies probably not involved except if they abut project site or except if one is the Federal Housing Authority

# LARGE-SCALE SITE CONCEPT DEVELOPMENT

To get started, let us assume that every cluster housing site plan must satisfy the FUNCTIONAL requirements of its residents and abutting neighbors and must provide PLEASURABLE qualities. Functional necessities include access to each unit, adequate parking, police and fire access, proper drainage, sunlight, and a measure of safety, while pleasurable qualities satisfy the need for identity, privacy, amenity, and orientation, and include preserving views, natural areas, human scale, water access, quiet, and so on. Since no two sites are the same and no two regions or climates are the same, every building problem must be solved individually.

Four factors traditionally guide a site planner in designing cluster housing:

1. What future residents desire in the way of a home: how much privacy, open space, identity, and yard; what activity needs to satisfy; how many cars to park, etc.
2. What the "character of site" suggests. Opportunities and constraints to development must be used to enhance the quality of the overall project.
3. What can be afforded. With rising costs this is becoming a great problem in site planning. Any designer can "create" a masterpiece with a large budget, but most people who need housing don't have large budgets.
4. What the local government will allow to be built, including density, setbacks, mix, height limitations, and open space requirements. This requires judgmental assessment, for many restrictions can be traded for other advantages.

At the suburban site scale, _topography_ guides development. Amenity, view, and orientation refine the plan and community structure is the end result. The desired community structure contains all values discussed in relation to the urban site: clustering units tightly to conserve open space; leaving some land undivided for common use; organizing open space into a general system rather than having isolated leftover spaces; separating pedestrian and auto circulation; interconnecting pedestrian circulation with nearby parks, schools, and shopping; and designing the total community to serve activities of all residents in a "stay-at-home community" approach.

Development Program. If the site planner has not been given a development program by the developers, he must participate in its preparation. The program must not be specific at the onset, but must take form during the site planning process according to the given physical environment.

The planner works initially with the developers to establish a feeling for their expectations, keeping decisions flexible, covering: approximate number of units; approximate ratio of resident, guest, and recreational vehicle parking spaces; anticipated household mix; desired community feeling, and recreation and service facilities to be included.

Programs are usually based on a financial evaluation of all developmental costs measured against anticipated sales or rental receipts. However, since costs can be balanced in many ways, site planners are becoming involved in the cost/ benefit process as a more effective way to justify certain site-related decisions.

A minimum unit count can often be determined from existing zoning (developers *never* build less than the allowable density); sewer or water capacity; what nearby developers have done; or what the developers have built in the past.

A complete range of household types is theoretically possible on most larger sites. However, since developers usually have experience with only a limited range of household types, they may have to be convinced of a more balanced community structure. Ideally, the mix should approximate the normal percentages in each group in the market area.

The United States breakdown of household types is:

15 % singles
15 % young couples
30 % couples with young children
12% couples with teenagers
18% couples with grown children
5% elderly couples
5% elderly singles

Desired variations of income, education, or ethnicity within a cluster should be discussed and strategies for attracting residents implemented.

Parking count depends on accessibility between the site and shopping, jobs and schools. If there is good public transportation, one car per family, with .5 guest parking per unit may do. If not, 1.5 to 2 cars plus .5 guest parking per unit may be required. Elderly need only one parking space per unit, while two or more singles living together may need one car per occupant. The planner should avoid committing to a precise number of parking spaces, instead look for a range which can later be refined.

Functional diagrams should be prepared of alternative ways to incorporate each household type within a cluster or development. Theoretically all household types can live together, but some separation often makes life more comfortable. Thus, which household types complement each other and which types may cause each other problems if they live side by side need to be considered. Generally, elderly people and young singles prefer to be separated from families with children. On the other hand, young couples or couples with grown children may serve as reasonable buffers between families with children and elderly or singles.

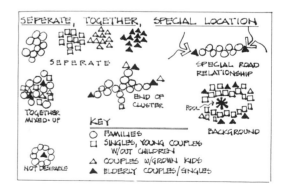

## SUBTRACTIVE PROCESS—WHAT SHOULD BE RESERVED

Land inappropriate for housing may be "subtracted" from the site. This includes all steep land, using two slope categories: 10 to 25 percent as "maybe" and 25 percent as "too steep." The 10 to 25 percent category may be refined by eliminating those areas with soil conditions subject to slippage. Also to be subtracted are major site amenities which convey an essential character or quality of the land, for instance, a meadow, a stand of trees, land bordering streams, steep cliffs, rock outcrops, old buildings, and prime vistas. Other land to be "subtracted" for preservation includes habitat areas likely to support diversity of wildlife: streams, edges of forests, bogs, or ponds. An overlap among drainage, wildlife, steep slopes, and amenity may be good because the amount of land to be reserved is minimized.

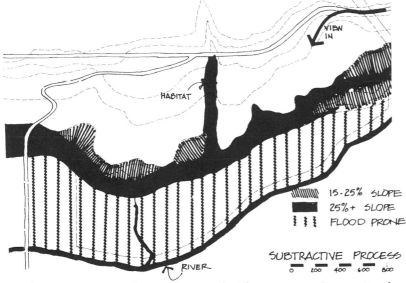

Each category to be subtracted (slope, amenity, natural process) should be outlined on the plan with a different color marker. If the diagram becomes confusing, separate plans may be drawn for each characteristic. Because the process of subtracting valued features is judgmental, each category should be accompanied with a list of implications and directions for development. Implications relate to increased construction and maintenance costs, amenity or sense of place values, or to intangible environmental factors associated with balance of life. Development directions describe actions, such as save, enhance, eliminate, relate to, use, protect, plant, extend, and so forth. Thus, each site feature becomes a guiding constraint and simplifies the decision-making process. Design becomes easier as the number of options decreases.

> In simplest terms, good ecological site planning is **doing the least to the land.** This is opposite to most suburban development standards which require wide roads, tree removal, artificial drainage structures, and uniform lotting. The less clearing, grading and disturbance you do, the better; the less disturbance to natural drainage, the better.

COMMUNITY OPEN SPACE is inextricably associated with the notion of amenity and natural factors and is the single most important environmental image maker. Determining its shape and location is the first step in concept development. At this point, we as planners select the most outstanding natural or cultural site amenities and plan the open space to include and enhance them. We should plan to make generally available the site areas most suited for public or resident use, reserving and supplementing existing vegetation. Neglected areas of the site should be improved through landscape development programs.

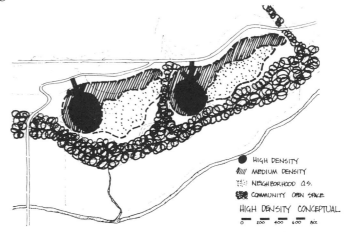

The *subtracted* elements discussed above should be linked together, attempting to create an identifiable, visible open space network. Two extreme solutions are possible:

1. An active, resident use open space system for children's play, bike riding, walking, sports, and so on. These activities are enhanced by a continual, linear open space system, free from auto intrusion, with level areas for specific activities.

2. Visual open space for light, air, amenity, and views. Very steep land, areas rich in wildlife, or fragile land may be best looked at and not made easily accessible. This approach limits resident mix to young working couples, elderly, or those without children or suggests providing a centralized recreation facility elsewhere on the site for those needing active recreation.

Recreation Facilities. Level open space should be examined for its potential as location for some community recreation

facility. Although specific facilities will be discussed later, for now it is necessary to consider only ACTIVE or PASSIVE and CENTRALIZED or DECENTRALIZED. Active implies specialization, requiring facilities such as tennis courts, basketball courts, swimming pools or ponds, horseshoe courts, etc., which may be disruptive to nearby residents. Passive recreation, such as picnicking or walking, may happen anywhere on the site, needs no facilities, and is not disruptive to nearby residents. Centralized means that most active facilities are located in one place and a community recreational focus developed. Decentralized means that the active facilities are spread out more evenly throughout the site.

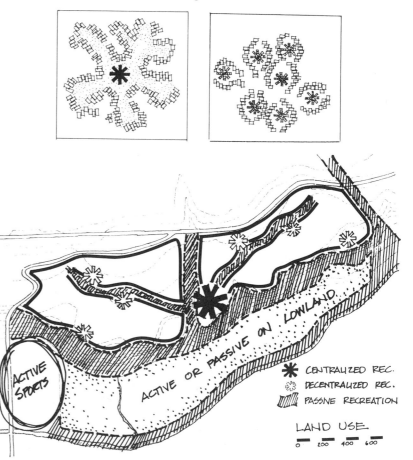

The decision to centralize or decentralize is based on a combination of site factors and program requirements which include the following.

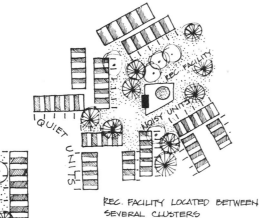

REC. FACILITY LOCATED BETWEEN
SEVERAL CLUSTERS

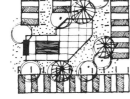

DECENTRALIZED - REC. FACILITY
IN EACH CLUSTER

1. Sites with several large level areas may use a decentralized approach with small active recreational facilities located on a number of small level areas throughout the site.
2. Small developments often benefit from grouping all facilities together to make them appear larger and to reduce construction and maintenance costs.
3. Clusters may focus on special recreational facilities in a decentralized system. In this approach, each cluster would have one special facility, such as a swimming pool, tennis court, children's play area, etc.
4. Sites with a large, level area may benefit from a centralized facility, particularly if the open space is a valley overlooked by the units. In addition, each individual cluster would have some open space around and within it. The advantage of allocating all the funds to one complex is efficiency in both construction and operation. Further, the complex can be located far enough from units to ensure privacy and quiet for all.

205

Some typical locations for recreation facilities include:

1. At the entrance, where residents and guests can see them upon entry. Recreation facilities can offer a degree of status.
2. On a high point overlooking the development.
3. In a valley, overlooked by housing units.
4. At the apex of pedestrian or auto circulation.
5. Alongside or near a natural amenity. Open space enlarges and enhances the recreation experience. It is essential not to surround recreation facilities with roadways.

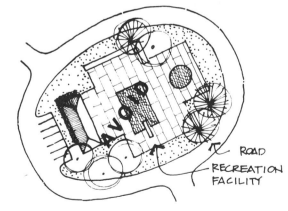

ROAD

RECREATION
FACILITY

# COMMUNITY STRUCTURE

By this time the planner should understand the site and almost be able to see community structure emerging. Four community structures are possible.

GRADUATED has a center (or several centers) from which units move out in concentric rings. Typically density decreases from the center out, and unit mix changes depending on how urban or rural the site is.

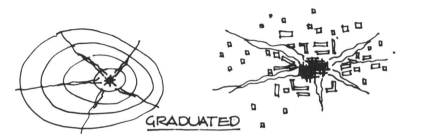

LINEAR unites the level areas with circulation in a linear pattern.

FOCUS relates each cluster of level space to the open space which formerly separated it. Open space can either separate or bind clusters. In this case clusters are bound together by their focusing on open space.

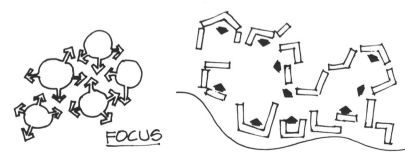

NODAL relates each cluster to itself using the open space for buffer and separation.

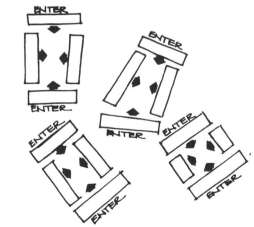

*Sense of Place,* or fundamental essence of a site, usually implies how the site might be best developed and used. If the sense of place is strongly related to a valley, meadow, or forest and the site's character would be diminished by con-

struction on it, development plans should preserve it. How closely houses may abut natural features is judgmental. However, if the feature is important enough to be shared by all residents, adequate room for a public walk should be provided and privacy in adjacent gardens maintained.

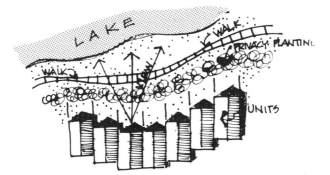

What to do:

- build heavily in impermeable soils
- use surface drainage for impermeable soils
- collect roof water runoff for site distribution
- use porous pavement, or porous paving blocks
- use swales and berms to direct runoff
- use vegetation to slow runoff
- select valuable trees for preservation
- determine "preservation strip" width for streams (100 -500')
- create storm water retention ponds
- keep roadways away from drainage swales or creeks

Design Objectives

- Minimizing disturbance to natural drainage patterns
- Reducing erosion
- Maintaining ground water balance
- Preserving biologically productive areas
- Protecting habitats of fauna and birds
- Maintaining diversity of vegetation
- Maintaining strength through size
- Maintaining continuity of the natural features
- Preventing slippage/LANDSLIDE
- Preventing flooding
- Avoiding stream degradation
- Maintaining water quality
- Maintaining the overall quality or character of the land

One word of caution at this point. The subtractive process leaves predominantly level areas with little natural attractiveness. The authors are not suggesting these are the only areas to build on. In fact, it may be best to build on more difficult areas, leaving level areas for active recreation; or to build at high densities on a small portion of sensitive land to take advantage of a dramatic view; or any of a hundred other design alternatives. Therefore, the choice is to:

> _Avoid_ potentially hazardous or ecologically productive land, or;

> _Build_ on these lands with an understanding of the risks, and design to minimize them.

FOCUSING DOWN. Once site amenities and development constraints have been identified, site planning is a matter of simultaneously interrelating several levels of design, from the total development at the largest scale to specific concerns of each cluster and unit. Each unit must become a perfect environment in every way, while clusters of units must become a perfect neighborhood.

## AUTO ACCESS

External connections to the nearest municipality should be considered next. If several existing roads abut the development, the planner should determine the most effective route based on the following criteria:

- Which road connects most directly to the nearest town?
- Which road has sufficient capacity to handle additional traffic?
- Which road could be connected to the site at the lowest cost?
- Which is the most visually pleasant route?
- Which road has adequate sight distance for moving into or away from the site?

Main entrance roads meeting existing roads should: (1) intersect at right angles, assuring visibility both ways and reducing the chance of "slipping" dangerously into traffic from an angled intersection, and (2) be long enough to allow stacking while cars wait to enter the main road. Judgment is required to anticipate the number of cars leaving the development during commuting hours and to gauge traffic levels on the existing road. Twenty feet of stacking distance should be allowed per car with no intersections crossing this space. In

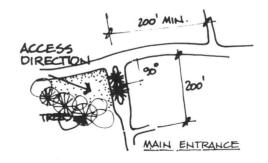

addition, main entrance roads should be located no closer than 200 feet from any existing intersection; (3) be opened visually to alert drivers to their location and allow them time to slow down; (4) serve developments up to 200 units in size per single entrance; (5) be approached from the driver's right side, enabling a free right turn into the development. If left turns are necessary, the possibilities of a left turn lane should be explored.

Small-scale developments should use the dead-end *branching pattern*, which by limiting unnecessary traffic enhances the development's environmental quality. Larger complexes of over 500 units probably require a combination of *grid and branching* patterns. The grid allows easy auto access between major living clusters, while the branching assures higher environmental quality immediately adjacent to internal clusters.

## ROADWAY LOCATION

The road is the most difficult and disruptive site planning element. Minimizing or eliminating the road will usually improve the site plan. The planner should determine how extensive a road system is required for his site, using the three road categories discussed in Chapter 4—*Major, Local, and Access.* Large sites may require all three, while smaller sites may need only an extensive Access road system. Avoiding or minimizing Major roads will make the development a better place to live.

Conceptually there are only two road patterns:

1. Branching pattern—like a tree with wide trunk and main branches accommodating large volumes of traffic, and smaller branches where theoretically traffic diminishes.
2. Grid pattern—a network of roads forming squares, rectangles, or triangles, allowing uniform through traffic on all roads. In a sense, this pattern turns its back on the issue of controlling auto traffic by saying, "let the motorist decide where to go."

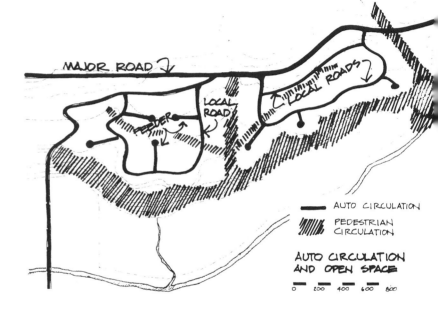

AUTO CIRCULATION

PEDESTRIAN CIRCULATION

AUTO CIRCULATION AND OPEN SPACE

0   200   400   600   800

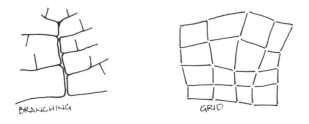

BRANCHING          GRID

All elements of the design need to be tackled at the same time without worrying about detail, size or exact scale. Broad felt tipped pens and easy flowing lines may be used to create bubble diagrams of road and cluster locations.

*Topography* is the significant design determinant because it must be considered in all circulation, open space, and house layouts. A coordinated response to topography automatically and naturally brings each system into accord with other elements of the environment; i.e., all elements of the scheme flow together. Topography is also a structuring device which gives form to any community.

Roads may be located either parallel or perpendicular to the contours. Roads *parallel* to the contours require extensive cross-sectional grading but allow easy access to downhill units and open views for all units, while roads *perpendicular* to the contours minimize grading but cause difficult unit access problems and limit views. As with all extremes, there are compromise solutions, such as a diagonal street. Other aspects of road alignment the planner should consider are:

- Avoiding difficult topography where possible, and trying not to cross streams or steep valleys with roads. If they must be crossed, the feasibility of a bridge crossing, with pedestrians moving under the road, should be explored.
- Relating roads to topography. If land forms are hilly, a curvilinear route paralleling one contour may be appropriate. Following the contours with an easy gradient provides comfort for pedestrians. Steep roads or long grades require extra power for the auto to traverse, creating bothersome noise.
- Designing roads to take advantage of unfolding views and vistas and focusing attention on desirable visual elements.
- Determining the natural drainage pattern and siting roads so the drainage pattern can be maintained.

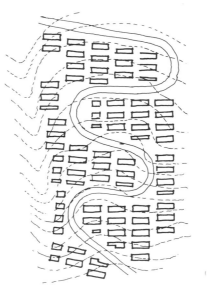

ROAD PATTERNS FOR SMALL SITES. A prime site planning objective is to combine the space allocated for housing, open space, and circulation into arrangements separating pedestrian traffic from automobile traffic. Although this is rarely possible, conflicts between pedestrians and automobiles can be minimized and roads treated according to the severity of

PARALLEL TO CONTOURS

PERPENDICULAR TO CONTOURS

the problem. Separating auto from pedestrian traffic should occur when large numbers of pedestrians are forced regularly to cross a street or when large numbers of autos conflict with pedestrian movement.

Although many sites abutting an existing county road are easiest to develop by connecting several cul-de-sac access roads to the county road, development identity will be difficult to achieve because the access roads won't be connected to each other. If suburban clusters are to relate to each other, an internal Local road is in order.

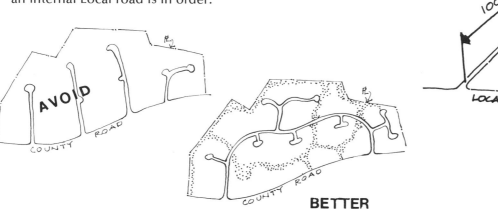

deep penetration into the site, opens up pedestrian areas, and minimizes the need for local roads. However, 1000 feet requires careful planning to prevent confusion and to assure safety and convenience. A mid-way cul-de-sac would allow some people to turn around without traveling the entire length.

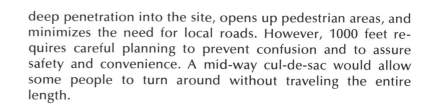

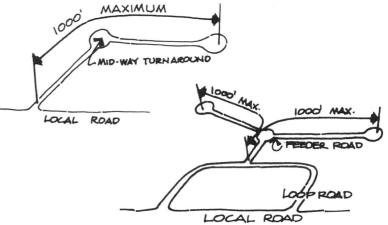

## LONG CULS-DE-SAC

Confining automobiles to the periphery of the site on long culs-de-sac is one way to create interconnected, separate pedestrian ways. This branching pattern is highly efficient and desirable. But, because it has only one exit, auto traffic can become congested.

How long is a long cul-de-sac? The FHA suggests 400 feet maximum, but the authors suggest 1,000 feet which allows

Fire trucks must have adequate passage in every site plan. (It should be pointed out that fire trucks are becoming smaller in size, and more flexible in turning, and that most firemen reach a fire even if they have to cross lawns or other landscaping.) Often the open space system can be used for emergency access.

At this point it is worth mentioning that road alignments should allow enough room for development, with the road either along *the edge* of the development serving one direction, or entering *near the center* and serving both directions. Often there is no choice since topography forces roads along more level portions for cost efficiency and ease of use. Roads in the middle of the site divide it into two open space systems with half the units relating to each space, rather than to the whole. If the site is large, this is not a problem, but if it is small, the road should be aligned closer to one side and a single centralized open space developed.

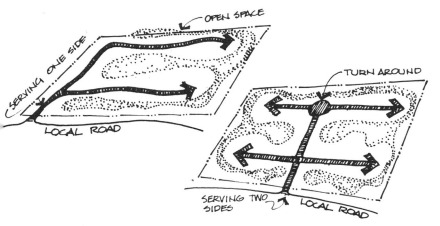

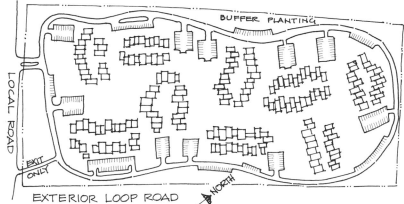

EXTERIOR LOOP ROAD

The road may be single loaded or double loaded. Double-loaded roads, which should be used where possible, are more efficient and cheaper to build since costs are shared by units on both sides. The site planner must be prepared to defend the use of a single-loaded roadway.

are seldom adequately maintained. Locating units between a ring road and the property line is a tricky task, which can most easily be accomplished by placing large family units outside the ring road, with direct auto access and oversized private gardens. Large private gardens take the place of public open

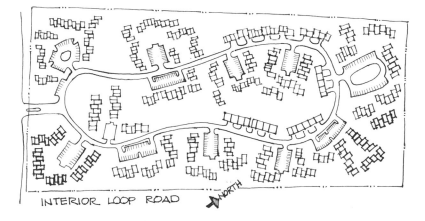

INTERIOR LOOP ROAD

*THE RING ROAD*, related to the grid, encircles the site as a large loop near its perimeter and serves interior units, or as a tighter loop closer to the center, it serves units on both sides. If the road is placed next to the property line, at least 15 feet of buffer should be left and the space carefully planted. Native plant materials are most appropriate since property line edges

space for these units. A row of single-family units also softens the transition between two properties, and often eases neighborhood concerns about higher density development. If the property abuts a park or other open space, at least 25 feet should be reserved for pedestrian circulation and units faced onto the adjoining space. Roads serving a small number of these units may weave around trees, be narrow in places, or be looped with one-way traffic. *All culs-de-sac must be two-way.* A design speed of 10-15 mph may improve abutting environmental conditions.

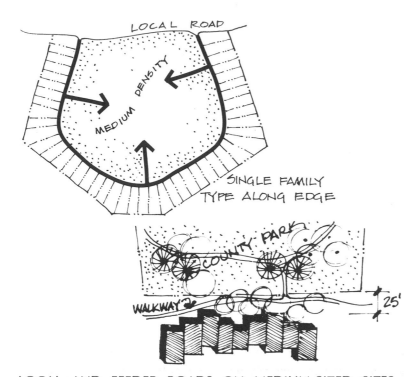

LOCAL AND FEEDER ROADS ON MEDIUM-SIZED SITES.
Local roads usually connect two major roads with a curvilinear alignment that keeps speeds down, assures a level of automobile inconvenience, and reduces short-cutting. Houses or clusters of units may front directly on local roads, although the majority of units should be served by feeder roads which are connected to a local road.

As the road system becomes larger and more complex, the number of pedestrian/auto conflicts and noise problems also increases. A principal site planning goal is to develop patterns which minimize environmental nuisances to residents. Balanced neighborhood traffic plans, called "Environmental Areas" by the Buchanan report *Traffic in Towns*, are defined as "having no extraneous traffic," and as areas within which considerations of environment predominate over the use of vehicles." The exact size of an environmental area is partly dependent on size, density, and auto use, and is governed by the need to prevent traffic from building up to a volume that causes irritation. British housing experts suggest that traffic on local roads in environmental areas should not exceed 120 vehicles per hour. Translated into houses that means 200 to 300 houses comprise an identifiable environmental area.

MAJOR ROADS form the bulkiest but shortest element of our travel network serving as efficient distributors of *auto* traffic. They provide optimum routes from any point within the site to any other point that is more than a short distance away and tend to reduce travel time for longer distances, but should not be freeways. The closest American road type is the boulevard, followed by the arterial which in its truest form is sup-

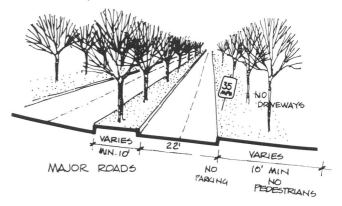

posed to serve similar purposes. Since suburban neighborhoods are likely to have existing networks of arterials, many developments may be able to connect one or two major roads running through the property, these arterials thus complementing or extending the existing road network.

Major roadway locations are determined by:

- Existing and potential connections
- Physiography
- Location of facilities and amenities
- Intensity of residential development

The GRID PATTERN, whether slightly modified or bent around topography, is the basis for a Major road system. Grid patterns distribute traffic uniformly, serve large areas, have flexibility since they are infinitely divisible into smaller units, and can be adjusted to avoid natural features or topography. The planner should first block out a basic grid, say at 2500 foot intervals, and evaluate its usefulness. Adjustments have to be made to avoid unique areas, forests, streams, and steep topography. Precise dimensions or details aren't important at this stage because the design will be adjusted and refined.

The process is one of trial and error, combining the planner's best intuition about the site with standard roadway layout patterns. While the planner is siting roads, he should remember to favor the pedestrian by developing large, auto-free areas for pedestrian activity.

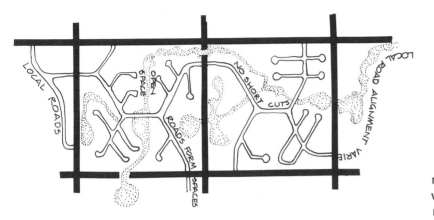

Intersections of major roads should be a minimum ¼ mile apart, with no direct access to business or residential clusters. This last point is worth repeating; if driveways interrupt major roads, traffic is slowed down and drivers use local roads, causing congestion and noise closer to the neighborhoods. Travel speed should be maximum 35 mph on major roads with no parking or sidewalks allowed alongside.

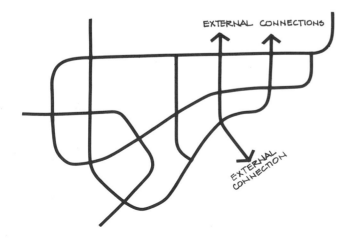

LINEAR ROAD PATTERNS may be used on narrow sites, serving development on one or two sides. A linear Major road may be aligned alongside but at some distance from a stream or natural feature. If the road is to abut a natural feature di-

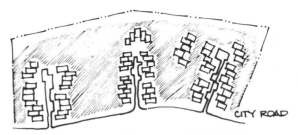

OPEN SPACE UNITES CLUSTERS NOT SERVED BY INTERNALIZED AUTO CIRCULATION

rectly, it can be relatively close allowing room for pedestrian walks. But if units are to be placed between the road and the natural feature, the distance must be greater to allow local or feeder road penetration into the site. The approximate distance can be quickly calculated by adding up assigned widths for each unit.

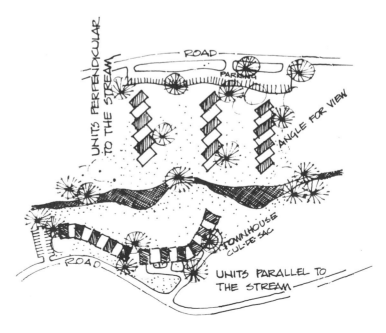

215

In summary, an ideal circulation diagram may consist of a large circular or grid loop for travel flexibility and reduction of congestion, with branching dead end streets penetrating into the center to serve housing clusters. Open space fills internal spaces between the branches, completing the travel network via pedestrian movement. Minimizing the length of road reduces costs substantially since utilities, sidewalks, lighting, and landscaping are also reduced. As many units as possible should be located *off* the road. Adequate room should be maintained for units not directly on the road. Internal circulation should be varied to match accessibility requirements. On nearing housing units, circulation should become _less_ efficient

and environmental conditions should improve. The farther from main auto access points, the fewer houses are served and the narrower roads can become.

## CLUSTER ARRANGEMENTS

The total site should now appear as a number of individual clusters, categorized according to the most appropriate user, anticipated densities, and desired environmental character. We are now ready to work within each cluster to determine the most appropriate distribution of units and the cluster arrangement. Three general arrangements related to topography, land size, amenity, orientation, and life style emerge:

LINEAR—Units in a row, either parallel or perpendicular to contours work well on steeper sites. Since access from adjacent roads or parking courts is direct, the pattern suggests individuality and dependence on the car.

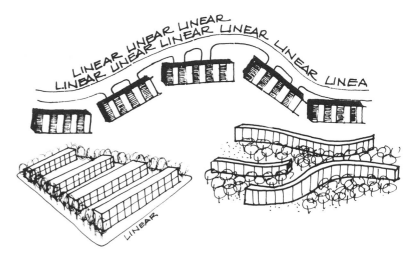

FOCUS—Court or cul-de-sac arrangements are organized around a shared access or interior space. This pattern creates the greatest sense of community.

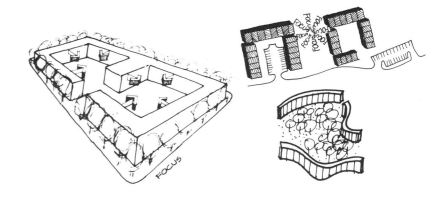

CARPET—Internal individually focused units such as patio houses or bungalows stress private space and cover large areas, particularly land without natural amenities. The pattern is rolled out like a carpet, adjustable at the edges to conform to unusual boundaries.

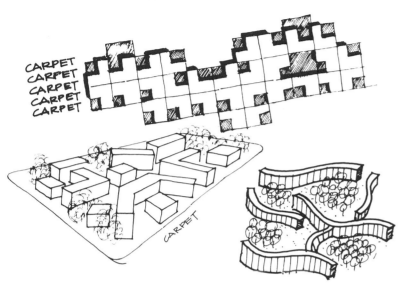

The cluster arrangements we have been talking about are superblocks, layouts with auto-free internal pedestrian spaces and with auto penetration from the perimeter. In suburban communities the designer has more opportunity to determine the size and shape of superblocks than in urban areas where existing street patterns and other constraints force the superblock to be regular and small in size. How large can superblocks be? They can be large enough for pedestrian enjoyment—for long uninterrupted walks, for play facilities and socializing areas—and at the same time small enough for automobile flexibility.

Superblocks have two dimensions, length and width, the width being critical. To determine minimum widths we should diagram several possible housing arrangements including:

1. Units parallel to the road. To approximate the space needed, we should start with an adequate setback, parking if necessary, the width of the building, a small space for private gardens, and an adequate amount of common open space, and repeat the section on the other side with backyard, house, front yard or setback, parking, and roadway. Main disadvantages are that unit backyards face each other directly. One row receives insufficient sunshine, if the open space is not aligned north and south. In addition, views from the road and pedestrian spaces are likely to be boring.

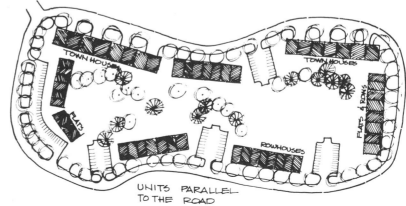

UNITS PARALLEL TO THE ROAD

217

2. <u>Units perpendicular to the road.</u> This suggests small parking courts or rear entrance roads serving single or double rows of units. A full range of open spaces, including private gardens, space between buildings, and large internal open space, is possible. The width of the superblock must be wider than that with units aligned parallel to the road.

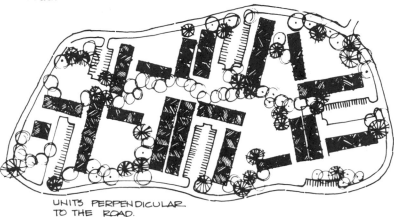

UNITS PERPENDICULAR TO THE ROAD.

3. <u>Rows of units parallel and perpendicular to roads</u> can be adjusted to fit around desirable existing site factors. Wide sections should be used for units perpendicular to the road and narrow portions for units parallel to the road. Parking arrangements may vary: for row houses or units perpendicular to the road, parking in separate lots or under buildings; for units parallel to the road, internal parking. Parking lots at one end also work well for units parallel to the road.

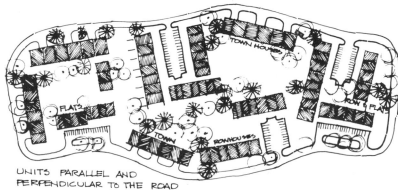

UNITS PARALLEL AND PERPENDICULAR TO THE ROAD

218

PARKING. In suburban locations auto access for residents and guests is necessary, although it is important that pedestrian routes be clear and comfortable for those preferring public transit to the automobile. Auto arrival sequences necessitate a visual connection between parking and final destination, which can be either bold and direct or subtle and indirect.

The bold approach is one in which the final destination can be seen from the parking area, while with the subtle approach the driver can see the destination *before* parking and can orientate to it after parking.

The planner should experiment with different parking arrangements described below.

1. Parking between units and the roadway is convenient since each unit has its parking space immediately in front. The major disadvantage is the relatively poor visual appearance created by a large parking lot at the entrance.

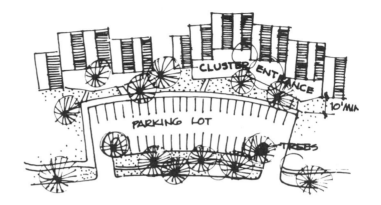

2. Parking at the ends of the buildings in small lots of 10 or 12 cars works for units parallel or perpendicular to the road, is readily accessible, and minimizes walking distances. In addition, it looks better than parking immediately in front of houses.

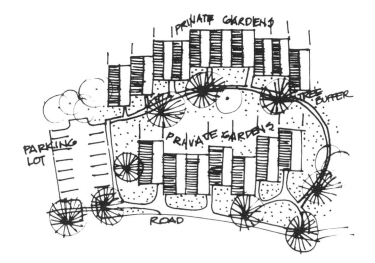

3. Parking in individual or group garages under the units conserves open space and is convenient for residents. The driveways to these garages create visual and functional dis-

ruption and must be wide for back-out safety. Since there is no central entrance, a sense of community is difficult to achieve with this arrangement.

4. Parking in large, shared garages either detached from or under a medium-density building is another parking arrangement. In considering the detached garage, centrality and land-use efficiency advantages must be weighed against the disadvantages of higher construction costs, impersonal parking, disorientation, and lack of clarity between the garage and the housing units. Detached garages don't work well for guest parking.

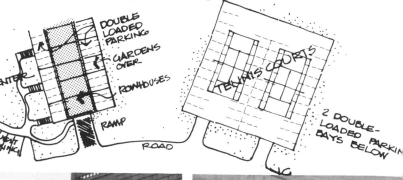

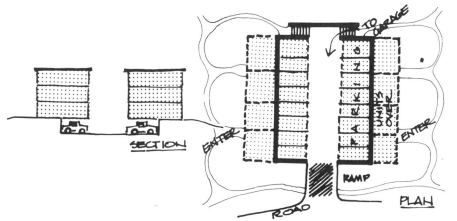

Court yard parking on suburban sites needn't be as compact and efficient as in urban developments. Parking may be around an informal center island, or may serve town houses off an entrance court using an end entrance (I or U shapes). The court may be extended as a cul-de-sac serving three or four units in a hard-to-reach corner of the site.

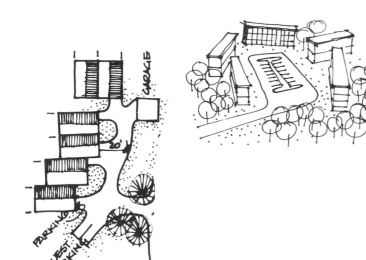

A planter strip separating sidewalk from road has been forgotten in most higher density developments. This slight luxury says OPEN SPACE, and probably isn't really a luxury.

ROAD/UNIT RELATIONSHIP. Now the planner should relate the road system to the housing program. How close should each road come to the house? Will people be willing to walk 100 feet? 100 yards? Upstairs? Along a covered path? How far people will walk varies with their age, health, family composition, and attitude. In general a 200-foot walk is maximum. A factor to consider is the distance garbagemen and tradesmen are willing to walk from their vehicles, usually 150-200 feet. If stairs are necessary, the distance may have to be shortened.

The cluster entrance sequence should be considered next. Where should cars leave the road and enter the cluster? This, of course, relates to parking arrangements. Long linear sites or steep sites suggest parking near the road rather than pene-

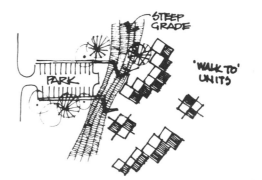

trating the site with a feeder road. Conversely, deep sites are best served by a feeder road leading to parking courts or individual drives. Town houses with internal parking require road access. Patio and row houses can be located off the road, with parking handled nearby in grouped arrangements.

The highest density units should be located so they connect efficiently to the external road/transit system and lower density units located toward distant edges. It would be desirable to designate buffer zones to separate living areas from busy roads.

TOPOGRAPHY. Sites with steep topography or unique natural features benefit from clustered units because density is concentrated so some areas are left free from development. Conversely, level sites or those without unique features may be developed more uniformly over the entire site, with open space allocated privately or for a group of units. Although steep land is more expensive to build on, it may be necessary if level land is scarce. If there is *only* enough level land for either recreational uses or housing, it is more acceptable to spend money to create level areas for houses than to create level areas for recreation and open space. With population mixes requiring large, level areas for open space use, the best land must be selected for that use first and slightly steeper slopes used for clusters of living units.

UPHILL VERSUS DOWNHILL—Roads paralleling contours have an uphill and downhill side, which can create difficulties for cluster access. Generally, downhill access is preferred since the cluster is overviewed from the car and is more imageable. Access is direct and change of grade can be accommodated within individual units instead of in public circulation routes.

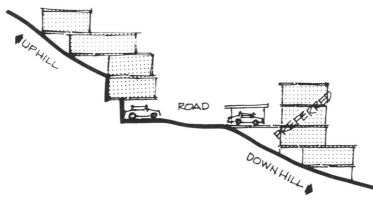

VIEWS—Units whose major living areas have a view are always the first units sold or rented. We, as planners, should consider the following questions regarding views. Is there a dramatic view which should be shared by all units? Is there a unique land form such as a meadow, lake, forest, hillside or stream which should be reserved for all, and might determine the clustering arrangement? Are there scattered small features such as clumps of trees, outcrops, or small glens providing a pleasant close-up view around which housing units might be clustered? Is there a *best orientation* providing sunlight, winter wind protection, and view? We should study each slope with sections to find ways to use distant views without retaining walls or steep banks. We should note carefully the exact percent of slope so that building spacing can be determined to assure views to units behind. Figuring floor-to-floor heights at 9 feet, we may experiment with using half-levels created by living spaces above one-floor units.

- Territorial views suggest arranging units along the edge of the level land, giving each part of the view.

- Dramatic views suggest tall, compact units, giving all units an uninterrupted view.
- Views into a valley are preferable to views out from a valley.

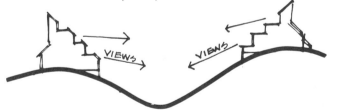

- Panoramic views suggest tall buildings on the higher elevations, with lower units terracing down the slope.

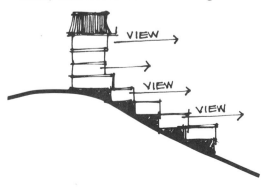

- V-shaped clusters can be oriented so each unit looks out on the view.

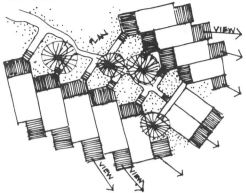

- Natural attractions, such as trees, interesting topography, or rock outcrops, relate well as a focus for small clusters of units.

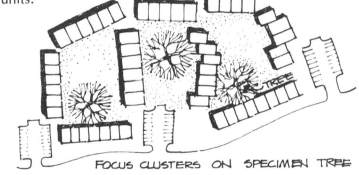

FOCUS CLUSTERS ON SPECIMEN TREE

223

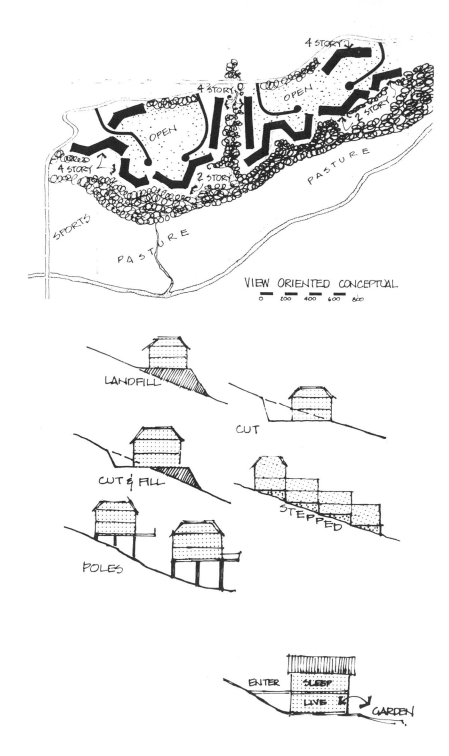

VIEW ORIENTED CONCEPTUAL

0  200  400  600  800

LANDFILL

CUT

CUT & FILL

STEPPED

POLES

ENTER  SLEEP
LIVE
GARDEN

## PLACING BUILDINGS ON SLOPING LAND

We should avoid placing buildings exactly on top of a hill. Since the top of a hill is likely to be windy, it is best to build on the brow, just before the grade steepens, so that protection against the wind will be gained and the hill's intrinsic quality saved.

Siting houses on steep slopes is conceptually quite simple; it involves constructing a level area with foundations, framing, or grading and constructing a house on the level area. Five approaches are possible.

_Land fill_—Grading soil out from a slope to create a level area. There may be problems: first, fill material may be expensive to acquire; second, sloping between level pads consumes land which is costly; third, the chance of erosion is increased; and lastly, fill may settle causing structural problems within the building.

_Cut_—Cut, the opposite of fill, is created by carving a level area from a slope. The level area, then, is on existing stable soil, erosion is minimized, and slopes can be steeper. The only problem is how to dispose of the dirt removed.

_Cut and fill_—This is the in-between or balanced solution. If structures are constructed on cut areas, and parking, roads, or other activity areas are relegated to fill area, a balanced grading scheme can be developed.

_Stepped foundations_—Working up a slope with stepped concrete foundations creates voids beneath the main floors. This method can be environmentally sound, though contractors tend to tackle the job with oversized equipment causing erosion and displacing vegetation.

_Pole Foundations_—Telephone or concrete poles are the least disruptive to the landscape if properly installed, and are relatively inexpensive.

Units running parallel to the contours have all entrances and gardens at approximately the same elevation. Entrances on steep slopes are on an upper floor, while living/eating rooms are on a lower floor with direct access to the garden. On the other hand, in units running perpendicular to the contours each entrance is at a different elevation. Units should be fit to the site, terracing down the hill to minimize cut and fill, and to add variety.

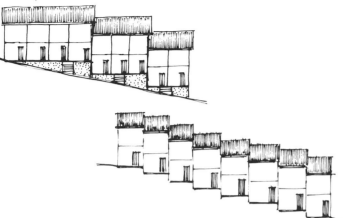

If soil and geologic conditions indicate no slippage problems, building on steep slopes can work. Since steep land suggests no direct auto access to units, walking may be required. Thus, steep developments may not be good for large families, elderly, or the handicapped, but work well for more agile resident types.

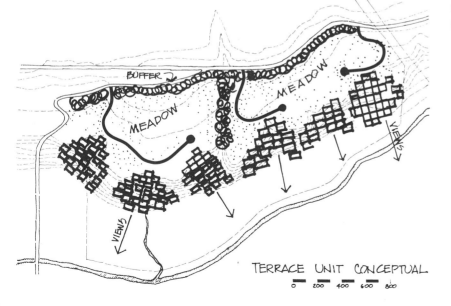

TERRACE UNIT CONCEPTUAL

0   200   400   600   800

LOOK, DO NOT TOUCH. At high densities, fragile landscapes may not recover from overuse and should be treated as visual rather than usable areas. The secret to preservation lies in limiting or eliminating access by:

- Planting with impenetrable vegetation.
- Dividing fragile lands into private ownership with individual responsibility for maintaining the land. Determining where people should and should not go is a prime site planning function.
- Aligning walkways and use areas away from fragile land. Most people are instinctively attracted to fragile areas; we are all intrigued by steep cliffs, marshy areas, small creeks, and unique vegetation. A walk might be constructed through a portion of the fragile areas and residents allowed some access in trade for no access elsewhere.

## ACCESS ROADS

Access roads are laid out last—inserted after open space and house type have been determined. In principle, feeder roads are located in the worst location environmentally, to the north, and away from desirable views. This low priority doesn't mean we can ignore it as a site planning problem since adequate space for maneuvering, parking, and buffer must be provided, and a careful relationship created between the auto and each unit. Enough room for access roads must be reserved during the early site planning phases.

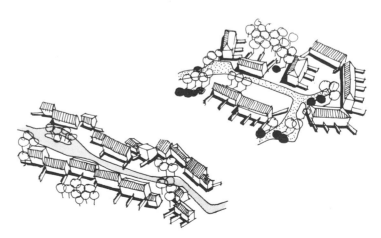

225

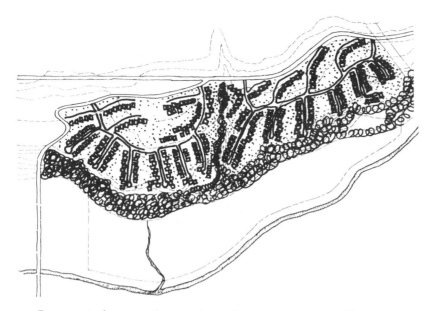

Design, and not just traffic considerations, plays a major role in local and access road layout. The site planner is orchestrating a sequence of open space views from the auto, eliminating the view in places and opening it up elsewhere. By simulating an auto trip through the site during design, we can sense where logical open space expansion is appropriate, e.g., at the development entrance, at bends in roads, at view spots, or at recreational facilities. Auto efficiency may be low as long as experience is high.

The right-of-way width may be varied to relate to abutting features. For instance, the road may be widened to include a grove of trees, stream, meadow, or view of an interesting natural feature. Portions of open space should be allocated to roadways, so that part of the feeling of an open space community is experienced from the automobile. Two opposite open space solutions are presented here, with numerous compromises possible.

For most clusters, the road needn't serve autos efficiently. In other words, roads may be narrow and turning radius small, so that overall pedestrian safety and use increase. Parking must be organized to minimize conflict, and defined with expanded sidewalk or planter areas. Major pedestrian walks may cross access roads as raised speed bumps or paved with different materials. Pavement widths for two-way access roads may be as little as 18 feet, certainly no wider than 20 feet. Parking bays should be 7 feet wide for parallel parking, and 20 feet for perpendicular. And, turning radius at corners may be as little as 2 feet, to limit travel speed.

A loop cul-de-sac is different from the cul-de-sac discussed earlier in that the loop is larger and facilitates traffic flow. Internal parking courts for small clusters (10 to 12) may wrap around a lawn area.

First, pedestrian and auto circulation may be _combined_ with the open space allocated along the roadways. This maximizes pleasant views from the auto, and minimizes construction and maintenance costs since only one pedestrian walk system has to be provided. However, resident recreational needs, as well as peace, quiet, and safety, are often not best served by open

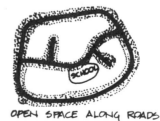

OPEN SPACE ALONG ROADS

INTERNAL OPEN SPACE

space adjacent to a road. Second, _separating_ most of the pedestrian system from the roadway ensures privacy, quiet, and safety for residents. Open space may be linked to roads in key locations such as at a school, park, recreation center, or pedestrian drop-off space.

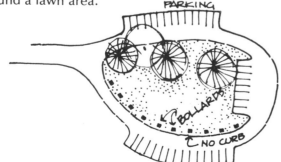

PARKING

BOLLARDS

NO CURB

On the other hand, separating pedestrians from vehicular traffic reduces surveillance potential, places pedestrians on both sides of houses, but provides more protection from automobile dangers.

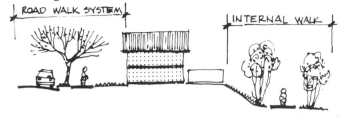

Open Space serves three broad functions which when related to architecture create a total unified environment. These functions may overlap for multiple use. The three functions are:

1. Pleasurable Open Space. This space is necessary to ensure a desirable quality of living and includes walks, malls, greenways, parks, and play areas.
2. Service Open Space. This functional open space includes streets, parking areas, roadways, and service space. These areas, often only marginally developed, must be totally landscaped to become an integral and pleasant part of the environment.
3. Open Space to Create Form and Image. The appearance and feeling of the community is determined by a combination of buildings and landscape. In higher density areas, buildings and building groupings dominate the landscape, forming the identifiable spaces. Here, open space plays a minor role as form giver, but is vitally important for recreation, service, and continuity. In less dense areas, where buildings tend to be separate and lack identifiable form, open spaces provide the unifying element.

Safety tradeoffs must be considered in determining the best location for pedestrian circulation. The road, our most public zone, is easy to survey and control, and therefore provides more safety for pedestrians from attack; yet it is not safe from autos and the dangers they imply. Pedestrian circulation adjacent to a road has many surveillance possibilities: from passing autos, nearby front doors, windows of adjacent buildings, or other pedestrians. Additionally, night walking is lit by street lights and emergency call boxes are nearby. Abutting residents can count on pedestrian traffic being on only one side of their homes.

For interest, tight spaces should be contrasted with larger open areas. Contrast is a basic principle in medium-density design; that is, making each area identifiable. The open space system should be extended to all areas of the site: over land reserved for utilities, along peripheral barriers or screens, along roadways, and around (as screening) site services such as parking, garbage disposal, and laundry. Open space should integrate all portions of the site as part of a pedestrian or bicycle path, or be used for community gardens, or even for wildlife habitat. The hierarchy of open spaces should be developed as discussed in Chapter 4 where it was considered in three categories: *Community Open Space*, consisting of the largest scale elements and amenities relating to the whole community; *Neighborhood Open Space*, consisting of smaller scaled elements oriented to the immediate residential community; and *Development Open Space*, consisting of public components immediately around a cluster such as streets, sidewalks, playgrounds, meeting places, and even private gardens.

CREATING OPEN SPACE AMENITY. If a site has open space with no character, elements of interest and focus may be added. For instance, a lake might be created as the central focus if soil conditions and topography are right and there is a

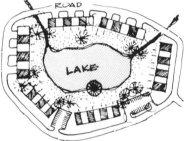

source of water. Public circulation must be provided along any amenity, even if it must pass near residential units. If this circulation is placed *below* units, on a hill, there is little loss of privacy for residents.

Focus may be on recreational spaces (pool, sauna, recreation building, and outdoor activity areas) or on natural elements (such as streams, or drainage routes) which can be adapted to passive recreational purpose. For instance, a path system might be designed along and across a stream which might be dammed in places to create ponds; the stream might serve the dual purpose of providing views for units.

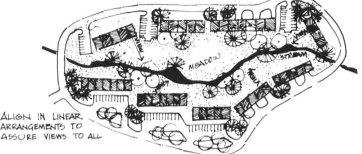

ALIGN IN LINEAR ARRANGEMENTS TO ASSURE VIEWS TO ALL

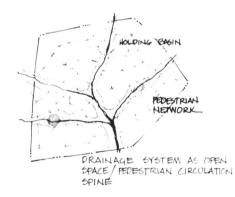

DRAINAGE SYSTEM AS OPEN SPACE / PEDESTRIAN CIRCULATION SPINE

228

A golf course, though expensive to construct, serves as an open space focus and as a promotional feature. Paths can be worked in carefully for long walks (though golfers usually aren't happy sharing their space with nongolfers), views opened from the road, and high density units placed strategically around it, with low-density units in areas with less amenity. Since an 18-hole golf course needs approximately 140 acres, the total development size would have to be substantial.

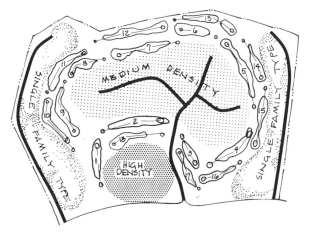

HOLLOW CORE SITE MODEL. Sites with varied or complex topography may be more easily understood by building a study model constructed of chipboard or corregated cardboard using the HOLLOW CORE technique. This technique uses less material than the solid core method and is quick to build, but requires care during fabrication. The chipboard should approximate or slightly exaggerate the contour interval. All contours should be traced onto *two sheets* of chipboard using carbon paper,,and each numbered. For very steep sites with small contour intervals, it may be necessary to use four sheets, skipping a contour between and allowing additional room for gluing. All *even* numbered contours should be cut from one sheet and all odd contours from the other. The contours placed one on top of the other should be aligned with the traced line and glued together. A thick coat of white glue works well. As the model becomes tall, it will need internal support from cardboard scraps.

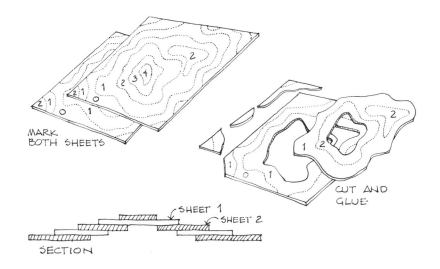

## SITE CONCEPT DEVELOPMENT—SUMMARY

The site planning proces we have been discussing is meant to be logical and rational in contrast to the intuitive design process which seemingly does not rely on reason. Not knowing why but sensing correctness, however, is a powerful design tool which can be used to establish how we feel about the site. Intuition utilizes the power of mind to perceive proper solutions, to respond to certain situations or conditions based on experience. This intuitive design method does have two problems, both of which can be overcome:

• The process limits solutions to those experienced by the designer and tends to repeat existing conditions and past mistakes.
• As the scale of projects increases, the complications and cause/effect relationships increase geometrically, resulting in situations so complex and interrelated as to be beyond the capability of our intuitive skills.

To guard against these problems, intuition should be used as a brainstorming, motivational process; an easy way to begin. We might start with a sketch solution to the problem, a two-hour stab without any analysis or baseline data, and ask ourselves these questions: How do we feel about the land? What should go where? What should be preserved? What is not important? We should generate ideas quickly and test each idea in a systematic manner. Schemes should be altered and reconsidered. All information generated during the site analysis and programming process becomes accessible as part of the intuitive process, as does every experience of our past.

One last comment on intuition is that it works well in noncritical situations where budget is generous and errors of judgment can be corrected. If, however, the budget is tight or there are critical natural and social concerns, intuition should be used carefully.

Site Concept Development involves interrelating your best judgments on maximizing 1. *Future resident needs, and 2. The Character of the Site* within costs affordable by residents and as allowed by local jurisdictions. The process involves first weaving unique and fragile lands into an open space system for resident use. Access, circulation patterns, and cluster locations are then added and interrelated. These first bold diagrams can then be refined by focusing down and studying individual clusters, detail road alignments and open space. The following suggestions outline considerations in this focusing process.

- Start with a higher density than necessary, with the idea that density might be decreased later.
- Provide a private, identifiable ground-level front door access to each unit. Ground-oriented access is the easiest access for most Americans to relate to.
- Block buildings first in bold form, forgetting about detail variations.
- Insert special units—single-family, attached villas, or patio houses—in odd spots where nothing else seems to work.

- Try various parking arrangements—open lots, garages, and group lots under buildings.
- Select and draw both the inside and outside of each unit, not the entire detail floorplan but at least room names, and placement of exterior doors and windows.
- Grade each building site as a small, level terrace, and avoiding extensive retaining walls.
- Adjust unit types, setback, and heights to reduce density to the desired level.
- Design low-cost developments around one or two basic, trailable modules, 12 feet wide by 30 feet long for a utility core and 60 feet long for living/sleep areas.
- Attach four to ten units. Attaching units together in a continuous building reduces side yard space and construction costs.
- Make sure units are open on at least two opposite sides, to ensure ventilation and arranging units so views are of open space, not other units.
- Draw a design section through each building and assess its desirability.
- Avoid locating roads between units and a site amenity. Never locate pedestrian facilities on an island surrounded by roads.
- Assure public pedestrian access to communal amenity, even between units and the amenity. A walk between units and an amenity makes the connection between the two public so the walk should be far enough from units to prevent loss of privacy.
- Face some clusters inward on planted and paved courts where young children play. Connect each by pedestrian pathways through the site.
- Provide one-story units for the elderly. If that isn't possible, design units with a bedroom and most living space on the ground floor.
- Where possible, create a single-family home feeling. Instead of conventional rows of similar units around a large common area, create a series of mini-clusters of 4-20 units.

# SITE REFINEMENT

By now the planner should have a conceptual site plan, or series of alternative plans, worked out in overall scale but not in detail. The following should have been identified or located diagrammatically:

- Site planning program requirements
- Development concept
- Entrance points and major circulation patterns
- Community open space

And the following should have been identified roughly:

- Cluster locations
- A housing approach, including

    unit types
    best orientations
    access and parking

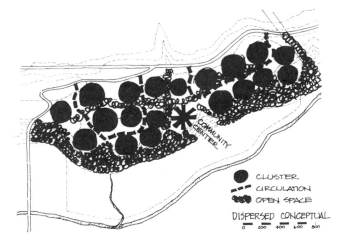

The task ahead involves refining each cluster, adjusting the relationship of cluster to cluster, and making adjustments to the overall plan. The refinement process consists of identifying and designing each cluster, the space and relationships between clusters, each individual unit, the circulation system, and the overall open space system.

# CLUSTERS

Before beginning the refinement process, let us review for a moment. Individual units are clustered when they visually and functionally relate to one another. Clusters may be bound together by:

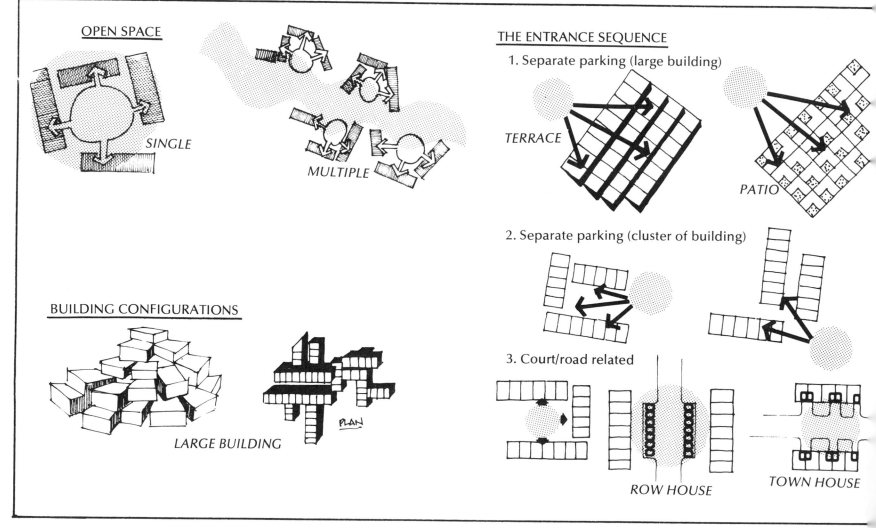

OPEN SPACE

SINGLE

MULTIPLE

BUILDING CONFIGURATIONS

LARGE BUILDING

PLAN

THE ENTRANCE SEQUENCE

1. Separate parking (large building)

TERRACE

PATIO

2. Separate parking (cluster of building)

3. Court/road related

ROW HOUSE

TOWN HOUSE

This is a judgmental process with a number of possible arrangements. For instance, all units may be focused on the entry space, units may be focused on interior open spaces, or the arrangements of units may be mixed. It is often possible for units to have several different focuses; an entry shared with one cluster and a rear yard shared with another.

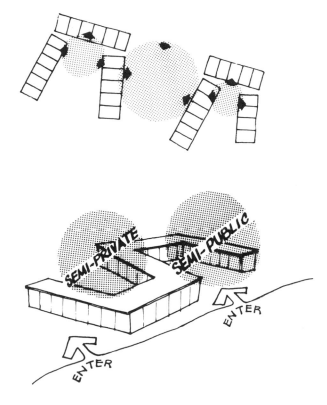

Through the refinement process, the concerns expressed earlier are still valid. Each unit must:

- Achieve privacy at the entrance and garden
- Have an outdoor space which receives some sunshine daily (south, southeast, southwest preferred)
- Be provided with as good a view as possible.

Each cluster should be reviewed to determine if it is in an area that would be expensive to develop such as steep slopes or flood prone areas, or it infringes on amenity such as trees, streams, etc. It is important to realize the vegetation within a construction zone is difficult to save because of the considerable grading and moving of heavy materials needed to construct reasonably priced medium-density housing. To keep expenses down and to preserve amenities, these adjustments may be made to clusters

- Reducing density near sensitive areas
- Stepping or turning buildings to avoid a condition
- Increasing or decreasing building heights
- Varying unit types
- Removing parking from near the units

DENSITY. Density may be varied from cluster to cluster in response to site conditions. Higher density may be desirable:

- Near the entrance of the development, thereby minimizing traffic in the interior of the site.
- Overlooking a major visual amenity, with all units receiving a view.
- Near public congregation areas—a transit stop, shopping, office complex, or recreational facility. Some residents are willing to give up the serenity of a natural landscape for the convenience of public and cultural facilities.
- Clustered near a sensitive area, with the remainder left undisturbed. It may be desirable to locate one high-density cluster along a lake, river, or stream leaving the remainder open.

# High Density Arrangements

High density housing means primarily:

Using high rise

Using stacked flats

Using maisonettes

Using back-to-back units

Parking in communal garages

235

"Look at every Main Street of every town in America and ask yourself 'who cares?' Nobody cares about community, divinity and humanity, and you can prove it by asking people what they care about. In terms of shelter they care about downpayment and location. Give me downpayment and location and I'll outsell community, divinity and humanity on any street corner."

Victor H. Palmiere
Pres. James Corporation
Land Developers

CLUSTER AND COMMUNITY. Cluster implies community, individuals living in a common location. Community requires a certain density, order, and beauty, and should be a source of pride. Community means lack of isolation, and familiar contacts and experiences. Community becomes a socializing factor; people need other people to talk to and share experiences with. Community is usually territorial, people identifying with other people within a specific area and sharing with each other the growth and health of their common territory.

A designer's task is twofold: first, to create an imageable territory which can be appreciated, enjoyed, and protected; and second, to create arrangements which allow residents to meet, share experiences, and converse with each other.

Identity of Clusters. Most people want their house, or at least immediate neighborhood, to stand out and be recognizable. Clusters of units within a development should appear as a unified whole, yet each cluster should in some way be distinguishable from other nearby clusters. There are several design approaches to create distinction.

1. The most positive approach is to separate clusters with an expanse of open space including tall trees. Other forms of open space (a buffer, stream, road, playfield, or schoolyard) may make a cluster recognizable.

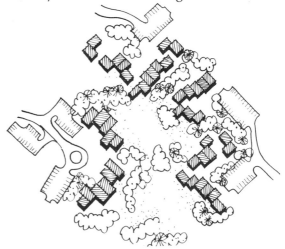

2. Paint, even slight variations of the same color, may help create a distinction between clusters of units with similar architectural forms.

3. The architectural theme may vary from cluster to cluster. Architectural forms may be used to distinguish clusters and provide identity—cantilevered forms; vertical or horizontal massing; traditional or contemporary arrangements. Variations in architectural arrangement (but with the same architectural style) create subtle differences.

> Mass, silhouette and spatial variations are qualities which can be manipulated. Unity can be achieved with similar color, material, architectural detailing, and fences.

4. Planting can distinguish clusters—a thematic tree or ground cover, carefully placed specimen trees, or just the extensiveness and maintenance of a well cared for garden.
5. A housing cluster with only *one* access point increases identity and promotes interactions of residents.
6. Compact clusters separated by open, natural areas, provide cohesion in the development because of contrast between built and unbuilt. The *edge* becomes the distinguishing element.

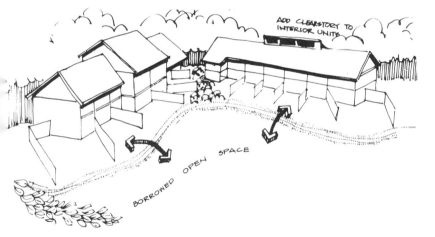

7. Lastly, compact development with amenities in easy walking distance fosters neighborhood identity. If the development is so large that a car is necessary, the trip gives a feeling of going somewhere and identity is diminished.

DEFENSIBLE SPACE. Allocating definable spaces to adjacent housing clusters creates *defensible space* according to Oscar Newman. Defensible space is an environment which induces hidden territoriality and sense of community in the inhabitants, creating a safe, productive, and well-maintained living space. Theoretically, outsiders perceive the open space as belonging to its residents, leaving him a foreigner and easily recognized as an intruder.

How can defensible space be created? The key lies in Separating public and private space, creating a feeling in outsiders that the land belongs to residents. At the same time, residents can feel their space is extended in the street if their windows overlook it, their entrances are on or near it, or their open space abuts it. This extension of defensible space causes residents to care about and protect the street near their clusters, but it also causes them to lose some privacy. Thus, the designer must resolve this dilemma in creating defensible space.

Define communal spaces with buildings.

Separate and identify individual or cluster entrance with a change in grade.

Separate and identify public from commun—al space with a change in grade.

Relate some entries directly to public spaces or the street.

Minimize the number of families using each cluster entry.

Visually extend private space to the street.

Face some windows onto common open spaces.

Newman, Oscar
*Defensible Space*
New York, The Mac Millan Co., 1972

Use low or perforated fences.

Create a single family image.

238

Communities with complete services tend to stimulate the sense of community—that is, with all necessary elements of life present, you can devote your full energies to that community. A walk to work community furthers this—placing emphasis and commitment in the home community. Easy access to good public transportation contributes to an improved life style.

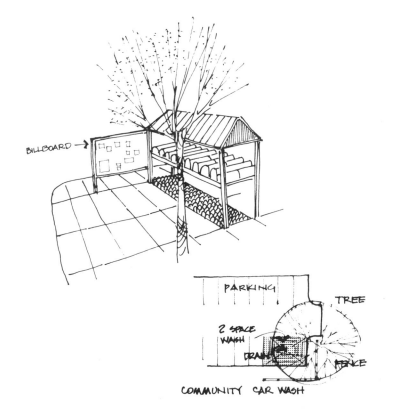

BILLBOARD →

PARKING

2 SPACE WASH

DRAIN

TREE

FENCE

COMMUNITY CAR WASH

At the other extreme, many new communities are ignoring the defensible space concept and are instead relying for security on enclosed, fortified spaces complete with gates, closed circuit television, and security guards. The two concepts are not necessarily incompatible; it is possible to provide a defensible open space focus inside "enclosed communities." The biggest roadblock is the attitude of the people who seek an enclosed community for prestige, as well as security, and are neither flexible nor anxious to socialize with their neighbors.

CLUSTERING FOR SOCIAL CONTACT. There are many ways in which a site planner may arrange clusters and other spaces to allow for social contacts and to encourage congeniality. Auto parking, cluster entrance, services, private gardens, and common open space are places where neighbors might meet. Meeting is more likely if residents spend a good portion of their leisure time in the development and if the development is oriented to pedestrians. Pedestrian orientation requires compact arrangements and short distances between amenities and shared facilities so people can meet freely and comfortably. Some typical meeting places include:

*Common Laundry.* The laundry is another likely place for neighbors to meet. The laundry room should be pleasant and comfortable, possibly related to an outdoor garden.

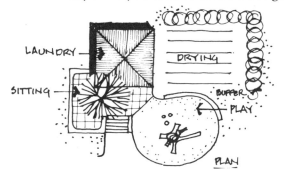

LAUNDRY

DRYING

SITTING

BUFFER

PLAY

PLAN

*Community Mailboxes.* Clustering mailboxes allows neighbors to meet "accidentally" while picking up their mail. A small board for messages enhances the community role of mailboxes.

*Car Wash Facility.* The facility, which need be little more than a shaded area designated for car wash with several hoses and

239

a drain, is a good place for neighbors to meet while pursuing a common interest—taking care of the car.

*Centralized Bus Station*-covered, well lit, with benches and message board allows residents to visit while waiting for the bus.

*Allotment Gardens.* Small garden plots for residents living on upper floors or those without a large enough garden space.

*Recreation Facilities.* Complete recreation facilities tailored to expected resident needs serves as a focus for social interactions.

*Entrance Gardens* with low fences so residents using them can visit with passing neighbors.

BUILDING VARIATIONS. Row and town houses have developed a reputation for being primarily cost-efficient house types necessary to solve low income housing needs. Far from it, both now serve increasing numbers of families in all income ranges who insist on high quality design and who want their no-maintenance advantage.

When cost is a problem, variations and extensions beyond the basic box should be kept to a minimum. When cost isn't the principal concern, variations turn the stereotypical box into exciting living. In addition, many architectural and landscape elements can be used to enrich the development without adding excessive costs.

- A flat roofed carport may be connected to a second-floor master bedroom with a bridge to be used as a roof garden.

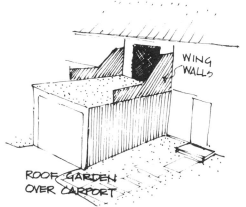

- The size and shape of walled garden patios may be altered to achieve variety. Also, fences extend the apparent size of buildings if the same material is used. Constructing repetitive units makes sense from a cost standpoint, with varied fence locations individualizing the units.

- Buildings may be connected by skybridge at the second and third story allowing horizontal movement above the ground floor.

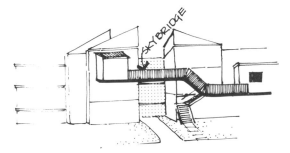

- Carports are separable from the unit and can be used to enlarge or diminish the apparent size of a building complex, create new spaces, or provide needed privacy. Auto entrances can be straight in (minimizing driveway length) or from the side (requiring more paving).

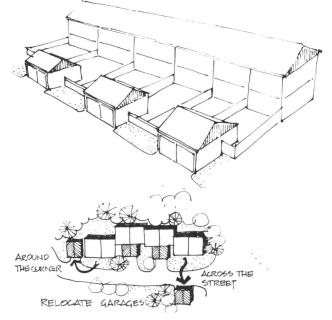

- Since covered parking is always preferred, carports may be added to some spaces in parking courts. The parking bay should be widened to at least 10 feet (11 or 12 is better) and the roof constructed. The carport may be tied to the building architecturally by roof shape, material, or color.

GARDEN APARTMENTS ARE NOT ENOUGH—Most garden apartments end up two stories high with uniform small private gardens resulting in an overall boring and dull development. Any contrast helps, including the following variations:

- using different shaped and sized buildings
- adding extra floors
- adding windows to the end unit
- mixing units (3 bedroom plus 1 bedroom)
- alternating units
- reversing unit
- flopping unit
- zig zagging units
- staggering units

- Covered walks connecting parking to units both shelter residents and create new spatial configurations. Although, it may be too expensive to shelter the entire distance, covering the busiest portion helps.
- Storage sheds for prams, bicycles, garden tools, and lawn furniture, are useful elements in defining space and adding variety to the entrance or private garden.

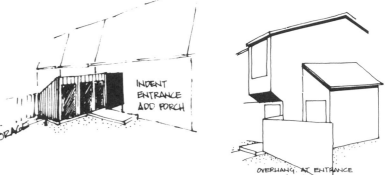

- Cantilevered space over an entrance shelters guests from rain and increases apparent interior space. Cantilevers may extend to 4 feet, with posts required for longer distances.
- Pierce end walls with windows or doors, or add a room or bay window for a more spacious dining, den or bedroom.

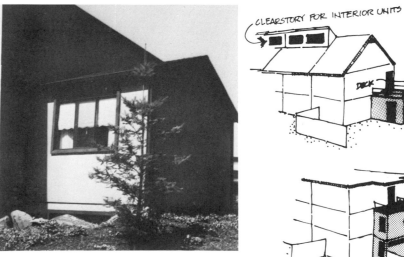

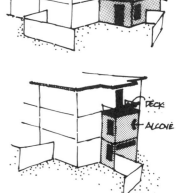

- Fin walls may be extended through the roof to further identify each unit. Roof lines and facades may be varied to identify individual units, while coherence is maintained with uniform materials or colors.

- Stacked flats may be combined with town houses to eliminate a driveway and avoid the look of sameness.

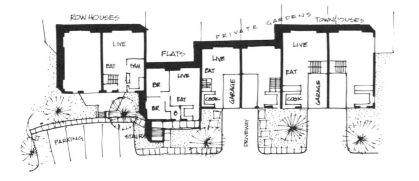

- One row house unit may be turned sideways, to combine a long side with the typical narrow fronts. Row and town houses may function with either the narrow or deep side out; the narrow side is normally used to conserve space with the deep side used minimally as a variation.

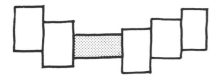

TURN ONE UNIT SIDEWAY

BACK-BACK UNITS. The authors recommend against arrangements which join on three sides because of problems with ventilation, daylight, and proper orientation. For example, the principal culprit is the double-loaded corridor apartment, where entrance noise, lack of privacy and poor orientation are almost unsurmountable problems. The fourplex is an exception, since two sides are always exposed to daylight, thereby assuring interior lighting and ventilation.

Some portions of a site may not lend themselves to attached row blocks, but are still worthwhile developing with some form of housing. Floating units, small buildings placed alone in the landscape, may be just the solution. The floating fourplex, a single-story building approximately 50 feet square with four one-bedroom units, is very flexible. Adding a second floor increases the unit count to eight or enlarges the units to two bedrooms.

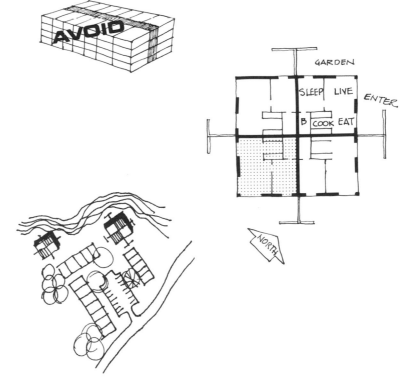

If fourplexes utilities, which may be prefabricated, are grouped efficiently around the core. Private gardens may be located off living and dining rooms or bedrooms by adding a door, a small fence, and some planting. Sun may be a problem, since each unit has a different orientation, but aligning the building 45 degrees to north assures some sunlight in all units. Indenting with an atrium on one wall allows more light into the deepest rooms.

Single-family arrangements may be created using a pinwheel fourplex serviced directly by a loop road. This arragement is road extensive and has little community open space, but all the qualities of a single-family residence are duplicated.

Two other variations which avoid double loaded corridor access problems are:

1. Separating the rows slightly and entering via an open air access.
2. Back-to-back row houses with entrance and garden combined on opposite sides of the building.

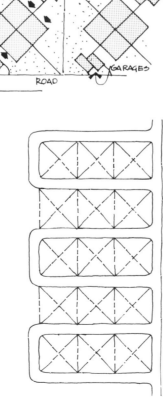

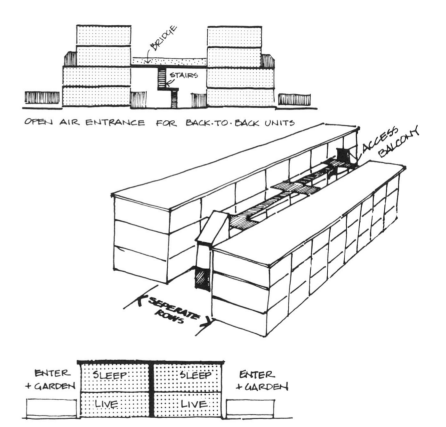

OPEN AIR ENTRANCE FOR BACK-TO-BACK UNITS

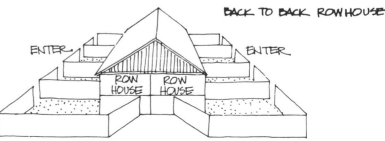

BACK TO BACK ROWHOUSE

# CLUSTERS ON SLOPING SITES

<u>Terrace Units.</u> Tall buildings may increase the heights of hills, and the remainder of development arranged around them in a variety of subsidiary groups. Buildings may cascade down a slope and split at half levels to take up grade. Thus, through terracing, all units are able to enjoy ground orientation, view, and proper sunlight. Slopes allow an increase in density without sacrificing privacy or increasing noise.

The conventional way to handle residential development on steep slopes is to use pads, which require extensive grading, can result in loss of vegetation and topsoil through erosion, and create visual degradation. Building on poles or extended foundations may be better, with units terracing down the slope to minimize foundation height.

The unit width-to-depth ratio should be varied until it steps uniformly down the hill. Theoretically, the roof of a unit below may become a private garden for a unit above. In testing, a nine foot change in grade may be used for floor-to-floor calculations. It is important to remember that there are usually no rear windows in terrace units, so the unit must not be deeper than 20 to 25 feet. Shallow units work best on steep slopes. Where the grade is not steep, units should have less than a complete overlap and a two or three-foot step up to the roof garden. Auto access should be tested from above, below, and at the midpoint.

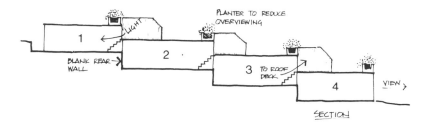

To figure out how to place units, we should draw an exact topographic section through the cluster and work with various unit arrangements on the slope until we find the best solution.

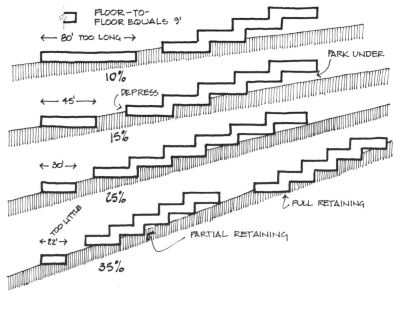

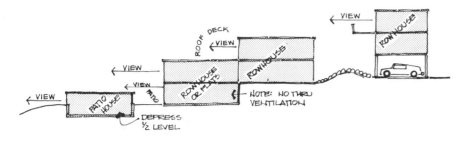

Terrace units can run as grouped blocks horizontal with the contours, at a right angle to them or in a controlled stagger at 45degrees to the slope. The steeper the slope, the higher the densities (remember land is measured horizontally rather than along the angle). In any case, it is always possible to site greater densities on sloping land than on level land, hence a weighting of the economical scale.

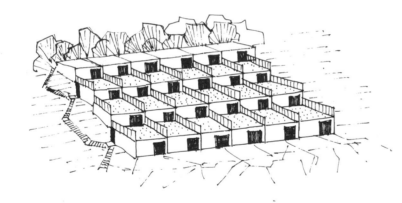

Sewer locations are important considerations in uphill/downhill situations. Sewers for uphill units can be located in the street, while sewers for downhill units have to be at the bottom of the hill with long connector lines.

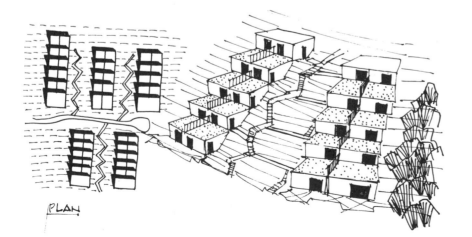

PLAN

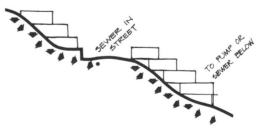

Finicular Railways-or diagonal elevators are useful, though expensive ways to serve units on a steep slope. Roads and parking are usually the limiting factor for development of steep hillsides. By parking at the top or bottom of a road, it may be possible to site units carefully on the hill, and access them with finicular rail. Units can be constructed on pole foundations further minimizing site disturbance, and can be staggered to provide unobstructed views to all units. The railway can be centrally located serving double loaded units at various levels. Access to each unit would be via a pathway or walk on the uphill side of each row, thereby maximizing privacy and views on the downhill site.

Combine up and downhill units when terracing. Keep access roads narrow and weave through existing vegetation along the levelest route.

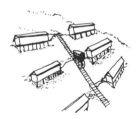

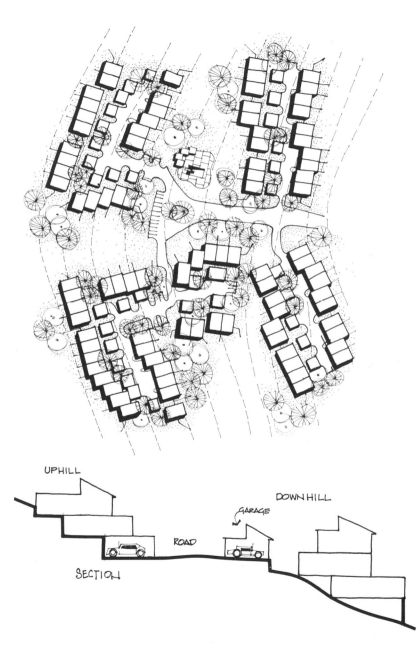

This solution is expensive. First, constructing units on steep slopes requires additional handwork in hauling supplies, excavation, etc. Second, steep slopes can slide, and engineered foundations may be necessary. Lastly, the railway is a tricky design problem, requiring safety precautions, care in installation and continued maintenance. The railway will be attractive to neighborhood kids, and even curious adults. For some household types, such as young unmarried, married without children, or for short hillsides, a solution using stairs may suffice. For elderly or families, a railway may be necessary. However, the benefits of using a hill providing views to many units and saving vegetation, may exceed the cost when considered over the long term.

UPHILL

DOWN HILL

GARAGE

ROAD

SECTION

Cabin Clusters. Used on steep sites, cabin clusters allow up to twice as many units as possible under traditional development. Boardwalks lead from external parking to each cluster of 6 to 10 units. Units may be arranged to secure individual privacy and views, and may be tucked neatly between trees on pole foundations. Parking is grouped above or below, with access on foot.

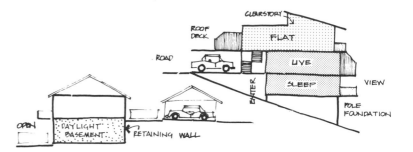

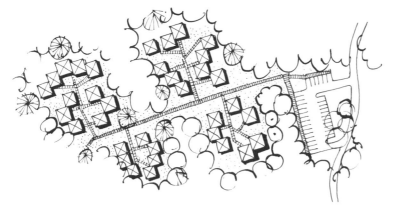

Uphill/Downhill Units. Downhill units are often reversed, with living-cooking areas on the upper floor and sleeping below. Decks cantilevered out over the downhill side, or resting on firm ground on the uphill side serve as gardens. A downhill unit may be floated free of the road and be connected with a bridge. Downhill units may be raised slightly to take advantage of a view or allow a full floor below.

Conversely, uphill units usually have living-cooking on the lower floor to shorten access from the road below. The carport is at the lowest level, while the private garden is at a higher level. A deck cantilevered over the carport may serve as a garden, but with a view of the road.

In uphill/downhill units, it is possible to have split levels, where residents enter into the living room level and go up half a level to sleeping quarters or down a half level to cooking/eating. The disadvantage is that variations in floor level cause increased construction costs.

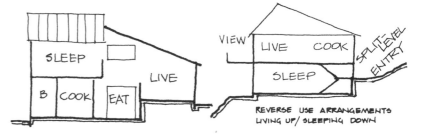

REVERSE USE ARRANGEMENTS LIVING UP/ SLEEPING DOWN

Roads should be designed to work with the grade to take advantage of views; i.e., a sloping cul-de-sac gives all units a view. Another way to gain views is to stagger units and align them at 45 degrees to the road. For maximum views greenspace may be tapered, opening up downslope. Since units at the top of the sloping culs-de-sac are prime sites, developers are tempted to crowd units there unnecessarily. Room for one public walk between units might be provided.

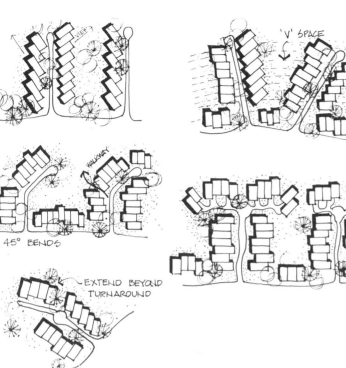

45° BENDS

EXTEND BEYOND TURNAROUND

4. Locate recreation facilities—play areas, swimming pool, laundry, patio, etc.—in the center of a development to create an open effect.
5. Lower patio fences and eliminate unnecessary fences. Borrowing private space for public use works; fences can be as low as 4 feet and still provide privacy.

6. Use open, exterior stairs (constructed of a steel frame with precast concrete treads).
7. Retain all trees, working buildings around them. Small, continuous and unfolding spaces are usually better than one large space.

TO AVOID A CROWDED LOOK, the planner should

1. Minimize interior roads and outdoor parking.
2. Make walkways and greenways long, so they feel spacious even though buildings may be close together.
3. Use one-story buildings to open up an area, particularly at the ends of a row of units.

8. Park as many cars under buildings as possible.
9. Provide a central open space—but allocate a large part to smaller courts that serve individual clusters. Create smaller courts by placing buildings at right angles to one another, therefore avoiding the slablike look of many projects.

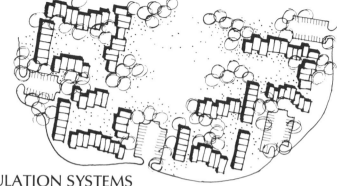

## CIRCULATION SYSTEMS

Cluster housing requires a completely new approach to circulation—one which measures more carefully the relationship between designs for accessibility and the resulting environment. While user preference suggests that people want to drive their cars to their dwellings, they also want quiet, pleasant surroundings and safe, enjoyable pedestrian routes.

Typically a cluster is served from a main cul-de-sac or loop road connected to a busier local road. Total cul-de-sac length may be quite long, up to 1000 feet with proper turn-arounds. Road/parking relationships should graduate over the length, with, for instance, the first few clusters served by parking courts or short culs-de-sac, town houses served by private drives, and finally row, patio or flats served by an end parking court. Culs-

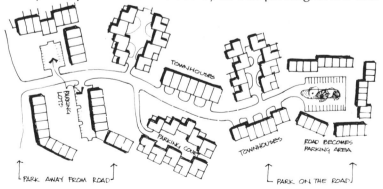

de-sac should be short enough so the driver can see its end before turning in and should have a narrow entrance with a sign of residents' names. Important roads should always be obvious, so drivers won't become confused and make wrong turns.

The cul-de-sac offers many design variations:

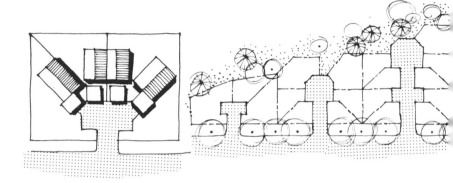

- Left-over portions of developable lands may be used for several single family units served by a cul-de-sac.
- A slanted cul-de-sac may be extended from a parking court to serve several units, or conversely, a parking court may be extended from a cul-de-sac.

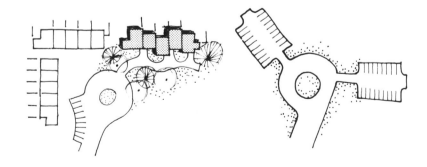

- Turn arounds may be added along the way to reduce through traffic.

250

- A small square may be formed by narrowing the road to one lane between clusters; one and two storied houses might be arranged in a somewhat formal way around the square. Building placement may prevent corridor views from square to square.

- A traffic island may be placed in the center of the turnaround. Other turnaround configurations include: (1) informally developed squares along a road with units shifting forward and back, and with trees planted in the middle of the street; and (2) buildings of two or three store stories arranged in a loop, with an interior service road. The end of

the road faced by most houses becomes the focal point of activity.

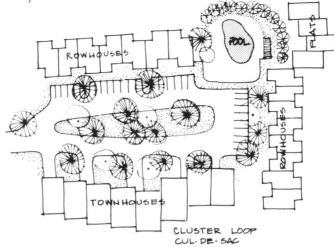

- Add pedestrian throughways connecting cul-de-sac to open space. These can be as narrow as 10 feet, but if carefully combined with the planning of each cluster, may be wider.

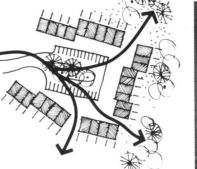 

DIFFERENTIATING AMONG ROAD TYPES. A marked contrast in width and character among Major, Local, and Feeder roads should be immediately evident in any cluster/open space development. Major roads should be boulevard-like and not serve any units directly. Local roads must be designed not only for good sight lines and easy curves, but for pedestrians' safety and experience as well. Feeder roads, narrow meandering roads for short distance travel, are meant for slow speeds and pedestrian safety.

Recommended street widths are:

l0 foot min. travel lane width
7 foot parallel parking width
l0 foot min. setback (walk plus planter width).
Access Road - 20' min. plus parking and setback
Local Road - 22' min. plus parking and setback
Major Road - two 22' lanes plus setback

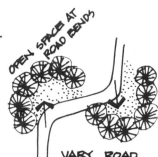

VARY ROAD ALIGNMENTS

VIEW IN

LOCATE RECREATION FACILITIES AT BEND IN ROADS

Travel is not solely for getting somewhere; it can be pleasant. Alignment should balance functional site problems with a visually pleasant route. Some simple road alignment variations include:

- The width of a route may be varied to miss a tree, steep terrain, or valley bottom.

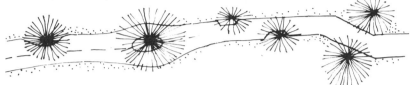

- A roadway may be split to avoid unique landscape features.
- Bridges and walls may be used to minimize landscape disruption.
- A route may steepen sharply for a short distance to climb a grade.
- Scenic views may be taken advantage of from the road. The roadway may be aligned along a portion of the open space. Distant views may be captured between buildings or bends in the road.
- Units at local road corners may be set back to allow drivers better view. This is particularly important for developments with children.

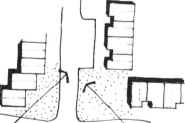

- The entrance road may be aligned to show off development amenities such as a lake or open meadow.

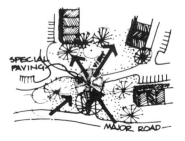

SPECIAL PAVING

MAJOR ROAD

In contrast for the circuitous feeder roads, pedestrian ways must be direct and criss-cross the entire layout, traveling through spaces under large buildings, along roads, and between units. Easy access to routes promotes walking.

CLUSTER ENTRANCES AND PARKING ROADS should be varied with width and direction to fit unusual spaces, to match the geometry of clusters, and to improve the visual image.

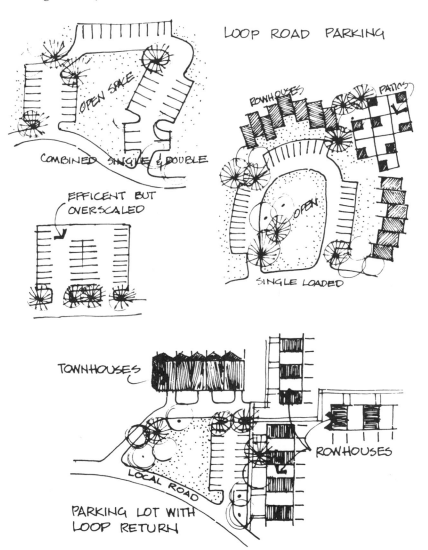

PARKING DOWN/BUILDING UP. To reduce grading and construction costs of traditional garage parking, the lot could be depressed two to four feet and the building a like amount to allow seven feet of parking headroom. Units are placed half over the parking and half over solid ground, with soil from the parking area raising gardens to floor level. A ramp 20 to 30 feet long connects street to parking, while entrances are on the garden side. Several steps are necessary at the entrance, and fences can be used to separate gardens from entrances.

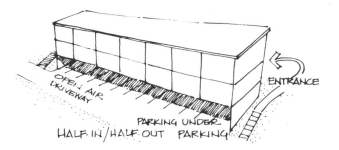

To increase the parking court efficiency, the lot may be double loaded by the addition of another building. Efficiency in parking is traded for high construction costs and siting demands. The narrow space between buildings is difficult to deal with, since trees cannot be planted there. Roofing the backout area and using the roof as an entrance court for both buildings leaves the opposite garden free of entrance functions. Moreover, a north/south axis is necessary for sunlight in all gardens.

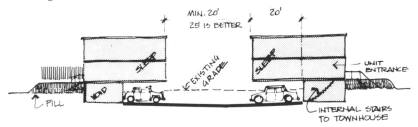

Several architectural problems are associated with parking under buildings. First, the dimensions of a parked car are usually narrower and more slender than a parked car. Each parking space should be 11 feet wide to accommodate structural supports. Two bays, or 22 feet, can be spanned structurally, but 22 feet is an unusual construction width. In depth, a car occupies about 20 feet, while a building is 30 to 40 feet deep. The extra footage may be used for several purposes.

1. For tandem parking; 40 feet of space serves the principal car plus a second car, recreational vehicle, or trailer.
2. As slope to take up grade between the depressed parking and existing grade, eliminating expensive retaining walls.
3. For specialized facilities such as laundry, shop, gym, or storage.
4. As interior access via a stairway to units overhead. Stairs serve the first floor, but serving a unit on the second floor is more difficult

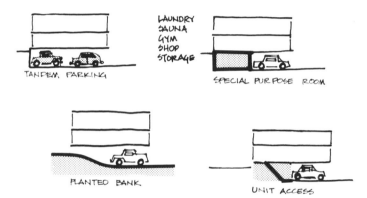

## GETTING FROM HERE TO THERE

The site plan is actually many mini-environments and sequences of activities. A site planner should be able to diagram all the major functions of a site.

- How do residents move from parking to their homes?
- How do guests move from parking to their host's house?
- How do kids move from home to play spaces?
- Where do residents go to empty garbage?
- Where are bicycles and prams stored?
- How are deliveries made?
- Where do residents pick up their mail?
- Where do residents wash their cars?
- Are there areas residents can walk their animals?
- Are there community garden allotments?
- Are there individual storage areas?
- How does a resident move from his home to the laundry?
- How do residents move to a community center?
- How do guests on foot or bicycle move to their host's house?

The final test for a site plan is for the designer to walk and drive the site imaginatively, trying to experience it as a future resident might. The two-dimensional plan must be thought of in terms of volumes and spaces, textures and colors, sun and shade, heat and cold, i.e., in terms of the conditions that might exist.

Parking for each unit should be located and the entrance route to each unit determined. Units have two entrance requirements—auto and pedestrian. If the neighborhood has a good bus system and people can walk home, then more units should be pedestrian orientated and located away from the road. On the other hand, areas with poor public transportation should be serviced more directly by automobiles.

ENTRANCES. Entrances should relate directly to an auto street, a pedestrian street, or an internal courtyard connected to a pedestrian street. The entrance court may be tight with only enough room to comfortably serve each unit, or it can be open combining small private gardens. Which one is best depends on resident mix and available open space. If the cluster is for families with young children, then a larger entry court could provide a play area; if there is no other common open space, then a larger space is necessary for congregating. The pattern could change over the years, beginning as an open court, with residents defining use spaces as they become necessary. A plan allocating each unit space for private entrance garden might be used as a guide for dividing the space later.

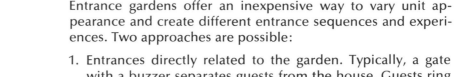

Entrance gardens offer an inexpensive way to vary unit appearance and create different entrance sequences and experiences. Two approaches are possible:

1. Entrances directly related to the garden. Typically, a gate with a buzzer separates guests from the house. Guests ring for entry at the garden gate, and once identified would walk through the garden to reach the front door. For more open living, no gate is used and visitors walk directly to the front door.

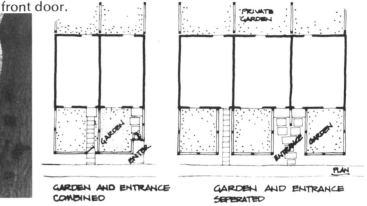

GARDEN AND ENTRANCE COMBINED

GARDEN AND ENTRANCE SEPERATED

2. For row-house units wider than 20 feet, a separate entrance next to the private garden is possible. A fence between entrance and garden assures privacy.

Town houses create unique entry problems since parking takes up most of the front yard. If parking is inside the unit, the driveway can be used for pedestrian entrance, but the more desirable approach is to narrow the drive to its absolute minimum (say, 8 feet) and capture the wasted space for use as a separate pedestrian entrance. If a front garden is desirable, the entrance may be combined with the garden to save space. Some other entrance considerations include the following:

- Separating front doors by a wall or planter makes each entrance private and identifiable. If an entrance path serves two units, it must divide comfortably at the door.
- Stepping up at the entrance emphasizes entry and separates the entrance from public space. If the entrance is elevated one foot (two steps), the garden fence should be at least four feet high for privacy.
- Varying the depth of row house units, creates protected space for entrances.
- Locating public walks below the entrance, with ramps or

255

steps leading up to each unit, clearly separates private from public spaces and prevents overviewing into units from the pathway.

- Switching the entrance in end units from the front to the side, varies the entrance path pattern, allows for a front garden, separates the entrance from neighboring entries, and adds distinction.

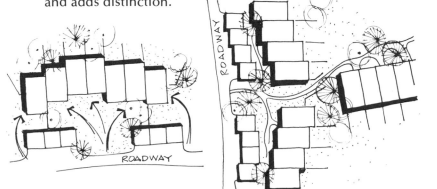

- Stepping units back to open the path serving units beyond.
- Setting units at an angle to the road or parking court, creating a small angular entry court. The angle allows a different view from the road, while providing an enlarged space at the entrance.

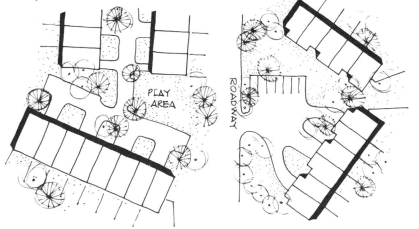

The combinations of elements for entrances are many; they must be combined to create a pleasurable entrance sequence of experiences. Some suggestions for good entry design include:

1. Making entry treatment affordable, which suggests that a minimum amount of space be used.
2. Separating clearly the realms of automobiles and pedestrians; Providing direct, safe, separate pedestrian routes; Aligning parking so pedestrian routes relate to units. Providing visibility, clarity and directness to each entrance is important.
3. Buffering views of autos by planting, fencing, or grading.

FROM UNIT TO OPEN SPACE. The ideal arrangement is direct access from a private rear garden to the community open space. Other ways of relating unit to open space include:

1. Connecting a front entry court to community open space and recreation systems.
2. Devising a second stair—the back door—leading from upper story units to the community open space.
3. Providing views to the open space, that is, indirect contact.
4. Designating an allotment garden somewhere on the property for units without private gardens. Having your own territory to go to is an "excuse" to go outside.

Which room should connect to the outside? That depends on how residents use their living, kitchen or dining room. Families may prefer to connect their private garden to the kitchen/dining room for informal use, and leave the living room as a deadend room with little through traffic. Singles and elderly couples may prefer the main garden off the living room, with a small service garden off the kitchen.

A busy road should be avoided between units and open space. However, roads needn't be barriers to open space access, but they must be safe. To insure an easy connection, two suggestions are given:

1. Keep the access road narrow. A short driveway to each garage, serving as backout space, allows narrower roads. A 20-foot-long driveway provides room for parking a second car and allows the road to be as narrow as 18 feet.

2. Avoid Curbs. Keep feeder roads level with adjacent ground. A curb is always a psychological barrier, suggesting the space is really not for people but for cars. If the road flows into the adjacent open space, it can serve visually as part of the open space. Two problems must be solved:

how to drain the road and how to keep cars from driving in the open space.

Ideally the natural open space beyond the road could be used for drainage with the road tipped slightly in that direction and runoff allowed to dissipate over the landscape. This requires a gravelly soil that perks well, vegetation to slow runoff, a narrow roadway, and removal of roof runoff through a storm drainage system. If there isn't room enough for runoff to dissipate, the road should have center drains and water should be collected in catch basins and disposed of in the best manner available, probably into a storm drain and holding pond.

Preventing autos from being driven on lawns is a little more difficult; part of the solution lies in developing community pride. Also, trees may be planted and bollards installed—about 15 feet apart—to prohibit access. Bollards (wood poles, timber, or cast concrete) may be alternated with trees to create an informal arrangement. Trees and bollards needn't be aligned in a straight row; they can be staggered or clumped.

Where possible, two pedestrian routes should be provided—one along the road system and another internally as a separate system. Road and internal pedestrian systems should join at a recreation complex, school, shopping area, or at places where the auto drops off or picks up pedestrians.

The amount of open space along each road should be determined. Certain portions of the road benefit by a slight widening of open space alongside.

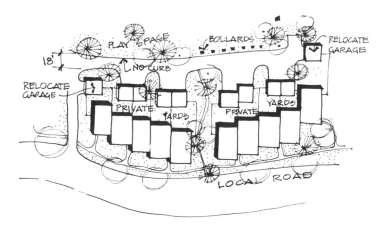

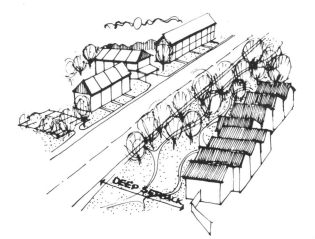

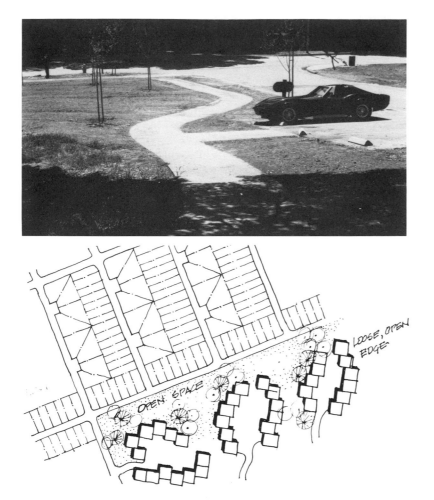

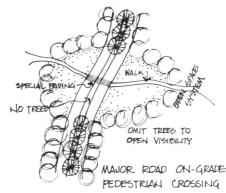

- When the open space system crosses a road, by extending it alongside the road in one direction a greater distance than actually required.

This may occur:

- Along heavy pedestrian routes of travel—near a high density cluster, shopping area, or school.
- Near the entrance, where additional open space visible to passing motorists helps convey the message that this is an open-space community.
- Internally on occasions when the road system seems boring and views of open space would be rewarding.

RECREATIONAL FACILITIES. Each active recreational facility should be integrated with its surroundings. Units should be protected from noisy facilities. Because it provides adequate buffer space, a centralized facility is easiest to plan. Decentralized facilities located adjacent to a cluster or shared by several clusters are more difficult to plan. If the facility is to be used by residents other than those of the cluster, pedestrian access must be clearly shown. The facility should be located below nearby units, separated by at least 20 feet of planted buffer. Where possible, active facilities should be located *between* several clusters, since this is semi-public space, easily integrated into the pedestrian system.

Centralizing recreational elements requires a complete pedestrian/bicycle access system so all residents can walk or bike to the facility. The pedestrian system should branch and become progressively wider as it approaches the recreation complex. Ideally it shouldn't cross roads, but this may not be possible in the low-density ends of large projects. Lastly, the recreational complex should not be surrounded by roads.

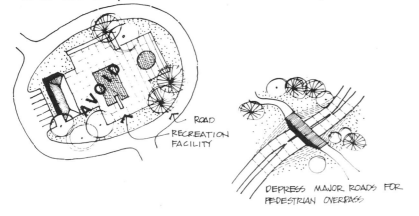

ROAD
RECREATION FACILITY

DEPRESS MAJOR ROADS FOR PEDESTRIAN OVERPASS

Review each major pedestrian road crossing for safety and continuity. Should any be grade separated? Grade separation is expensive, and unless well designed, may not be used by residents. Grade separation should occur only when sufficient pedestrians must regularly cross a busy road—as to reach a school, shopping, public transit or recreation complex. Though construction costs are usually high, they will never be cheaper than during the initial site preparation phase. Pedestrian bridges are more pleasant to cross than underpasses if the grade change can be solved to minimize stairs. Try depressing the road, and mounding the pedestrian crossing up.

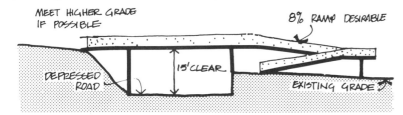

MEET HIGHER GRADE IF POSSIBLE

8% RAMP DESIRABLE

DEPRESSED ROAD

15' CLEAR

EXISTING GRADE

Conversely, large diameter galvanized drainpipe can be buried beneath a road serving as a pedestrian underpass.

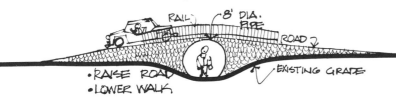

RAIL

8' DIA. PIPE

ROAD

EXISTING GRADE

• RAISE ROAD
• LOWER WALK

SUMMARY - THINGS TO AVOID.

All two story buildings.

Exterior 'Motel Type' entrance balcony.

Balconies overlooking parking areas.

Combining pedestrian entrances and auto driveways.

Noisy swim pool in the center of all units.

Cluster entry inundated by automobiles.

Garden areas too close to roads.

Buildings spaced too close.

# WHAT GOES WHERE?

At higher densities, the location of all site elements becomes crucial, lest the privacy and quality of living in some units be diminished. For medium density developments to work, each element or activity must be located to satisfy:

*Specific resident activities*, such as emptying garbage, washing laundry, walking, swimming, etc. The location and treatment of each facility must satisfy specific purposes efficiently.

*Experience*. At higher densities, it is seldom possible for each element to serve only one purpose. At the very least, each element must (1) service its own purpose, (2) be attractive, (3) not create disturbance for nearby units or activity areas, and (4) serve as a social catalyst.

*Minimum intrusion to other residents*. At higher densities, someone has to live near a communal laundry, a garbage collecting area, or swimming pool. Thus the chance of these residents being bothered by the activity noise of others is great unless each location and detail is carefully planned.

A word of caution, we don't yet know what results certain locational decisions have on community structure. Designers often create social problems by basing location and program decisions on their own experience, which may not relate to the needs or desires of future residents. The most risky practice is trying to interpret the life styles of expected residents without first observing them. When observing different resident groups, we should consider

- What locational factors bring people of different backgrounds together?
- What factors tend to split them?

Centralize or decentralize—Many community services are being centralized, i.e., garbage collection in large containers at centralized points adjacent to a road, and mail delivered to central boxes. Moreover, one large laundry room is cheaper to install and maintain than several dispersed ones. Responsi-

- Where should the launary room be located?
- What type of residents are inappropriate next to a swim pool?
- Where should the garbage cans be located?
- How far will residents walk from their car to the house?
- Where should swimming pools be located?
- Where do 5 to 12 year-olds go to? And what do they have to do?

bility for maintenance of facilities is an important consideration. Privately owned facilities are clearly the owner's responsibility, while centralized facilities may be shared by enough users to justify a hired maintenance service. Responsibility for maintenance of decentralized facilities shared by a small number of people is often unclear, with residents often assuming the management maintains them.

The decentralized, middle range is most important, for if a group of residents can bind together to carry out management responsibilities for their common facility, they will have formed a vital social organization.

LOCATIONAL TENDENCIES OF HOUSING TYPES. Each house type has inherent locational tendencies based on household user needs which can be used to determine housing distribution patterns. Locational tendencies are expressed in terms of

(1) accessibility to facilities such as schools, play areas, recreation areas; (2) relationship to natural features such as view, slope, vegetation, microclimate; and (3) general environmental quality such as privacy, noise, seclusion, homogenous or heterogeneous compatability.

Since it is impossible to design the perfect environment for everyone, the next step is to decide *who gets what?* For instance, elderly may spend a great amount of time in and around their unit and benefit from a small garden, while a single working person may find a second-floor deck perfectly acceptable. Panoramic views may be desirable, but most people will settle for a pleasant close-up view of a garden or communal open space.

We should consider how the following might relate to the needs of certain household types:

| | |
|---|---|
| convenience | activity |
| safety | long-term use |
| sociability | identity |
| noise | quiet use |

This chart summarizes some suggested locational relationships.

## HOUSING TYPES

| | STEPPED HOUSING | MAISONETTES | TOWN HOUSES | ROW HOUSES | PATIO HOUSES | SEMI-DETACHED | SINGLE DETACHED | TENDENCIES |
|---|---|---|---|---|---|---|---|---|
| **ACCESSIBILITY** | | | | | | | | |
| TO PRIMARY SCHOOLS | ● | | ● | ● | ● | ● | ● | |
| TO MAJOR CENTRE | | | | | | | | |
| TO CONVENIENCE SHOPPING | | ● | | | | | | |
| TO MAJOR RECREATION | | ● | | | | | | |
| TO NEIGHBOURHOOD RECREATION | | | ● | ● | | | | |
| TO PLAY AREAS | | | | | | | | |
| **NAT. FEATURES** | | | | | | | | |
| PRIME VEGETATION | | | | ● | | ● | | |
| GOOD VEGETATION | ● | ● | ● | ● | | ● | | |
| VIEW | | | ● | ● | | ● | ● | |
| SLOPE | ● | | | | | ● | ● | |
| GOOD MICROCLIMATE | ● | ● | ● | ● | | ● | | |
| **QUALITY** | | | | | | | | |
| SECLUSION FROM MAJOR TRAFFIC | ● | ● | ● | | | ● | ● | |
| VISUALLY SECLUDED | | | ● | ● | | ● | ● | |
| AURALLY SECLUDED | ● | ● | ● | ● | | ● | ● | |
| LAND USE HOMOGENEITY | | | | ● | ● | ● | ● | |
| LAND USE MIX | | | ● | | | | | |
| ACTIVE ENVIRONMENT | | ● | | | | | | |
| HEIGHT RESTRICTION 1-3 FLOOR | | | ● | ● | ● | ● | ● | |

In addition, we might examine what prevents close physical integration of the housing fabric including:

> space for expansion
> privacy
> non-quiet use
> auto-access

OTHER POSSIBILITIES We might examine housing location in relation to access and movement systems.

Natural amenity and seclusion are important for ground-oriented structures, which depend on the private garden for image and amenity.

View and convenience to major communal facilities are important to smaller units in compact, taller structures.

Who lives on what floor? Common sense prevails. Elderly generally prefer the first floor with easy street access and no stairs. Families should also be located on the ground floor with easy access to the garden for kids' play and family activity. Young married and single adults should be quite comfortable on the upper floors, with an outdoor deck or roof garden for barbecuing and other activities.

Terracing can change locational patterns extensively. With pedestrian access parallel to the contours, it is possible for every unit to be accessible without going up or down stairs and for each unit to have ground orientation to small gardens.

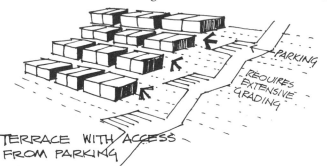

TERRACE WITH ACCESS FROM PARKING

Mix-em up, but aim to satisfy specific user requirements within the cluster. For instance, a small first floor unit for retirees, with second floor for entertainment-oriented mature couples.

A row of single-family units with large gardens around the perimeter of a site acts as a visual buffer between adjacent development, and keeps the development low and open at the edge. Zero lot line platting should be used to increase efficiency.

Household types require, or are best served by, different densities. For instance, a family of growing children might be happier at a lower density than a young single professional or a retired couple.

The following list of traditional household types and density requirements is in chronological sequence.

1. Young single person rents a small furnished apartment, perhaps shared with a friend.
2. Young married couple rents a small furnished apartment.
3. Married couple rents a larger unfurnished apartment. The move might be related to a change in job.
4. Married couple purchases a small house.
5. Married couple with small children purchases a larger house. This move might be related to need for more space, change of job, or increase in income.
6. Married couple with children expands house by remodeling.
7. For a few couples, the custom building of a house.
8. Couples whose children have left home, sell house and purchase a smaller house or rent an apartment.
9. Single person whose spouse is deceased retains separate home for a while before selling it.
10. Single person moves into an apartment, in with a child, or to a retirement home.

Certainly, there are many exceptions to this list of typical housing situations. This list is important for understanding the variety of housing requirements that have to be satisfied.

## LOCATING GUEST PARKING

It would be best if site planners considered guest parking during the entire design process, but most of us don't. Instead, we review the semi-finished plan adding guest parking here and there, changing original design intentions by adding parking to open space. As early as possible, the plan should be reviewed to ensure an adequate and workable guest parking arrangement.

Determining the number and location of guest parking depends on:

*Resident mix.* Are tenants to be young people with full entertainment schedules, necessitating extra guest parking stalls? Singles compound the parking problem, since two or three single people, each with his own car and individual sets of friends, are likely to share a unit. Elderly people, with less demanding entertainments schedules, generally require fewer guest parking stalls. Large families ideally are located at a lower density, allowing more room for guest parking in driveways or on the street.

*Public transit.* A well-used bus system may reduce the need for extensive guest parking facilities. Although public transportation is still not generally accepted in suburban communities, it may have to be relied on more in the future.

*Peak load/low load compromise.* Guest parking demand increases on weekends, particularly during evenings. During the rest of the week, guest parking is a small problem. The question is: do we design for peak period efficiency, and live with empty stalls during the week, or do we accept the possibility of confusion and illegal parking on the weekend, allowing more open space during the week? For instance, to solve this dilemma it may be possible to plan for parking on one side of a "no parking street" on Friday, Saturday, and Sunday evenings, forcing traffic to slow down while passing.

*The size of the community.* Is the community population large enough to allow the formation of many friendships, thus reducing dependence on outside visitors? This is an iffy approach, for typically best friends are not neighbors. In theory, as a planned community becomes larger and self-sufficient, the need for guest parking decreases slightly.

There are two conceptual ways to route guests from car to unit: *externally or internally*.

1. External implies road-related parking. This approach is clear, direct, and has few disadvantages except the visual clutter of parked cars and a slight decrease in pedestrian safety and experience. In theory, every Town house can have one guest parking space in the driveway, plus one on the street.

2. Internal suggests an open-space related route. For complex site plans, guest parking should be centrally located and the final portion of the journey made on foot through open space. This doesn't necessarily mean one huge guest parking area should be provided; several small lots located throughout the community, with letter or number identification, are better. A 200 to 300 foot walk one to two minutes long isn't unreasonable, and can be quite pleasant. While this approach decreases auto convenience, it allows a safer quieter overall environment.

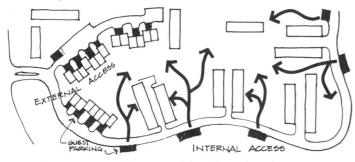

Some other guest parking considerations involve:

- Deciding on which streets parking will be allowed, and which streets are to remain free of parked cars. Nonparking roads should be designed by planting trees in the right of way to narrow the street or by pedestrian safe-cross zones.
- Avoiding guest parking in communal garages. Garages are disorienting, expensive, and easily congested.
- Marking guest parking spaces clearly with signs. Typically guest parking should be less convenient than resident parking, should be grouped in clusters, and should be the first spaces in the parking lot to reduce through traffic.
- Adding signs to direct drivers to each resident's entrance. Nonentry points should be marked with signs reading "private drive," "resident," or "assigned parking." .

LOCATING RECREATION FACILITIES

Recreation is considered a key factor in the success of cluster housing, with open space necessarily designed as a leisure-time resource. The trend towards shorter work weeks and increased leisure time must be met with more extensive recreational and educational opportunities. Additionally, so much of our work week is spent in sedentary indoor activity that we want to spend leisure time out of doors.

Traditionally, recreation, especially tennis, swimming and other club-related activities, has been organized with set hours. With more extensive open space development, residents should have the opportunity for recreation at any time. Ideally, residents would be able to engage in recreation on their way to shopping, work, school.

Recreation can be divided into two broad categories— *active and passive*. Active recreation requires a deliberate effort— running, swimming, bicycling, tennis, etc.— and often a special facility. Passive recreation is possible whenever one is out of doors and includes walking, sitting, viewing, driving, and just relaxing.

Open space users may be generally grouped according to their special needs (physical, mental, social, and creative) which must be satisfied. Some recreation such as walking, bicycling, bowling, etc. can satisfy many basic needs simultaneously, including relaxation, creation, fellowship, adventure, achievement, service, physical and mental development.

To accommodate community recreational needs, a diverse and intricately developed park system should form the backbone of the community. The space should be a linear and continuous system connecting all residential units with different recreational facilities. Linear means the open space system is long—with many edges capable of reaching all residents at some point. The system should enlarge in selected areas to allow inclusion of special facilities for organized sport, play, rest, etc. The location of these facilities should be based on population densities, with more facilities within the high density core and fewer in single-family areas. Existing topography, land form, and tree cover must also be locational determinants.

A recreational system must:

> Provide recreation opportunities to serve everyone, regardless of age or sex.
>
> Provide facilities and areas to make possible a great variety of recreational activities serving a wide range of recreational interests.
>
> Include areas that differ widely in size, location, natural features, potentials, etc. thereby serving different recreation needs.
>
> Provide equitable distribution of recreation areas to the community.
>
> Provide neighborhood recreational focus.

Six types of developed recreation areas are typically located along the open space system within the public way. These relate directly to user needs and include:

1. Small facilities for very young and the elderly
2. Children's play areas
3. Individual pieces of play apparatus and sculpture
4. Parks
5. Special recreational spaces
6. Rural parks (for large developments)

These six recreation areas are discussed in more detail below.

1. SMALL FACILITIES FOR THE VERY YOUNG AND THE ELDERLY. These should be located along the linear park system close to apartments and dwellings, more frequently in the dense areas and less often in single-family areas. They require only a simple widening of the pathway. Equipment may include several benches, trees, a sand box, and small play apparatus tables or a rain-sun shelter.

2. PLAY AREAS FOR CHILDREN. These more formalized play areas serve as a substitute for backyard space. They should

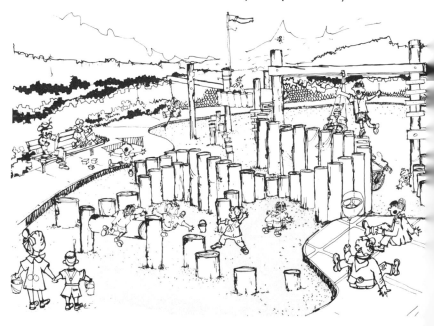

be within three minutes' walking distance of home for all children; spacing may be greater in single-family areas. These play areas should include play apparatus necessary for children's physical development, open paved areas for semiorganized sports, a park-like setting including seating, landscaping, etc., all integrated into a total design. The secret of success of these play areas is in the way they are designed, developed, and maintained; they may be stimulating, exciting, and challenging or a dull failure.

3. INDIVIDUAL PIECES OF PLAY EQUIPMENT OR SCULPTURE. Play apparatus of this type might augment the play area described in 2 above. They should be located in enlarged path areas or where interesting site conditions prevail, allowing children to stop and play if they are intrigued, then proceed along to another area of the open space system.

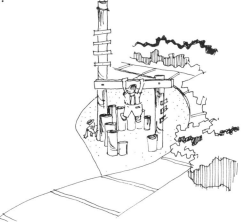

4. PARKS. These are for general relaxation, picnicking, resting, and represent small green retreats from the busy world. Although the linear park generally serves this purpose, it is important to have larger areas of land set aside for passive enjoyment.

5. SPECIAL RECREATIONAL SPACES. Gathering places for teenagers, crafts area, civic gathering plazas, malls, etc., all fit into this category.

6. RURAL PARKS. These parks are for passive use, with many community amenities such as major grassed playfields; tennis courts; horse, bicycle, and walking trails; family picnic areas; allotment gardens; and other special facilities.

While categorizing recreation spaces according to age or sex groups is helpful at the planning stage, it must be carefully avoided in actual practice. Recreation areas, differing in function, size, location, etc., can be combined on the same piece of land. For instance, a section of children's playground can be developed as a tot lot, while another area is used as sitting space for the elderly, etc.

SHORT PITCH FOR PLAY AREA NEAR THE STREET. Even though adults would like kids to play in safe areas away from the dangers of cars, they like to play near the street. So why not accommodate them by locating play areas adjacent to access roads and near parking areas (but not near major roads and busy local roads)? Street play facilities may be as simple as a basketball hoop mounted so that the street becomes the court. (Better yet if it is under a streetlight so play can continue during dark winter months.); a fire hydrant modified to doubl as spray pool with nearby drain; painted games in or near the street, and so on. If it is not desirable for kids to play in the street, a wide sidewalk or planter strip allows safer play near the street.

It is essential that traffic travel at slow speeds and be warned that kids may be playing in or near the street. Speed bumps, signs, and street diverters help. Temporary barriers or even gates which kids could close when they wanted to play (and drivers could open when they wanted to drive through) further protect kids at play and open the entire street for games of street hockey, football, baseball, etc. A side benefit is that the road doubles as open space and can take the rough play activity.

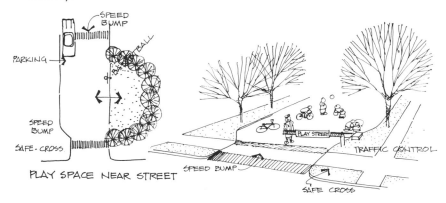

PLAY SPACE NEAR STREET

# COMMUNITY FACILITIES ANALYSIS

**Column groups:**

- **PARTICIPATION:** INDIVIDUAL · FAMILY GROUP · SMALL GROUP · LARGE GROUP · NECESSARY PARTICIPATION · OPTIONAL PARTICIPATION · DAILY · WEEKLY · WEEK-END · MONTHLY · OCCASIONAL · SEASONAL · DAY · NIGHT · SHORT-TERM · LONG-TERM
- **PARTICIPANTS:** YOUNG CHILDREN · TEENAGE BOYS · TEENAGE GIRLS · MEN · WOMEN · ELDERLY MEN · ELDERLY WOMEN · MODERATE INCOME · MIDDLE INCOME · UPPER INCOME
- **ORGANIZATIONAL:** PRIVATE · PUBLIC · EXCLUSIVE · INCLUSIVE · UNIQUE TO CITY · MULTIPLE TO CITY · LARGE MEMBERSHIP REQUIRED · PART OF SYSTEM · PRE-ESTABLISHED ORGANIZATION · REQUIRING FORMATION · TRANSITORY INTEREST
- **SPATIAL:** REQUIRING SPECIAL FACILITIES · PERMANENT FACILITIES · TEMPORARY FACILITIES · USING PUBLIC SPACES · SPATIALLY EXTENSIVE · SPATIALLY INTENSIVE · SUSCEPTIBLE TO MULTIPLE USE · INDOOR · OUTDOOR
- **LOCAT:** "URBAN" · "NON-URBAN" · LOCATIONALLY SPECIFIC · LOCATIONALLY NON-SPECIFIC
- **EXTENT:** HOUSEHOLD RELATED · IMMEDIATE NEIGHBOURHOOD · NEIGHBOURHOOD · SITE

## FACILITIES

### INFORMAL ACTIVITIES
- CHILDRENS PLAY
- TEENAGE PLAY
- BABY-SITTING
- INFORMAL SOCIALIZING
- PARTIES
- TENNIS
- SWIMMING
- WALKING
- BALL PLAYING
- CYCLING
- SIGHT-SEEING
- OBSERVATION
- HORSE RIDING

### ENTERTAIN
- COMMERCIAL ENTERTAINMENT
- SPECTATOR SPORTS
- FAIRS/FETES/SHOWS
- ZOOS/BOTANICAL GARDENS
- HORSE RACING

### ORGANIZED SPORT
- GOLF CLUBS
- CRICKET CLUBS
- RUGBY CLUBS
- SOCCER CLUBS
- BOWLING CLUBS
- TENNIS CLUBS
- GENERAL SPORTS CLUB
- ATHLETICS
- GYMNASIUMS
- HEALTH STUDIOS
- ACQUATIC SPORTS CLUB
- PUBLIC SWIMMING BATHS
- RIDING STABLES
- ICE SKATING RINK
- SKI SLOPES
- BOWLING ALLEYS
- MINIATURE GOLF
- GO-CART TRACK

● APPLICABLE · ■ POSSIBLY APPLICABLE

Matrixes in this chapter from: *Crown Mines Project, Major Report, 1969* prepared by Urban Design Consultant.

# LOCATIONAL TENDENCIES – COMMUNITY FACILITIES

| FACILITIES \ TENDENCIES | REGIONAL | SOUTHERN SUBURBS | NEIGHBOURING AREA | SITE | LOCAL | BY RAPID TRANSIT | BY BUS | BY CAR | BY CYCLE | ON FOOT | FLAT LAND IMPORTANT | GOOD VEGETATION | WATER ASSOCIATION | GOOD MICRO-CLIMATE | HIGHLY IDENTIFIABLE | HIGHLY VISIBLE | SYSTEMATIC DISTRIBUTION | ANONYMITY | PRIVACY | COMPATIBLE WITH RESID. | QUIET | ACTIVE | SAFE | ASSOCIATED OPEN SPACE | SEPARATE SITE | INTENSIVE | EXTENSIVE | HORIZONTAL EXPANSION POSS. | STRUCTURAL CHANGE POSS. |
|---|---|---|---|---|---|---|---|---|---|---|---|---|---|---|---|---|---|---|---|---|---|---|---|---|---|---|---|---|---|
| ACCESSIBILITY | | | | | | MODE | | | | | NAT. FEATURES | | | | IDENTITY | | | | | | QUALITY | | | DEMARKATION | | | | RESTR | |
| DAY CARE | | | | | ● | | ● | | ● | | | | | | | | ● | ● | | ● | ● | | ● | ● | | ● | | | |
| PLAYGROUNDS | | | | | ● | | | ● | ● | | | ● | | ● | | | ● | ● | ● | ● | ● | | ● | ● | | ● | | | |
| PRIVATE SPORTS | | | | | ● | | | ● | ● | ● | ● | | ● | | | | ● | ● | ● | ● | ● | | ● | ● | | ● | | | |
| OPEN SPACE | | | | | ● | | | | ● | ● | | ● | ● | ● | | | ● | ● | | ● | ● | | ● | ● | | ● | | | |
| NURSERY SCHOOLS | | | | ● | | | ● | ● | | | | | | | | | ● | | | ● | ● | | ● | ● | | ● | | | |
| PRIMARY SCHOOLS | | | ● | ● | | ● | ● | ● | | | | | | | | ● | ● | | | ● | ● | | ● | ● | ● | ● | | | |
| RELIGIOUS | | | ● | ● | | ● | ● | ● | | | | | | | ● | ● | | | | | | ● | | | ● | ● | | | |
| LOCAL COMMERCIAL | | | ● | ● | | ● | ● | ● | ● | | | | | | | | ● | | | ● | | | | | ● | | | | ● |
| SPORTS & SOCIAL CLUBS | | | | ● | | ● | ● | ● | ● | | ● | | ● | | | | ● | ● | ● | | | ● | | ● | | ● | | | |
| SECONDARY SCHOOLS | | ● | | | | ● | ● | ● | ● | | ● | | | | | ● | | | | | | ● | | ● | ● | ● | | | |
| VOCATIONAL EDUCATION | | ● | | | | ● | ● | ● | | | ● | | | | | ● | | | | | | ● | | ● | ● | ● | | | ● |
| CULTURAL ACTIVITIES | | | ● | | | | ● | | | | | | | | | ● | | | | ● | | ● | | ● | | | | | ● |
| CLINICS & WELFARE | | ● | | | | | ● | | | | | | | | | | | | | ● | | ● | | ● | | | | | ● |
| SPECIALIZED COMMERCIAL | ● | | | | | ● | ● | ● | | | ● | | | | ● | ● | | | | ● | | ● | | ● | | | | ● | ● |
| COMMERCIAL ENTERTAINMENT | ● | | | | | | ● | | | | | | | | ● | ● | | | | | | ● | | | | | | | ● |
| SPORTS & SOCIAL CLUBS | ● | | | | | | ● | ● | ● | | ● | | ● | | | | | | ● | | | ● | | ● | ● | ● | | | |
| RIDING STABLES | ● | | | | | | ● | ● | | | | | | | | | | | | | | | ● | | ● | ● | | | |
| HOSPITALS | ● | | | | | ● | ● | ● | | | | | | | ● | ● | | | | | ● | | | | ● | ● | | ● | ● |
| SPECTATOR SPORTS | ● | | | | | ● | ● | ● | | | | | | ● | ● | ● | | | | | | ● | | ● | ● | ● | | | |
| ZOOLOGICAL, BOTANICAL GARDENS | ● | | | | | ● | ● | ● | | | | ● | ● | ● | ● | ● | | | | | | | | | ● | ● | ● | ● | ● |
| PICNIC AREAS | ● | | | | | | ● | ● | | | | ● | ● | | | | | | | | ● | | ● | | ● | ● | | | |
| SHOW GROUNDS | ● | | | | | ● | ● | ● | | | ● | | ● | ● | | | | | | | | ● | | | ● | ● | ● | ● | ● |
| HORSE RACING | ● | | | | | | | ● | | | | | | | ● | ● | | | | | | | | | ● | ● | | | |
| AQUATIC SPORTS | ● | | | | | | ● | ● | | | | | ● | ● | ● | ● | | | | | | | | ● | ● | ● | | | |

269

ADVENTURE PLAYGROUND. An adventure playground provides the ultimate play experience. Both constructive and destructive kinds of play are possible and the child is free to use his imagination. It provides the opportunity for the child to organize and to order his own experiences. Materials in an adventure playground are basic ones such as soil, stones, wood, water, fire, and everyday articles, which are assigned a purpose only by the imagination of the children using the playground at a given moment. Thus, the structure, form, and use are infinitely variable.

COMMUNITY RECREATION FACILITIES. One benefit of medium-density cluster living is access to facilities not affordable to most families such as swimming pools, baseball or soccer fields, tennis courts, and so on. But most people don't want these community facilities too close to their homes because of noise and visual intrusion. The extent of problems associated with these factors depends on resident mix; if all residents around a facility are of the same age or family type—that is, all young families, all elderly, or all young unmarried, the problems are simpler as use patterns are similar and noise generating conflicts usually don't exist.

Conceptually, recreation facilities are usually located near the highest density areas, close to units with minimum-sized private gardens. Large units or units with large private gardens needn't be adjacent to communal recreation facilities— trading private for public space.

Some locational options for recreational facilities include the following.

- NEAR THE MAIN ENTRANCE and visible to all as they arrive. This location solves two problems: first the developer's need to create a marketable image to sell or rent the units; second, residents often rely on their surrounding landscape as a status symbol. Putting these amenities out front, so to speak, is the best way to impress friends. The reverse is true in many higher income communities, where residents prefer anonymity and seek to keep community amenity private; located out of sight of passing traffic.

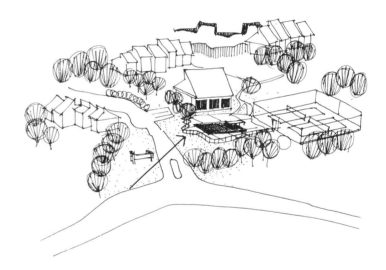

- DECENTRALIZED. A recreation complex for each cluster creates its own internal focus. The major advantage is that residents use facilities nearby with far greater frequency than those even a short distance away. How many units can efficiently support a complex depends on the rent/sales price structure; it could be as few as six or seven units, but more likely will be a 12 to 20 unit cluster. Operation of a shared club/pool complex is complicated and expensive unless residents agree to share cleaning and maintenance tasks, and unless a solar heating system is installed.

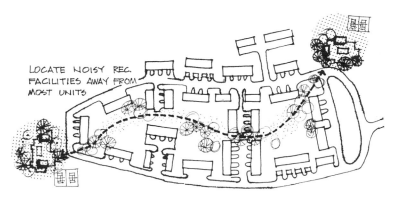

LOCATE NOISY REC. FACILITIES AWAY FROM MOST UNITS

- A MIDDLE POSITION. This is a compromise for large communities, with one major recreation/social club for all to share and several smaller pool or club facilities scattered throughout the development. Having several facilities allows flexibility in scheduling use for competing age groups, e.g., ensuring a child-free time for exclusive adult use. Auxiliary pools need not include changing rooms or extensive club facilities, although a toilet may be necessary.

ARE SWIMMING POOLS NECESSARY? Swimming pools are appealing to prospective residents. However, many who think they might use a pool don't because time schedules don't allow it, the weather isn't right, the pool is too crowded with kids, etc. Since pools are expensive to construct and operate, user frequency should be estimated before pools are included in a design. Some considerations about pools are:

- In hot climates (such as in southern California, Arizona, Florida) swimming pools are an accepted and desirable part of life. The question in hot climates is probably not whether but how many pools to install.
- The same is true of luxury developments, whose prospective residents demand a choice of activities and might not settle in a development without a pool.
- On the opposite end of the scale, sites with nearby public swimming facilities might not need their own pools.
- Developments with predominantly elderly residents might not have a pool or might have an indoor pool for year-round use and weather protection.
- Developments attempting to keep rents as low as possible should not include a swimming pool.
- Developments with only north or east orientation and little direct sunlight should not include a pool.
- Often the housing market dictates the need for developments to have pools to compete with other nearby developments.
- Covered pools extend the usefulness of pools in colder climates, with additional construction expenses but lower heating costs. The problem with covered pools is loss of enjoyment of the sun in the summer. Removable roofs haven't yet been perfected, although sliding doors can open the pool to an adjacent outdoor sun pocket.
- An *indoor*/outdoor pool half open and half covered solves some of the problem. Swimmers are able to enter the water from a warm interior, and fences block cold winds. An industrial garage door can be raised in summer to open the pool up.

Other desirable recreational amenities include:

*Golf courses* have become associated with cluster housing, and for good reason. Fairways tend to tie a development together and offer numerous views; the long length assures privacy to each cluster and allows different types of clusters; natural drainage and space for some natural processes; and keen resident interest in golf binds the community together socially.

However, costs of buying land, developing and setting up a club house/recreation facility usually range between $1 million and $3 million. A small par-3 18-hole course or a regulation 9-hole course requires about 45 to 50 acres, while a regulation 18-hole course requires between 130 and 140 acres. Finding club members who can afford initiation and maintenance fees for an investment of that size is difficult.

*Pitch-n-Putt golf* This is an inexpensive solution for the golfer where open space is limited. Pitch-N-Putts require approximately 1 to 10 acres of land and can create a focus for several clusters of units.

*Practice Tees.* This is even less space consuming than Pitch-n-Putt, requiring only a 50 by 100 foot piece of land. To function properly, all golf-related facilities must be properly constructed and maintained; costs are relatively high.

*Dual use of school yards.* If possible, schools should be included as part of the community open space system. It might be located centrally in the development with paths leading to and through it. In addition, school yards should be made available for community recreation during off-school hours.

*Recreational Space for Teenagers.* In addition to organized sport and formal meeting places, teenagers need informal spaces where they can congregate after school and in the evenings. Since outdoor space is needed, an area adjacent to a club house, a small store with coffee or ice cream, a book store, etc., might be provided with a few benches and tables with good visibility from paths and roads.

To encourage walking within the community, convenient parking around recreation facilities may be limited to cars for

staff, delivery, and handicapped. An auto/passenger drop-off lane is helpful. Locate facilities near the street to encourage surveillance from passing motorists. Locate club facilities along routes used daily, so residents may stop by on their way to somewhere else.

CONVENIENCE SHOPPING. When a community reaches about 200 units, it is possible to include a grocery/general store. Convenience shopping, though generally more expensive, makes living pleasant, particularly for elderly or young working people who may do all their shopping there. Where should it go? That depends on whether it is to serve *only* residents of that community or if it will also serve a clientele beyond the development. The store may be located:

- In the community center, serving only residents of the defined community. It might be managed by the community center's management or it might be run as a community cooperative.
- Along a busy, external street serving both residents and non-residents. A direct pedestrian/bicycle route is necessary to serve residents, as well as external auto access for service and non-resident use. The store location should be planned so non-residents do not drive through the community to shop. A store serving both resident and non-resident populations has a larger clientele and a greater chance of success.

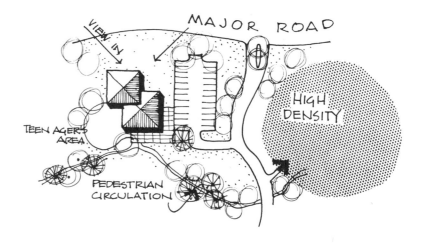

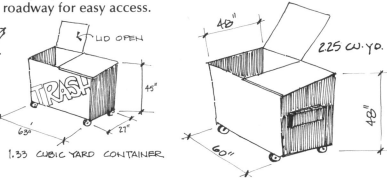

## GARBAGE AND TRASH COLLECTION AREAS.

Though a small consideration, garbage and trash storage should be planned in advance. At higher densities it is necessary to centralize garbage collection, utilizing containers that serve a number of units instead of cans. Metal trash containers vary slightly in size, but are approximately 3 feet wide, 4 feet high, and 6 feet long. They are mounted on wheels, and trash is dropped into the container through top hinged doors. The containers are not very attractive and are difficult to buffer. But, the main design problem is that the containers must be next to a roadway for easy access.

LID OPEN

45"

63"    27"

1.33 CUBIC YARD CONTAINER

48"

2.25 CU. YD.

48"

60"

Where should the collection area be located? It must (1) be located alongside a roadway for easy pickup, (2) be close and convenient for those using it, (3) must not interfere with nearby units, and (4) must be carefully buffered by fences and landscaping. A collection area might replace a parking space,

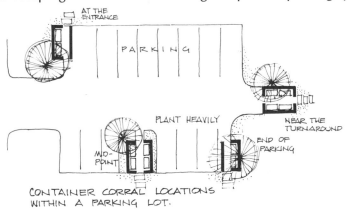

AT THE ENTRANCE

PARKING

PLANT HEAVILY

NEAR THE TURNAROUND

MID-POINT

END OF PARKING

CONTAINER CORRAL LOCATIONS WITHIN A PARKING LOT.

particularly if next to a planter. Several questions become obvious: How far will (should) people walk to dispose of garbage? What opportunities for engaging in conversation are present or can be enhanced by design? Should residents empty garbage through their front or rear door? How many units should each collection area serve? What access is necessary for garbage trucks?

A standard one and a third yard container emptied once a week will service about 6 to 8 mixed units and twice a week, 12 to 16 units. Mixed units include one, two, three, four bedrooms; obviously six four-bedroom units generate more garbage than six one-bedroom units. Because of their size, two containers are about the limit for each collection area. Any fencing must be extremely durable to withstand the treatment of hurried collectors. The authors suggest cast concrete or 2x12 lumber and a construction technique similar to that used to build a cattle corral.

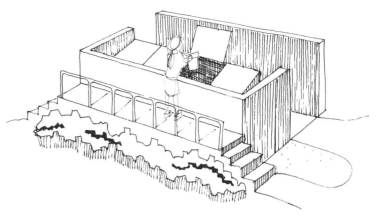

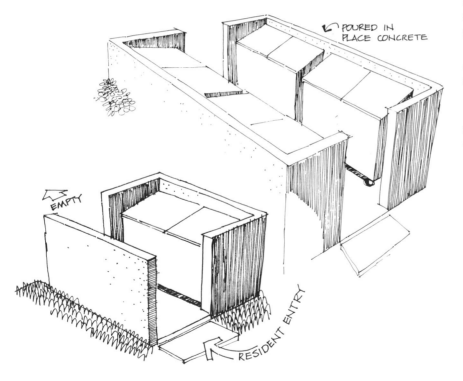

POURED IN PLACE CONCRETE

EMPTY

RESIDENT ENTRY

Because of the height of the lid, an arrangement using a raised walk on one side for easy drop-off works best. The fenced area should be larger than that needed for the container for maneuverability and for storage of boxes and other trash that won't fit.

*Trash Recycling.* We are nearing the day when residents will be asked to separate recyclable waste into bins for later collection by the disposal company. While this has obvious societal values, it creates a problem of providing enough space for a number of different bins.

*Individual garbage cans.* The alternative to garbage collection areas is each resident having his own garbage cans which he rolls to a collection point on garbage collection day and which he rolls back to his home in the evening. The responsibility for storing garbage cans during the rest of the week is the resident's.

LAUNDRY ROOMS. Most larger family units should have built-in space for washer and dryer. The same is true of luxury units, where residents expect and will pay for washer/dryer space within their unit. Smaller or less luxurious, units generally have community laundry rooms which may be located:

1. Within a cluster of units, usually in the basement or in space created by converting a three bedroom to a one bedroom unit. There are some advantages to locating a laundry room in a cluster of units: residents don't have to walk far; a smaller number of users per laundry facility instills some responsibility for maintenance and care of other neighbors' clothes; the facility can be small with one washer/dryer per 6 to 9 mixed units (efficiency to three bedrooms); and lastly, it creates another opportunity for cluster residents to meet each other. The principal site planning problem is noise. Washer/dryer rooms are noisy, and must be carefully located and insulated to protect the privacy of adjacent neighbors.

2. In a separate communal facility building somewhere on the site. A laundry facility may be an extension of a rec room, next to a shop, part of a day care facility, or alone in its own small building. A facility separate from living units minimizes the noise and disturbance problems, but is less likely to be resident maintained. It must be fairly large, serving up to 50 units, with at least six washers and four dryers.

In either case, there are several site planning considerations that can make the laundry facility pleasant.

- A small outdoor patio area adjacent to the laundry room may be provided for resident use during good weather. Several benches, a table/bench, trees, a small patch of lawn, and maybe even a sand play area for tots may be included.

- The room itself must be inviting with windows, a small locker for each family, and chairs.

- Laundry buildings may be located next to another activity area: tennis courts, recreation room, sauna, pool, community center, etc.

- An outdoor drying area might be designed for use in good weather. We have become accustomed to putting laundry directly into the dryer, but with higher energy costs, the clothes line is a must. Communal clothes drying areas create some problems such as laundry being stolen, kids accidentally getting it dirty, animals damaging it; in addition, many people don't like to look at drying clothes. Keeping a communal drying area small helps; careful siting is a must with kids' play areas and circulation kept at a distance; landscaping and maintenance creates an air of respectability and may reduce vandalism. An alternative is a small clothes line in each private garden.

STORAGE. Medium-density housing is reputed to have limited storage; small closets, no basement, no tool shed. Since storage space is costly, some developers choose to reduce storage in order paraphernalia necessary to operate a single family house isn't necessary in cluster living and needn't be stored. Some typical storage arrangements include:

*Space attached to carport*/garage. Storage units can be added to the end or placed between cars. Units should be a minimum of three feet wide and have a door three feet wide. Sometimes two units can occupy the space at the end of a parking bay, allowing the next space to be vacant, or planted. Conversely, the carport end could be enlarged ten feet providing a comfortable shop for resident use.

*Basement storage.* Storage space may be provided in basement areas, especially in buildings with parking in the basement. The decision is one of priorities: is storage more important than, say, additional recreation space or larger living space?

*Locker storage.* This may be provided for each unit in communal facilities such as laundry room, recreation room, shop, and swimming pool changing room.

*Tool shed as part of yard fence.* If the private garden is to be fenced, a small tool shed can be easily built in. A simple concrete floor, with walls to match the fence, and a pitched roof works well. The storage unit needn't be tall; six feet sloping to four feet is adequate.

*Boat, trailer, and second-car storage.* It is not desirable for residents to park a second, seldom-used vehicle next to their units. A better solution is a fenced and lighted parking lot somewhere on the property where vehicles and trailers can be parked closely, perhaps in tandem, to conserve space.

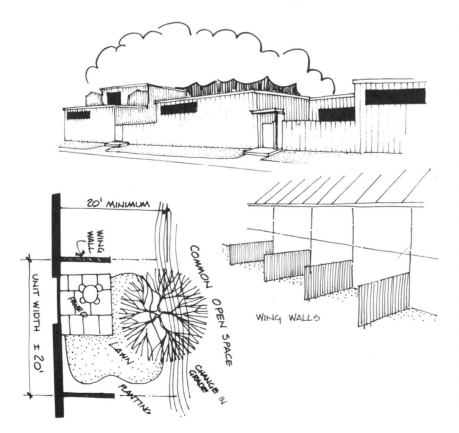

20' MINIMUM

WING WALL

COMMON OPEN SPACE

UNIT WIDTH ± 20'

PAVED

LAWN

PLANTING

CHANGE IN GRADE

WING WALLS

## OTHER SITE PLANNING DILEMMAS AND TRADEOFFS

PRIVATE GARDENS—TO FENCE OR NOT TO. The landscape will generally look more spacious and open without fences, yet most families prefer some privacy in their own garden. At medium density, privacy is not always assured by simply building a fence. Overviewing is a prime privacy problem which can't be controlled by fencing, though it can be controlled somewhat by tree planting.

Patio houses, which are meant to have defined gardens, should be fenced. Sometimes low fences are appropriate for garden ends where units face onto an open space.

Adjacent row units usually require wing walls to prevent sideways viewing between adjacent gardens. Generally the most used portion of a garden, where privacy is sought, is the part immediately adjacent to the door. As one moves farther away from the door, the need for privacy seems to decrease. Thus, wing walls may be quite high, six to eight feet at the building, decreasing to a height of five to six feet. The wall may be constructed of the same material as the building and needn't protrude more than eight feet to provide a sense of privacy. Wing walls with no end fence increase the visual size of the open space and provide the most privacy relative to the length of fence. Providing privacy from people in the open space isn't overly complex, but requires some planning. Raising the garden three feet above surrounding open space places the garden at a "superior" level and creates a feeling of privacy and security. Planting low shrubs at the periphery of the garden eliminates view in from the adjacent open space. Depending on grades it may be possible to depress the surrounding open space three feet, or use a combination of cut and fill to mound.

Earth mounding is relatively inexpensive and can create a completely new landscape. All topsoil should be stripped and stockpiled for later use. Lastly, the mounds should be large enough to appear natural and graded gently. Shrub planting between private garden and semi-public portions of open space helps ensure privacy. The planting, particularly if thick and thorny, directs people away from the private gardens and provides some visual screening.

SOME "FENCE" SOLUTIONS. Private gardens facing the street should be fenced. Space, about three feet, between the fence and sidewalks, should be saved for planting. The planting strip protects the fence and assures a pleasant walk for passing pedestrians. Street trees in the planting strip should be planted to allow sunlight to penetrate into the garden. Fences along the street must be more carefully designed and constructed than internal fences. Raising the garden several feet by retaining wall or sloped bank insures greater privacy for roadside units.

*Large Family Units*, particularly with young children, may require a fenced garden. Generally gardens for children should be slightly larger than other gardens. Try to use large fenced units to define other open space areas. For instance, fenced

One detail—residential fences are normally constructed inexpensively, look bad and won't stand up to public wear. Where possible, separate fences from public walls by a small planter—even just two feet wide.

gardens on the end of a row can enclose the total internal area and perhaps minimize the need for other fences. There is an opposite point of view—that large families do not really need privacy (or cannot easily get it) and would benefit from being directly attached to the open space for easy access by the kids.

*Fence When Open Space Is Limited.* Tight urban sites sometimes contain insufficient open space to provide private, semi-private, and public spaces. In some cases it may be better to divide left-over space between the units, and fence each yard for privacy. In such a situation the fences become important visual elements and should be carefully designed. Large trees should be planted in some yards to emphasize the presence of adjacent open space.

*Resident-Built Fences.* Residents may want to decide on the location and height of fences. And they might choose from prefabricated panels. With fence panels available, the residents could install fences during summer or winter as required. There are some problems: cost of prefabrication is more than the cost of constructing a fence; storage of unused fences is difficult (although a development need not store enough for everyone); and assembly and support systems are difficult to develop.

*Movable Panels* might be used so fences could be changed from time to time. For instance, four might be provided per unit, two used for wing walls and two staggered across the yard width. With planting, the system could insure adequate privacy without being completely fenced.

*Overhead Trellis.* A light frame, perhaps with climbing vine, provides sun protection to inside rooms as well as privacy from overviewing from units above.

CONFUSION BETWEEN THE FRONT AND REAR ENTRANCE. Guests and tradespeople may be confused by double entrances to units (one on the parking side and one on the open space side) and not know which entrance to use. Likely, the entrance nearest the road will be considered by most people as the main entrance, the front door. One possible solution to confusing entrance is to construct a hallway between the two entrances with both doors opening onto it. Other solutions to the dilemma include:

*Signs and Maps.* Large developments benefit from a comprehensive sign/map near the main entrance depicting routes and locations of various clusters. Clusters and street names should be identified. Nearer each cluster signs with unit numbers and resident names can eliminate confusion. Signs may also be used to identify guest parking lots and pathways through open space.

*Construct Fences* to discourage wrong entry. How the gate is designed, a fenced garden can be made welcoming or unwelcoming. If the gate is camouflaged, it is not inviting, whereas a gate that is lower or inset slightly , constructed of a different material, or has a sign with unit number and occupants' names and door bell welcomes the visitor.

PROVIDING A GARDEN FOR EVERY UNIT AT MEDIUM DENSITY. A one or two-story development generally allows room for a ground-oriented garden at each unit. However, if units are stacked two, three, or four floors, ground-oriented gardens for all units are not possible. However, ground-level garden space may be traded for roof garden, a deck space. Cost and functional problems prohibit decks from being as large as on-grade gardens, so container gardening has to substitute for "real dirt" gardening.

*Roof Garden.* An outdoor space over a room below creates a garden, varies the building, and utilizes available land efficiently. Privacy from overviewing is easy to solve with a wide planter rail and wing walks. The main problem with roof gardens is waterproofing, which tends to increase construction and maintenance costs considerably. For small roof gardens with light use, a heavy built-up tar and gravel roof with deck boards can work. Larger roof gardens or those extensively used need surfacing, such as concrete, over the waterproofing. Again, surfaces of concrete are expensive because of weight, drainage problems, and the complicated process of laying the concrete. Roof gardens over garages, tool sheds, or other nonliving spaces simplify construction demands and should be examined for potential use.

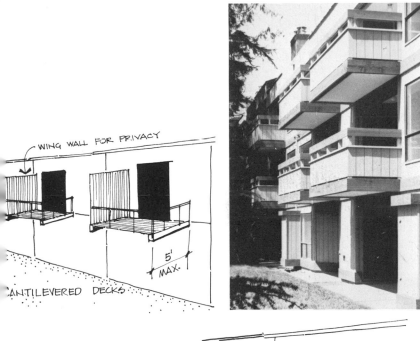

WING WALL FOR PRIVACY

5' MAX.

CANTILEVERED DECKS

*Cantilevered Deck.* Wood-frame construction allows decks to be cantilevered (using extended floor joists) to a distance of about five feet with varying lengths, although five feet wide by ten feet long is large enough for many outdoor activities. Decking may be fir, cedar, or redwood. In addition, a rail at least three feet high should be provided. Wing walls ensure privacy from adjacent units, though privacy can be increased by separating adjacent decks some distance. Cost of cantilevered deck are considerably less than the cost of roof decks.

Small cantilevered decks may be constructed inexpensively off a number of rooms; a three-foot by six-foot long deck from dining or bedroom allows residents to step outside for a moment of sunshine or fresh air. Such a deck could be waterproofed to act as a rain shield for a door below.

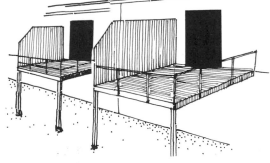

*Post and Beam Balcony.* Since balcony widths exceeding five feet cannot be easily cantilevered, post and beam construction must be used. The main advantage of this form of con-

279

struction is its ability to support more deck space; an outdoor space at least 10 feet square can accommodate many family needs. The main disadvantage lies in the extensive support structure of posts, which interferes with activities below and looks awkward when more than one story tall.

*Inward Cast Deck.* For rainy areas or where setback requirements prohibit decks extending beyond the building line, a deck may be carved out of the living space. Limitations in size depend only on how much living space can be given up. Construction costs are minimal, although waterproofing may be a problem. Privacy is certain, and, there are no shadows cast or other interference with units below.

*Pea Patch or Allotment Gardens.* Allotment gardens can easily be worked into the communal open space system. What is needed is a level, sunny area that can be divided into smaller plots. Ten feet square is minimum for each plot, although 15 to 20 feet square is preferred. Developing the allotment garden requires systems for dividing plots and tilling and enriching the soil, as well as installation of water faucets, small tool sheds, benches, and possibly a comfort station. Since the communal activity provides self-policing and adequate maintenance, fencing is seldom necessary.

TYPICAL APARTMENT ARRANGEMENTS. Any housing complex benefits from larger sites. The larger the site, the more flexibility a designer has to integrate all functions of a site plan. What happens on a very small site, where circulation, open space, and housing units must somehow be squeezed in?

First, most apartment complexes use stacked flats instead of row or town houses. Entries are usually double loaded to save additional space. Orientation and identity are usually sacrificed, with units receiving whatever sun is possible. Private gardens are almost always eliminated, though often small balconies are provided. Entry is usually combined with the parking lot and is seldom pleasant.

In most western states, a 50 foot by 100 foot apartment lot is zoned for six units. This is equivalent to a gross density of 50 d/u per acre! A standard solution, if there is an alley behind is to park three cars in front, three cars behind, divide the remaining 60 feet in two, enter in the center, and stack two sets of flats three stories high. One set overlooks the street, the other the alley. Entrance is down one side in the required 5 foot setback. There is no common open space or landscaping, and protection of privacy is difficult. Parking perpendi-

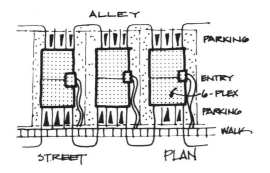

ALLEY

PARKING

ENTRY

6-PLEX

PARKING

WALK

STREET    PLAN

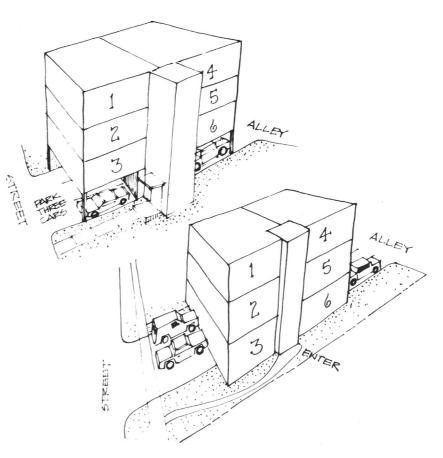

STREET

PARK THREE CARS

ALLEY

1  4
2  5
3  6

ALLEY

1  4
2  5
3  6

STREET

ENTER

cular to and across the sidewalk diminishes the passing pedestrians' experience and creates a parking lot image. Again, the main advantage is that this type of development is less expensive than row or town houses.

A variation of this plan, when no alley exists or where perpendicular parking off a main road is not allowed, is to park all six cars under the building in a 90° arrangement. This requires a 40-foot wide parking lot (allowing the 5 foot setback on either side) by 60 feet long with single road access. The same six-unit complex is then built over the parking.

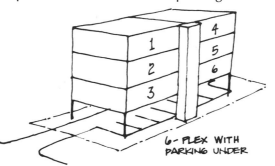

1  4
2  5
3  6

6-PLEX WITH
PARKING UNDER

281

Stacking units one on top of another up to four floors creates some undesirable features. First, one unit directly over another creates a noise problem which is expensive to lessen since the sound of walking is easily transmitted through most floor systems. Secondly, ground floor access is available only to the first floor. Third, identity tends to be related to the ground floor, with units "in the sky" having less identity. Fourth, the internal separation of living and sleeping is difficult in a compact plan all on one floor. Lastly, some rooms, particularly baths, may not have windows while others may have less than desirable views. The principal advantage of stacked flats is cost in that they are less expensive to construct than row or town houses.

continually curtained. Furthermore, units face onto the side yard which usually is not wide enough for privacy or sunlight.

Motel type units are a popular developer's special, particularly for one bedroom units. "Motel type" derives its name from the typical motel exterior access balcony on each floor serving stacked flats. Parking is usually under, the entrance is at the street, with units running from the entrance balcony to the other property line. Entrance along a balcony is noisy and reduces privacy to units. Most windows along the entrance balcony cannot be opened for fear of intrusion and must be

The Donut Plan derives its name from an arrangement which consists of a ring of parking surrounding a ring of buildings which surrounds a small court. This arrangement requires a large piece of property and has as its main drawback the parking lot surrounding the units, creating a difficult entry sequence. Typically there is little planting and no entrance garden between units and parking. However, the interior court is relatively free of outside intrusion and can be quite pleasant.

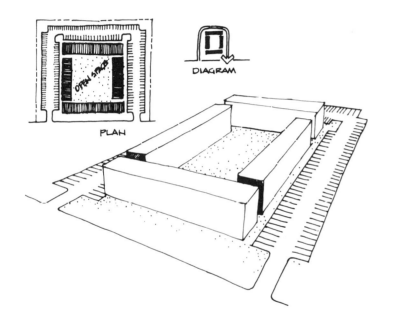

OPEN SPACE

PLAN

DIAGRAM

In summary, although we may try to assure each unit the best view, proper sun orientation, privacy, connection to the open space, and easy access, it is impossible to provide everything. Thus, we reach a dilemma that must be solved through tradeoff. The dilemma may be: (1) a *density dilemma*, making accomplishing all goals impossible because of high density; (2) an *efficiency versus amenity dilemma*, usually involving the automobile; and (3) a *cost dilemma*, where just a few more dollars would make a great deal of difference. The site planner's task is to expose and resolve each dilemma.

# IMPLEMENTING THE SITE PLAN

As the preliminary site plan takes shape, the planner, or planning team, faces a series of legal and technical situations including how to best deliver site services (sewer, gas, water, etc.); how to deal with zoning and ownership regulations; how to comply with environmental impact assessments; and how to reduce the cost of housing, which regardless of the projected market income seems always to be too high. These situations and alternative solutions are discussed in some detail in this chapter.

## DELIVERING SITE SERVICES

Circulation and open space systems serve not only for recreation, movement, community structure, and amenity, but also as a *location for all site utilities*. Generally, though, site utilities are not prime determinants of site form, but adequate

space must be provided for them to function efficiently. Since the final detailed utility plan will be laid out by a civil engineer in consultation with the site planner, only a general approach needs to be considered at this stage. Each site plan must contain an infrastructure with the following systems:

| | |
|---|---|
| Movement Systems | auto |
| | bicycle |
| | pedestrian |
| | public transit |
| Energy Systems | gas |
| | electricity |
| | steam |
| Communication Systems | telephone |
| | CC TV |
| | cable |
| Waste Management Systems | trash |
| | sewer |
| | garbage |
| Water Systems | delivery |
| | storage |
| | fire fighting |
| Public Safety Systems | fire call boxes |
| | police call boxes |
| Recreation Systems | facilities for active recreation |
| | facilities for passive recreation |
| Street Furniture Systems | lighting |
| | seating |
| | signs |

Besides movement and recreation systems which are integral to site planning, waste management systems need to be considered. The other systems, while important, are flexible and do not pose important site planning constraints.

UTILITY AVAILABILITY. Large suburban developments on underdeveloped land may not be conveniently served by all necessary utilities. Sewer and water are the most important utilities; most others either are available, can be lived without, or are easily installed. If service is not available at the property line, the feasibility and costs of extending it to the site should be investigated. If sewer and water are not accessible or if trunk line capacity is inadequate, the site may have to be abandoned as undevelopable, a decision that should be made prior to extensive site planning studies.

WHERE SHALL WE PUT THEM? Utilities are typically located in road rights-of-way with most utilities located directly under the roadway. It is advantageous to place utilities in the street because repair is easy since there is plenty of room to manipulate equipment and ownership is usually public; no cluster or unit need be disturbed during construction or repair.

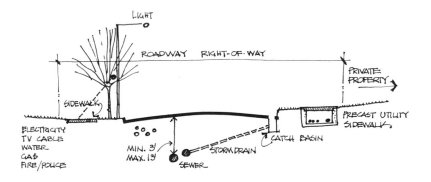

An alternative is to bury utilities in the sidewalk, as is done in many European cities. The disadvantages of this approach are that utilities often interfere with street furniture, street trees, and light standards, and disruption is greater when repairs need to be made. A third alternative is to locate portions of the utility system in community open space. Its main advantages are efficiency and lower construction costs. However, since this approach is potentially disruptive to landscape development during construction or repair, the authors suggest keeping utilities out of the open space system unless the cost advantage is high.

If the site is isolated (i.e., if other property must be crossed to reach it), an easement may be required. Easements are

deeded rights-of-way to use a specific portion of a piece of private property for some specific purpose, i.e., for a sewer line. They must be purchased if they cross other privately owned land, and may be difficult and expensive to obtain. For this reason, they are usually narrow, seldom wider than necessary to allow construction equipment to operate. Trees and permanent structures should not be located on the easement, although grass, shrubs, removable fences, and open space activities are usually permissible.

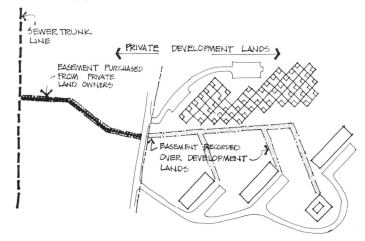

Any proposed utility line within the development boundary that crosses what will be future residents' property should be recorded as an easement. This includes lines crossing communal open space. Internal easements are determined during design and show up as deed restrictions when the property is sold.

COMBINED STORM AND SANITARY SEWERS. In the past most sewer systems were constructed with sanitary waste and storm water runoff in the same system. This practice is no longer allowed in most communities to protect environmental quality. Now storm water systems have to be separate. Since storm water does not need to be treated, it may be returned to the natural drainage system.

RUNOFF DISPOSAL. The authors recommend devising systems of storm water disposal which minimize the number of catch basins and underground drain lines, and which use swales, holding basins, ground-water recharge devices, and simple dispersal directly over the ground. These alternatives will work for most areas except those which receive continual rain, have poor soil percolation, are prone to flash floods, and have developments with densities higher than 15 d.u./acre.

*Why Is Runoff a Problem?* When a site is developed and surfaces are paved or covered (roads, parking areas, buildings), water is not allowed to percolate into the ground. Then the speed and amount of runoff increases; runoff is almost 100 percent over paved surfaces, compared with only 40 percent over undeveloped land. The result is more water moving faster down streams causing flooding, erosion and a decrease in water quantity. Many communities have spent a great deal of money channeling streams in pipes to prevent these problems, which could have been solved following natural drainage patterns. The concept is quite simple: more paving means more runoff which means more storm water management.

A site may be divided into small watersheds of wide planted swales and holding ponds. Holding ponds should be designed to store all runoff from paved surfaces for the duration of an average storm, and then slowly release water following the storm. Planting is essential in decreasing runoff. Water is held in the dense matting of plants' roots or absorbed into their leaves, lessening the amount of water running across the surface of the ground.

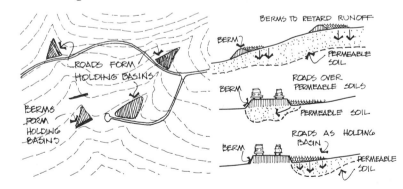

The basic principle in developing systems for runoff disposal is to maintain runoff volume and speeds at predevelopment levels, called zero-percent increased runoff; then existing drainage patterns can be maintained. Runoff disposal systems allow storm water to percolate into the ground or be detained in holding basins until a storm subsides when it can be re-

turned to the natural drainage system without causing erosion and flooding. To minimize the amounts of runoff from extensively paved areas such as roads and parking lots it is best to keep road widths and parking areas as small as possible, no wider than minimum requirements and perhaps even narrower. On small access roads, curbs may be eliminated and replaced with wide planted swales which absorb and disperse some of the runoff. Dry wells and drain fields may be constructed beneath road surfaces, with runoff diverted into them. Since this method is complex, it requires the assistance of a creative civil engineer. Although similar systems may be used along the planted edges and median strips of Local and Major roads, most have to be drained with a storm system transporting runoff from the road to a dispersal site, a creek, stream, river, or holding pond.

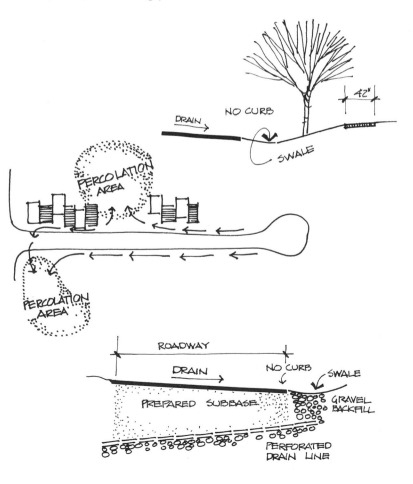

Small parking areas may be paved with gravel, instead of asphalt, allowing more percolation. Since compaction of gravel by parked cars is possible, the lot must be carefully designed to prevent this. On the other hand, heavily used lots, requiring asphalt paving, may be designed to slow runoff by diverting it into planted areas for percolation, with a catch basin placed in the low spot to pick up any overflow.

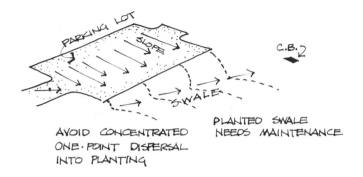

AVOID CONCENTRATED ONE-POINT DISPERSAL INTO PLANTING

PLANTED SWALE NEEDS MAINTENANCE

*Now a word of caution*, if all runoff is diverted into planted open space, the result may be a muddy mess instead of usable parkland. Therefore, it is essential that the planner use good judgment and make exact calculations of quantity of runoff and percolation potential.

SEPTIC TANKS. New environmental protection regulations severely limit the use of individual septic tanks at higher densities. The principal problem with septic waste disposal is the large quantity of effluent that must be absorbed by ground percola tion. If a site has a high water table or is near a body of water, septic disposal is not feasible.

COMMUNITY SANITARY SYSTEMS. In areas without sewer systems small community sanitary systems may be used to handle sewage on a temporary basis until hookup to a permanent system is possible. Two systems are presently available:

*Community septic system*. This is essentially a large version of an individual septic system with several settling tanks and a large drainfield. A sewer system is installed throughout the development leading to the septic area. Space requirements are usually not too great, and the drainfield may be planted in grass and used for recreation. Although the installation process is simple, it usually takes time to obtain the approvals needed for implementation. In addition, close coordination with the local health district is essential to insure adequate percolation. Community septic systems have been used in developments up to several hundred units, and are often installed, as a temporary system, until a municipal system is available.

*Secondary sewage treatment facility*. This is often necessary in areas with a high ground water table or with nearby bodies of water. A secondary sewage treatment facility makes the effluent safe to dispose of either in a river or underground, and replaces the settling tanks of a septic system. If effluent discharge is to be underground, a drainfield is still required. If it is to be into a stream or body of water, an outfall or pipe outlet is necessary. As with the septic system, these facilities require cooperation with health officials and a complex set of approvals.

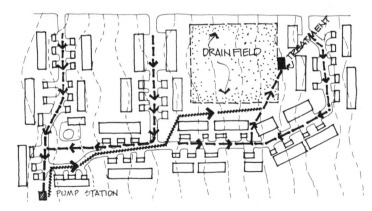

SEWER LINES. If sewer lines are available for hookup to the site, the planner should be aware of a number of factors. Typically public sewer lines are precast concrete, though tile is sometimes used, and all pipes are at least 10 inches in diameter for easy cleaning. Sewer lines run in straight or almost straight lines; a slight bend is permissible. Each major bend or connection of several pipes requires a manhole cleanout in addition to the manhole cleanouts required by code at set distances, usually every 400 feet.

Determining the depth of sewer lines is a design problem. The discharge elevation is one determinant; a line may not be lower than this point unless a pumping station is installed. If basements are built, the sewer line must be lower than basement level. Another determinant is that sewer lines must flow somewhat uniformly to the lowest elevation, which may be between three and 13 feet. To verify locations and potential conflicts, a quick section should be drawn through the proposed sewer route. Two variations on developments of sewer systems are mentioned briefly.

*Pumping stations.* Level sites or sites with extreme topography may require pumping stations to lift sanitary or storm wastes to a higher elevation so the force of gravity can move them downhill. These systems are expensive to install and operate (the pumps clog easily), and should be used only where essential.

*Vacuum sewers.* Small diameter, pressure lines have been introduced successfully in several developments. Though more costly to install and operate, they do allow greater location flexibility, eliminate the need for deep lines, and permit lines to move more freely within a development. They could even be installed in a common utility trench, as discussed below.

OTHER SITE SERVICES. All other site services are pressure fed and therefore easier to lay out. Most services utilize the hierarchial branching pattern, decreasing in size from the main connection to the development boundary. The exception is the water system which must loop to keep pressure in the pipes equal.

A utility trench cast of concrete under removable sidewalk sections is an excellent location for services which don't have to be buried deeply such as electricity, telephone, television cable, police and fire call lines, and in warmer climates domestic water supply. The box trench should be about two feet deep with service holes in the side to feed utilities to abutting uses. Special sections are available for street crossings, but curvilinear sections are not yet available. Although utility trenches are expensive to install, they are easy to reach so future servicing and repair costs should be low.

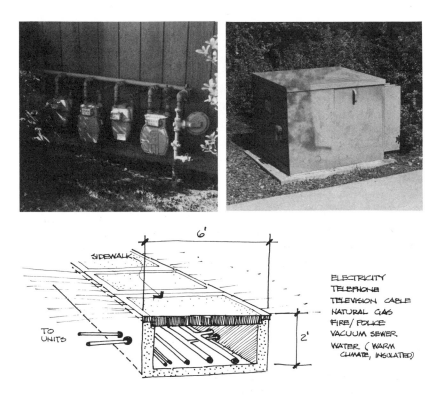

CALCULATING COSTS. Like other linear elements, construction costs of site utilities are based primarily on the *length* of run; that is, the longer the line the greater the expense. Obviously factors such as the steepness of terrain, depth of burial, and presence of underground rock obstructions increase costs and should be avoided in selection of utility lines.

Preliminary cost estimates may be prepared using *relative costs,* in other words, designing and refining alternative locations until one appears relatively less expensive than the others. The least expensive line would be the one running the shortest distance through best site conditions from service stub to all units with minimum intrusion into public open spaces. Although relative costs and utility locations should be studied by the site planner early in the process, they must be verified by a civil engineer before the plan is finalized.

WHO PAYS FOR WHAT? Typically a developer must finance all non-profit utility lines such as sanitary sewers and water mains. Roads and sidewalks are also almost always installed by the developer, with construction costs added to the unit

289

cost or rent. Private utility companies (gas, electric, television, and telephone) install their own services and recover costs through monthly fees. Lastly, installation of public safety elements, such as fire hydrants, call boxes, and street lights, varies from place to place. Either the developer installs them or the municipality installs them and backcharges the developer or future owners.

## ZONING

The site planner must be familiar with existing zoning requirements and the procedures for changing conditions that present unworkable problems. Zoning, like other legal matters, appears difficult but can be understood by mastery of some basic principles.

First, zoning is a form of police control enacted to assure public health, safety, and welfare. All requirements and controls of the zoning code are supposedly important in this respect so that any proposed change must be in the public interest. Zoning controls three factors of the site plan: use, intensity of use, and configuration.

*Use* divides land uses into categories: residential, commercial, industrial, institutional, rural, unclassified, etc. In most areas land is assigned a zone, in which uses are permitted, excluded or permitted with stipulations.

*Intensity* describes how much a site may be developed. In housing, the measure of intensity is usually dwelling units per acre, but may be a minimum lot size, a parking requirement, or a floor-area ratio (FAR). Parking requirements and floor-area ratio don't specify maximum intensity directly, but tend to place limits based on design skills—for instance a FAR of 2 means a floor area equal to two times the lot area can be built. The number of units is dependent on how many the site planner can design into that maximum floor area.

*Configuration* describes physical limitations in the way a site may be developed, including setbacks, height restrictions, points of access, etc.

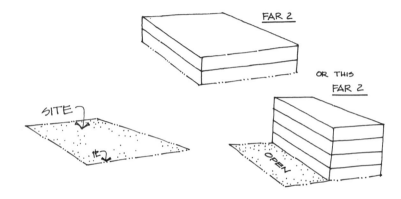

Local land-use regulations—subdivision regulations to govern lot division and zoning to control building configuration constricts the opportunity for imaginative building.

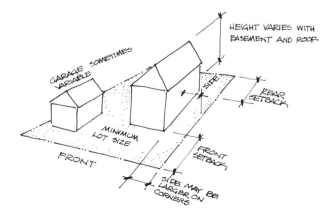

A site planner's first task is to assess existing zoning to determine if it allows adequate flexibility to meet program demands. Development is easier if the site plan conforms to existing zoning, since any zoning change is expensive, time consuming, and uncertain. Should change be necessary there are three techniques that can be employed.

Rezoning. Everyone has the right to apply for rezoning, generally for change in use. Specific application procedures listed in the local zoning ordinance usually involve an application, a fee, and documented justifications for the change. Review by the controlling agency planning staff and public hearings follow. Approval is often politically motivated, always controversial, results in increased property value, and is subject to review by courts. The illegality of spot zoning makes many rezones questionable and unsure. Furthermore, while rezones are easier to obtain on large parcels of land or in areas of absentee ownership, they are very difficult to obtain in stable neighborhoods. They seldom produce ideal environments, since use is often in excess of desirable conditions and since no mechanisms are provided to insure that a specific plan will be implemented.

Variance. Variance is a procedure used to relax certain zoning conditions if a hardship exists. Most hardships are the result of physical site conditions such as a steep cliff, or irregular lot shape, poor soil, that together with a setback requirement make the site unusable.

The procedure for approval of a variance is usually simpler than for rezoning. It costs less, is not politically motivated, and is more likely to be approved if the hardship actually exists. Developers sometimes apply for a variance to increase the intensity of use based on economic hardship. They have to prove that some economic reason (high cost of land, unusual soil condition, etc.) makes development of the land unprofitable unless a higher density is allowed. Even though this use of the variance procedure has been shown to work, it is questionable, since the change is actually a form of rezoning.

Planned Unit Development. A Planned Unit Development (also known as PUD, planned unit, planned development, or planned community) is a parcel of land planned as a single unit rather than as an aggregate of individual lots, with increased flexibility in siting regulations (such as setbacks, height restrictions) or land use restrictions (such as mixing land uses). The greater flexibility in locating buildings and combining land uses often makes it possible to achieve economics of construction as well as to preserve open space and other amenities. Thus, the Planned Unit Development designation, in a conceptual sense, allows the site planner to propose the best use and arrangement of the land, with fewer constraints than those imposed by existing zoning. The P.U.D. does, however, continue to protect the public against unscrupulous developers.

In most areas, the P.U.D. is an overzone or contract zone placed, upon approval, over the existing zone. Site planners can, theoretically, propose to arrange buildings in any desirable manner, eliminating setbacks to save natural features, reducing the length and width of roads, clustering without side yards, etc. In exchange for allowing this flexibility, the local government expects: 1) an understanding of exactly what the finished product will be, that is, complete plans of all buildings and landscaping, including quality of materials and construction procedures. 2) a development that preserves and provides certain amenities, natural features, recreation facilities, and plantings. 3) a development that will not unnecessarily change the life style or economic condition of the neighborhood or city.

Each locality has its own P.U.D. ordinance, which should be checked for procedural and site restraint conditions. Most P.U.D. ordinances require a minimum site (2 acres, 5 acres, etc.) and state whether existing density or use can be changed. Although the P.U.D. overzone was not intended to allow an increase in density, it is common for developers to seek an increase. In order to obtain P.U.D. designation a developer must prepare a proposal with documentation; it is reviewed by the planning staff and at public hearings before approval is granted. The process is seldom that simple since the planning staff generally suggests changes and the public forces other changes. The process does allow a site planner to consider both client and larger public needs in devising the scheme. When plans are finally approved, they form a contract which must be adhered to within an agreed-upon time period.

DENSITY. Density describes how heavily we use our land, that is, how intensely a unit of land is used. Residential density is measured by two scales: dwelling units per acre and people per acre. Dwelling units per acre is the most common measure. The concept is simple, direct, easy to manage although somewhat arbitrary. Densities are established and applied in blanket fashion over the land as either dwelling units per acre (D.U./acre) or a minimum lot size. This form of control is workable for low densities (below six D.U./acre) but becomes imprecise at higher densities where overcrowding and small units may cause social problems. The people per acre measure, a more precise scale, can minimize the effects of overcrowding. This measure is used extensively in England and follows a systematic set of guidelines which assures certain amenities per resident.

Most people in the West prefer to live at relatively low densities, yet rising costs and low public amenities are beginning to alter this feeling. The "proper" density varies from site to site and household type to household type, but should balance the advantages and disadvantages of high and low density.

Medium density results in lower unit costs and lower quality private amenities but high quality public amenities, while low density results in high unit costs, high quality private amenities but low quality public amenities.

The Land Use Intensity formula devised by the Federal Housing Administration (FHA) emphasizes the importance of basic amenity by relating amenity to density in a mathematical ratio. The formula assigns density by comparing rights-of way for cars, car parking spaces, building area, recreation, play and planting space. The formula is complicated, but allows adjustment of each factor, which theoretically affects density, while keeping amenity in balance.

Density and Feasibility.

A decisive criterion is how dense does a development need to be to support public facilities and public transportation. Only at the density of row, town or patio houses, do people live close enough for public transportation to be efficient.

Design plays an important part in how successful development of a specific density will be. The arrangement, location, views, and sequence of a well designed medium-density development can enable it to function better than a poorly designed low-density development.

Parking Space increases as density increases to a point where surface parking can seriously reduce usable open space. As a general rule, surface parking becomes disadvantageous above 15 D.U./acre. The alternatives are to provide multistory garage parking, reduce open space, or limit density to balance open space and on-grade parking.

Sewers. Areas served by sewage treatment plants have no definable upper density limits; however, areas served by septic systems do have severe limitations on density. Septic systems, dependent on the percolation capability of the soil, are generaly limited to one per minimun lot size of 10,000 square feet or approximately one-quarter area.

Available Open Space. Building sites adjacent to large public open spaces (parks, playgrounds, schoolyards, etc.) often are capable of sustaining increased density, by "borrowing land" from the adjacent open space. Likewise, building sites near

good public transportation or adjacent to convenient shopping or employment can often sustain higher densities because of reduced reliance on the private automobile.

Durability of Open Space. Children in their normal play patterns are hard on open space; newly installed landscapes and lawns can support only a limited number of children. Normal landscape development can handle a maximum density of approximately 15 D.U./acre. Obviously, a development without children could exceed that density without undue harm to landscape development.

Ground Orientation, Privacy, and Identity. These become difficult and expensive at densities in excess of 18 to 20 D.U./acre. Up to that point it is possible for all units to have privacy, identity, easy access, and private outdoor space.

In cluster development density varies according to physical conditions and household types. Some areas in the development may have as many as 50 D.U./acre on a net basis (for singles, young married couples, and elderly people) while others may have only one D.U./acre. To ensure a healthy environment, however, overall density generally should not exceed 10 D.U./acre in suburban conditions or 15 D.U./acre in urban conditions. In many suburban conditions overall density should not exceed 7 D.U./acre.

There is a lower end to density—a matter of practicality. Low density means large investment for roads and services, long travel distances to commercial and civic center and to work.

The upper limit of density is set by problems of congestion.

FHA regulations prohibit families with children from being located in high-rise buildings unless no other options are available.

## OWNERSHIP

During program development it is important to determine whether the units will be resident owned or rented. People look more carefully at the size of closets, the quality of construction, and the overall environment when purchasing than when renting. The difference between expectations of owners and renters is subtle and affects social relationships, marketing strategy, and development economics. Thus, the different forms of tenure available to medium-density cluster housing are:

Fee Ownership. This means outright ownership of a parcel of land and house, and includes most single-family houses with an identifiable properly line and access directly from a public street. The owner is responsible for maintenance, payment of taxes, and management of the property, and typically all property in the development is divided and owned by either a homeowner or the city.

Rental. Units owned by a landlord, are rented by a tenant generally on a monthly or yearly basis. Maintenance, management, payment of taxes, etc., are the responsibility of the owner who pays for them from the rental fee.

Two newer forms of home ownership have been developed to handle the problems of cluster housing developments, since cluster houses do not fit the definition of fee-owned houses. For instance, a unit may not connect to a public road and open space associated with the development is jointly owned and managed by all the residents.

Condominium Ownership. This form of ownership is similar to fee ownership in that each owner possesses an identifiable and legally defined house (not a stacked or interlocked unit), plus a share in the development's common open space. Typically each unit is located on a public street, commonly owned street, or path system. Generally, condominium units are easily sold and financed.

Cooperative Ownership. Developments with interlocked units, units in tall buildings, or other units which can't be easily identified or related to a street or path are sold as cooperatives. Cooperative ownership is an undividable share of the development. Each unit has a share with certain rights describing which unit you own and your rights to common areas and facilities.

It is typical for condominium and cooperative residents to belong to a home-owners' association and pay a monthly management and maintenance fee to cover costs for upkeep of the common land. The fee covers taxes on common property, insurance, maintenance of the garden, pool, etc. and often has an amount designated for repair and upkeep of the outside of all units (that is, painting every 5 to 10 years or a new roof in 20 years). Monthly fees vary from $10 to $120 and are tax deductible. Residents elect home-owner association officers, who are responsible for overseeing management of the common areas. Some recreational cluster developments are experimenting with time-sharing or joint venture ownership, in which several families jointly own a unit and each is able to use it for a specifc length of time per year. For instance, four owners may share it, each for one week a month or for three months of the year. The principal advantages are a reduction in the cost and use time of the house or unit for each family.

LOT LINES. Lot lines should be determined at the end of the site planning process. After all planning has been done, land may be allocated to individual units and common open areas. Lot lines may twist and turn, and needn't follow the standard rectangular pattern. A lawyer can describe each lot legally regardless of its shape.

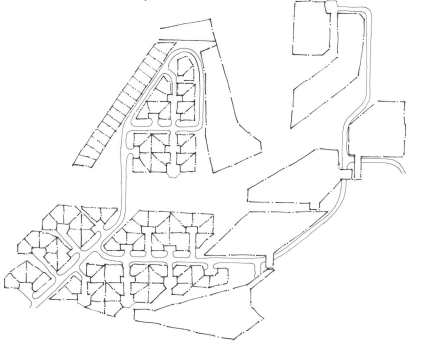

## ENVIRONMENT IMPACT ASSESSMENT

Impact assessment is now an operative part of most approval procedures required for larger developments. Assessment involves determining impacts caused by the development on the long-and short-term quality of the environment. Many state laws have been written using federal N.E.P.A. (National Environmental Policy Act) guidelines which require an evaluation of:

1. The environmental impact of the proposed action
2. Any adverse environmental effects which cannot be avoided should the proposal be implemented
3. Alternatives to the proposed action
4. The relationship between local short-term uses of man's environment and the maintenance and enhancement of long-term productivity
5. Any irreversible and irretrievable commitments of resources which would be involved in the proposed action should it be implemented

Many recent developments have designated impact assessment as the final planning step, uncovering impacts after all decisions have been made and monies exhausted. At this point designers and developers are unwilling to make changes, resulting in counterproductive gamesmanship to justify a bad project, reworking portions of the project, or even abandoning the entire effort because of unreconcilable problems. Although many bad developments have been constructed, they are becoming fewer as the general public becomes more enlightened and demanding and as the quality of assessment increases.

Impact assessment was instituted to improve the quality of our planning, which theoretically would improve the quality of our environment. The procedure is essentially a record keeping process requiring the testing of many alternatives, even those counter to stated goals. Assessment is meant to be incorporated *early* enough in the site planning process to ensure the correctness of major decisions and to allow changes in development direction if conditions warrant it. Long-term impacts are the most difficult to determine but should not be avoided by conscientious planners or developers.

COMPLYING WITH IMPACT ASSESSMENT—At the largest scale impact assessment is concerned with beneficial and detrimental economic, social, physical, and environmental effects of a project. For housing the concern focuses on four factors:

- The capability of a community's physical infrastructure to support the development; in other words, can existing water, sewer, electricity, and road systems support the new development?
- The ability of the community's social services (schools, fire, police, health, etc.) to support the new project within proposed property tax revenues
- The relationship of the proposed development to the long-term growth rate and expectations of the community
- The project's impact on the natural processes of the site and surrounding area

The site planner who has assessed the site's natural processes carefully and understands their ecological integrity should have no trouble complying with the intent of impact assessment. The first three factors listed above will not be considered here, because it is assumed they will be addressed by a consortium of professionals including the site planner. At least 20 documented approaches to impact assessment addressing the five basic concerns listed earlier are summarized below:

- Developing baseline lists and maps of existing natural process conditions; determining location, quantity, and types of biological and physical processes; determining the interrelations, linkages, and dependencies of each element and the possible limits of disturbance. This step involves judgment, experience, and scientific knowledge, which may be supplied by an ecologist or other natural scientist.
- Through creative site planning devising alternative schemes that minimize disturbances to ecologically valued elements.

With many housing projects requiring Environmental Impact Statements, it is essential for site planner and ecologist to learn each other's language and habits so the team can function properly.

- Devising "mitigating responses" to remedy detrimental conditions that cannot be avoided. This may include creating new habitats, planting special trees, providing sources of food or water, duplicating natural drainage patterns, etc. "Mitigating responses" is still a controversial approach, since so little is known about long-term effects.

One of the most positive aspects of the new environmental impact assessment law has been the elimination of the traditional rift between designers wanting to preserve environmental quality and developers not showing enough concern. The site planner now has the legal backing to design well and still maintain a reasonable relationship with his clients.

## REDUCING THE COST OF HOUSING

In studying the cost of housing, there are two traditional but opposite approaches to consider: the filtering-down process and the cost-reduction process. The filtering-down process assumes that if houses are built for those who can afford better housing, someone from a slightly lower income level will move into their old houses. The theory presumes the process will work all the way down to the lowest income level. The flaws in this theory are obvious: first, there are many more families in the lower than upper income range, so adequate supply is never available; second, the supply of houses varies according to conditions far beyond anyone's control; third, lower priced houses are often built away from employment and away from good public transportation and services. In addition, the filtering process often never reaches the lower levels, with houses being bought by people in upper and middle levels. So this is a process over which the site planner has little control or involvement. The cost reduction approach, on the other hand, can be influenced by everyone involved in housing. Bankers can seek ways to lower interest rates and closing costs, architects can devise new techniques and materials to reduce construction costs, lawyers can perhaps shorten the bureaucratic process involved in approvals, municipalities can find ways to reduce property taxes, etc. The site planner has many important cost-reducing opportunities available to him including reducing the cost of land, reducing the cost of construction, saving amenities and thus reducing the cost of creating open space and recreational facilities.

Unattached individuals—particularly in the older age brackets—are most likely to spend a greater than average proportion of their income for housing.

HOW IS OUR HOUSING DOLLAR SPENT? The most valid assessment of the cost of housing is a long-range one that accounts for the direct and indirect cost to both the user and the community over the lifetime of the housing development, but the cost of housing must also be assessed in terms of the individual consumer and his ability to afford housing today. Accelerating costs plus a shortage of homes is making the dream of home ownership less and less a reality for more Americans. This includes people with moderate as well as those with low incomes; it includes families as well as elderly people on fixed incomes. Whether this is a sign of future conditions is hard to predict, but based on past trends, it seems likely that housing costs will rise at least in proportion to the costs of other consumer items. Let's now look at how our housing dollar is spent, and what increases have occurred over the years.

INCREASED LAND COSTS. There is general agreement that land has been the fastest rising major cost element in housing over the last several decades. The average value of land in all metropolitan areas more than doubled between 1950 and 1965, with many areas receiving as much as a five-fold increase. Site value as a percent of total house value for F.H.A. single family homes increased from 12 percent in 1950 to 20 percent in 1970. For higher priced houses, site values may account for 30 percent of the total value of house; this is partially the result of speculation, larger lot sizes, and a lack of control of where growth should occur. It has been estimated that we have used enough land through poor management, etc., in the last 10 years to satisfy our actual need for the next 50 years. The cost of land for housing is attributable to three factors:

1. Price of raw land
2. Cost of land development
3. Amount of land used per unit

The major reason for increased land costs is probably the rise in the costs of raw land. With land considered a "sure profit," many pieces of land are passed from speculator to speculator, escalating in price with each transaction. Other important reasons are the rising costs of planning land development, rising standard of land development, and increased land consumption per unit. In addition, since most easily developed or highly accessible land around urban areas has been developed, only difficult sites or distant land are left.

INCREASED LABOR AND MATERIAL COSTS. The effect of wage increases for on-site labor on total housing costs is hard to calculate. Even though hourly wage rates paid to building trades workers have gone up extremely fast, roughly tripling between 1950 and 1972 and still climbing, labor's share of housing dollar *actually declined* over the same period. This relative decline can be attributed to rising labor productivity, former on-site tasks being done in factories, and a disproportionately rapid increase in land prices.

The construction industry believes that the most improved technology can do is to clip 15% off construction cost of a housing unit.

Prices for building materials have been relatively more stable —rising about 30 percent between 1950 and 1970, but the last few years has seen an annual increase of 10 percent. However, the proportion of total housing costs used for building materials remains high since builders are using more factory finished products.

HIGHER FRONT END COSTS. The greatest percentage cost increase is in the area of financing and closing costs. Although these costs (higher interest rates, professional services, larger discounts, title searches, escrow fees) do not affect construction costs, they do raise occupancy costs. Front end costs, or professional services (finsncial, legal, design, etc.) for necessary costs, they do raise occupancy costs. Front end costs now account for appxoimately eight percent of development costs and are increasing. As many as 36 different agencies may be involved in the approval process for a major land development.

Other factors contributing to increased housing costs are increased size of homes, higher quality of construction and materials, and the demand for more labor-saving appliances (dishwashers, grabage disposals). Cost reductions in the future could be gained through the building of smaller homes with fewer rooms. Our new houses have grown on the average 40 percent in size since World War II adding additional baths, spare rooms, larger halls, closets, etc. While the advantage of increased size is obvious, it is also a possible area to reduce costs in the future.

> It is very probable that about 75% of the living space of the middle income dwelling is not used more than a few hours a day.

Rough breakdown of initial development and construction costs for a conventional single-family unit in 1970 are:

| | |
|---|---|
| Developed land | 25% |
| Construction materials | 36% |
| On-site labor | 19% |
| Overhead and profit | 14% |
| Miscellaneous | 6% |
| TOTAL | 100% |

ADDITIONAL COSTS TO RESIDENTS. Beyond construction and development costs, the home buyer or renter is faced with additional operating expenses, including:

1. Financing and real estate taxes which add approximately 40 percent to the cost of housing and are continuing to rise. A 1 percent rise in mortgage rate equals a 10 percent rise in housing costs over the life of the mortgage.
2. Servicing which includes municipal and state costs associated with suburban development. These too are continuing to rise. The cost of freeways, arterials, police and fire protection, sewers, light, schools, etc., must be added to the initial cost of housing, though the consumer pays for them indirectly.

REDUCING DEVELOPMENT COSTS

Typical ways to reduce costs other than unit and landscaping costs, in cluster developments include:

- Shortening the length of roadways. Roadways are the principal infrastructure expense because they include in addition to the roadway: street lighting, sidewalks, sewers, water, gas, electricity, and landscaping. Every lineal foot of roadway that can be eliminated will reduce overall development costs.
- Narrowing building widths reduces the length of road required.
- Eliminating roadway frontage by using patio houses, houses on key shaped lots, units perpendicular to the road, and stacked maisonettes. All decrease the proportionate amount of roadway related to each unit. Using culs-de-sac which are generally narrower than local roads, and do not need sidewalks, curbs, or storm gutters.
- Centralizing parking to reduce the length of roadway necessary to serve the total development. Besides decreasing initial construction costs, shorter roadways reduce future maintenance costs.

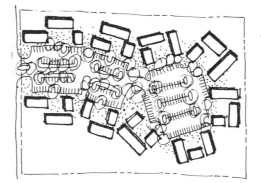

- PLANT 2 TREES PER 3 CARS
- AVOID PLACING CARS ON BOTH SIDES OF UNITS

- Narrowing roadway width to the minimum necessary for a road's intended function. Since utilities are not eliminated, narrowing a road does not reduce costs as dramatically as shortening it. Unfortunately most engineering standards require wider roads than necessary for safe travel, so any proposal to narrow the road may entail a battle with the local engineering department—a battle worth the effort.

Narrowing access and local roads should be given top priority, as they directly affect living conditions. /Access roads with no through circulation may be 20 to 26 feet wide. The twenty-six foot width allows parking on one side with traffic moving at a reasonable speed in both directions, while the twenty-foot width allows free flowing two-way traffic without parking or if parking is allowed, a car moving in one direction must wait until a car in other direction passes.

- Eliminating roadway curbs. This can be done by draining the road to the center, eliminating both curbs, or draining the road to one side, eliminating one curb. A center-drained road is less costly to construct than a road draining

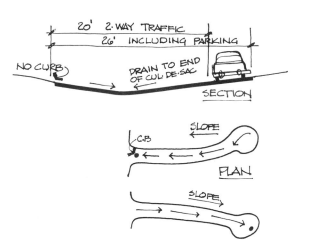

to one side; but both are less than the standard crowned roadway. Curbs, however, have inherent problems since they tend to concentrate runoff, causing increased volumes and velocities, making extensive drainage systems necessary

- Eliminating drainage structures. Curbs and gutters may be replaced with wide flat swales on roads that do not serve driveways. Swales should not exceed 5 percent slope, and must be planted immediately following construction. Slopes steeper than 5 percent or areas handling more runoff may require occasional rip-rap or gravel bottoms, and periodic discharge into larger open areas for ground water absorption. The swale system is not without prob-

lems: many soils will not absorb a sufficient quantity of water to allow the system to work and future maintenance will be necessary.

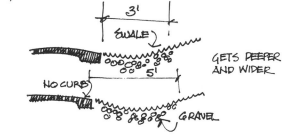

- Constructing single sidewalks instead of walks on both sides of the street. This reduces costs somewhat and on lightly traveled roads presents little disadvantage to pedestrians.
- Large parking lots—low budget development can reduce costs with large parking lots detached from the unit. This eliminates road length, and the cost of serving each unit with the automobile, but lots should be heavily landscaped.
- Working with the contours. On sloping sites, the least expensive solution is to site blocks of units along the contours in terraced fashion' thus avoiding retaining walls. On the other hand, change of level between attached houses or the use of split levels increases construction costs because of internal retaining walls.

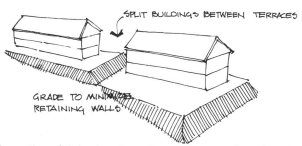

- Locating high-density clusters near the development entrance to minimize the length of roadway and utilities.
- Increasing density to offset high land costs. Sometimes even one or two units per acre can make a big difference.
- Avoiding costly facilities if there's uncertainty about their being fully used (such as swimming pools and recreation centers).

## REDUCING UNIT COSTS

Over the years, the size of suburban houses has increased with more bedrooms, guest space, spare rooms, bathrooms, dining rooms, libraries, and other little used spaces. Probably 75 percent of the space of the middle income dwelling is not used more than a few hours a day. The principal unit cost reduction technique is to *reduce interior spaces*—make it smaller. Units should be laid out efficiently, shortening or eliminating halls, adjusting entrances to minimize through traffic from a room, thereby making the room more efficient, and so on. Other cost-reducing techniques include:

- Building to fit present needs. Many American houses are constructed to meet people's anticipated future needs. It is

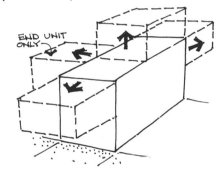

Buildings taller than four floors usually require an elevator, which adds considerable cost, and may even necessitate 4-6 additional floors to justify it.

more reasonable to build for present needs and leave room for future expansion.
- Adding carports later. Space 10 feet x 20 feet for carports may be allocated initially.
- Using systems building including planned coordination of building design, manufacture and construction within the constraints of cost, resource availability, and standards of acceptability.
- The least-used rooms should be the first to be eliminated or reduced, bedrooms and dining rooms next. Main living areas should be the last to be reduced, if at all. Efficiency may be gained through interrelating spaces, for instance, borrowing dining space from living space or an extra bedroom serve as guest room, hobby room, study, television room, studio or office.

- Using even modules. Construct row and town houses in even modules of four, six, or eight units in one building and all on one level. The greater the number of units in a building on one level the less construction costs will be, since utility services can be reduced, or combined in back-to-back arrangements.
- Stacking utilities. Bathroom over kitchen reduces construction costs by concentrating the work area, minimizing the length of plumbing materials, and simplifying framing problems. Prefabricated plumbing walls are available.

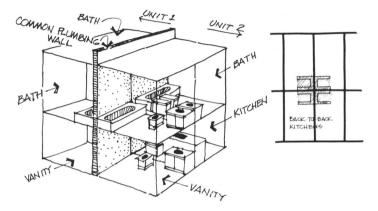

- Arranging utilities back to back. Utilities arranged with bath to kitchen or bath to bath reduce cost. Although building design becomes more difficult, it may be justified by cost savings. Back to back fourplexes allow utilities to be easily combined.
- Eliminating variations. A long straight wall, with no jogs or staggering, is easiest (therefore least expensive) to build. Each corner adds to the cost, from foundation to roof, but may be worthwhile as a device to insure privacy and create individual identity.
- Avoiding roof gardens. Waterproofing is complicated and expensive. Balconies or decks, which are less expensive, work almost as well.
- Making the unit simpler. Costs may be reduced by eliminating any nonessential plumbing or kitchen fixtures and by simplifying interior elements such as dropped or raised ceilings, multilevel layouts, or nonstandard ceiling heights.
- Shifting to modular or factory assembled units at the start if budget is tight. Savings may be gained by working with the realities of modular systems.

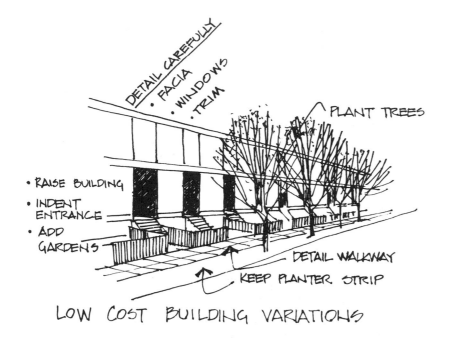

LOW COST BUILDING VARIATIONS

Labels in image: DETAIL CAREFULLY • FACIA • WINDOWS • TRIM; PLANT TREES; • RAISE BUILDING; • INDENT ENTRANCE; • ADD GARDENS; DETAIL WALKWAY; KEEP PLANTER STRIP

## REDUCING LANDSCAPE COSTS

While the authors do not feel comfortable suggesting a reduction in the scope of landscape treatment, it is possible to use smaller trees and shrubs as a cost reduction method. Small trees and shrubs should be avoided in heavily traveled areas where they are likely to be trampled and in children's play areas where they are likely to be destroyed.

This is a decision that must be weighted carefully, extensive tree planting can sometimes correct deficiencies of a poor site plan. One *large* tree is sometimes sufficient to identify a cluster, while a small tree would not help the space. Large open spaces may be mass planted with inexpensive seedlings; this means overplanting by perhaps 100 percent, assuming that many will not survive and that the rest may be thinned later. Other landscape cost reduction techniques include:

• Eliminating ambiguous open space reduces costs for the developer. Ambiguous open space may be made part of adjacent private gardens. As private open space it is planted and maintained by the unit owner rather than the developer.

• Saving costs of street lights. Incandescent light fixtures, which give off the warmest and most pleasant light, are not economical when compared with mercury or sodium vapor fixtures. Mercury vapor (MV) and sodium vapor (SV) shine at a higher intensity, burn longer between bulb changes, and consume less energy per unit output, making them more feasible for developments. The higher the light standard, the greater the coverage of light; therefore, the farther apart light standards may be placed. Although placing light standards farther apart reduces cost, tall light standards tend to be out of scale with residential development and may cast light into nearby houses.

• Reducing the level of outdoor light. Most recommended light levels tend to be higher than is actually required. In neighborhood clusters, light levels can generally be reduced by up to 50 percent of the recommended standards, without severe loss of safety. It is best to avoid reductions at intersections and other areas of pedestrian/auto conflict or intensive use.

• Using yard lights. Small courtyards and culs-de-sac may be lit with residential scale light fixtures attached to the exterior of buildings. Installation costs are lower and the scale of fixtures is compatible with a small neighborhood cluster. One disadvantage is that residents control the lights and can turn them off.

• Eliminating retaining walls and steps. Use banks and ramps instead.

• Switching to gravel or compacted fines in parking areas or for walks. Asphalt and concrete are initially more expensive, but require less long-term maintenance, while gravel is cheap to install, but requires continual maintenance.

• Transferring landscape and recreational development costs to others. It used to be easy for a developer to give open space to the local Parks Department for development. Now, however, this practice is discouraged by these already overburdened public agencies, although if a piece of land away from the central part of the housing community is particularly nice, they might make an exception

Saving existing healthy vegetation can sometimes reduce costs. However, on small sites, saving vegetation constrains the contractor, which may more than offset the savings. Some suggestions for saving vegetation include:

- Leaving where possible a 10-foot work space around each row or unit.
- Planning carefully for utilities to avoid placement near valuable vegetation.
- Moving desirable trees which are in the way of development.
- Saving a number of trees in larger areas rather than isolating them.
- Avoiding unnecessary soil compaction around existing trees or in areas to be planted. The fewer times trucks drive over an area the better.
- Planning construction staging areas for materials storage and layout during construction. Future parking areas often serve this purpose well.

Construction controls outlined by the planner should include:

- Preparing a contractor's "do's and don'ts" plan for fencing, compaction, replacements, and elements to be destroyed, saved, or moved.
- Constructing a temporary fence around all trees which should be saved to prevent contractors from accidentally injuring them.
- Devising a clearing plan based on realities of the construction process. A logical division might categorize the site into total clearing (building pads, roads, active use areas),selective clearing (adjacent to buildings and roads, parking areas, etc.) and no clearing (between units).

- Stripping and stockpiling all topsoil for later reuse.

PRIVATE CONSTRUCTION IS CHEAPER. On the whole, construction of the same facility in the public sector is more expensive than in the private sector. Public construction standards are usually higher than private standards to minimize long-term maintenance costs. Homeowners generally prefer to pay lower initial and higher maintenance costs over the years.

This is true in road construction as well as building construction. Roads ownership is a little less obvious. Generally Major and Local roads, serving large numbers of autos, are thought to have a "public purpose" and are held in public ownership, while Access roads, serving a small number of autos and leading to housing units, are owned jointly by the units they serve and are therefore private roads.

As with public buildings, public roads must be constructed to a high standard, which is expensive. This usually includes a wider cross-section, complicated construction techniques, complete curbs and gutters, and elaborate drainage systems. The rationale is that proper installation, though more expensive, is safer and will require less maintenance over the years. Private roads, on the other hand, may be constructed at a narrower width and to lower construction standards reducing initial costs; however, maintenance and repairs must be borne by the private owners. The developer is responsible for constructing the private road initially and the cost of construction is transferred to future residents through sales or rent prices. .

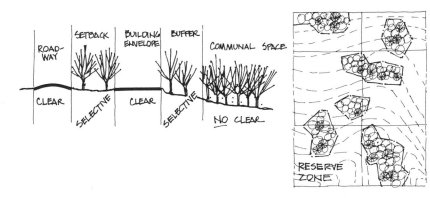

AREAS WHERE REDUCTIONS SHOULD NOT BE MADE. Soundproofing should not be minimized since privacy between units is essential at higher densities. Extensive tree planting, which creates a pleasant environment more cheaply and completely than any other means, should not be reduced.

FHA requirements state "The appeal and character of the site shall be preserved and enhanced by retaining and protecting existing trees and other site features."
(M319-1)

In conclusion, while cost reduction is important, the designer should be careful not to let efficiency overcome livability with short-term benefits outweighed by long-term costs. For instance, it may be more economical to leave room for future expansion than to assume people won't have a need for more space and provide no options .

It should be obvious that six techniques are used to reduce cluster housing costs:

1. Postponing nonessential elements until they are absolutely necessary or affordable.
2. Lowering quality by installing less expensive fittings and materials.
3. Reducing the size of buildings and roads.
4. Clustering and sharing facilities (laundry, parking, storage, shops, play space, etc.)
5. Designing so that layouts and materials provide maximum benefit per cost.
6. Transferring costs to the owner or some local municipality.

Each approach must be evaluated for both shortand long-term cost/benefits. For instance, eliminating a room but providing a way to add the room later may serve short-and long-term goals better than reducing the size of a bedroom without providing for expansion

# INDEX

# INDEX